Advance Praise for
30/30: Thirty American Stories
from the Last Thirty Years

"This anthology brings together a diverse montage of distinct and diverse voices—a mosaic of America."

Susan Isaak Lolis
Florida Atlantic University

"It has all the apparatus you need to cover the elements of fiction, a very good history of the short story, and lively author bios, along with good hints for writing prompts."

Michael Wilkerson
Indiana University

"The most distinctive benefit of this book is that it offers good contemporary fiction at an affordable price—stories that students love and teachers appreciate."

Andrew Scott
Ball State University

"The 'Elements' section seems a well organized, thoroughly explained, and adequately exampled section that would serve well for undergrads in the intro or intermediate sections of workshop courses."

William Miller
George Mason University

"The strength of the book is clearly in its stated intention to combine a range of voices and narrative structures that speak to evolving American identities. . . . The focus on narrative voice is particularly engaging, and the stories that are selected demonstrate the rich variety of voices and narrative directions and indirections that characterize the American short story."

Victoria Aarons
Trinity University

"It provides something new to the current market: craft analysis in Appendix II—using the published stories as springboards for study and writing . . . no other reader I've ever come across does that."

Cathy Day
University of Pittsburgh

"I'm especially taken with the editors' approach in regards to discussion of the history of the short story and its place in our lives."

Mary Darlin Neal
James Madison University

Porter Shreve and **B. Minh Nguyen** have co-edited *The Contemporary American Short Story* and *Contemporary Creative Nonfiction: I & Eye*. Shreve has also coedited three additional anthologies and has published two novels: *Drives Like a Dream* and *The Obituary Writer*, a *New York Times* Notable Book. His short stories and nonfiction have appeared in *Witness*, *Northwest Review*, the *Chicago Tribune*, the *New York Times*, the *Boston Globe* and *Salon*.

Nguyen is the author of a forthcoming memoir, *Stealing Buddha's Dinner*, and a novel, *Short Girls*. Winner of the 2005 PEN/Jerard Award in nonfiction, her work has been published in *Scribner's Best of the Fiction Workshops*, the *Chicago Tribune*, *Gourmet Magazine*, and several anthologies. Shreve and Nguyen are on the English and Creative Writing faculty at Purdue University.

30/30:

Thirty American Stories
from the Last Thirty Years

Edited by

Porter Shreve
Purdue University

B. Minh Nguyen
Purdue University

PENGUIN ACADEMICS

PEARSON
Longman

New York   San Francisco   Boston
London   Toronto   Sydney   Tokyo   Singapore   Madrid
Mexico City   Munich   Paris   Cape Town   Hong Kong   Montreal

Managing Editor: Erika Berg
Executive Marketing Manager: Ann Stypuloski
Production Manager: Denise Phillip
Project Coordination, Text Design, and Electronic Page Makeup: Pre-Press
  Company, Inc.
Cover Designer/Manager: Wendy Ann Fredericks
Cover Photo: © Mark Wilson/Getty Images
Manufacturing Buyer: Roy Pickering
Printer and Binder: Edwards Brothers Malloy
Cover Printer: Edwards Brothers Malloy

For permission to use copyrighted material, grateful acknowledgment is made
to the copyright holders on pp. 303–304, which are hereby made part of this
copyright page.

Library of Congress Cataloging-in-Publication Data
30/30: thirty American stories from the last thirty years / edited by Porter
Shreve, B. Minh Nguyen.
        p. cm.
    ISBN 0-321-33898-7
    1. Short stories, American. 2. American fiction–20th century. 3. American
fiction–21st century. 4. United States–Social life and customs–Fiction. I. Shreve,
Porter. II. Nguyen, B. Minh. III. Title: Thirty American stories from the last 30
years. IV. Title: Thirty/thirty.
PS648.S5A1425 2006
813'.0108054—dc22

                                                                2005051455

Copyright © 2006 by Pearson Education, Inc.

For more information about the Penguin Academics series, please contact us by
mail at Longman Publishers, attn. Marketing Department, 1185 Avenue of the
Americas, 25th Floor, New York, NY 10036, or by e-mail at www.ablongman.com.

Please visit us at www.ablongman.com

ISBN 0-321-33898-7

17 18 19 20—EBM—15 14 13 12

Contents

Preface

As writing and literature instructors, we have seen an increasing need for an anthology of contemporary short stories that is diverse and fresh, with selections geared toward both creative writing and literature courses. This anthology is designed to meet that need, presenting an array of fiction that not only teaches craft, but also provides a context in which to study formal and thematic trends of the past 30 years.

The stories in this anthology are all published after the bicentennial, and each decade since 1976 is represented by well-established authors such as Sandra Cisneros, Raymond Carver, and Donald Barthelme, plus newer voices such as Aleksandar Hemon, Jhumpa Lahiri, and Z. Z. Packer. The anthology offers a stylistic range, from the traditional narrative to experimental forms, and a thematic range as well, with stories that address issues including family and culture, love and loss, ethnicity and gender.

Our objective in choosing these 30 stories was to bring together the fullest possible range of forms, styles, and voices that comprise the contemporary American short story, all in a compact and affordable edition. We have blended a small number of "contemporary classics" by Tim O'Brien, Jamaica Kincaid, and Ursula K. Le Guin with the work of less frequently anthologized authors, among them David Wong Louie, June Spence, and Reginald McKnight. The result, we hope, is not only a composite picture of North American life since 1976 but a measure of the scope and depth of the short story as art form.

Besides its range and diversity, *30/30: Thirty American Stories from the Last Thirty Years* is a flexible text. It could be used as a primary or a supplementary text in a wide range of courses. It is well suited for creative writing courses, providing excellent models of narrative technique. The author biographies give biographical and social context and include quotations from the authors themselves on their narrative process and strategies. By combining established and new authors, *30/30* is equally useful for short-story genre courses and, as a supplement, in introductory literature courses.

We have also included a range of apparatus to enrich the teaching and reading of the stories.

- The **Introduction** provides useful background information for readers, particularly those who are in introductory literature and writing courses. After presenting a brief discussion of the status of the contemporary American short story, we discuss the elements of fiction, including character, voice, and language, giving examples from different selections in the anthology.
- The detailed **author bios** that precede each story provide biographical and social context.
- **Appendix I** provides a condensed and accessible "Brief History of the Short Story" to help students understand how the form developed, and how various movements in literature and critical theory evolved.
- **Appendix II** offers ten substantial and adaptable "Writing Prompts," arranged to coordinate with major elements of fiction: Character, Voice and Point of View, Setting, Plot, and Image and Symbol. Nearly all of the prompts are inspired by or drawn from the selections in the anthology, and serve as springboards for student writing and discussion.

We would like to thank the instructors who reviewed our preliminary materials and offered invaluable recommendations and advice: Victoria Aarons, Trinity University; Lavonne Adams, University of North Carolina—Wilmington; Greg Bills, University of Redlands; Kevin Boyle, Elon University; Cathy Day, University of Pittsburgh; Richard Fine, Virginia Commonwealth University; Scott Garson, Santa Clara University; Hans Carrol Hetrick, Minnesota State University—Mankato; John Hildebidle, MIT; Susan M. Isaak, Florida Atlantic University; James Kastely, University of Houston; Phil LaMarche, Syracuse University; Mark Leichliter, University of Northern Colorado; Mike Magnuson, Southern Illinois University—Carbondale; William Miller, George Mason University; Brian Mooney, Marlboro College; Scott Nadelson, Willamette University; Mary Darlin Neal, James Madison University; Pat O'Donnell, University of Maine—Farmington; Andrew Perry, Elon University; John Peterson, Stanford University; Daniel Pinkerton, Pennsylvania State University; Jim Plath, Illinois Wesleyan University; Andrew Porter, University of Maryland—Baltimore County; Mike Raymond, Stetson University; William Ryan, University of Louisiana—Monroe; Andrew Scott, Ball State University; Alex Shakar, University of Illinois—Champaign-Urbana; Cheryl Slean, University of Washington; Erika Solberg, Monmouth College; John Tait, University of North Texas; Michael Wilkerson, Indiana University; Austin Wilson, Millsaps College. Thanks also go to the English Department and M.F.A. Program in Creative Writing at Purdue University for their generous support. Special thanks to Ruth Curry, Christopher Myers, Beth Keister, Sam Blake, and our editor Erika Berg.

PORTER SHREVE

B. MINH NGUYEN

Introduction

Why Short Stories?

Everyone loves a good story. "What's the latest?" someone asks us. "Did you hear what happened to . . . ?" From gossip to meaningful conversation, the answer comes in the form of narrative, storytelling, the construction of feelings and relationships, the events and details that make meaning of our lives. The short story form—more precise and compressed than a novel yet similarly rich in character, voice, and situation—captures the distilled essence of our narrative impulse.

Throughout the 19th and early 20th centuries, Americans could find stories in newspapers and all manner of magazines, from dime Westerns to *The Saturday Evening Post* to *The New Yorker*. With the emergence of modernism after World War I, stories gained wider attention from critics as an essential part of literary study. Writers as varied as Sherwood Anderson, Katherine Ann Porter, and Richard Wright used the short story form as a particular means for interpreting experience and establishing their voices.

Today, short stories continue to redefine and reshape the boundaries of literary fiction. Many of America's finest prose stylists have broadened the story's scope, expanding the canon with such contemporary classics as "The Things They Carried" by Tim O'Brien and "The House on Mango Street" by Sandra Cisneros. In recent years, literary journals such as *McSweeney's* and *Zoetrope* have brought more attention to the field; short story collections by writers such as Z. Z. Packer and Jhumpa Lahiri have won wide praise and large audiences; and the number of creative writing classes and programs in American universities has grown dramatically in the past 30 years. Colleges, bookstores, and coffeehouses increasingly sponsor author readings, giving the public an opportunity to meet writers and hear how a story is also an individual's voice speaking to a community. Whether on the page or heard out loud, stories remain a dynamic and powerful way to develop, through compression and immediacy, a sense of narrative time, character, meaning, and event. With their brevity, short stories can readily inspire, teach technique and craft, and show us different uses of voice, style, and language.

In 30/30, we have brought together a handful of contemporary classics such as Cynthia Ozick's "The Shawl" and Raymond Carver's "Cathedral" with newer works such as David Wong Louie's "Cold-hearted" and Aleksandar Hemon's "A Coin." Several of the stories here follow the familiar arcs of rising action, crisis and falling action, while others experiment liberally with form. Whether traditional or innovative, each of the pieces we have collected defies simple summary; the stories seek the original, unpredictable, and challenging, and will immerse you in the field of contemporary short story writing in America. We hope these stories will inspire debate, engage your sympathies, and make you want to rush home and write.

The Elements of Fiction

We read first, undeniably, for pleasure: to see what happens, to feel something, to live inside someone else's life for a while, to gain different ideas and perspectives, to linger over a writer's language and style. Good stories engage our senses and our imaginations. At some level, the essence of a story—its emotional effect and resonance—may remain mysterious and wonderful. Yet as critical readers, thinkers, and writers, we seek to understand the craft of writing, the techniques, processes, and acts of revision that go into the making of a good story.

Beyond the first enjoyment of reading, what we are really looking to understand is what a story "means": How does a story render a particular experience or voice in an engaging, emotionally significant way? How do characters come to life through vivid language and dialogue? To find answers we close-read, going beyond the literal and the face value, and ask questions about how and why a story is plotted, how characters are developed, and how a story reaches its conclusion. The act of reading becomes an act of interpreting. Instead of regarding characters as good, bad, right, or wrong, we consider them in terms of the story's elements, such as language, character, setting, motivation, and conflict. These elements combine in various ways to reflect the particular style of a story or writer. Some stories, such as Ron Carlson's "Milk," are driven as much by a character's voice, a particular way of articulating experience, as they are by external conflicts. In "Milk," the conflict—the narrator and his wife's disagreement about having their children fingerprinted—is played out and escalated through the narrator's increasingly obsessive viewpoint.

By examining the way the elements of fiction work in a story, we can understand how central themes and ideas emerge. Let's look, for instance, at Jamaica Kincaid's "Girl." At first glimpse we might say that it is about a girl whose mother is lecturing her on how to be a proper lady. This meaning occurs on the literal level of plot. If we go beyond plot, we note how the story uses language, imagery, and tone to generate issues of power, domination, and the struggle for a voice. This non-literal approach gives us a way to understand a story beneath its surface.

Plot

Plot, simply defined, is what happens in a story. If you've ever felt suspense while reading, wondering what's going to happen next or how a character is going to respond to something that just happened, then you have felt the power of plot.

Plot is developed through a complex coordination of language, characterization, and voice. An action or event may reveal a character's emotion, state of mind, or motivation; the event may also be of metaphorical significance. Exposition and dramatization are two components of plot. *Exposition* includes background, context, introduction, and summary; it tells rather than shows what happened. In Raymond Carver's "Cathedral," for example, much of the background information concerning the narrator's wife and Robert is relayed to the reader through exposition. When Robert arrives, the story shifts toward *dramatization,* also known as *scene,* which involves dialogue, description, action, and a greater sense of urgency. The plot of a story tends to strike a balance between exposition and dramatization, often using the former to contextualize and set up the latter. Exposition and *flashbacks,* memories or moments from past events, also help establish character motivation and show how the past has influenced the current dramatization. In Dorothy Allison's "River of Names," flashbacks are used to show the contrasts between the narrator's past and present lives. *Foreshadowing* is another device that can add depth to a story; here, images, events, and dialogue are used to anticipate and suggest later events. An example of foreshadowing occurs in Gish Jen's "Birthmates" when Art Woo, checking into a hotel, sees a plaque that reads "Fewest Customer Injuries, 1972–1973." His anxiety about what this plaque means foreshadows the injury he will soon sustain.

A traditional plot progression is set into motion by establishing the story's *conflict*. This problem or tension, often between characters, propels actions and reactions. The development of conflict and tension is called the *complication,* or *rising action.* When the story reaches the height of its tension it arrives at its *turning point,* sometimes referred to as the *climax.* Here something significant is decided or not decided, acted upon or not acted upon, and the results lead to the *falling action,* where the narrative winds toward its *resolution* or *denouement.* Reginald McKnight's "The Kind of Light That Shines on Texas" is an example of a story that follows this traditional plot line. Many contemporary stories, on the other hand, eschew traditional plot and clear turning points; one example is Rick Moody's "Boys," which builds upon the repeated line "Boys enter the house" into a kind of chant. Stories also usually contain a *subplot,* a minor or secondary plot line that may be used to further conflicts or to contrast or parallel the central plot. McKnight's use of the secondary character Marvin Pruitt, whom the narrator at first dislikes but who eventually comes to the narrator's defense, is an example.

One marker of some modern and contemporary stories is the moment of *epiphany,* in which a character reaches a realization or moment of insight. A term closely associated with the stories in James Joyce's *Dubliners* (1922), an epiphany or "showing forth" refers to a character's realization about something true, important, or meaningful about him/herself or his/her world. We can see a famous example in Raymond Carver's "Cathedral," when the isolated, friendless narrator experiences a moment of community and spirituality with "the blind man." Alternately, a story might play with or challenge that idea of epiphany to generate a sense of uncertainty, chaos, displacement, or inevitability. Annie Proulx's "Job History," for example, consciously avoids an encapsulated emotional summary; the story's protagonist is detached, a part of the indifferent environment that shaped him.

Conflict

Conflict is central to the development of character and plot. It builds emotion, tension, and drama, giving us a sense of what is at stake in a story. Most stories give us glimpses of both internal and external conflict. *External conflict* can occur between characters or between a character and an outward source; *internal conflict* occurs within a character and might be shown through his or her self-doubt, insecurity, and fear. Characters might be grappling with their pasts, the decisions they have made, or their own sense of identity. Internal conflicts are usually expressed, in some way, through external conflicts. In Mary Gaitskill's "Tiny, Smiling Daddy," Stew's internal conflict concerns his troubled relationships with his daughter Kitty and with his father. This internal anguish is expressed through external tension with his wife. As with many stories, the conflicts here reach no clear resolution. This technique gives us a way to examine ideas and questions such as: Why must the conflicts remain unresolved? What might a story be saying about the clash of values and beliefs?

Character

While plot is what happens in a story, *character* determines what happens. When you feel something about a character, be it like, dislike, fear, distrust, or sympathy, you are responding to characterization. We read stories and interpret them in ways that are not so different from how we read and interpret our everyday lives. We observe, listen, feel emotions, make observations and weigh decisions. What do characters want? What are they after? What is at stake for them? Ultimately, understanding character is important not only as a way to understand a story but also as a way to think critically about a story's themes; a character is not just a character, but a reflection of nonliteral ideas as well.

E. M. Forster, in his *Aspects of the Novel* (1927), famously established the distinction between flat and round characters. *Round* characters are like human beings—complex creations who are capable of change. *Flat* characters seem one dimensional, with easily summed-up personalities. Often, flat characters perform stock or background roles in a story, like acquaintances at a big party. *Dynamic* characters, on the other hand, change over the course of a story. Most often a story's main character will be the most dynamic in the story because, in dealing with a conflict, he or she must undergo some kind of change in order to reach a resolution. Forster's classifications are useful in getting us to think about character development in terms of the way characters play off each other through their conflicts, tensions, and symbolic representations. In Junot Díaz's "Fiesta, 1980," for instance, the principal characters—Yunior, the narrator, and his father, Papi—are complex and round; the main conflict of the story exists between them. As the tension grows, we see Yunior gaining a deeper understanding of his family life and of who his parents are; in this way, he can be seen as a dynamic character. Papi, on the other hand, does not gain understanding, and remains the same, intimidating figure throughout the story. "Fiesta, 1980" also gives us necessary *secondary characters* in the rest of the family; their interactions with Yunior and Papi increase tension and are integral to the development of Yunior's voice, character, and inner thoughts.

Another facet of character development is *motivation*, or the internal and external causes that propel a character to act. Motivation contributes to the story's conflict and addresses the reasoning behind a character's progress in a story. In David Leavitt's "Gravity," for instance, we might say that Sylvia throws the crystal bowl to Theo because she wants to see him catch it; she is motivated by a wish to see him save something, which in turn parallels her own wish to save him from dying.

The main character of a story is the *protagonist*, and how he or she is revealed depends a good deal on the narrator's *point of view* and *voice*. Whose perception are we being given, and why? When and how is the story being told? The narrator holds the responsibility of describing, observing, and shaping the world of the story.

Point of View and Voice

A story told from the *first-person* "I" can establish intimacy and the narrator's voice immediately; we may feel that the narrator is speaking directly and openly to us, as in Charles Baxter's "Snow," which begins with this line: "Twelve years old, and I was so bored I was combing my hair just for the hell of it." In first-person stories the narrator is often the protagonist, but not always. Indeed, the first-person narrator as observer rather than protagonist, exemplified in novel form in F. Scott Fitzgerald's *The Great Gatsby* (1925) and shown here in Percival Everett's "The Fix," can be a rich source for narrative. Here, narrators are watching from the sidelines, watching the main character go through events and changes; they are often outsiders in their society, community, family, or group. Or they may exist in an in-between state—belonging yet not belonging—giving them the ability to observe multiple sides of a situation.

This theme of narrative dislocation has grown into a major subject in contemporary fiction. In particular, writers from historically marginalized communities—including immigrant, ethnic, and gay and lesbian—have published a wealth of stories that show us the in-betweenness of worlds and identities. Here, the use of the first-person "I" can be a way to get us thinking about voices we may not have heard before. In Sherman Alexie's "What You Pawn I Will Redeem," for example, the narrator belongs to his Indian tribe and appears to be a known figure in his community; at the same time, because he is homeless—a condition connected to his Indianness, the story suggests—he belongs nowhere. Yet his voice, the very fact of his role as narrator of the story, insists that we pay attention to his life.

A *second-person* narrative puts "you" in the position of narrator, as in Jamaica Kincaid's "Girl" and Lorrie Moore's "How to Talk to Your Mother (Notes)." A fairly recent innovation in fiction, the second-person point of view closes the distance between reader and character, making the reader both a part of the story—often in a deliberately self-conscious way—yet also hyper-aware of the narrative technique. The *third-person* point of view tells the story from outside the narrative. Most third-person perspectives are limited, meaning they reveal a story from one character's perspective. In David Wong Louie's "Cold-hearted," for example, the third-person point of view emphasizes how the protagonist, Lawrence, feels set apart from the rest of his family. The third-person omniscient point of view, as seen in Tim O'Brien's "The Things They Carried," can slip into the mind of any and every character. This perspective has become increasingly rare in contemporary short fiction, perhaps because literature has come to favor the subjectivity of individual perception and experience. At the same time, some postmodern works employ an insider's "I" or collective third-person "we" point of view to emphasize a sense of satire or social commentary. Ursula K. Le Guin's "The Ones Who Walk Away from Omelas" and June Spence's "Missing Women" are two examples.

Consider also the *time frame* of the point of view. Is it traditional past tense? Is the narrator telling the story while looking back from a distance of years? Is the story present tense, generating a sense of immediacy? Perhaps it switches back and forth between past tense and present tense episodes. Point of view and voice shape how we experience a story and how characters and conflicts are revealed to us. First-person point of view gives us a specific, narrow perception; we are in on the narrator's thoughts. Yet we should also consider what the narrator doesn't tell us, as well as how his or her emotions affect the movement of the story. We might be skeptical or kept off balance by the narrator's perspective. What is the state of mind of the narrator in T.C. Boyle's "Greasy Lake"? Why does Dorothy Allison's "River of Names" rely on a narrator who admits "But I lie"?

Voice is the distinctive way in which a narrator tells a story. Combined with point of view, it creates a relationship between reader and narrator that may be direct and confidential, as in Lydia Davis's "Story," or perhaps more arch and distant, as in Annie Proulx's "Job History." The "voice-driven" story, as seen in Sherman Alexie's "What You Pawn I

Will Redeem," usually relies on the first-person narrator, and his or her particular language, diction, and identity, to propel the story's events and emotions. In Alexie's story, the very first sentence establishes the narrative style: "One day you have a home and the next you don't, but I'm not going to tell you my particular reasons for being homeless, because it's my secret story, and Indians have to work hard to keep secrets from hungry white folks."

As we read and immerse ourselves in a story's narrative voice and point of view, we should be mulling over questions such as: Why are we getting this particular view? What do we gain from experiencing a first-person narrator's life versus seeing a third-person limited view of another character's experience? In what ways does a particular point of view skew the narrative? What feelings are shown through voice?

Setting

Setting, or time and place, gives us a way to visualize a story. By having a literal context for plot, character, and dialogue, we can find meaning between an action and when and where it occurs. Setting provides an immediate sign-post, an introduction to the world of each story, and metaphorical possibility. For example, to fully understand Reginald McKnight's "The Kind of Light That Shines on Texas," we need to know that it takes place in a southwestern school struggling with integration. Tim O'Brien's "The Things They Carried" uses setting literally, to show the landscape of the war, and metaphorically, to show the soldiers' emotions. Setting also helps create *atmosphere,* which is the mood of a story and its emotional impact on us. Atmosphere emerges from the story's situations and locations. For instance, the setting and situation of Jhumpa Lahiri's "Interpreter of Maladies"—an Indian American family visiting ruins in India as tourists; hot weather and a long car trip—create an atmosphere of restlessness and isolation, reflecting Mrs. Das's sense of loss and not belonging.

Language, Symbol, and Tone

At the foundation of every story is its *language*—how a writer makes use of diction, imagery, metaphors, symbolism, irony, and tone. Each word in a story has a *denotative* and *connotative* effect. Consider the title of Jamaica Kincaid's "Girl." It literally denotes the girl whom the mother is addressing. At the same time, the word also connotes the very idea of girlhood and what it means to be a girl. The sentence structure of the story is also significant: almost the entire story is one long sentence, generating tension and a sense of endless demand. Writers may draw on poetic elements such as lyricism and rhythm to create emotional intensity, as we see in Sandra Cisneros's "The House on Mango Street" and Rick Moody's "Boys." Writers rely on the power of descriptive language to depict scenes and characters as well as to create depth of emotion, voice, and meaning, as seen in this example from Stuart Dybek's "We Didn't": "We didn't in your mother's Buick Eight where a rosary twined the rearview mirror like a beaded black snake with silver, cruciform fangs."

Description involves the vivid, precise use of *imagery* to describe what characters, places, and landscapes look like. Images can set up a literal vision of the story's world via verisimilitude, the use of real-life details to ground the story in a sense of reality. It also gives us a way to understand the story on a nonliteral level. When we reread and analyze a story, we see how every concrete image can become a symbol or a *metaphor,* a description of an object, person, or moment through terms of comparison. This example from Louise Erdrich's "Saint Marie" contains first a simile then a metaphor: "her fingers were like a burdle of broom straws...her eye sockets were two deep lashless hollows in a taut skull." Through such figurative language we see how the narrator perceives Sister Leopolda both visually and emotionally.

Like metaphors, *symbols* rely on a comparison between two different things, but symbols use a concrete object to represent an idea or feeling. Take a look, for instance, at how Charles Baxter and Ann Beattie use snow as a symbol in their respective stories, both titled "Snow." In Baxter's story snow is connected to a moment of childhood awareness and responsibility; in Beattie's story snow is connected to memories of a romantic relationship. To some extent both stories use snow as a symbol of temporality and stillness, but the resulting effects, meanings, and styles are very different. This is not to say, however, that stories must revolve around one singular symbol, meaning, or "message." Symbols are just one aspect of language used to create character, voice, and conflict, and to create another layer of a story—another way to understand it.

Another technique of language is *irony,* which points out the gap between what is anticipated or expected, and what actually happens or is revealed; a note of surprise, bittersweetness, or humor emerges when we or the characters realize that a reversal has occurred. Z. Z. Packer's "Every Tongue Shall Confess" uses irony to point out moments of hypocrisy, such as Deacon Julian's behavior, in the main character's church.

Language, style, and point of view all combine to establish *tone,* the overall feeling the narrator has toward the characters, events, setting, and even the reader. The impact of a word often relies on its circumstances; whether you read the statement "you're a genius" as sincere or sarcastic depends on its context. The desperate tone in Lydia Davis's "Story" is established through the rapid succession and accumulation of sentences filled with "I," detailing all of the narrator's obsessive thoughts and actions.

Structure

Every story has a particular *structure* or organization, the way in which the narrative develops. Some stories move in a traditional linear chronology; others skew time, jumping from moment to moment as in Tim O'Brien's "The Things They Carried," which employs repetition to depict the soldiers' daily lives of isolation, fear, uncertainty, and continuous marching. This story also uses segmentation and section breaks to create transitions and signify jumps in narration or time period. Aleksandar Hemon's "A Coin" also uses segmentation to suggest the fragmentation of memory and experience.

The structure of a story, whether it involves a traditional or nontraditional sense of time and plot, helps us understand a story on its own terms. As readers we follow the path—the structure—of each story and see where it takes us and what we can uncover. When a story jumps into a flashback or memory, we follow, knowing we are going to find out necessary background. When we see a section break, we take a breath and pause, as the page is telling us to do. When we encounter a long paragraph filled with long sentences, we read on, breathlessly. Along the way all of the elements of short story writing unfold, and the process of reading becomes a process of gathering together the strands of narrative, language, and ideas.

Ever since Edgar Allan Poe defined the short story as a work that has a "unity of effect," other writers have been trying to redefine what a story is. Thus you will see a wide variety of stories here, from traditional structures to innovative forms; they reflect the range of styles and voices that characterize contemporary American short fiction. Poe's demand for unity applies well to some of the stories in this collection; others stretch the boundaries of assumptions we might have about what makes a story a story.

The elements of fiction can work together in an endless number of ways, and it is this multiplicity that makes the contemporary American short story such a dynamic field. Just as we learn to appreciate the discipline of the craft, we recognize the wealth of new possibilities that lie ahead for readers and writers of this most vital form.

Sherman Alexie

Sherman Alexie, a Spokane/Coeur d'Alene Indian, was born in 1966 and grew up on the Spokane Indian Reservation in Washington. Alexie's work spans the genres of fiction, essay, poetry, and filmmaking. He has published three collections of poetry: The Business of Fancydancing *(1991),* I Would Steal Horses *(1993), and* One Stick Song *(2000). His first collection of short stories,* The Lone Ranger and Tonto Fistfight in Heaven *(1993) received the PEN/Hemingway Award; his other collections are* The Toughest Indian in the World *(2000) and* Ten Little Indians *(2003). He has also published the novels* Reservation Blues *(1995) and* Indian Killer *(1996). His film* Smoke Signals *won several awards at the Sundance Film Festival. On the role of being a writer, Alexie has said: "I've made mistakes about subject matter, things I probably shouldn't have written about. I wrote about events I shouldn't have written about. And that was a personal moral choice to stop writing about those events. I didn't have to, and even if I had continued to write about them, it was my prerogative. You know, as an artist, it's not my job to fit in; it's not my job to belong. I'm not a social worker; I'm not a therapist. It's my job to beat the shit out of the world. I'm not here to make people feel good."*

What You Pawn
I Will Redeem

NOON

One day you have a home and the next you don't, but I'm not going to tell you my particular reasons for being homeless, because it's my secret story, and Indians have to work hard to keep secrets from hungry white folks.

I'm a Spokane Indian boy, an Interior Salish, and my people have lived within a hundred-mile radius of Spokane, Washington, for at least ten thousand years. I grew up in Spokane, moved to Seattle twenty-three years ago for college, flunked out after two semesters, worked various blue- and bluer-collar jobs, married two or three times, fathered two or three kids, and then went crazy. Of course, crazy is not the official definition of my mental problem, but I don't think asocial disorder fits it, either, because that makes me sound like I'm a serial killer or something. I've never hurt another human being, or, at least, not physically. I've broken a few hearts in my time, but we've all done that, so I'm nothing special in that regard. I'm a boring heartbreaker, too. I never dated or married more than one woman at a time. I didn't break hearts into pieces overnight. I broke them slowly and carefully. And I didn't set any land-speed records running out the door. Piece by piece, I disappeared. I've been disappearing ever since.

I've been homeless for six years now. If there's such a thing as an effective homeless man, then I suppose I'm effective. Being homeless is probably the only thing I've ever been good at. I know where to get the best free food. I've made friends with restaurant and convenience store managers who let me use their bathrooms. And I don't mean the public bathrooms, either. I mean the employees' bathrooms, the clean ones hidden behind the kitchen or the pantry or the cooler. I know it sounds strange to be proud of this, but it means a lot to me, being trustworthy enough to piss in somebody else's clean bathroom. Maybe you don't understand the value of a clean bathroom, but I do.

Probably none of this interests you. Homeless Indians are everywhere in Seattle. We're common and boring, and you walk right on by us, with maybe a look of anger or disgust or even sadness at the terrible fate of the noble savage. But we have dreams and families. I'm friends with a homeless Plains Indian man whose son is the editor of a bigtime newspaper back east. Of course, that's his story, but we Indians are great storytellers and liars and mythmakers, so maybe that Plains Indian hobo is just a plain old everyday Indian. I'm kind of suspicious of him, because he identifies himself only as Plains Indian, a genetic term, and not by a specific tribe. When I asked him why he wouldn't tell me exactly what he is, he said, "Do any of us know exactly what we are?" Yeah, great, a philosophizing Indian. "Hey," I said, "you got to have a home to be that homely." He just laughed and flipped me the eagle and walked away.

I wander the streets with a regular crew—my teammates, my defenders, my posse. It's Rose of Sharon, Junior, and me. We matter to one another if we don't matter to anybody else. Rose of Sharon is a big woman, about seven feet tall if you're measuring overall effect and about five feet tall if you're only talking about the physical. She's a Yakama Indian of the Wishram variety. Junior is a Colville, but there are about 199 tribes that make up the Colville, so he could be anything. He's good-looking, though, like he just stepped out of some "Don't Litter the Earth" public service advertisement. He's got those great big cheekbones that are like planets, you know, with little moons orbiting them. He gets me jealous, jealous, and jealous. If you put Junior and me next to each other, he's the Before Columbus Arrived Indian and I'm the After Columbus Arrived Indian. I am living proof of the horrible damage that colonialism has done to us Skins. But I'm not going to let you know how scared I sometimes get of history and its ways. I'm a strong man, and I know that silence is the best method of dealing with white folks.

This whole story really started at lunchtime, when Rose of Sharon, Junior, and I were panning the handle down at Pike Place Market. After about two hours of negotiating, we earned five dollars—good enough for a bottle of fortified courage from the most beautiful 7-Eleven in the world. So we headed over that way, feeling like warrior drunks, and we walked past this pawnshop I'd never noticed before. And that was strange, because we Indians have built-in pawnshop radar. But the strangest thing of all was the old powwow-dance regalia I saw hanging in the window.

"That's my grandmother's regalia," I said to Rose of Sharon and Junior.

"How you know for sure?" Junior asked.

I didn't know for sure, because I hadn't seen that regalia in person ever. I'd only seen photographs of my grandmother dancing in it, And those were taken before somebody stole it from her, fifty years ago. But it sure looked like my memory of it, and it had all the same color feathers and beads that my family sewed into our powwow regalia.

"There's only one way to know for sure," I said.

So Rose of Sharon, Junior, and I walked into the pawnshop and greeted the old white man working behind the counter.

"How can I help you?" he asked.

"That's my grandmother's powwow regalia in your window," I said. "Somebody stole it from her fifty years ago, and my family has been searching for it ever since."

The pawnbroker looked at me like I was a liar. I understood. Pawnshops are filled with liars.

"I'm not lying," I said. "Ask my friends here. They'll tell you."

"He's the most honest Indian I know," Rose of Sharon said.

"All right, honest Indian," the pawnbroker said. "I'll give you the benefit of the doubt. Can you prove it's your grandmother's regalia?"

Because they don't want to be perfect, because only God is perfect, Indian people sew flaws into their powwow regalia. My family always sewed one yellow bead somewhere on our regalia. But we always hid it so that you had to search really hard to find it.

"If it really is my grandmother's," I said, "there will be one yellow bead hidden somewhere on it."

"All right, then," the pawnbroker said. "Let's take a look."

He pulled the regalia out of the window, laid it down on the glass counter, and we searched for that yellow bead and found it hidden beneath the armpit.

"There it is," the pawnbroker said. He didn't sound surprised. "You were right. This is your grandmother's regalia."

"It's been missing for fifty years," Junior said.

"Hey, Junior," I said. "It's my family's story. Let me tell it."

"All right," he said. "I apologize. You go ahead."

"It's been missing for fifty years," I said.

"That's his family's sad story," Rose of Sharon said. "Are you going to give it back to him?"

"That would be the right thing to do," the pawnbroker said. "But I can't afford to do the right thing. I paid a thousand dollars for this. I can't just give away a thousand dollars."

"We could go to the cops and tell them it was stolen," Rose of Sharon said.

"Hey," I said to her. "Don't go threatening people."

The pawnbroker sighed. He was thinking about the possibilities.

"Well, I suppose you could go to the cops," he said. "But I don't think they'd believe a word you said."

He sounded sad about that. As if he was sorry for taking advantage of our disadvantages.

"What's your name?" the pawnbroker asked me.

"Jackson," I said.

"Is that first or last?"

"Both," I said.

"Are you serious?"

"Yes, it's true. My mother and father named me Jackson Jackson. My family nickname is Jackson Squared. My family is funny."

"All right, Jackson Jackson," the pawnbroker said. "You wouldn't happen to have a thousand dollars, would you?"

"We've got five dollars total," I said.

"That's too bad," he said, and thought hard about the possibilities. "I'd sell it to you for a thousand dollars if you had it. Heck, to make it fair, I'd sell it to you for nine hundred and ninety-nine dollars. I'd lose a dollar. That would be the moral thing to do in this case. To lose a dollar would be the right thing."

"We've got five dollars total," I said again.

"That's too bad," he said once more, and thought harder about the possibilities. "How about this? I'll give you twenty-four hours to come up with nine hundred and ninety-nine dollars. You come back here at lunchtime tomorrow with the money and I'll sell it back to you. How does that sound?"

"It sounds all right," I said.

"All right, then," he said. "We have a deal. And I'll get you started. Here's twenty bucks."

He opened up his wallet and pulled out a crisp twenty-dollar bill and gave it to me. And Rose of Sharon, Junior, and I walked out into the daylight to search for nine hundred and seventy-four more dollars.

1 P.M.

Rose of Sharon, Junior, and I carried our twenty-dollar bill and our five dollars in loose change over to the 7-Eleven and bought three bottles of imagination. We needed to figure out how to raise all that money in only one day. Thinking hard, we huddled in an alley beneath the Alaska Way Viaduct and finished off those bottles—one, two, and three.

2 P.M.

Rose of Sharon was gone when I woke up. I heard later that she had hitchhiked back to Toppenish and was living with her sister on the reservation.

Junior had passed out beside me and was covered in his own vomit, or maybe somebody else's vomit, and my head hurt from thinking, so I left him alone and walked down to the water. I love the smell of ocean water. Salt always smells like memory.

When I got to the wharf, I ran into three Aleut cousins, who sat on a wooden bench and stared out at the bay and cried. Most of the homeless Indians in Seattle come from Alaska. One by one, each of them hopped a big working boat in Anchorage or Barrow or Juneau, fished his way south to Seattle, jumped off the boat with a pocketful of cash to party hard at one of the highly sacred and traditional Indian bars, went broke and broker, and has been trying to find his way back to the boat and the frozen north ever since.

These Aleuts smelled like salmon, I thought, and they told me they were going to sit on that wooden bench until their boat came back.

"How long has your boat been gone?" I asked.

"Eleven years," the elder Aleut said.

I cried with them for a while.

"Hey," I said. "Do you guys have any money I can borrow?"

They didn't.

3 P.M.

I walked back to Junior. He was still out cold. I put my face down near his mouth to make sure he was breathing. He was alive, so I dug around in his blue jeans pockets and found half a cigarette. I smoked it all the way down and thought about my grandmother.

Her name was Agnes, and she died of breast cancer when I was fourteen. My father always thought Agnes caught her tumors from the uranium mine on the reservation. But my mother said the disease started when Agnes was walking back from a powwow one night and got run over by a motorcycle. She broke three ribs, and my mother always said those ribs never healed right, and tumors take over when you don't heal right.

Sitting beside Junior, smelling the smoke and the salt and the vomit, I wondered if my grandmother's cancer started when somebody stole her powwow regalia. Maybe the cancer started in her broken heart and then leaked out into her breasts. I know it's crazy, but I wondered whether I could bring my grandmother back to life if I bought back her regalia.

I needed money, big money, so I left Junior and walked over to the Real Change office.

4 P.M.

Real Change is a multifaceted organization that publishes a newspaper, supports cultural projects that empower the poor and the homeless, and mobilizes the public around poverty issues. Real Change's mission is to organize, educate, and build alliances to create solutions to homelessness and poverty. It exists to provide a voice for poor people in our community.

I memorized Real Change's mission statement because I sometimes sell the newspaper on the streets. But you have to stay sober to sell it, and I'm not always good at staying sober. Anybody can sell the paper. You buy each copy for thirty cents and sell it for a dollar, and you keep the profit.

"I need one thousand four hundred and thirty papers," I said to the Big Boss.

"That's a strange number," he said. "And that's a lot of papers."

"I need them."

The Big Boss pulled out his calculator and did the math.

"It will cost you four hundred and twenty-nine dollars for that many," he said.

"If I had that kind of money, I wouldn't need to sell the papers."

"What's going on, Jackson-to-the-Second-Power?" he asked. He is the only person who calls me that. He's a funny and kind man.

I told him about my grandmother's powwow regalia and how much money I needed in order to buy it back.

"We should call the police," he said.

"I don't want to do that," I said. "It's a quest now. I need to win it back by myself."

"I understand," he said. "And, to be honest, I'd give you the papers to sell if I thought it would work. But the record for the most papers sold in one day by one vender is only three hundred and two."

"That would net me about two hundred bucks," I said.

The Big Boss used his calculator. "Two hundred and eleven dollars and forty cents," he said.

"That's not enough," I said.

"And the most money anybody has made in one day is five hundred and twenty-five. And that's because somebody gave Old Blue five hundred-dollar bills for some dang reason. The average daily net is about thirty dollars."

"This isn't going to work."

"No."

"Can you lend me some money?"

"I can't do that," he said. "If I lend you money, I have to lend money to everybody."

"What can you do?"

"I'll give you fifty papers for free. But don't tell anybody I did it."

"O.K," I said.

He gathered up the newspapers and handed them to me. I held them to my chest. He hugged me. I carried the newspapers back toward the water.

5 P.M.

Back on the wharf, I stood near the Bainbridge Island Terminal and tried to sell papers to business commuters boarding the ferry.

I sold five in one hour, dumped the other forty-five in a garbage can, and walked into McDonald's, ordered four cheeseburgers for a dollar each, and slowly ate them.

After eating, I walked outside and vomited on the sidewalk. I hated to lose my food so soon after eating it. As an alcoholic Indian with a busted stomach, I always hope I can keep enough food in me to stay alive.

6 P.M.

With one dollar in my pocket, I walked back to Junior. He was still passed out, and I put my car to his chest and listened for his heartbeat. He was alive, so I took off his shoes and socks and found one dollar in his left sock and fifty cents in his right sock.

With two dollars and fifty cents in my hand, I sat beside Junior and thought about my grandmother and her stories.

When I was thirteen, my grandmother told me a story about the Second World War. She was a nurse at a military hospital in Sydney, Australia. For two years, she healed and comforted American and Australian soldiers.

One day, she tended to a wounded Maori soldier, who had lost his legs to an artillery attack. He was very dark-skinned. His hair was black and curly and his eyes were black and warm. His face was covered with bright tattoos.

"Are you Maori?" he asked my grandmother.

"No," she said. "I'm Spokane Indian. From the United States."

"Ah, yes," he said. "I have heard of your tribes. But you are the first American Indian I have ever met."

"There's a lot of Indian soldiers fighting for the United States," she said. "I have a brother fighting in Germany, and I lost another brother on Okinawa."

"I am sorry," he said. "I was on Okinawa as well. It was terrible."

"I am sorry about your legs," my grandmother said.

"It's funny, isn't it?" he said.

"What's funny?"

"How we brown people are killing other brown people so white people will remain free."

"I hadn't thought of it that way."

"Well, sometimes I think of it that way. And other times I think of it the way they want me to think of it. I get confused."

She fed him morphine.

"Do you believe in heaven?" he asked.

"Which heaven?" she asked.

"I'm talking about the heaven where my legs are waiting for me."

They laughed.

"Of course," he said, "my legs will probably run away from me when I get to heaven. And how will I ever catch them?"

"You have to get your arms strong," my grandmother said, "So you can run on your hands."

They laughed again.

Sitting beside Junior, I laughed at the memory of my grand-mother's story. I put my hand close to Junior's mouth to make sure he was still breathing. Yes, Junior was alive, so I took my two dollars and fifty cents and walked to the Korean grocery store in Pioneer Square.

7 P.M.

At the Korean grocery store, I bought a fifty-cent cigar and two scratch lottery tickets for a dollar each. The maximum cash prize was five hundred dollars a ticket. If I won both, I would have enough money to buy back the regalia.

I loved Mary, the young Korean woman who worked the register. She was the daughter of the owners, and she sang all day.

"I love you," I said when I handed her the money.

"You always say you love me," she said.

"That's because I will always love you."

"You are a sentimental fool."

"I'm a romantic old man."

"Too old for me."

"I know I'm too old for you, but I can dream."

"O.K.," she said. "I agree to be a part of your dreams, but I will only hold your hand in your dreams. No kissing and no sex. Not even in your dreams."

"O.K.," I said. "No sex. Just romance."

"Goodbye, Jackson Jackson, my love. I will see you soon."

I left the store, walked over to Occidental Park, sat on a bench, and smoked my cigar all the way down.

Ten minutes after I finished the cigar, I scratched my first lottery ticket and won nothing. I could win only five hundred dollars now, and that would be only half of what I needed.

Ten minutes after I lost, I scratched the other ticket and won a free ticket—a small consolation and one more chance to win some money.

I walked back to Mary.

"Jackson Jackson," she said. "Have you come back to claim my heart?"

"I won a free ticket," I said.

"Just like a man," she said. "You love money and power more than you love me."

"It's true," I said. "And I'm sorry it's true."

She gave me another scratch ticket, and I took it outside. I like to scratch my tickets in private. Hopeful and sad, I scratched that third ticket and won real money. I carried it back inside to Mary.

"I won a hundred dollars," I said.

She examined the ticket and laughed.

"That's a fortune," she said, and counted out five twenties. Our fingertips touched as she handed me the money. I felt electric and constant.

"Thank you," I said, and gave her one of the bills.

"I can't take that," she said. "It's your money."

"No, it's tribal. It's an Indian thing. When you win, you're supposed to share with your family."

"I'm not your family."

"Yes, you are."

She smiled. She kept the money. With eighty dollars in my pocket, I said goodbye to my dear Mary and walked out into the cold night air.

8 P.M.

I wanted to share the good news with Junior. I walked back to him, but he was gone. I heard later that he had hitchhiked down to Portland, Oregon, and died of exposure in an alley behind the Hilton Hotel.

9 P.M.

Lonesome for Indians, I carried my eighty dollars over to Big Heart's in South Downtown. Big Heart's is an all-Indian bar. Nobody knows how or why Indians migrate to one bar and turn it into an official Indian bar. But Big Heart's has been an Indian bar for twenty-three years. It used to be way up on Aurora Avenue, but a crazy Lummi Indian burned that one down, and the owners moved to the new location, a few blocks south of Safeco Field.

I walked into Big Heart's and counted fifteen Indians—eight men and seven women. I didn't know any of them, but Indians like to belong, so we all pretended to be cousins.

"How much for whiskey shots?" I asked the bartender, a fat white guy.

"You want the bad stuff or the badder stuff?"

"As bad as you got."

"One dollar a shot."

I laid my eighty dollars on the bar top.

"All right," I said. "Me and all my cousins here are going to be drinking eighty shots. How many is that apiece?"

"Counting you," a woman shouted from behind me, "that's five shots for everybody."

I turned to look at her. She was a chubby and pale Indian woman, sitting with a tall and skinny Indian man.

"All right, math genius," I said to her, and then shouted for the whole bar to hear. "Five drinks for everybody!"

All the other Indians rushed the bar, but I sat with the mathematician and her skinny friend. We took our time with our whiskey shots.

"What's your tribe?" I asked.

"I'm Duwamish," she said. "And he's Crow."

"You're a long way from Montana," I said to him.

"I'm Crow," he said. "I flew here."

"What's your name?" I asked them.

"I'm Irene Muse," she said. "And this is Honey Boy."

She shook my hand hard, but he offered his hand as if I was supposed to kiss it. So I did. He giggled and blushed, as much as a dark-skinned Crow can blush.

"You're one of them two-spirits, aren't you?" I asked him.

"I love women," he said. "And I love men."

"Sometimes both at the same time," Irene said.

We laughed.

"Man," I said to Honey Boy. "So you must have about eight or nine spirits going on inside you, enit?"

"Sweetie," he said. "I'll be whatever you want me to be."

"Oh, no," Irene said. "Honey Boy is falling in love."

"It has nothing to do with love," he said.

We laughed.

"Wow," I said. "I'm flattered, Honey Boy, but I don't play on your team."

"Never say never," he said.

"You better be careful," Irene said. "Honey Boy knows all sorts of magic."

"Honey Boy," I said, "you can try to seduce me, but my heart belongs to a woman named Mary."

"Is your Mary a virgin?" Honey Boy asked.

We laughed.

And we drank our whiskey shots until they were gone. But the other Indians bought me more whiskey shots, because I'd been so generous with my money. And Honey Boy pulled out his credit card, and I drank and sailed on that plastic boat.

After a dozen shots, I asked Irene to dance. She refused. But Honey Boy shuffled over to the jukebox, dropped in a quarter, and selected Willie Nelson's "Help Me Make It Through the Night." As Irene and I sat at the table and laughed and drank more whiskey, Honey Boy danced a slow circle around us and sang along with Willie.

"Are you serenading me?" I asked him.

He kept singing and dancing.

"Are you serenading me?" I asked him again.

"He's going to put a spell on you," Irene said.

I leaned over the table, spilling a few drinks, and kissed Irene hard. She kissed me back.

10 P.M.

Irene pushed me into the women's bathroom, into a stall, shut the door behind us, and shoved her hand down my pants. She was short, so I had to lean over to kiss her. I grabbed and squeezed her everywhere I could reach, and she was wonderfully fat, and every part of her body felt like a large, warm, soft breast.

MIDNIGHT

Nearly blind with alcohol, I stood alone at the bar and swore I had been standing in the bathroom with Irene only a minute ago.

"One more shot!" I yelled at the bartender.

"You've got no more money!" he yelled back.

"Somebody buy me a drink!" I shouted.

"They've got no more money!"

"Where are Irene and Honey Boy?"

"Long gone!"

2 A.M.

"Closing time!" the bartender shouted at the three or four Indians who were still drinking hard after a long, hard day of drinking. Indian alcoholics are either sprinters or marathoners.

"Where are Irene and Honey Boy?" I asked.

"They've been gone for hours," the bartender said.

"Where'd they go?"

"I told you a hundred times, I don't know."

"What am I supposed to do?"

"It's closing time. I don't care where you go, but you're not staying here."

"You are an ungrateful bastard. I've been good to you."

"You don't leave right now, I'm going to kick your ass."

"Come on, I know how to fight."

He came at me. I don't remember what happened after that.

4 A.M.

I emerged from the blackness and discovered myself walking behind a big warehouse. I didn't know where I was. My face hurt. I felt my nose and decided that it might be broken. Exhausted and cold, I pulled a plastic tarp from a truck bed, wrapped it around me like a faithful lover, and fell asleep in the dirt.

6 A.M.

Somebody kicked me in the ribs. I opened my eyes and looked up at a white cop.

"Jackson," the cop said. "Is that you?"

"Officer Williams," I said. He was a good cop with a sweet tooth. He'd given me hundreds of candy bars over the years. I wonder if he knew I was diabetic.

"What the hell are you doing here?" he asked.

"I was cold and sleepy," I said. "So I lay down."

"You dumb-ass, you passed out on the railroad tracks."

I sat up and looked around. I was lying on the railroad tracks. Dockworkers stared at me. I should have been a railroad-track pizza, a double Indian pepperoni with extra cheese. Sick and scared, I leaned over and puked whiskey.

"What the hell's wrong with you?" Officer Williams asked. "You've never been this stupid."

"It's my grandmother," I said. "She died."

"I'm sorry, man. When did she die?"

"Nineteen seventy-two."

"And you're killing yourself now?"

"I've been killing myself ever since she died."

He shook his head. He was sad for me. Like I said, he was a good cop.

"And somebody beat the hell out of you," he said. "You remember who?"

"Mr. Grief and I went a few rounds."

"It looks like Mr. Grief knocked you out."

"Mr. Grief always wins."

"Come on," he said. "Let's get you out of here."

He helped me up and led me over to his squad car. He put me in the back. "You throw up in there and you're cleaning it up," he said.

"That's fair."

He walked around the car and sat in the driver's seat. "I'm taking you over to detox," he said.

"No, man, that place is awful," I said. "It's full of drunk Indians."

We laughed. He drove away from the docks.

"I don't know how you guys do it," he said.

"What guys?" I asked.

"You Indians. How the hell do you laugh so much? I just picked your ass off the railroad tracks, and you're making jokes. Why the hell do you do that?"

"The two funniest tribes I've ever been around are Indians and Jews, so I guess that says something about the inherent humor of genocide."

We laughed.

"Listen to you, Jackson. You're so smart. Why the hell are you on the street?"

"Give me a thousand dollars and I'll tell you."

"You bet I'd give you a thousand dollars if I knew you'd straighten up your life."

He meant it. He was the second-best cop I'd ever known.

"You're a good cop," I said.

"Come on, Jackson," he said. "Don't blow smoke up my ass."

"No, really, you remind me of my grandfather."

"Yeah, that's what you Indians always tell me."

"No, man, my grandfather was a tribal cop. He was a good cop. He never arrested people. He took care of them. Just like you."

"I've arrested hundreds of scumbags, Jackson. And I've shot a couple in the ass."

"It don't matter. You're not a killer."

"I didn't kill them. I killed their asses. I'm an ass-killer."

We drove through downtown. The missions and shelters had already released their overnighters. Sleepy homeless men and women stood on street corners and stared up at a gray sky. It was the morning after the night of the living dead.

"Do you ever get scared?" I asked Officer Williams.

"What do you mean?"

"I mean, being a cop, is it scary?"

He thought about that for a while. He contemplated it. I liked that about him.

"I guess I try not to think too much about being afraid," he said. "If you think about fear, then you'll be afraid. The job is boring most of the time. Just driving and looking into dark corners, you know, and seeing nothing. But then things get heavy. You're chasing somebody, or fighting them or walking around a dark house, and you just know some crazy guy is hiding around a corner, and hell, yes, it's scary."

"My grandfather was killed in the line of duty," I said.

"I'm sorry. How'd it happen?"

I knew he'd listen closely to my story.

"He worked on the reservation. Everybody knew everybody. It was safe. We aren't like those crazy Sioux or Apache or any of those other warrior tribes. There've only been three murders on my reservation in the last hundred years."

"That is safe."

"Yeah, we Spokane, we're passive, you know. We're mean with words. And we'll cuss out anybody. But we don't shoot people. Or stab them. Not much, anyway."

"So what happened to your grandfather?"

"This man and his girlfriend were fighting down by Little Falls."

"Domestic dispute. Those are the worst."

"Yeah, but this guy was my grandfather's brother. My great-uncle."

"Oh, no."

"Yeah, it was awful. My grandfather just strolled into the house. He'd been there a thousand times. And his brother and his girlfriend were drunk and beating on each other. And my grandfather stepped between them, just as he'd done a hundred times before. And the girlfriend tripped or something. She fell down and hit her head and started crying. And my grandfather kneeled down beside her to make sure she was all right. And for some reason my great-uncle reached down, pulled my grandfather's pistol out of the holster, and shot him in the head."

"That's terrible. I'm sorry."

"Yeah, my great-uncle could never figure out why he did it. He went to prison forever, you know, and he always wrote these long let-

ters. Like fifty pages of tiny little handwriting. And he was always trying to figure out why he did it. He'd write and write and write and try
to figure it out. He never did. It's a great big mystery."

"Do you remember your grandfather?"

"A little bit. I remember the funeral. My grandmother wouldn't let
them bury him. My father had to drag her away from the grave."

"I don't know what to say."

"I don't, either."

We stopped in front of the detox center.

"We're here," Officer Williams said.

"I can't go in there," I said.

"You have to."

"Please, no. They'll keep me for twenty-four hours. And then it will
be too late."

"Too late for what?"

I told him about my grandmother's regalia and the deadline for
buying it back.

"If it was stolen, you need to file a report," he said. "I'll investigate
it myself. If that thing is really your grandmother's, I'll get it back for
you. Legally."

"No," I said. "That's not fair. The pawnbroker didn't know it was
stolen. And, besides, I'm on a mission here. I want to be a hero, you
know? I want to win it back, like a knight."

"That's romantic crap."

"That may be. But I care about it. It's been a long time since I really
cared about something."

Officer Williams turned around in his seat and stared at me. He
studied me.

"I'll give you some money," he said. "I don't have much. Only
thirty bucks. I'm short until payday. And it's not enough to get back the
regalia. But it's something."

"I'll take it," I said.

"I'm giving it to you because I believe in what you believe. I'm hoping, and I don't know why I'm hoping it, but I hope you can turn thirty
bucks into a thousand somehow."

"I believe in magic."

"I believe you'll take my money and get drunk on it."

"Then why are you giving it to me?"

"There ain't no such thing as an atheist cop."

"Sure, there is."

"Yeah, well, I'm not an atheist cop."

He let me out of the car, handed me two fivers and a twenty, and shook my hand.

"Take care of yourself, Jackson," he said. "Stay off the railroad tracks."

"I'll try," I said.

He drove away. Carrying my money, I headed back toward the water.

8 A.M.

On the wharf, those three Aleuts still waited on the wooden bench.

"Have you seen your ship?" I asked.

"Seen a lot of ships," the elder Aleut said. "But not our ship."

I sat on the bench with them. We sat in silence for a long time. I wondered if we would fossilize if we sat there long enough.

I thought about my grandmother. I'd never seen her dance in her regalia. And, more than anything, I wished I'd seen her dance at a pow-wow.

"Do you guys know any songs?" I asked the Aleuts.

"I know all of Hank Williams," the elder Aleut said.

"How about Indian songs?"

"Hank Williams is Indian."

"How about sacred songs?"

"Hank Williams is sacred."

"I'm talking about ceremonial songs. You know, religious ones. The songs you sing back home when you're wishing and hoping."

"What are you wishing and hoping for?"

"I'm wishing my grandmother was still alive."

"Every song I know is about that."

"Well, sing me as many as you can."

The Aleuts sang their strange and beautiful songs. I listened. They sang about my grandmother and about their grandmothers. They were lonesome for the cold and the snow. I was lonesome for everything.

10 A.M.

After the Aleuts finished their last song, we sat in silence for a while. Indians are good at silence.

"Was that the last song?" I asked.

"We sang all the ones we could," the elder Aleut said. "The others are just for our people."

I understood. We Indians have to keep our secrets. And these Aleuts were so secretive they didn't refer to themselves as Indians.

"Are you guys hungry?" I asked.

They looked at one another and communicated without talking.

"We could eat," the elder Aleut said.

11 A.M.

The Aleuts and I walked over to the Big Kitchen, a greasy diner in the International District. I knew they served homeless Indians who'd lucked into money.

"Four for breakfast?" the waitress asked when we stepped inside.

"Yes, we're very hungry," the elder Aleut said.

She took us to a booth near the kitchen. I could smell the food cooking. My stomach growled.

"You guys want separate checks?" the waitress asked.

"No, I'm paying," I said.

"Aren't you the generous one," she said.

"Don't do that," I said.

"Do what?" she asked.

"Don't ask me rhetorical questions. They scare me."

She looked puzzled, and then she laughed.

"O.K., professor," she said. "I'll only ask you real questions from now on."

"Thank you."

"What do you guys want to eat?"

"That's the best question anybody can ask anybody," I said. "What have you got?"

"How much money you got?" she asked.

"Another good question," I said. "I've got twenty-five dollars I can spend. Bring us all the breakfast you can, plus your tip."

She knew the math.

"All right, that's four specials and four coffees and fifteen percent for me."

The Aleuts and I waited in silence. Soon enough, the waitress returned and poured us four coffees, and we sipped at them until she returned again, with four plates of food. Eggs, bacon, toast, hash brown potatoes. It's amazing how much food you can buy for so little money.

Grateful, we feasted.

NOON

I said farewell to the Aleuts and walked toward the pawnshop. I heard later that the Aleuts had waded into the saltwater near Dock 47 and disappeared. Some Indians swore they had walked on the water and headed north. Other Indians saw the Aleuts drown. I don't know what happened to them.

I looked for the pawnshop and couldn't find it. I swear it wasn't in the place where it had been before. I walked twenty or thirty blocks looking for the pawnshop, turned corners and bisected intersections, and looked up its name in the phone books and asked people walking past me if they'd ever heard of it. But that pawnshop seemed to have sailed away like a ghost ship. I wanted to cry. And just when I'd given up, when I turned one last corner and thought I might die if I didn't find that pawnshop, there it was, in a space I swear it hadn't occupied a few minutes ago.

I walked inside and greeted the pawnbroker, who looked a little younger than he had before.

"It's you," he said.

"Yes, it's me," I said.

"Jackson Jackson."

"That is my name."

"Where are your friends?"

"They went traveling. But it's O.K. Indians are everywhere."

"Do you have the money?"

"How much do you need again?" I asked, and hoped the price had changed.

"Nine hundred and ninety-nine dollars."

It was still the same price. Of course, it was the same price. Why would it change?

"I don't have that," I said.

"What do you have?"

"Five dollars."

I set the crumpled Lincoln on the countertop. The pawnbroker studied it.

"Is that the same five dollars from yesterday?"

"No, it's different."

He thought about the possibilities.

"Did you work hard for this money?" he asked.

"Yes," I said.

He closed his eyes and thought harder about the possibilities. Then he stepped into the back room and returned with my grandmother's regalia.

"Take it," he said, and held it out to me.

"I don't have the money."

"I don't want your money."

"But I wanted to win it."

"You did win it. Now take it before I change my mind."

Do you know how many good men live in this world? Too many to count!

I took my grandmother's regalia and walked outside. I knew that solitary yellow bead was part of me. I knew I was that yellow bead in part. Outside, I wrapped myself in my grandmother's regalia and breathed her in. I stepped off the sidewalk and into the intersection. Pedestrians stopped. Cars stopped. The city stopped. They all watched me dance with my grandmother. I was my grandmother, dancing.

Dorothy Allison

Dorothy Allison was born in 1949. Raised in Greenville, South Carolina, she grew up in poverty and has written candidly about being physically and sexually abused by her stepfather. Allison has described those years as a "long terrible struggle to simply survive, to escape my stepfather, uncles, speeding Pontiacs, broken glass, and rotten floorboards." Her childhood is the subject of much of her work, including the novel Bastard Out of Carolina *(1992), which was a National Book Award finalist and winner of the Lambda Literary Award for best lesbian fiction of the year. Known for her feminism, which she has called "a substitute religion that made sense," Allison's other publications include the short story collection* Trash *(1988), the poetry collection* The Women Who Hate Me *(1991), the memoir* Two or Three Things I Know for Sure *(1994), the essay collection* Skin: Talking about Sex, Class, and Literature *(1994), and the novel* Cavedweller *(1998). Allison's work deals directly with issues of gender, class, and sexual orientation. In an essay published in the* New York Times Book Review, *she comments on the importance of literature that deals honestly with such themes: "We are the ones they make fiction of— we gay and disenfranchised and female—and we have the right to demand our full, nasty, complicated lives."*

River of Names

At a picnic at my aunt's farm, the only time the whole family ever gathered, my sister Billie and I chased chickens into the barn. Billie ran right through the open doors and out again, but I stopped, caught by a shadow moving over me. My cousin, Tommy, eight years old as I was, swung in the sunlight with his face as black as his shoes—the rope around his neck pulled up into the sunlit heights of the barn, fascinating, horrible. Wasn't he running ahead of us? Someone came up behind me. Someone began to scream. My mama took my head in her hands and turned my eyes away.

Jesse and I have been lovers for a year now. She tells me stories about her childhood, about her father going off each day to the university, her mother who made all her dresses, her grandmother who always smelled of dill bread and vanilla. I listen with my mouth open, not believing but wanting, aching for the fairy tale she thinks is everyone's life.

"What did your grandmother smell like?"

I lie to her the way I always do, a lie stolen from a book. "Like lavender," stomach churning over the memory of sour sweat and snuff.

I realize I do not really know what lavender smells like, and I am for a moment afraid she will ask something else, some question that will betray me. But Jesse slides over to hug me, to press her face against my ear, to whisper, "How wonderful to be part of such a large family."

I hug her back and close my eyes. I cannot say a word.

I was born between the older cousins and the younger, born in a pause of babies and therefore outside, always watching. Once, way before Tommy died, I was pushed out on the steps while everyone stood listening to my Cousin Barbara. Her screams went up and down in the back of the house. Cousin Cora brought buckets of bloody rags out to be burned. The other cousins all ran off to catch the sparks or poke the fire with dogwood sticks. I waited on the porch making up words to the shouts around me. I did not understand what was happening. Some of the older cousins obviously did, their strange expressions broken by stranger laughs. I had seen them helping her up the stairs while the thick blood ran down her legs. After a while the blood on the rags was thin, watery, almost pink. Cora threw them on the fire and stood motionless in the stinking smoke.

Randall went by and said there'd be a baby, a hatched egg to throw out with the rags, but there wasn't. I watched to see and there wasn't; nothing but the blood, thinning out desperately while the house slowed down and grew quiet, hours of cries growing soft and low, moaning under the smoke. My Aunt Raylene came out on the porch and almost fell on me, not seeing me, not seeing anything at all. She beat on the post until there were knuckle-sized dents in the peeling paint, beat on that post like it could feel, cursing it and herself and every child in the yard, singing up and down, "Goddamn, goddamn, that girl . . . no sense . . . goddamn!"

I've these pictures my mama gave me—stained sepia prints of bare dirt yards, plank porches, and step after step of children—cousins, uncles, aunts; mysteries. The mystery is how many no one remembers. I show them to Jesse, not saying who they are, and when she laughs at the broken teeth, torn overalls, the dirt, I set my teeth at what I do not want to remember and cannot forget.

We were so many we were without number and, like tadpoles, if there was one less from time to time, who counted? My maternal great-grandmother had eleven daughters, seven sons; my grand-mother, six sons, five daughters. Each one made at least six. Some made nine. Six times six, eleven times nine. They went on like multi-plication tables. They died and were not missed. I come of an enor-mous family and I cannot tell half their stories. Somehow it was al-ways made to seem they killed themselves: car wrecks, shotguns, dusty ropes, screaming, falling out of windows, things inside them. I am the point of a pyramid, sliding back under the weight of the ones who came after, and it does not matter that I am the lesbian, the one who will not have children.

I tell the stories and it comes out funny. I drink bourbon and make myself drawl, tell all those old funny stories. Someone always seems to ask me, which one was that? I show the pictures and she says, "Wasn't she the one in the story about the bridge?" I put the pictures away, drink more, and someone always finds them, then says, "Goddamn! How many of you were there anyway?"

I don't answer.

Jesse used to say, "You've got such a fascination with violence. You've got so many terrible stories."

She said it with her smooth mouth, that chin nobody ever slapped, and I love that chin, but when Jesse spoke then, my hands shook and I wanted nothing so much as to tell her terrible stories.

So I made a list. I told her: that one went insane—got her little brother with a tire iron; the three of them slit their arms, not the wrists but the bigger veins up near the elbow; she, now *she* strangled the boy she was sleeping with and got sent away; that one drank lye and died laughing soundlessly. In one year I lost eight cousins. It was the year everybody ran away. Four disappeared and were never found. One fell in the river and was drowned. One was run down hitchhiking north. One was shot running through the woods, while Grace, the last one, tried to walk from Greenville to Greer for some reason nobody knew. She fell off the overpass a mile down from the Sears, Roebuck ware-house and lay there for hunger and heat and dying.

Later, sleeping, but not sleeping, I found that my hands were up under Jesse's chin. I rolled away, but I didn't cry. I almost never let my-self cry.

Almost always, we were raped, my cousins and I. That was some kind of joke, too.

What's a South Carolina virgin?

'At's a ten-year-old can run fast.

It wasn't funny for me in my mama's bed with my stepfather, not for my cousin, Billie, in the attic with my uncle, not for Lucille in the woods with another cousin, for Danny with four strangers in a parking lot, or for Pammie who made the papers. Cora read it out loud: "Repeatedly by persons unknown." They stayed unknown since Pammie never spoke again. Perforations, lacerations, contusions, and bruises. I heard all the words, big words, little words, words too terrible to understand. DEAD BY AN ACT OF MAN. With the prick still in them, the broom handle, the tree branch, the grease gun . . . objects, things not to be believed . . . whiskey bottles, can openers, grass shears, glass, metal, vegetables . . . not to be believed, not to be believed.

Jesse says, "You've got a gift for words."

"Don't talk," I beg her, "don't talk." And this once, she just holds me blessedly silent.

I dig out the pictures, stare into the faces. Which one was I? Survivors do hate themselves, I know, over the core of fierce self-love, never understanding, always asking, "Why me and not her, not him?" There is such mystery in it, and I have hated myself as much as I have loved others, hated the simple fact of my own survival. Having survived, am I supposed to say something, do something, be something?

I loved my Cousin Butch. He had this big old head, pale thin hair, and enormous, watery eyes. All the cousins did, though Butch's head was the largest, his hair the palest. I was the dark-headed one. All the rest of the family seemed pale carbons of each other in shades of blond, though later on everybody's hair went brown or red and I didn't stand out so. Butch and I stood out then—I because I was so dark and fast, and he because of that big head and the crazy things he did. Butch used to climb on the back of my Uncle Lucius's truck, open the gas tank and hang his head over, breathe deeply, strangle, gag, vomit, and breathe again. It went so deep, it tingled in your toes. I climbed up after him and tried it myself, but I was too young to hang on long, and I fell heavily to the ground, dizzy and giggling. Butch could hang on, put his hand down into the tank and pull up a cupped palm of gas, breathe deep and laugh. He would climb down roughly, swinging down from the door handle, laughing, staggering, and stinking of gasoline. Someone caught him at it. Someone threw a match. "I'll teach you."

Just like that, gone before you understand.

I wake up in the night screaming, "No, no, I won't!" Dirty water rises in the back of my throat, the liquid language of my own terror and rage. "Hold me. Hold me." Jesse rolls over on me; her hands grip my hipbones tightly.

"I love you. I love you. I'm here," she repeats.

I stare up into her dark eyes, puzzled, afraid. I draw a breath in deeply, smile my bland smile. "Did I fool you?" I laugh, rolling away from her. Jesse punches me playfully, and I catch her hand in the air.

"My love," she whispers, and cups her body against my hip, closes her eyes. I bring my hand up in front of my face and watch the knuckles, the nails as they tremble, tremble. I watch for a long time while she sleeps, warm and still against me.

James went blind. One of the uncles got him in the face with home-brewed alcohol.

Lucille climbed out the front window of Aunt Raylene's house and jumped. They said she jumped. No one said why.

My Uncle Matthew used to beat my Aunt Raylene. The twins, Mark and Luke, swore to stop him, pulled him out in the yard one time, throwing him between them like a loose bag of grain. Uncle Matthew screamed like a pig coming up for slaughter. I got both my sisters in the tool shed for safety, but I hung back to watch. Little Bo came running out of the house, off the porch, feet first into his daddy's arms. Uncle Matthew started swinging him like a scythe, going after the bigger boys, Bo's head thudding their shoulders, their hips. Afterward, Bo crawled around in the dirt, the blood running out of his ears and his tongue hanging out of his mouth, while Mark and Luke finally got their daddy down. It was a long time before I realized that they never told anybody else what had happened to Bo.

Randall tried to teach Lucille and me to wrestle. "Put your hands up." His legs were wide apart, his torso bobbing up and down, his head moving constantly. Then his hand flashed at my face. I threw myself back into the dirt, lay still. He turned to Lucille, not noticing that I didn't get up. He punched at her, laughing. She wrapped her hands around her head, curled over so her knees were up against her throat.

"No, no," he yelled. "Move like her." He turned to me. "Move." He kicked at me. I rocked into a ball, froze.

"No, no!" He kicked me. I grunted, didn't move. He turned to Lucille. "You." Her teeth were chattering but she held herself still, wrapped up tighter than bacon slices.

"You move!" he shouted. Lucille just hugged her head tighter and started to sob.

"Son of a bitch," Randall grumbled, "you two will never be any good."

He walked away. Very slowly we stood up, embarrassed, looked at each other. We knew.

If you fight back, they kill you.

My sister was seven. She was screaming. My stepfather picked her up by her left arm, swung her forward and back. It gave. The arm went around loosely. She just kept screaming. I didn't know you could break it like that.

I was running up the hall. He was right behind me. "Mama! Mama!" His left hand—he was left-handed—closed around my throat, pushed me against the wall, and then he lifted me that way. I kicked, but I couldn't reach him. He was yelling, but there was so much noise in my ears I couldn't hear him.

"Please, Daddy. Please, Daddy. I'll do anything, I promise. Daddy, anything you want. Please, Daddy."

I couldn't have said that. I couldn't talk around that fist at my throat, couldn't breathe. I woke up when I hit the floor. I looked up at him.

"If I live long enough, I'll fucking kill you."

He picked me up by my throat again.

What's wrong with her?
Why's she always following you around?
Nobody really wanted answers.

A full bottle of vodka will kill you when you're nine and the bottle is a quart. It was a third cousin proved that. We learned what that and other things could do. Every year there was something new.

You're growing up.
My big girl.

There was codeine in the cabinet, paregoric for the baby's teeth, whiskey, beer, and wine in the house. Jeanne brought home MDA, PCP, acid; Randall, grass, speed, and mescaline. It all worked to dull things down, to pass the time.

Stealing was a way to pass the time. Things we needed, things we didn't, for the nerve of it, the anger, the need. *You're growing up,* we told each other. But sooner or later, we all got caught. Then it was, *When are you going to learn?*

Caught, nightmares happened. *Razorback desperate,* was the conclusion of the man down at the county farm where Mark and Luke were
sent at fifteen. They both got their heads shaved, their earlobes sliced.
What's the matter, kid? Can't you take it?

Caught at sixteen, June was sent to Jessup County Girls' Home
where the baby was adopted out and she slashed her wrists on the bed-
springs.

Lou got caught at seventeen and held in the station downtown,
raped on the floor of the holding tank.

Are you a boy or are you a girl?

On your knees, kid, can you take it?

Caught at eighteen and sent to prison, Jack came back seven years
later blank-faced, understanding nothing. He married a quiet girl from
out of town, had three babies in four years. Then Jack came home one
night from the textile mill, carrying one of those big handles off the
high-speed spindle machine. He used it to beat them all to death and
went back to work in the morning.

Cousin Melvina married at fourteen, had three kids in two and a
half years, and welfare took them all away. She ran off with a carnival
mechanic, had three more babies before he left her for a motorcycle ac-
robat. Welfare took those, too. But the next baby was hydrocephalic, a
little waterhead they left with her, and the three that followed, even the
one she used to hate so—the one she had after she fell off the porch and
couldn't remember whose child it was.

"How many children do you have?" I asked her.

"You mean the ones I have, or the ones I had? Four," she told me,
"or eleven."

My aunt, the one I was named for, tried to take off for Oklahoma.
That was after she'd lost the youngest girl and they told her Bo would
never be "right." She packed up biscuits, cold chicken, and Coca-Cola,
a lot of loose clothes, Cora and her new baby, Cy, and the four
youngest girls. They set off from Greenville in the afternoon, hoping to
make Oklahoma by the weekend, *but they only got as far as Augusta.*
The bridge there went out under them.

"An Act of God," my uncle said.

My aunt and Cora crawled out down river, and two of the girls
turned up in the weeds, screaming loud enough to be found in the dark.
But one of the girls never came up out of that dark water, and Nancy,
who had been holding Cy, was found still wrapped around the baby, in
the water, under the car.

"An Act of God," my aunt said. "God's got one damn sense of humor."

My sister had her baby in a bad year. Before he was born we had talked about it. "Are you afraid?" I asked.

"He'll be fine," she'd replied, not understanding, speaking instead to the other fear. "Don't we have a tradition of bastards?"

He was fine, a classically ugly healthy little boy with that shock of white hair that marked so many of us. But afterward, it was that bad year with my sister down with pleurisy, then cystitis, and no work, no money, having to move back home with my cold-eyed stepfather. I would come home to see her, from the woman I could not admit I'd been with, and take my infinitely fragile nephew and hold him, rocking him, rocking myself.

One night I came home to screaming—the baby, my sister, no one else there. She was standing by the crib, bent over, screaming red-faced, "Shut up! Shut up!" With each word her fist slammed the mattress fanning the baby's ear.

"Don't!" I grabbed her, pulling her back, doing it as gently as I could so I wouldn't break the stitches from her operation. She had her other arm clamped across her abdomen and couldn't fight me at all. She just kept shrieking.

"That little bastard just screams and screams. That little bastard. I'll kill him."

Then the words seeped in and she looked at me while her son kept crying and kicking his feet. By his head the mattress still showed the impact of her fist.

"Oh no," she moaned, "I wasn't going to be like that. I always promised myself." She started to cry, holding her belly and sobbing. "We an't no different. We an't no different."

Jesse wraps her arm around my stomach, presses her belly into my back. I relax against her. "You sure you can't have children?" she asks. "I sure would like to see what your kids would turn out to be like."

I stiffen, say, "I can't have children. I've never wanted children."

"Still," she says, "you're so good with children, so gentle."

I think of all the times my hands have curled into fists, when I have just barely held on. I open my mouth, close it, can't speak. What could I say now? All the times I have not spoken before, all the things I just could not tell her, the shame, the self-hatred, the fear; all of that hangs between us now—a wall I cannot tear down.

I would like to turn around and talk to her, tell her . . . "I've got a dust river in my head, a river of names endlessly repeating. That dirty water rises in me, all those children screaming out their lives in my memory, and I become someone else, someone I have tried so hard not to be."

But I don't say anything, and I know, as surely as I know I will never have a child, that by not speaking I am condemning us, that I cannot go on loving you and hating you for your fairy-tale life, for not asking about what you have no reason to imagine, for that soft-chinned innocence I love.

Jesse puts her hands behind my neck, smiles and says, "You tell the funniest stories."

I put my hands behind her back, feeling the ridges of my knuckles pulsing.

"Yeah," I tell her. "But I lie."

Donald Barthelme

Donald Barthelme (1931–1989) was born in Philadelphia, grew up in Texas, lived for many years in New York City, and taught for much of his career at the University of Houston. His experimental fictions use humor, social satire, a nonconventional minimalist style, and a collage technique that reflects the disconnected chaos of sound and image characteristic of contemporary life. Barthelme published two novels, Snow White *(1967) and* The Dead Father *(1975), as well as eight short story collections, including* Sixty Stories *(1981), which won the PEN/Faulkner Award for fiction. His essays and interviews are collected in* The Teachings of Donald Barthelme *(1992) and* Not Knowing *(1997). In the essay "Not Knowing," he describes his own approach to creative art: "Writing is a process of dealing with not-knowing, a forcing of what and how. . . . The not-knowing is crucial to art, is what permits art to be made. Without the scanning process engendered by not-knowing, without the possibility of having the mind move in unanticipated directions, there would be no invention. . . . The not knowing is not simple, because it's hedged about with prohibitions, roads that may not be taken. The more serious the artist, the more problems he takes into account and the more considerations limit his possible initiatives."*

The School

Well, we had all these children out planting trees, see, because we figured that . . . that was part of their education, to see how, you know, the root systems . . . and also the sense of responsibility, taking care of things, being individually responsible. You know what I mean. And the trees all died. They were orange trees. I don't know why they died, they just died. Something wrong with the soil possibly or maybe the stuff we got from the nursery wasn't the best. We complained about it. So we've got thirty kids there, each kid had his or her own little tree to plant, and we've got these thirty dead trees. All these kids looking at these little brown sticks, it was depressing.

It wouldn't have been so bad except that just a couple of weeks before the thing with the trees, the snakes all died. But I think that the snakes—well, the reason that the snakes kicked off was that . . . you remember, the boiler was shut off for four days because of the strike, and that was explicable. It was something you could explain to the kids because of the strike. I mean, none of their parents would let them cross the picket line and they knew there was a strike going on and what it meant. So when things got started up again and we found the snakes they weren't too disturbed.

With the herb gardens it was probably a case of overwatering, and at least now they know not to overwater. The children were very conscientious with the herb gardens and some of them probably . . . you know, slipped them a little extra water when we weren't looking. Or maybe . . . well, I don't like to think about sabotage, although it did occur to us. I mean, it was something that crossed our minds. We were thinking that way probably because before that the gerbils had died, and the white mice had died, and the salamander . . . well, now they know not to carry them around in plastic bags.

Of course we *expected* the tropical fish to die, that was no surprise. Those numbers, you look at them crooked and they're belly-up on the surface. But the lesson plan called for a tropical-fish input at that point, there was nothing we could do, it happens every year, you just have to hurry past it.

We weren't even supposed to have a puppy.

We weren't even supposed to have one, it was just a puppy the Murdoch girl found under a Gristede's truck one day and she was afraid the truck would run over it when the driver had finished making his delivery, so she stuck it in her knapsack and brought it to school with her. So we had this puppy. As soon as I saw the puppy I thought, Oh Christ, I bet it will live for about two weeks and then . . . And that's what it did. It wasn't supposed to be in the classroom at all, there's some kind of regulation about it, but you can't tell them they can't have a puppy when the puppy is already there, right in front of them, running around on the floor and yap yap yapping. They named it Edgar—that is, they named it after me. They had a lot of fun running after it and yelling, "Here, Edgar! Nice Edgar!" Then they'd laugh like hell. They enjoyed the ambiguity. I enjoyed it myself. I don't mind being kidded. They made a little house for it in the supply closet and all that. I don't know what it died of. Distemper, I guess. It probably hadn't had any shots. I got it out of there before the kids got to school. I checked the supply closet each morning, routinely, because I knew what was going to happen. I gave it to the custodian.

And then there was this Korean orphan that the class adopted through the Help the Children program, all the kids brought in a quarter a month, that was the idea. It was an unfortunate thing, the kid's name was Kim and maybe we adopted him too late or something. The cause of death was not stated in the letter we got, they suggested we adopt another child instead and sent us some interesting case histories, but we didn't have the heart. The class took it pretty hard, they began (I think; nobody ever said anything to me directly) to feel that maybe there was something wrong with the school. But I don't think there's anything wrong with the school, particularly, I've seen better and I've seen worse. It was just a run of bad luck. We had an extraordinary number of parents passing away, for instance. There were I think two heart attacks and two suicides, one drowning, and four killed together in a car accident. One stroke. And we had the usual heavy mortality rate among the grandparents, or maybe it was heavier this year, it seemed so. And finally the tragedy.

The tragedy occurred when Matthew Wein and Tony Mavrogordo were playing over where they're excavating for the new federal office building. There were all these big wooden beams stacked, you know, at the edge of the excavation. There's a court case coming out of that, the parents are claiming that the beams were poorly stacked. I don't know what's true and what's not. It's been a strange year.

I forgot to mention Billy Brandt's father, who was knifed fatally when he grappled with a masked intruder in his home.

One day, we had a discussion in class. They asked me, where did they go? The trees, the salamander, the tropical fish, Edgar, the poppas and mommas, Matthew and Tony, where did they go? And I said, I don't know, I don't know. And they said, who knows? and I said, nobody knows. And they said, is death that which gives meaning to life? and I said, no, life is that which gives meaning to life. Then they said, but isn't death, considered as a fundamental datum, the means by which the taken-for-granted mundanity of the everyday may be transcended in the direction of—

I said, yes, maybe.

They said, we don't like it.

I said, that's sound.

They said, it's a bloody shame!

I said, it is.

They said, will you make love now with Helen (our teaching assistant) so that we can see how it is done? We know you like Helen.

I do like Helen but I said that I would not.

We've heard so much about it, they said, but we've never seen it.

I said I would be fired and that it was never, or almost never, done as a demonstration. Helen looked out of the window.

They said, please, please make love with Helen, we require an assertion of value, we are frightened.

I said that they shouldn't be frightened (although I am often frightened) and that there was value everywhere. Helen came and embraced me. I kissed her a few times on the brow. We held each other. The children were excited. Then there was a knock on the door, I opened the door, and the new gerbil walked in. The children cheered wildly.

Charles Baxter

Charles Baxter was born in 1947 and raised in Minneapolis. He has written three novels: First Light *(1994), the National Book Award Finalist* The Feast of Love *(2000), and* Saul and Patsy *(2003); and four short story collections:* Harmony of the World *(1984),* Through the Safety Net *(1985),* A Relative Stranger *(1990), and* Believers *(1997). He has written two collections of poetry, edited three literary anthologies, and written a book of essays on writing and craft,* Burning Down the House *(1997). Baxter has set nearly all of his work in the Midwest, often in or near the fictional town of Five Oaks, Michigan. In an interview with the* Atlantic, *he discussed his method for triggering a short story: "I like to throw characters together into situations that create stress so that as the story goes forward, something in the situation or the characters is forced to reveal itself. I put characters under stress until something rises to the surface. Some hidden thing or beautiful action or enactment of desire or frustration. . . . I've always thought that one way to achieve this is to use characters who are strangers—they don't know anything more about themselves than the reader does, so the story has to move itself along from that point on."*

Snow

Twelve years old, and I was so bored I was combing my hair just for the hell of it. This particular Saturday afternoon, time was stretching out unpleasantly in front of me. I held the comb under the tap and then stared into the bathroom mirror as I raked the wave at the front of my scalp upward so that it would look casual and sharp and perfect. For inspiration I had my transistor radio, balanced on the doorknob, tuned to an AM Top Forty station. But the music was making me jumpy, and instead of looking casual my hair, soaking wet, had the metallic curve of the rear fins of a De Soto. I looked aerodynamic but not handsome. I dropped the comb into the sink and went down the hallway to my brother's room.

Ben was sitting at his desk, crumpling up papers and tossing them into a wastebasket near the window. He was a great shot, particularly when he was throwing away his homework. His stainless-steel sword, a souvenir of military school, was leaning against the bookcase, and I could see my pencil-thin reflection in it as I stood in his doorway. "Did you hear about the car?" Ben asked, not bothering to look at me. He was gazing through his window at Five Oaks Lake.

"What car?"

"The car that went through the ice two nights ago. Thursday, Look. You can see the pressure ridge near Eagle Island."

I couldn't see any pressure ridge; it was too far away. Cars belonging to ice fishermen were always breaking through the ice, but swallowing up a car was a slow process in January, though not in March or April, and the drivers usually got out safely. The clear lake ice reflected perfectly the flat gray sky this drought winter, and we could still see the spiky brown grass on our back lawn. It crackled and crunched whenever I walked on it.

"I don't see it," I said. "I can't see the hole. Where did you hear about this car? Did Pop tell you?"

"No," Ben said. "Other sources." Ben's sources, his network of friends and enemies, were always calling him on the telephone to tell him things. He basked in information. Now he gave me a quick glance. "Holy smoke," he said. "What did you do to your hair?"

"Nothing," I said. "I was just combing it."

"You look like that guy," he said. "The one in the movies."

"Which guy?"

"That Harvey guy."

"Jimmy Stewart?"

"Of course not," he said. "You know the one I mean. Everybody knows that guy. The Harvey guy." When I looked blank, he said, "Never mind. Let's go down to the lake and look at that car. You'd better tell them we're going." He gestured toward the other end of the house.

In the kitchen I informed my parents that I was headed somewhere with my brother, and my mother, chopping carrots for one of her stews, looked up at me and my hair. "Be back by five," she said. "Where did you say you were off to?"

"We're driving to Navarre," I said. "Ben has to get his skates sharpened."

My stepfather's eyebrows started to go up; he exchanged a glance with my mother—the usual pantomime of skepticism. I turned around and ran out of the kitchen before they could stop me. I put on my boots, overcoat, and gloves, and hurried outside to my brother's car, a 1952 Rocket 88. He was already inside. The motor roared.

The interior of the car smelled of gum, cigarettes, wet wool, analgesic balm, and after-shave. "What'd you tell them?" my brother asked.

"I said you were going to Navarre to get your skates sharpened."

He put the car into first gear, then sighed. "Why'd you do that? I have to explain everything to you. Number one: my skates aren't in the car. What if they ask to see them when we get home? I won't have them. That's a problem, isn't it? Number two: when you lie about being somewhere, you make sure you have a friend who's there who can say you *were* there, even if you weren't. Unfortunately, we don't have any friends in Navarre."

"Then we're safe," I said. "No one will say we *weren't* there."

He shook his head. Then he took off his glasses and examined them as if my odd ideas were visible right there on the frames. I was just doing my job, being his private fool, but I knew he liked me and liked to have me around. My unworldliness amused him; it gave him a chance to lecture me. But now, tired of wasting words on me, he turned on the radio. Pulling out onto the highway, he steered the car in his customary way. He had explained to me that only very old or very sick people actually grip steering wheels. You didn't have to hold the wheel to drive a car. Resting your arm over the top of the wheel gave a better appearance. You dangled your hand down, preferably with a cigarette in it, so that the car, the entire car, responded to the mere pressure of your wrist.

"Hey," I said. "Where are we going? This isn't the way to the lake."

"We're not going there first. We're going there second."

"Where are we going first?"

"We're going to Five Oaks. We're going to get Stephanie. Then we'll see the car."

"How come we're getting her?"

"Because she wants to see it. She's never seen a car underneath the ice before. She'll be impressed."

"Does she know we're coming?"

He gave me that look again. "What do they teach you at that school you go to? Of course she knows. We have a date."

"A date? It's three o'clock in the afternoon," I said. "You can't have a date at three in the afternoon. Besides, I'm along."

"Don't argue," Ben said. "Pay attention."

By the time we reached Five Oaks, the heater in my brother's car was blowing out warm air in tentative gusts. If we were going to get Stephanie, his current girlfriend, it was fine with me. I liked her smile—she had an overbite, the same as I did, but she didn't seem self-conscious about it—and I liked the way she shut her eyes when she laughed. She had listened to my crystal radio set and admired my collection of igneous rocks on one of her two visits to our house. My brother liked to bring his girlfriends over to our house because the house was old and large and, my brother said, they would be impressed by the empty rooms and the long hallways and the laundry chutes that dropped down into nowhere. They'd be snowed. Snowing girls was something I knew better than to ask my brother about. You had to learn about it by watching and listening. That's why he had brought me along.

Ben parked outside Stephanie's house and told me to wait in the car. I had nothing to do but look at houses and telephone poles. Stephanie's front-porch swing had rusted chains, and the paint around her house seemed to have blistered in cobweb patterns. One drab lamp with a low-wattage bulb was on near an upstairs window. I could see the lampshade: birds—I couldn't tell what kind—had been painted on it. I adjusted the dashboard clock. It didn't run, but I liked to have it seem accurate. My brother had said that anyone who invented a clock that would really work in a car would become a multimillionaire. Clocks in cars never work, he said, because the mainsprings can't stand the shock of potholes. I checked my wristwatch and yawned. The inside of the front window began to frost over with my breath. I decided that when I grew up I would invent a new kind of timepiece for cars, without springs or gears. At three-twenty I adjusted the clock again. One minute later, my brother came out of the house with Stephanie. She saw me in the car, and she smiled.

I opened the door and got out. "Hi, Steph," I said. "I'll get in the backseat."

"That's okay, Russell," she said, smiling, showing her overbite. "Sit up in front with us."

"Really?"

She nodded. "Yeah. Keep us warm."

She scuttled in next to my brother, and I squeezed in on her right side, with my shoulder against the door. As soon as the car started, she and my brother began to hold hands: he steered with his left wrist over the steering wheel, and she held his right hand. I watched all this, and Stephanie noticed me watching. "Do you want one?" she asked me.

"What?"

"A hand." She gazed at me, perfectly serious. "My other hand."

"Sure," I said.

"Well, take my glove off," she said. "I can't do it by myself." My brother started chuckling, but she stopped him with a look. I took Stephanie's wrist in my left hand and removed her glove, finger by finger. I hadn't held hands with anyone since second grade. Her hand was not much larger than mine, but holding it gave me an odd sensation, because it was a woman's hand, and where my fingers were bony, hers were soft. She was wearing a bright-green cap, and when I glanced up at it she said, "I like your hair, Russell. It's kind of slummy. You're getting to look dangerous. Is there any gum?"

I figured she meant in the car. "There's some up there on the dashboard," Ben said. His car always had gum in it. It was a museum of gum. The ashtrays were full of cigarette butts and gum, mixed together, and the floor was flecked silver from the foil wrappers.

"I can't reach it," Stephanie said. "You two have both my hands tied down."

"Okay," I said. I reached up with my free hand and took a piece of gum and unwrapped it. The gum was light pink, a sunburn color.

"Now what?" I asked.

"What do you think?" She looked down at me, smiled again, then opened her mouth. I suddenly felt shy. "Come on, Russell," she said. "Haven't you ever given gum to a girl before?" I raised my hand with the gum in it. She kept her eyes open and on me. I reached forward, and just as I got the gum close to her mouth she opened wider, and I slid the gum in over her tongue without even brushing it against her lipstick. She closed and began chewing.

"Thank you," she said. Stephanie and my brother nudged each other. Then they broke out in short quick laughs—vacation laughter. I knew that what had happened hinged on my ignorance, but that I wasn't exactly the butt of the joke and could laugh, too, if I wanted. My palm was sweaty, and she could probably feel it. The sky had turned darker, and I wondered whether, if I was still alive fifty years from now, I would remember any of this. I saw an old house on the side of the highway with a cracked upstairs window, and I thought, that's what I'll remember from this whole day when I'm old—that one cracked window.

Stephanie was looking out at the dry winter fields and suddenly said, "The state of Michigan. You know who this state is for? You know who's really happy in this state?"

"No," I said. "Who?"

"Chickens and squirrels," she said. "They love it here."

My brother parked the car on the driveway down by our dock, and we walked out onto the ice on the bay. Stephanie was stepping awkwardly, a high-center-of-gravity shuffle. "Is it safe?" she asked.

"Sure, it's safe," my brother said. "Look." He began to jump up and down. Ben was heavy enough to be a tackle on his high-school football team, and sounds of ice cracking reverberated all through the bay and beyond into the center of the lake, a deep echo. Already, four ice fishermen's houses had been set up on the ice two hundred feet out—four brightly painted shacks, male hideaways—and I could see tire tracks over the thin layer of sprinkled snow. "Clear the snow and look down into it," he said.

After lowering herself to her knees, Stephanie dusted the snow away. She held her hands to the side of her head and looked. "It's real thick," she said. "Looks a foot thick. How come a car went through?"

"It went down in a channel," Ben said, walking ahead of us and calling backward so that his voice seemed to drift in and out of the wind. "It went over a pressure ridge, and that's all she wrote."

"Did anyone drown?"

He didn't answer. She ran ahead to catch up to him, slipping, losing her balance, then recovering it. In fact I knew that no one had drowned. My stepfather had told me that the man driving the car had somehow— I wasn't sure how a person did this—pulled himself out through the window. Apparently the front end dropped through the ice first, but the car had stayed up for a few minutes before it gradually eased itself into the lake. The last two nights had been very cold, with lows around fifteen below zero, and by now the hole the car had gone through had iced over.

Both my brother and Stephanie were quite far ahead of me, and I could see them clutching at each other, Stephanie leaning against him, and my brother trying out his military-school peacock walk. I attempted this walk for a moment, then thought better of it. The late-afternoon January light was getting very raw: the sun came out for a few seconds, lighting and coloring what there was, then disappeared again, closing up and leaving us in a kind of sour grayness. I wondered if my brother and Stephanie actually liked each other or whether they were friends because they had to be.

I ran to catch up to them. "We should have brought our skates," I said, but they weren't listening to me. Ben was pointing at some clear ice, and Stephanie was nodding.

"Quiet down," my brother said. "Quiet down and listen."

All three of us stood still. Some cloud or other was beginning to drop snow on us, and from the ice underneath our feet we heard a continual chinging and barking as the ice slowly shifted.

"This is exciting," Stephanie said.

My brother nodded, but instead of looking at her he turned slightly to glance at me. Our eyes met, and he smiled.

"It's over there," he said, after a moment. The index finger of his black leather glove pointed toward a spot in the channel between Eagle Island and Crane Island where the ice was ridged and unnaturally clear. "Come on," he said.

We walked. I was ready at any moment to throw myself flat if the ice broke beneath me. I was a good swimmer—Ben had taught me—but I wasn't sure how well I would swim wearing all my clothes. I was absorbent and would probably sink headfirst, like that car.

"Get down," my brother said.

We watched him lowering himself to his hands and knees, and we followed. This was probably something he had learned in military school, this crawling. "We're ambushing this car," Stephanie said, creeping in front of me.

"There it is," he said. He pointed down.

This new ice was so smooth that it reminded me of the thick glass in the Shedd Aquarium, in Chicago. But instead of seeing a loggerhead turtle or a barracuda I looked through the ice and saw this abandoned car, this two-door Impala. It was wonderful to see—white-painted steel filtered by ice and lake water—and I wanted to laugh out of sheer happiness at the craziness of it. Dimly lit but still visible through the murk, it sat down there, its huge trunk and the sloping fins just a bit green in the algae-colored light. This is a joke, I thought, a practical joke meant to confuse the fish. I could see the car well enough to notice its radio-antenna, and the windshield wipers halfway up the front window, and I could see the chrome of the front grille reflecting the dull light that ebbed down to it from where we were lying on our stomachs, ten feet above it.

"That is one unhappy automobile," Stephanie said. "Did anyone get caught inside?"

"No," I said, because no one had, and then my brother said, "Maybe."

I looked at him quickly. As usual, he wasn't looking back at me. "They aren't sure yet," he said. "They won't be able to tell until they bring the tow truck out here and pull it up."

Stephanie said, "Well, either they know or they don't. Someone's down there or not, right?"

Ben shook his head. "Maybe they don't know. Maybe there's a dead body in the backseat of that car. Or in the trunk."

"Oh, no," she said. She began to edge backward.

"I was just fooling you," my brother said. "There's nobody down there."

"What?" She was behind the area where the ice was smooth, and she stood up.

"I was just teasing you," Ben said. "The guy that was in the car got out. He got out through the window."

"Why did you lie to me?" Stephanie asked. Her arms were crossed in front of her chest.

"I just wanted to give you a thrill," he said. He stood up and walked over to where she was standing. He put his arm around her.

"I don't mind normal," she said. "Something could be normal and I'd like that, too." She glanced at me. Then she whispered into my brother's ear for about fifteen seconds, which is a long time if you're watching. Ben nodded and bent forward and whispered something in return, but I swiveled and looked around the bay at all the houses on the shore, and the old amusement park in the distance. Lights were beginning to go on, and, as if that weren't enough, it was snowing. As far as I was concerned, all those houses were guilty, both the houses and the people in them. The whole state of Michigan was guilty—all the adults, anyway—and I wanted to see them locked up.

"Wait here," my brother said. He turned and went quickly off toward the shore of the bay.

"Where's he going?" I asked.

"He's going to get his car," she said.

"What for?"

"He's going to bring it out on the ice. Then he's going to drive me home across the lake."

"That's really stupid!" I said. "That's really one of the dumbest things I ever heard! You'll go through the ice, just like that car down there did."

"No, we won't," she said. "I know we won't."

"How do you know?"

"Your brother understands this lake," she said. "He knows where the pressure ridges are and everything. He just *knows*, Russell. You have to trust him. And he can always get off the ice if he thinks it's not safe. He can always find a road."

"Well, I'm not going with you," I said. She nodded. I looked at her, and I wondered if she might be crazed with the bad judgment my parents had told me all teenagers had. Bad judgment of this kind was starting to interest me; it was a powerful antidote for boredom, which seemed worse.

"You don't want to come?"

"No," I said. "I'll walk home." I gazed up the hill, and in the distance I could see the lights of our house, a twenty-minute walk across the bay.

"Okay," Stephanie said. "I didn't think you'd want to come along." We waited. "Russell, do you think your brother is interested in me?"

"I guess so," I said. I wasn't sure what she meant by "interested." Anybody interested him, up to a point. "He says he likes you."

"That's funny, because I feel like something in the Lost and Found," she said, scratching her boot into the ice. "You know, one of those gloves that don't match anything." She put her hand on my shoulder. "One glove. One left-hand glove, with the thumb missing."

I could hear Ben's car starting, and then I saw it heading down Gallagher's boat landing. I was glad he was driving out toward us, because I didn't want to talk to her this way anymore.

Stephanie was now watching my brother's car. His headlights were on. It was odd to see a car with headlights on out on the ice, where there was no road. I saw my brother accelerate and fishtail the car, then slam on the brakes and do a 360-degree spin. He floored it, revving the back wheels, which made a high, whining sound on the ice, like a buzz saw working through wood. He was having a thrill and soon would give Stephanie another thrill by driving her home across ice that might break at any time. Thrills did it, whatever it was. Thrills led to other thrills.

"Would you look at that," I said.

She turned. After a moment she made a little sound in her throat. I remember that sound. When I see her now, she still makes it—a sign of impatience or worry. After all, she didn't go through the ice in my brother's car on the way home. She and my brother didn't drown, together or separately. Stephanie had two marriages and several children. Recently, she and her second husband adopted a Korean baby. She has the complex dignity of many small-town people who do not resort to alcohol until well after night has fallen. She continues to live in Five Oaks, Michigan, and she works behind the counter at the post office, where I buy stamps from her and gossip, holding up the line, trying to make her smile. She still has an overbite and she still laughs easily, despite the moody expression that comes over her when she relaxes. She has moved back to the same house she grew up in. Even now the exterior paint on that house blisters in cobweb patterns. I keep track of her. She and my brother certainly didn't get married; in fact, they broke up a few weeks after seeing the Chevrolet under ice.

"What are we doing out here?" Stephanie asked. I shook my head. "In the middle of winter, out here on this stupid lake? I'll tell you, Russell, I sure don't know. But I do know that your brother doesn't notice me enough, and I can't love him unless he notices me. You know your brother. You know what he pays attention to. What do I have to do to get him to notice me?"

I was twelve years old. I said, "Take off your shoes."

She stood there, thinking about what I had said, and then, quietly, she bent down and took off her boots, and, putting her hand on my shoulder to balance herself, she took off her brown loafers and her white socks. She stood there in front of me with her bare feet on the ice. I saw in the grayish January light that her toenails were painted. Bare feet with painted toenails on the ice—this was a desperate and beautiful sight, and I shivered and felt my fingers curling inside my gloves.

"How does it feel?" I asked.

"You'll know," she said. "You'll know in a few years."

My brother drove up close to us. He rolled down his window and opened the passenger-side door. He didn't say anything. I watched Stephanie get into the car, carrying her shoes and socks and boots, and then I waved goodbye to them before turning to walk back to our house. I heard the car heading north across the ice. My brother would be looking at Stephanie's bare feet on the floor of his car. He would probably not be saying anything just now.

When I reached our front lawn, I stood out in the dark and looked in through the kitchen window. My mother and stepfather were sitting at the kitchen counter; I couldn't be sure if they were speaking to each other, but then I saw my mother raise her arm in one of her can-you-believe-this gestures. I didn't want to go inside. I wanted to feel cold, so cold that the cold itself became permanently interesting. I took off my overcoat and my gloves. Tilting my head back, I felt some snow fall onto my face. I thought of the word "exposure" and of how once or twice a year deer hunters in the Upper Peninsula died of it, and I bent down and stuck my hand into the snow and frozen grass and held it there. The cold rose from my hand to my elbow, and when I had counted to forty and couldn't stand another second of it, I picked up my coat and gloves and walked into the bright heat of the front hallway.

Ann Beattie

Born in 1947 and raised in Washington, DC, Ann Beattie is known as a chronicler of the postwar baby boom generation. While a Ph.D. candidate at the University of Connecticut in the early seventies, she began writing and publishing stories in The New Yorker. *In 1976 she published a collection of stories,* Distortions, *as well as a novel,* Chilly Scenes of Winter. *More fiction followed, including the short story collections* The Burning House *(1982),* Where You'll Find Me *(1988),* What Was Mine *(1991),* Park City: New and Selected Stories *(1998),* Perfect Recall *(2001),* Follies: New Stories *(2005), and the novels* Falling in Place *(1980),* Picturing Will *(1990), and* The Doctor's House *(2002). In her essay "Where Characters Come From," first published in* The Mississippi Review, *Beattie writes, "My characters, who surprise, and enlighten, and dismay me so often, come from familiar worlds with unfamiliar subtexts. Similarly, they are 'real,—not made up—until the very early point in any story when they will not be contained, and then they are transformed so they are beyond my comprehension until the moment something clicks, and then I know what I did not know before, or did not articulate to myself. Inventing characters is for me no different from inventing any day. The best days, though, are the ones that contain real inventions. The days when I write stories."*

Snow

I remember the cold night you brought in a pile of logs and a chipmunk jumped off as you lowered your arms. "What do you think *you're* doing in here?" you said, as it ran through the living room. It went through the library and stopped at the front door as though it knew the house well. This would be difficult for anyone to believe, except perhaps as the subject of a poem. Our first week in the house was spent scraping, finding some of the house's secrets, like wallpaper underneath wallpaper. In the kitchen, a pattern of white-gold trellises supported purple grapes as big and round as Ping-Pong balls. When we painted the walls yellow, I thought of the bits of grape that remained underneath and imagined the vine popping through, the way some plants can tenaciously push through anything. The day of the big snow, when you had to shovel the walk and couldn't find your cap and asked me how to wind a towel so that it would stay on your head—you, in the white towel turban, like a crazy king of snow. People liked the idea of our being together, leaving the city for the country. So many people visited, and the fireplace made all of them want to tell amazing stories: the child who happened to be standing on the right corner when the door of the ice-cream truck came open and hundreds of Popsicles crashed out; the man standing on the beach, sand sparkling in the sun, one bit glinting more than the rest, stooping to find a diamond ring. Did they talk about amazing things because they thought we'd turn into one of them? Now I think they probably guessed it wouldn't work. It was as hopeless as giving a child a matched cup and saucer. Remember the night, out on the lawn, knee-deep in snow, chins pointed at the sky as the wind whirled down all that whiteness? It seemed that the world had been turned upside down, and we were looking into an enormous field of Queen Anne's lace. Later, headlights off, our car was the first to ride through the newly fallen snow. The world outside the car looked solarized.

You remember it differently. You remember that the cold settled in stages, that a small curve of light was shaved from the moon night after night, until you were no longer surprised the sky was black, that the chipmunk ran to hide in the dark, not simply to a door that led to its escape. Our visitors told the same stories people always tell. One night, giving me a lesson in storytelling, you said, "Any life will seem dramatic if you omit mention of most of it."

This, then, for drama: I drove back to that house not long ago. It was April, and Allen had died. In spite of all the visitors, Allen, next door, had been the good friend in bad times. I sat with his wife in their living room, looking out the glass doors to the backyard, and there was Allen's pool, still covered with black plastic that had been stretched across it for winter. It had rained, and as the rain fell, the cover collected more and more water until it finally spilled onto the concrete. When I left that day, I drove past what had been our house. Three or four crocuses were blooming in the front—just a few dots of white, no field of snow. I felt embarrassed for them. They couldn't compete.

This is a story, told the way you say stories should be told: Somebody grew up, fell in love, and spent a winter with her lover in the country. This, of course, is the barest outline, and futile to discuss. It's as pointless as throwing birdseed on the ground while snow still falls fast. Who expects small things to survive when even the largest get lost? People forget years and remember moments. Seconds and symbols are left to sum things up: the black shroud over the pool. Love, in its shortest form, becomes a word. What I remember about all that time is one winter. The snow. Even now, saying "snow," my lips move so that they kiss the air.

No mention has been made of the snowplow that seemed always to be there, scraping snow off our narrow road—an artery cleared, though neither of us could have said where the heart was.

T.C. Boyle

T. Coraghessan Boyle was born in 1948 in Peekskill, New York. He received an M.F.A. from the Iowa Writers' Workshop and a Ph.D. in Nineteenth Century British Literature from the University of Iowa. His 17 books of fiction include Tooth and Claw *(2005),* The Inner Circle *(2004), the National Book Award Finalist* Drop City *(2003),* The Road to Wellville *(1993), and the Pen/Faulkner Award-winning* World's End *(1987). In his essay "This Monkey, My Back," he discusses the ways in which his writing habit is stronger than any drug: "I can see how my books and stories are tied inextricably, how the themes and obsessions— the search for the father, racism, class and community, predetermination versus free will, cultural imperialism, sexual war, and sexual truce—keep repeating. I can see this, but only in retrospect. That's the beauty of this addiction—you have to move on, no retirement here, look out ahead, though you can't see where you're going. First you have nothing, and then, astonishingly, after ripping out your brain and your heart and betraying your friends and ex-lovers and dreaming like a zombie over the page till you can't see or hear or smell or taste, you have something. Something new. Something of value. Something to hold up and admire. And then? Well, you've got a jones, haven't you? And you start all over again, with nothing."*

Greasy Lake

> It's about a mile down on the dark side of Route 88.
> —*Bruce Springsteen*

There was a time when courtesy and winning ways went out of style, when it was good to be bad, when you cultivated decadence like a taste. We were all dangerous characters then. We wore torn-up leather jackets, slouched around with toothpicks in our mouths, sniffed glue and ether and what somebody claimed was cocaine. When we wheeled our parents' whining station wagons out into the street we left a patch of rubber half a block long. We drank gin and grape juice, Tango,

Thunderbird, and Bali Hai. We were nineteen. We were bad. We read André Gide and struck elaborate poses to show that we didn't give a shit about anything. At night, we went up to Greasy Lake.

Through the center of town, up the strip, past the housing developments and shopping malls, street lights giving way to the thin streaming illumination of the headlights, trees crowding the asphalt in a black unbroken wall: that was the way out to Greasy Lake. The Indians had called it Wakan, a reference to the clarity of its waters. Now it was fetid and murky, the mud banks glittering with broken glass and strewn with beer cans and the charred remains of bonfires. There was a single ravaged island a hundred yards from shore, so stripped of vegetation it looked as if the Air Force had strafed it. We went up to the lake because everyone went there, because we wanted to snuff the rich scent of possibility on the breeze, watch a girl take off her clothes and plunge into the festering murk, drink beer, smoke pot, howl at the stars, savor the incongruous full-throated roar of rock and roll against the primeval susurrus of frogs and crickets. This was nature.

I was there one night, late, in the company of two dangerous characters. Digby wore a gold star in his right ear and allowed his father to pay his tuition at Cornell; Jeff was thinking of quitting school to become a painter/musician/head-shop proprietor. They were both expert in the social graces, quick with a sneer, able to manage a Ford with lousy shocks over a rutted and gutted blacktop road at eighty-five while rolling a joint as compact as a Tootsie Roll Pop stick. They could lounge against a bank of booming speakers and trade "man"s with the best of them or roll out across the dance floor as if their joints worked on bearings. They were slick and quick and they wore their mirror shades at breakfast and dinner, in the shower, in closets and caves. In short, they were bad.

I drove. Digby pounded the dashboard and shouted along with Toots & the Maytals while Jeff hung his head out the window and streaked the side of my mother's Bel Air with vomit. It was early June, the air soft as a hand on your cheek, the third night of summer vacation. The first two nights we'd been out till dawn, looking for something we never found. On this, the third night, we'd cruised the strip sixty-seven times, been in and out of every bar and club we could think of in a twenty-mile radius, stopped twice for bucket chicken and forty-cent hamburgers, debated going to a party at the house of a girl Jeff's sister knew, and chucked two dozen raw eggs at mailboxes and hitchhikers. It was 2:00 A.M.; the bars were closing. There was nothing to do but take a bottle of lemon-flavored gin up to Greasy Lake.

The taillights of a single car winked at us as we swung into the dirt lot with its tufts of weed and washboard corrugations; '57 Chevy, mint, metallic blue. On the far side of the lot, like the exoskeleton of some gaunt chrome insect, a chopper leaned against its kickstand. And that was it for excitement: some junkie half-wit biker and a car freak pumping his girlfriend. Whatever it was we were looking for, we weren't about to find it at Greasy Lake. Not that night.

But then all of a sudden Digby was fighting for the wheel. "Hey, that's Tony Lovett's car! Hey!" he shouted, while I stabbed at the brake pedal and the Bel Air nosed up to the gleaming bumper of the parked Chevy. Digby leaned on the horn, laughing, and instructed me to put my brights on. I flicked on the brights. This was hilarious. A joke. Tony would experience premature withdrawal and expect to be confronted by grim-looking state troopers with flashlights. We hit the horn, strobed the lights, and then jumped out of the car to press our witty faces to Tony's windows; for all we knew we might even catch a glimpse of some little fox's tit, and then we could slap backs with red-faced Tony, rough-house a little, and go on to new heights of adventure and daring.

The first mistake, the one that opened the whole floodgate, was losing my grip on the keys. In the excitement, leaping from the car with the gin in one hand and a roach clip in the other, I spilled them in the grass—in the dark, rank, mysterious nighttime grass of Greasy Lake. This was a tactical error, as damaging and irreversible in its way as Westmoreland's decision to dig in at Khe Sanh. I felt it like a jab of intuition, and I stopped there by the open door, peering vaguely into the night that puddled up round my feet.

The second mistake—and this was inextricably bound up with the first—was identifying the car as Tony Lovett's. Even before the very bad character in greasy jeans and engineer boots ripped out of the driver's door, I began to realize that this chrome blue was much lighter than the robin's-egg of Tony's car, and that Tony's car didn't have rear-mounted speakers. Judging from their expressions, Digby and Jeff were privately groping toward the same inevitable and unsettling conclusion as I was.

In any case, there was no reasoning with this bad greasy character—clearly he was a man of action. The first lusty Rockette kick of his steel-toed boot caught me under the chin, chipped my favorite tooth, and left me sprawled in the dirt. Like a fool, I'd gone down on one knee to comb the stiff hacked grass for the keys, my mind making connections in the most dragged-out, testudineous way, knowing that things had gone wrong, that I was in a lot of trouble, and that the lost ignition key was my grail and my salvation. The three or four succeeding blows were mainly absorbed by my right buttock and the tough piece of bone at the base of my spine.

Meanwhile, Digby vaulted the kissing bumpers and delivered a savage kung-fu blow to the greasy character's collarbone. Digby had just finished a course in martial arts for phys-ed credit and had spent the better part of the past two nights telling us apocryphal tales of Bruce Lee types and of the raw power invested in lightning blows shot from coiled wrists, ankles, and elbows. The greasy character was unimpressed. He merely backed off a step, his face like a Toltec mask, and laid Digby out with a single whistling roundhouse blow . . . but by now Jeff had got into the act, and I was beginning to extricate myself from the dirt, a tinny compound of shock, rage, and impotence wadded in my throat.

Jeff was on the guy's back, biting at his ear. Digby was on the ground, cursing. I went for the tire iron I kept under the driver's seat. I kept it there because bad characters always keep tire irons under the driver's seat, for just such an occasion as this. Never mind that I hadn't been involved in a fight since sixth grade, when a kid with a sleepy eye and two streams of mucus depending from his nostrils hit me in the knee with a Louisville slugger; never mind that I'd touched the tire iron exactly twice before, to change tires: it was there. And I went for it.

I was terrified. Blood was beating in my ears, my hands were shaking, my heart turning over like a dirtbike in the wrong gear. My antagonist was shirtless, and a single cord of muscle flashed across his chest as he bent forward to peel Jeff from his back like a wet overcoat. "Motherfucker," he spat, over and over, and I was aware in that instant that all four of us—Digby, Jeff, and myself included—were chanting "motherfucker, motherfucker," as if it were a battle cry. (What happened next? the detective asks the murderer from beneath the turned-down brim of his porkpie hat. I don't know, the murderer says, something came over me. Exactly.)

Digby poked the flat of his hand in the bad character's face and I came at him like a kamikaze, mindless, raging, stung with humiliation—the whole thing, from the initial boot in the chin to this murderous primal instant involving no more than sixty hyperventilating, gland-flooding seconds—I came at him and brought the tire iron down across his ear. The effect was instantaneous, astonishing. He was a stunt man and this was Hollywood, he was a big grimacing toothy balloon and I was a man with a straight pin. He collapsed. Wet his pants. Went loose in his boots.

A single second, big as a zeppelin, floated by. We were standing over him in a circle, gritting our teeth, jerking our necks, our limbs and hands and feet twitching with glandular discharges. No one said anything. We just stared down at the guy, the car freak, the lover, the bad greasy character laid low. Digby looked at me; so did Jeff. I was still holding the tire iron, a tuft of hair clinging to the crook like dandelion fluff, like down. Rattled, I dropped it in the dirt, already envisioning the headlines, the pitted faces of the police inquisitors, the gleam of handcuffs, clank of bars, the big black shadows rising from the back of the cell . . . when suddenly a raw torn shriek cut through me like all the juice in all the electric chairs in the country.

It was the fox. She was short, barefoot, dressed in panties and a man's shirt. "Animals!" she screamed, running at us with her fists clenched and wisps of blow-dried hair in her face. There was a silver chain round her ankle, and her toenails flashed in the glare of the headlights. I think it was the toenails that did it. Sure, the gin and the cannabis and even the Kentucky Fried may have had a hand in it, but it was the sight of those flaming toes that set us off—the toad emerging from the loaf in *Virgin Spring,* lipstick smeared on a child: she was already tainted. We were on her like Bergman's deranged brothers— see no evil, hear none, speak none—panting, wheezing, tearing at her clothes, grabbing for flesh. We were bad characters, and we were scared and hot and three steps over the line—anything could have happened.

It didn't.

Before we could pin her to the hood of the car, our eyes masked with lust and greed and the purest primal badness, a pair of headlights swung into the lot. There we were, dirty, bloody, guilty, dissociated from humanity and civilization, the first of the Ur-crimes behind us, the second in progress, shreds of nylon panty and spandex brassiere dangling from our fingers, our flies open, lips licked—there we were, caught in the spotlight. Nailed.

We bolted. First for the car, and then, realizing we had no way of starting it, for the woods. I thought nothing. I thought escape. The headlights came at me like accusing fingers. I was gone.

Ram-bam-bam, across the parking lot, past the chopper and into the feculent undergrowth at the lake's edge, insects flying up in my face, weeds whipping, frogs and snakes and red-eyed turtles splashing off into the night: I was already ankle-deep in muck and tepid water and still going strong. Behind me, the girl's screams rose in intensity, disconsolate, incriminating, the screams of the Sabine women, the Christian martyrs, Anne Frank dragged from the garret. I kept going, pursued by those cries, imagining cops and bloodhounds. The water was up to my knees when I realized what I was doing: I was going to swim for it. Swim the breadth of Greasy Lake and hide myself in the thick clot of woods on the far side. They'd never find me there.

I was breathing in sobs, in gasps. The water lapped at my waist as I looked out over the moon-burnished ripples, the mats of algae that clung to the surface like scabs. Digby and Jeff had vanished. I paused. Listened. The girl was quieter now, screams tapering to sobs, but there were male voices, angry, excited, and the high-pitched ticking of the second car's engine. I waded deeper, stealthy, hunted, the ooze sucking at my sneakers. As I was about to take the plunge—at the very instant I dropped my shoulder for the first slashing stroke—I blundered into something. Something unspeakable, obscene, something soft, wet, moss-grown. A patch of weed? A log? When I reached out to touch it, it gave like a rubber duck, it gave like flesh.

In one of those nasty little epiphanies for which we are prepared by films and TV and childhood visits to the funeral home to ponder the shrunken painted forms of dead grandparents, I understood what it was that bobbed there so inadmissibly in the dark. Understood, and stumbled back in horror and revulsion, my mind yanked in six different directions (I was nineteen, a mere child, an infant, and here in the space of five minutes I'd struck down one greasy character and blundered into the waterlogged carcass of a second), thinking. The keys, the keys, why did I have to go and lose the keys? I stumbled back, but the muck took hold of my feet—a sneaker snagged, balance lost—and suddenly I was pitching face forward into the buoyant black mass, throwing out my hands in desperation while simultaneously conjuring the image of reeking frogs and muskrats revolving in slicks of their own deliquescing juices. AAAAArrrgh! I shot from the water like a torpedo, the dead man rotating to expose a mossy beard and eyes cold as the moon. I must have shouted out, thrashing around in the weeds, because the voices behind me suddenly became animated.

"What was that?"

"It's them, it's them: they tried to, tried to . . . *rape* me!" Sobs.

A man's voice, flat Midwestern accent. "You sons a bitches, we'll kill you!"

Frogs, crickets.

Then another voice, harsh, *r*-less, Lower East Side: "Motherfucker!" I recognized the verbal virtuosity of the bad greasy character in the engineer boots. Tooth chipped, sneakers gone, coated in mud and slime and worse, crouching breathless in the weeds waiting to have my ass thoroughly and definitively kicked and fresh from the hideous stinking embrace of a three-days-dead-corpse, I suddenly felt a rush of joy and vindication: the son of a bitch was alive! Just as quickly, my bowels turned to ice. "Come on out of there, you pansy mother-fuckers!" the bad greasy character was screaming. He shouted curses till he was out of breath.

The crickets started up again, then the frogs. I held my breath. All at once there was a sound in the reeds, a swishing, a splash: thunk-a-thunk. They were throwing rocks. The frogs fell silent. I cradled my head. Swish, swish, thunk-a-thunk. A wedge of feldspar the size of a cue ball glanced off my knee. I bit my finger.

It was then that they turned to the car. I heard a door slam, a curse, and then the sound of the headlights shattering—almost a good-natured sound, celebratory, like corks popping from the necks of bottles. This was succeeded by the dull booming of the fenders, metal on metal, and then the icy crash of the windshield. I inched forward, el-bows and knees, my belly pressed to the muck, thinking of guerrillas and commandos and *The Naked and the Dead*. I parted the weeds and squinted the length of the parking lot.

The second car—it was a Trans-Am—was still running, its high beams washing the scene in a lurid stagy light. Tire iron flailing, the greasy bad character was laying into the side of my mother's Bel Air like an avenging demon, his shadow riding up the trunks of the trees. Whomp. Whomp. Whomp-whomp. The other two guys—blond types, in fraternity jackets—were helping out with tree branches and skull-sized boulders. One of them was gathering up bottles, rocks, muck, candy wrappers, used condoms, poptops, and other refuse and pitching it through the window on the driver's side. I could see the fox, a white bulb behind the windshield of the '57 Chevy. "Bobbie," she whined over the thumping, "come on." The greasy character paused a mo-ment, took one good swipe at the left taillight, and then heaved the tire iron halfway across the lake. Then he fired up the '57 and was gone.

Blond head nodded at blond head. One said something to the other, too low for me to catch. They were no doubt thinking that in helping to annihilate my mother's car they'd committed a fairly rash act, and thinking too that there were three bad characters connected with that very car watching them from the woods. Perhaps other possibilities occurred to them as well—police, jail cells, justices of the peace, rep-arations, lawyers, irate parents, fraternal censure. Whatever they were thinking, they suddenly dropped branches, bottles, and rocks and sprang for their car in unison, as if they'd choreographed it. Five seconds. That's all it took. The engine shrieked, the tires squealed, a cloud of dust rose from the rutted lot and then settled back on darkness.

I don't know how long I lay there, the bad breath of decay all around me, my jacket heavy as a bear, the primordial ooze subtly reconstituting itself to accommodate my upper thighs and testicles. My jaws ached, my knee throbbed, my coccyx was on fire. I contemplated suicide, wondered if I'd need bridgework, scraped the recesses of my brain for some sort of excuse to give my parents—a tree had fallen on the car, I was blindsided by a bread truck, hit and run, vandals had got to it while we were playing chess at Digby's. Then I thought of the dead man. He was probably the only person on the planet worse off than I was. I thought about him, fog on the lake, insects chirring eerily, and felt the tug of fear, felt the darkness opening up inside me like a set of jaws. Who was he, I wondered, this victim of time and circumstance bobbing sorrowfully in the lake at my back. The owner of the chopper, no doubt, a bad older character come to this. Shot during a murky drug deal, drowned while drunkenly frolicking in the lake. Another headline. My car was wrecked; he was dead.

When the eastern half of the sky went from black to cobalt and the trees began to separate themselves from the shadows, I pushed myself up from the mud and stepped out into the open. By now the birds had begun to take over for the crickets, and dew lay slick on the leaves. There was a smell in the air, raw and sweet at the same time, the smell of the sun firing buds and opening blossoms. I contemplated the car. It lay there like a wreck along the highway, like a steel sculpture left over from a vanished civilization. Everything was still. This was nature.

I was circling the car, as dazed and bedraggled as the sole survivor of an air blitz, when Digby and Jeff emerged from the trees behind me. Digby's face was crosshatched with smears of dirt; Jeff's jacket was gone and his shirt was torn across the shoulder. They slouched across the lot, looking sheepish, and silently came up beside me to gape at the ravaged automobile. No one said a word. After a while Jeff swung open the driver's door and began to scoop the broken glass and garbage off the seat. I looked at Digby. He shrugged. "At least they didn't slash the tires," he said.

It was true: the tires were intact. There was no windshield, the headlights were staved in, and the body looked as if it had been sledge-hammered for a quarter a shot at the county fair, but the tires were inflated to regulation pressure. The car was drivable. In silence, all three of us bent to scrape the mud and shattered glass from the interior. I said nothing about the biker. When we were finished, I reached in my pocket for the keys, experienced a nasty stab of recollection, cursed myself, and turned to search the grass. I spotted them almost immediately, no more than five feet from the open door, glinting like jewels in the first tapering shaft of sunlight. There was no reason to get philosophical about it: I eased into the seat and turned the engine over.

It was at that precise moment that the silver Mustang with the flame decals rumbled into the lot. All three of us froze; then Digby and Jeff slid into the car and slammed the door. We watched as the Mustang rocked and bobbed across the ruts and finally jerked to a halt beside the forlorn chopper at the far end of the lot. "Let's go," Digby said. I hesitated, the Bel Air wheezing beneath me.

Two girls emerged from the Mustang. Tight jeans, stiletto heels, hair like frozen fur. They bent over the motorcycle, paced back and forth aimlessly, glanced once or twice at us, and then ambled over to where the reeds sprang up in a green fence round the perimeter of the lake. One of them cupped her hands to her mouth. "Al," she called. "Hey, Al!"

"Come on," Digby hissed. "Let's get out of here."

But it was too late. The second girl was picking her way across the lot, unsteady on her heels, looking up at us and then away. She was older—twenty-five or -six—and as she came closer we could see there was something wrong with her: she was stoned or drunk, lurching now and waving her arms for balance. I gripped the steering wheel as if it were the ejection lever of a flaming jet, and Digby spat out my name, twice, terse and impatient.

"Hi," the girl said.

We looked at her like zombies, like war veterans, like deaf-and-dumb pencil peddlers.

She smiled, her lips cracked and dry. "Listen," she said, bending from the waist to look in the window, "you guys seen Al?" Her pupils were pinpoints, her eyes glass. She jerked her neck. "That's his bike over there—Al's. You seen him?"

Al. I didn't know what to say. I wanted to get out of the car and retch. I wanted to go home to my parents' house and crawl into bed. Digby poked me in the ribs. "We haven't seen anybody," I said.

The girl seemed to consider this, reaching out a slim veiny arm to brace herself against the car. "No matter," she said, slurring the *t*'s "he'll turn up." And then, as if she'd just taken stock of the whole scene—the ravaged car and our battered faces, the desolation of the place—she said: "Hey, you guys look like some pretty bad characters—been fightin', huh?" We stared straight ahead, rigid as catatonics. She was fumbling in her pocket and muttering something. Finally she held out a handful of tablets in glassine wrappers: "Hey, you want to party, you want to do some of these with me and Sarah?"

I just looked at her. I thought I was going to cry. Digby broke the silence. "No, thanks," he said, leaning over me. "Some other time."

I put the car in gear and it inched forward with a groan, shaking off pellets of glass like an old dog shedding water after a bath, heaving over the ruts on its worn springs, creeping toward the highway. There was a sheen of sun on the lake. I looked back. The girl was still standing there, watching us, her shoulders slumped, hand outstretched.

Ron Carlson

Ron Carlson was born in 1947 in Logan, Utah. A contributor to The New Yorker, Harper's, Best American Short Stories, *and many other magazines and journals, Carlson is particularly well known for his funny and searing observations on adolescence. He has published the short story collections* The News of the World *(1987),* Plan B for the Middle Class *(1992),* The Hotel Eden *(1997),* At the Jim Bridger *(2002), and* A Kind of Flying *(2003). His novels include* Truants *(1981) and* The Speed of Light *(2003). In an interview in* Writers Ask, *Carlson spoke about the process and discipline of writing: "When you're a writer you spend days in the room without knowing what you've got, but you're still willing to keep reeling it in and following it. You're willing to be true to it. It may mean you have to write thirty pages to get fifteen. The big secret to such writing is the ability to stay in the room. The writer is the person who stays in the room . . . all the good writing I've done in the last ten years has been done in the first twenty minutes after the first time I wanted to leave the room. I've learned to stay there and keep writing."*

Milk

They almost fingerprint the children before I can stop them. Phyllis is making a rare personal appearance in my office to help me with a motorcycle injury claim, and I want to squeeze every minute out of her, and I'm taking no calls. We all call Phyllis "The Queen of Wrongful Death," which is the truest nickname in the firm. She likes being a hard case, and she's lording it over me a bit this morning, rereading a lot of the stuff that I'd summarized for her, when Tim buzzes and says Annie's on the line.

I almost wave it off. She probably wants to meet for lunch and today there's going to be no lunch, because I want to get this motorcycle case buttoned up so we can take the twins on a picnic this weekend. Now that they can walk, our house is getting real small. But it's not lunch. Annie's voice is down a note or two, stern, as she says she and my mother are going to take the boys down to Community Fuel, where there is another fingerprint program today. I listen to Annie tell the story and watch Phyllis frowning through the file. My mother read about the program in the paper and with so many children abducted and missing, etc. etc. etc. Annie closes with *I know what you think, but this is something we should do for your mother's sake.*

I don't say anything.

"Jim?" Annie says.

"Ann. You said it. You know what I think. *No way.* Not the twins. Not for my mother. Not for anybody."

"She's coming over to get us in half an hour."

"Ann," I say again. "Take her to lunch, but do not fingerprint the boys. Okay? Under no circumstances. That's all."

"It's no big deal . . ."

"Tell my mother that."

"I'm going to tell your mother that you're terrified and unable at this time to do the right thing."

When I hang up, Phyllis looks up. At thirty-four she wears those imperious half glasses, which, in a drunken moment at the firm barbeque last summer, she admitted to me are just part of her costume, "dress to win"; and I admit now that they intimidate me.

"Fingerprints?" she says. "Are the twins being booked?"

"It's that I.D. program at Community Fuel. My mother wants to take the kids."

"And . . .?"

"My kids are not being fingerprinted. I'm not caving in to this raging paranoia. It's a better world than people think."

Phyllis takes off her awful glasses and lets them drop on their necklace against her breast. "And you're not scared in the least, are you?"

When I come home from work, Lee and Bobby laugh their heads off. It has become my favorite part of the day. I peek into the kitchen and say, "Oh-oh!" and they amble in stiffly in their tiny overalls, arms up for balance. They start: "Oh-oh!" as I pick them up and they laugh and laugh as we do our entire repertoire of sounds: *Dadda, Momma, Baby,* and the eleven or twelve other syllables, as well as a good portion of growling, humming, meowing, mooing, and buzzing. When I whistle softly through my teeth, they hug me hard to make me stop.

They are fraternal twins. Bobby has a lot of hair and a full face. Lee, though he probably weighs the same, twenty-two pounds, seems slighter, more fragile. Ironically, Bobby cries more and easier. They can lie on a blanket with fists full of each other's hair, and only Bobby will fuss. They each have four and a half teeth and they call each other the same name: *Baby.*

Tonight I lift them up and the laughing intensifies as I tote them into the living room where Annie is picking up the blanket and toys.

She starts right in: "Well, boys, it's Daddy, the Rulemaker."

"Annie . . ."

"The lawgiver." She holds the bundle in her arms and stands to face me. She goes on in a gruff voice: "*No fingerprints. Not in this house! Not for anybody!*"

Bobby and Lee think this is wonderful and they laugh again. Each has a good hold on my hair and their laughing pulls my scalp in two directions. Annie comes right up to the boys and makes a mock frown, her nose against mine. She growls. "*Not even for my mother!*" She kisses me quickly and disappears into the boys' room. The boys snap around to watch her and the hair pulling brings tears to my eyes.

Annie's got me. We've been married nine years, and it's been a good marriage. We've grown up together really, and only since the boys have arrived have I started with this rule stuff. Annie and I used to go crazy after visiting our friends Stuart and Ruth and their kids. Everything was rules. *No baseball in the backyard. No jackets in the basement. No magazines in the kitchen. No loud talking in the hall. No snacks during homework.* We promised then never to post rules. Driving home from their house, Annie and I would make up rules and laugh until we'd have to pull over. *No hairdryers in the bathtub. No looking out the window while someone is talking to you. No peeking at the answers to the crossword puzzle. No shirt, no shoes, no service.* And Annie even gave Ruth one of our ridiculous lists, typed up as a joke (their lists were typed and posted on the refrigerator door), but Ruth did not think it was that funny. She said, "Wait until you have kids."

And now I have both kids in my arms when Annie comes back into the room. "Call your mother," she says, taking Lee from me and putting him in his high chair. "She wants to know why you're not looking out for the best interest of your children. Put Bobby in his chair before you call, okay?"

We've been through this all before, but I can see this week is going to be worse. I watched the news programs on television and saw the troops of children being fingerprinted. I made it clear from the beginning that we did not want to do that. Annie watched my opposition grow over the weeks, realizing that this was probably the biggest disagreement in our marriage.

"I don't understand you," she said. "You're a lawyer, for Petes' sakes. You like things nailed down. What's the problem?"

But she said it as: what's *your* problem? I watched the children, many babies, being fingerprinted. I couldn't express what my problem was.

And my mother wanted to know why, in light of all the missing children and the recent abductions, why wouldn't I do it *for their sake*.

"Because," I had explained to her at last, at the end of my patience: "Because the only use those prints will ever have is in identifying *a body*, okay? *Do you see?* They use them to identify the body. And my children will not need fingerprints, *because nothing is going to happen to my children*. Is that clear?" I had almost yelled at my mother. "We don't need fingerprints!"

Then my mother would be hurt for a few days and then silent for a few days, and then there'd be another news story and we'd do it all again.

Annie tried to intervene. "Stop being a jerk. It's not a big deal. It's not going to hurt the boys. They'll forget it. Your mother would feel better."

"No."

"Why not?"

I don't know how many times we had some version of that conversation, but I do know that once I took Annie's wrist and raged through the house like the sorry creature I can be at times, pointing to the low surfaces, "Because, we've got fingerprints! Look!" I made her look at the entryway door and the thousand hands printed there, at the car windows, and the front of the fridge, and finally the television, where a vivid hand printed in rice cereal made Tom Brokaw on the evening news look like he was growing a beard. "We have fingerprints. And I love these fingerprints. We don't need any others."

All Annie said was, "Can I have this now?" She indicated her arm. I let her go. She shook her head at me and went in to check on the boys.

And there was the milk.

I wanted Annie to change milk. We had been getting the Hilltop green half-gallon cartons. Then they started putting children on the back panels, missing children. Under the bold heading, MISSING, would be two green and white photographs of the children, their statistics printed underneath: date of birth; age; height; eyes; hair; weight; date missing; from. . . . The photographs themselves assumed a lurid, tabloid quality, and everytime I opened the fridge they scared me. I'd already seen ads for missing children on a weekly mailer we receive which offers—on the flip side—discount coupons for curtain and rug cleaning, optical services, and fast food, primarily chicken. And in Roy's Drug one night I dropped the Archie comic I was going to buy for the boys (to keep them from ripping up our art books), when I saw two missing children inside the front cover. It was all getting to me.

One night late, I went into Smith's Food King and turned all the Hilltop milk to the back panel so sixty children stared out from the dairy case. I started it as a statement of some kind, but when I stepped back across the aisle and saw their group sadness, all those green and white poor resolution smiles, wan even in the bright Food King light, I lost my breath. I fled the store and sulked home and asked Annie if we could buy another brand.

When I told her why, when I told her about the two kids taking a little starch out of the world for me when I opened the refrigerator at two A.M. to grab Bobby a bottle, those nights when he still fusses, Annie just said *No.*

Tonight after I have the fifteenth version of my fingerprint call with my mother, I am out of tolerance, reason, generosity, and any of their relatives. I never swear in the company of my mother, and as I sit down in the kitchen and watch Annie spoon the boys their macaroni and strained beef, I think perhaps I should. I might not have this knot in my neck. There on the table is the Hilltop milk with somebody's picture on the back.

I don't know why, but I start: "Annie, I don't want this milk in the house."

She's cool. "And is there a reason for that, oh powerful Rulemaker?"

"I've told you the reason. I'm not interested in being depressed or in having my children frightened by faces of lost souls in the refrigerator."

Annie says nothing. She spoons the macaroni into Bobby's open mouth. After each mouthful, he goes: "mmmmnnnnn!" and laughs. It's something I taught the boys with Milupa and bananas, but Lee's version is softer, almost a sigh of satisfaction.

"What is the point? There is no point in publishing these lurid photographs."

"They're not lurid."

"What's the point? I am supposed to study the carton, cruise the city, stop every child walking home from school: *is he missing? would he like to go home now?* Really, what? I see some girl playing tennis against the practice wall in Liberty Park, am I supposed to match her with my carton collection of missing children?" I've raised my voice a little, I can tell, because Annie looks narrow-eyed, stony.

She hands me the spoon for Lee, who is smiling at me for yelling. Annie rises and takes the milk and puts it in the refrigerator. "Missing children don't get to play tennis," she says quietly, wiping Bobby up and putting him on the floor. Bobby goes immediately to the one cupboard I haven't safety clipped, opens it, and pulls a large bottle of olives onto his foot.

He watches the bottle roll across the floor and when it stops against the stove, he looks up into my face with his beautiful face and he starts to cry.

"Bobby's first," Annie says, plucking him from the floor. "Bobby's first in bed tonight!"

When she carts Bobby off, I let Lee out of his chair. I hand him his bottle out of the fridge and he takes it with both hands as if it were an award. He starts to walk off, then realizes, I guess, that Mom isn't here and he doesn't really know where to go. So, he looks up at me, a child who resembles an angel so much it is troubling. Then Annie is behind him, lifting him away, and I am left alone in the kitchen.

I wipe up the chairs and the floor and cap the macaroni and strained beef, but when I put them away, I see that green Hilltop milk carton.

"You want to close the fridge?" Annie is behind me.

"No, look. Look at this."

"Close the fridge door."

"Look!" I point at the child, his green and white photograph so grim in the bright light of the fridge.

I take one carton of milk out and close the fridge. I read aloud: "MISSING: Name: Richard Tarrel. D.O.B.: 10/21/82. Age: 4. Height: 2 feet 8 inches. Eyes: blue. Hair: light brown. Weight: 27 pounds. Date missing: 6/24/86. From: Omaha. . . ." I mean to make a point by reading it, but the *twenty-seven pounds* gets me a little, and by the time I read *Omaha,* I stop and sit down and look across at Annie. She looks like she is going to cry. She looks a lot like I have made her cry again.

She firms her mouth once and shakes her head as she stands up to leave the room. "Nebraska," she whispers. "Omaha, Nebraska."

I sit at the kitchen table listening to Bobby and Lee murmuring toward sleep in their room, and I look at little twenty-seven-pound Richard Tarrel. Even in the poor quality photograph, he is beautiful, his eyes huge and dark, his lips pouted in a coy James Dean smile. There is no background in the photo, but I've been to Omaha. I can imagine the backyard somewhere out near 92nd Street, the swingset, the young peach tree Richard's father planted this summer, after the man at the nursery told him that though it was small, there would be peaches next fall.

The next morning, I've got the day trip to Denver, the quick deposition, and back on the nine o'clock. Annie is cordial to me in the morning, well, stern. I have a cup of coffee and pick at some of Bobby's scrambled eggs. Annie doesn't offer to have the whole gang drive me to the airport, which would have happened if we weren't fighting. I feel bad about it, kind of flat, but the boys will not have their fingerprints taken. I do not believe in it and it will not happen. Not my boys. It's a rule.

The flight over is rocky. The plane pitches heavily up the slope and then down, across the mountains to Denver. Sitting in the window seat of my row, one empty seat away, is a pale blond girl. I'm trying to fill in all the forms so I can maybe make the early plane tonight, but she stops me. I have to study her. She huddles to the window, her fragile face poised there, watching the unchanging grayness. Her Levi's are worn and the red plaid bag she clutches on her lap is years old. Her shirt is a blue stripe dress shirt that could have never, ever fit her; it is five sizes large. She sits in a linty, dark blue scrape. I can't stop myself from looking at her. Date of Birth: 1969. Age: 17; Height: 5 feet 9 inches; Eyes: brown; Hair: light blond; Weight: 120; Date Missing. . . .

The girl turns her face to me in the bouncing airplane and speaks, her lips barely moving: "Don't," she says. "Please. Just don't."

My deposition is a witness to a motorcycle accident, a sophomore in psychology, and I meet him at the University Union in Boulder just after noon. In our hour, I learn: both children moved to avoid the cycle, but they moved different ways and one, the victim, our client, was hit and injured. My witness was driving pizza delivery behind the motorcycle and saw it all. Daylight. Sun to his back. A simple story. After the witness leaves for class, I sit in the modular furniture mesmerized for a while by the young people streaming around me.

There are children everywhere. All the way down the highway from Boulder to Denver, I see them alone and in groups, kicking along in the gravel. They all seem to need haircuts. I check my watch: two o'clock on a school day. Why isn't anybody where he's supposed to be? I think about our case; it's a given. I wonder what help the settlement will be to the parents of the hurt girl. I try to make the equation in my mind. We'll ask for six hundred thousand and get two. The girl's eleven years old and has one complete knee and six-tenths of the other. Let's see: she'll have that limp for sixty-eight years, if she lives her statistic. That's three thousand dollars a year not to walk like everyone else, or play soccer, I guess, or tennis. I ditch my rental car at the Avis curb, and think: what a strange man I'm becoming. What's happening to me?

The six o'clock is full so I hit the little sky-lounge near the gate and have a Manhattan. I used to love having an hour or two to ransack the magazines and have a Manhattan, my little joke living in the West, but now it's not much fun. There seems some urgency about getting home. I can't really settle down. I want to get home.

Sometimes, driving home alone in the last two blocks before our house, a feeling descends upon me like a gift. It is as if a huge door opens and I can breathe differently, see the entire scope of our lives, and it makes me unreasonably happy. It makes me want to rush into the kitchen and sweep Annie up and cry: *forgive me, forgive us, let's never quarrel again, we have everything.* I don't know where the feeling comes from or how real it is, but I have it tonight as I turn into the driveway.

My mother's white Seville is parked to one side, something I didn't really want to see, but there's our house standing like a house in a story, an entire happy little world. The kitchen windows are beautiful yellow squares and a blue glow in the two small windows out front means they're watching television.

I vow to go in cheerfully and join them, open a beer, chat openly with the two women about everything. This fingerprint thing doesn't have to be such a big deal. We can agree. We can face the future without unreasonable fear.

In the kitchen, two blue Community Fuel Folders spill across the table. On the cover of each is a large white fingerprint the size of a head of lettuce. Underneath the print, it says: COMMUNITY I.D./PROJECT FINGERPRINT. I can hear the women talking in the other room under the television noises. I open the first folder and there it is in Annie's print-

ing: Bobby Hensley. Date of Birth. Age. Weight. Hair. There is an
empty square: place recent photograph here. And below: the ten
smudges of Bobby's fingers.

I reach two bottles out of the fridge, one Nuk, one yellow nipple for
Lee, and slip them inside my sportcoat. I tiptoe into the boys' room.
Lee is asleep in a knot of blanket; Bobby lies on his side with his thumb
loosely in his mouth experimenting with sounds: *doya, doya, moya*. He
looks up at me calmly and smiles and then rolls to a crawl and stands
in his crib. I pick him up and park him in a shoulder and then lift Lee
like a melon under my forearm. I sweep the boys noiselessly through
the kitchen and out to the car.

I am calm enough to strap them in their car seats, Lee asleep in the
back and Bobby on the seat next to me in the front. I coast back down
the driveway before starting the car, and I am on the road half a block
before I pull the lights on.

"Ba," Bobby says as we pass a city bus in front of East High. "Ba."

"Bus," I say, the first word I've said aloud since my plane landed.
"That's right. It's a bus."

The streets are luminous, wet and shiny, ticketed with early leaves,
and our tires make the friction I have always loved to hear after rain.
So the streets whisper darkly as we slow at each bright intersection, the
flaring Seven-Elevens, the flat white splash of a gas station. Then it is
dark again, and we are driving.

Lee starts to squeak, which means he will babble for a while and
then cry. He's a little tongue-tied and is gradually tearing the cord underneath by stretching his mouth in low squalls which becomes real
crying after about a minute. I stop at the light at Fourth and State and
give both boys their bottles.

We turn left onto State and head south, cruising by the jillion colored lights the kids love. In the rearview mirror, I can see Lee settled
now in his seat. He has learned to balance the bottle on the carseat
arm-tray, so his hands are free. Right now, they extend off to each side,
palms up, and Lee opens and closes his hands slowly as he watches
them and sucks on the bottle.

Bobby has his head tipped right to witness the spectacle of neon
from the bars and motels, the bright dragon above the Double Hey Rice
Palace, the pulsing tire in front of Big O. He has his bottle clutched in
both hands and set hard in the side of his mouth like a cigar.

When I was a boy I remember that my father would always pick up babies in restaurants. We'd go to Harmon's on North Temple about every

other Sunday as a treat. My brother and I always had the gorgeous shakes, strawberry and chocolate, too thick for the straw, my mother always wore one of her three pretty dresses and patted our faces with the corner of her napkin, and my father would always spot a baby three tables away. He would simply rise and go over to the little family and pick up their baby and bring it over to our table and talk to it, asking did it want to be ours and things like that, just loud enough for the parents to hear. I remember the parents always smiling, perhaps an older sister craning her neck to see where the baby had gone, and my father dipping a spoon into my strawberry shake for the child. Sometimes he'd keep the baby on his lap for half an hour, showing off, sometimes, he would return it right away, the baby squirming in his arms, fighting for a last glance at my strawberry shake. My father gave forty kids their first taste of ice cream at our table, and no one seemed to be scared of anything.

"Namma," Bobby says, lifting his bottle over the seat and dropping it. He places one hand on the window and says it again, "Namma."

Somewhere out in this garish Disneyland of light, he has spotted a bear, and now he wants "Namma," his bear, actually a stuffed toy raccoon. Namma is the one who taught us all *peek-a-boo* and *Where's-your-nose*. In my haste leaving the house, I have forgotten Namma.

In the backseat, Lee is again asleep, his arms limp at his sides, his bottle still protruding from his mouth.

"Namma," Bobby says, turning to me.

"Namma," I say back to him, and he smiles. We will have to go home. Namma is at home peeking out of a corner of the crib. Bobby is still smiling at me coyly, waiting for me to say something else, so I sing his favorite song: "The Lion Sleeps Tonight."

"Ooh Wimoweh. Wimoweh, O Wimoweh . . ." I sing, nodding my head so Bobby will nod his too. "In the jungle, the quiet jungle, the lion sleeps tonight. . . ."

Tired, he leans his head back against the car seat and watches me sing, his open-mouth grin never changing. I do a lot of extra "*O Wimoweh*"s, and the song ends somewhere in Murray. Bobby has closed his mouth now; his eyes are next. I look at my watch: ten to twelve; and I realize that this is the latest I've been out since the boys were born, and people are everywhere. We better go home.

I do a U-turn in the bright, crowded parking lot of a Seven-Eleven. A lone teenager leans against the phones, smoking a cigarette. He wears a Levi's jacket and a blue bandanna around his neck. I look at his face, the eyebrows almost grown together, the pretty lower lip. Date of Birth: 1971; Age: 15; Height: 5 feet 7 inches; Weight: 125; Eyes: blue; Hair: dark brown; Date missing: I don't know. On the milk carton there will be a date, but as I glance back at the boy, I can only see that it looks like he's been out in the night a long time.

Three blocks later, Bobby's asleep. It's late. The traffic is thick and bright. I pass a twenty-four hour Safeway and the parking lot is full. Behind me the headlights teem. A man cruises by us smoking a cigarette in a large Chevrolet. Two couples on motorcycles, the girls holding on, their faces turned out of the wind into their boyfriends' backs. A new station wagon, three girls bouncing in the front seat. Two boys in a Volkswagen bug, their elbows out the window as if summer weren't really over.

At home Annie has checked on the children by now and found them gone, and she has found my valise, and she has given my mother another drink and calmed her down. She knows I'm coming home. We have been safe all our lives. We've traveled: London, Tokyo, Paris, where we saw a diplomat shot down the block from us. Annie has broken her leg skiing. Our Cherokee was totaled by a street department truck two summers ago. We have always felt safe until the boys arrived, and now I am afraid of everything.

I start to sing. We're locked in, the windows are up. These are my boys. I sing softly: "Ooh Wimoweh. Wimoweh, O Wimoweh, Wimoweh," and on, even at a stoplight. I can feel people looking at me, and I lower my face onto the back of my hand on the steering wheel. It's so late. What is everybody doing up so late?

Raymond Carver

Raymond Carver (1938–1988) grew up in Eastern Oregon, where his father worked in a sawmill. At nineteen, he married, began a family, and embarked on long years working low-paying jobs while attending college, including the University of Iowa Writers' Workshop. His first collection of stories, Will You Please Be Quiet, Please? *(1978) was nominated for the National Book Award and established his highly influential minimalist literary style, which he further explored in* What We Talk About When We Talk About Love *(1981). In his last two collections,* Cathedral *(1983) and* Where I'm Calling From: New and Selected Stories *(1988), he continued his minimalism but in a more open and expansive style. Carver also published five books of poetry. Commenting on the requirements of the short story in an essay in the* New York Times, *he wrote: "There has to be tension, a sense that something is imminent, that certain things are in relentless motion, or else, most often, there simply won't be a story. What creates tension in a piece of fiction is partly the way the concrete words are linked together to make up the visible action of the story. But it's also the things that are left out, that are implied, the landscape just under the smooth (but sometimes broken and unsettled) surface of things."*

Cathedral

This blind man, an old friend of my wife's, he was on his way to spend the night. His wife had died. So he was visiting the dead wife's relatives in Connecticut. He called my wife from his in-laws'. Arrangements were made. He would come by train, a five-hour trip, and my wife would meet him at the station. She hadn't seen him since she worked for him one summer in Seattle ten years ago. But she and the blind man had kept in touch. They made tapes and mailed them back and forth. I wasn't enthusiastic about his visit. He was no one I knew. And his being blind bothered me. My idea of blindness came from the movies. In the movies, the blind moved slowly and never laughed. Sometimes they were led by seeing-eye dogs. A blind man in my house was not something I looked forward to.

That summer in Seattle she had needed a job. She didn't have any money. The man she was going to marry at the end of the summer was in officers' training school. He didn't have any money, either. But she was in love with the guy, and he was in love with her, etc. She'd seen something in the paper: HELP—*Reading to Blind Man*, and a telephone number. She phoned and went over, was hired on the spot. She'd worked with this blind man all summer. She read stuff to him, case studies, reports, that sort of thing. She helped him organize his little office in the county social-service department. They'd become good friends, my wife and the blind man. How do I know these things? She told me. And she told me something else. On her last day in the office, the blind man asked if he could touch her face. She agreed to this. She told me he touched his fingers to every part of her face, her nose— even her neck! She never forgot it. She even tried to write a poem about it. She was always trying to write a poem. She wrote a poem or two every year, usually after something really important had happened to her.

When we first started going out together, she showed me the poem. In the poem, she recalled his fingers and the way they had moved around over her face. In the poem, she talked about what she had felt at the time, about what went through her mind when the blind man touched her nose and lips. I can remember I didn't think much of the poem. Of course, I didn't tell her that. Maybe I just don't understand poetry. I admit it's not the first thing I reach for when I pick up something to read.

Anyway, this man who'd first enjoyed her favors, the officer-to-be, he'd been her childhood sweetheart. So okay. I'm saying that at the end of the summer she let the blind man run his hands over her face, said good-bye to him, married her childhood etc., who was now a commissioned officer, and she moved away from Seattle. But they'd kept in touch, she and the blind man. She made the first contact after a year or so. She called him up one night from an Air Force base in Alabama. She wanted to talk. They talked. He asked her to send a tape and tell him about her life. She did this. She sent the tape. On the tape, she told the blind man about her husband and about their life together in the military. She told the blind man she loved her husband but she didn't like it where they lived and she didn't like it that he was part of the military-industrial thing. She told the blind man she'd written a poem and he was in it. She told him that she was writing a poem about what it was like to be an Air Force officer's wife. The poem wasn't finished yet. She was still writing it. The blind man made a tape. He sent her the tape. She made a tape. This went on for years. My wife's officer was posted to one base and then another. She sent tapes from Moody AFB, McGuire, McConnell, and finally Travis, near Sacramento, where one night she got to feeling lonely and cut off from people she kept losing in that moving-around life. She got to feeling she couldn't go it another step. She went in and swallowed all the pills and capsules in the medicine chest and washed them down with a bottle of gin. Then she got into a hot bath and passed out.

But instead of dying, she got sick. She threw up. Her officer—why should he have a name? he was the childhood sweetheart, and what more does he want?—came home from somewhere, found her, and called the ambulance. In time, she put it all on a tape and sent the tape to the blind man. Over the years, she put all kinds of stuff on tapes and sent the tapes off lickety-split. Next to writing a poem every year, I think it was her chief means of recreation. On one tape, she told the blind man she'd decided to live away from her officer for a time. On another tape, she told him about her divorce. She and I began going out, and of course she told her blind man about it. She told him everything, or so it seemed to me. Once she asked me if I'd like to hear the latest tape from the blind man. This was a year ago. I was on the tape, she said. So I said okay, I'd listen to it. I got us drinks and we settled down in the living room. We made ready to listen. First she inserted the tape into the player and adjusted a couple of dials. Then she pushed a lever. The tape squeaked and someone began to talk in this loud voice. She lowered the volume. After a few minutes of harmless chitchat, I heard my own name in the mouth of this stranger, this blind man I didn't even know! And then this: "From all you've said about him, I can only conclude—" But we were interrupted, a knock at the door, something, and we didn't ever get back to the tape. Maybe it was just as well. I'd heard all I wanted to.

Now this same blind man was coming to sleep in my house.

"Maybe I could take him bowling," I said to my wife. She was at the draining board doing scalloped potatoes. She put down the knife she was using and turned around.

"If you love me," she said, "you can do this for me. If you don't love me, okay. But if you had a friend, any friend, and the friend came to visit, I'd make him feel comfortable." She wiped her hands with the dish towel.

"I don't have any blind friends," I said.

"You don't have *any* friends," she said. "Period. Besides," she said, "goddamn it, his wife's just died! Don't you understand that? The man's lost his wife!"

I didn't answer. She'd told me a little about the blind man's wife. Her name was Beulah. Beulah! That's a name for a colored woman.

"Was his wife a Negro?" I asked.

"Are you crazy?" my wife said. "Have you just flipped or something?" She picked up a potato. I saw it hit the floor, then roll under the stove. "What's wrong with you?" she said. "Are you drunk?"

"I'm just asking," I said.

Right then my wife filled me in with more detail than I cared to know. I made a drink and sat at the kitchen table to listen. Pieces of the story began to fall into place.

Beulah had gone to work for the blind man the summer after my wife had stopped working for him. Pretty soon Beulah and the blind man had themselves a church wedding. It was a little wedding—who'd want to go to such a wedding in the first place?—just the two of them, plus the minister and the minister's wife. But it was a church wedding just the same. It was what Beulah had wanted, he'd said. But even then Beulah must have been carrying the cancer in her glands. After they had been inseparable for eight years—my wife's word, *inseparable* – Beulah's health went into a rapid decline. She died in a Seattle hospital room, the blind man sitting beside the bed and holding on to her hand. They'd married, lived and worked together, slept together—had sex, sure—and then the blind man had to bury her. All this without his having ever seen what the goddamned woman looked like. It was beyond my understanding. Hearing this, I felt sorry for the blind man for a little bit. And then I found myself thinking what a pitiful life this woman must have led. Imagine a woman who could never see herself as she was seen in the eyes of her loved one. A woman who could go on day after day and never receive the smallest compliment from her beloved. A woman whose husband could never read the expression on her face, be it misery or something better. Someone who could wear makeup or not—what difference to him? She could, if she wanted, wear green eyeshadow around one eye, a straight pin in her nostril, yellow slacks, and purple shoes, no matter. And then to slip off into death, the blind man's hand on her hand, his blind eyes streaming tears—I'm imagining now—her last thought maybe this: that he never even knew what she looked like, and she on an express to the grave. Robert was left with a small insurance policy and a half of a twenty-peso Mexican coin. The other half of the coin went into the box with her. Pathetic.

So when the time rolled around, my wife went to the depot to pick him up. With nothing to do but wait—sure, I blamed him for that—I was having a drink and watching the TV when I heard the car pull into the drive. I got up from the sofa with my drink and went to the window to have a look.

I saw my wife laughing as she parked the car. I saw her get out of the car and shut the door. She was still wearing a smile. Just amazing. She went around to the other side of the car to where the blind man was already starting to get out. This blind man, feature this, he was wearing a full beard! A beard on a blind man! Too much, I say. The blind man reached into the backseat and dragged out a suitcase. My wife took his arm, shut the car door, and, talking all the way, moved him down the drive and then up the steps to the front porch. I turned off the TV. I finished my drink, rinsed the glass, dried my hands. Then I went to the door.

My wife said, "I want you to meet Robert. Robert, this is my husband. I've told you all about him." She was beaming. She had this blind man by his coat sleeve.

The blind man let go of his suitcase and up came his hand.

I took it. He squeezed hard, held my hand, and then he let it go.

"I feel like we've already met," he boomed.

"Likewise," I said. I didn't know what else to say. Then I said, "Welcome. I've heard a lot about you." We began to move then, a little group, from the porch into the living room, my wife guiding him by the arm. The blind man was carrying his suitcase in his other hand. My wife said things like, "To your left here, Robert. That's right. Now watch it, there's a chair. That's it. Sit down right here. This is the sofa. We just bought this sofa two weeks ago."

I started to say something about the old sofa. I'd liked that old sofa. But I didn't say anything. Then I wanted to say something else, small-talk, about the scenic ride along the Hudson. How going *to* New York, you should sit on the right-hand side of the train, and coming *from* New York, the left-hand side.

"Did you have a good train ride?" I said. "Which side of the train did you sit on, by the way?"

"What a question, which side!" my wife said. "What's it matter which side?" she said.

"I just asked," I said.

"Right side," the blind man said. "I hadn't been on a train in nearly forty years. Not since I was a kid. With my folks. That's been a long time. I'd nearly forgotten the sensation. I have winter in my beard now," he said. "So I've been told, anyway. Do I look distinguished, my dear?" the blind man said to my wife.

"You look distinguished, Robert," she said. "Robert," she said. "Robert, it's just so good to see you."

My wife finally took her eyes off the blind man and looked at me. I had the feeling she didn't like what she saw. I shrugged.

I've never met, or personally known, anyone who was blind. This blind man was late forties, a heavy-set, balding man with stooped shoulders, as if he carried a great weight there. He wore brown slacks, brown shoes, a light-brown shirt, a tie, a sports coat. Spiffy. He also had this full beard. But he didn't use a cane and he didn't wear dark glasses. I'd always thought dark glasses were a must for the blind. Fact was, I wished he had a pair. At first glance, his eyes looked like anyone else's eyes. But if you looked close, there was something different about them. Too much white in the iris, for one thing, and the pupils seemed to move around in the sockets without his knowing it or being able to stop it. Creepy. As I stared at his face, I saw the left pupil turn in toward his nose while the other made an effort to keep in one place. But it was only an effort, for that eye was on the roam without his knowing it or wanting it to be.

I said, "Let me get you a drink. What's your pleasure? We have a little of everything. It's one of our pastimes."

"Bub, I'm a Scotch man myself," he said fast enough in this big voice.

"Right," I said. Bub! "Sure you are. I knew it."

He let his fingers touch his suitcase, which was sitting alongside the sofa. He was taking his bearings. I didn't blame him for that.

"I'll move that up to your room," my wife said.

"No, that's fine," the blind man said loudly. "It can go up when I go up."

"A little water with the Scotch?" I said.

"Very little," he said.

"I knew it," I said.

He said, "Just a tad. The Irish actor, Barry Fitzgerald? I'm like that fellow. When I drink water, Fitzgerald said, I drink water. When I drink whiskey, I drink whiskey." My wife laughed. The blind man brought his hand up under his beard. He lifted his beard slowly and let it drop.

I did the drinks, three big glasses of Scotch with a splash of water in each. Then we made ourselves comfortable and talked about Robert's travels. First the long flight from the West Coast to Connecticut, we covered that. Then from Connecticut up here by train. We had another drink concerning that leg of the trip.

I remembered having read somewhere that the blind didn't smoke because, as speculation had it, they couldn't see the smoke they exhaled. I thought I knew that much and that much only about blind people. But this blind man smoked his cigarette down to the nubbin and then lit another one. This blind man filled his ashtray and my wife emptied it.

When we sat down at the table for dinner, we had another drink. My wife heaped Robert's plate with cube steak, scalloped potatoes, green beans. I buttered him up two slices of bread. I said, "Here's bread and butter for you." I swallowed some of my drink. "Now let us pray," I said, and the blind man lowered his head. My wife looked at me, her mouth agape. "Pray the phone won't ring and the food doesn't get cold," I said.

We dug in. We ate everything there was to eat on the table. We ate like there was no tomorrow. We didn't talk. We ate. We scarfed. We grazed that table. We were into serious eating. The blind man had right away located his foods, he knew just where everything was on his plate. I watched with admiration as he used his knife and fork on the meat. He'd cut two pieces of meat, fork the meat into his mouth, and then go all out for the scalloped potatoes, the beans next, and then he'd tear off a hunk of buttered bread and eat that. He'd follow this up with a big drink of milk. It didn't seem to bother him to use his fingers once in a while, either.

We finished everything, including half a strawberry pie. For a few moments, we sat as if stunned. Sweat beaded on our faces. Finally, we got up from the table and left the dirty plates. We didn't look back. We took ourselves into the living room and sank into our places again. Robert and my wife sat on the sofa. I took the big chair. We had us two or three more drinks while they talked about the major things that had come to pass for them in the past ten years. For the most part, I just listened. Now and then I joined in. I didn't want him to think I'd left the room, and I didn't want her to think I was feeling left out. They talked of things that had happened to them—to them!—these past ten years. I waited in vain to hear my name on my wife's sweet lips: "And then my dear husband came into my life"— something like that. But I heard nothing of the sort. More talk of Robert. Robert had done a little of everything, it seemed, a regular blind jack-of-all-trades. But most recently he and his wife had had an Amway distributorship, from which, I gathered, they'd earned their living, such as it was. The blind man was also a ham radio operator. He talked in his loud voice about conversations he'd had with fellow operators in Guam, in the Philippines, in Alaska, and even in Tahiti. He said he'd have a lot of friends there if he ever wanted to go visit those places. From time to time, he'd turn his blind face toward me, put his hand under his beard, ask me something. How long had I been in my present position? (Three years.) Did I like my work? (I didn't.) Was I going to stay with it? (What were the options?) Finally, when I thought he was beginning to run down, I got up and turned on the TV.

My wife looked at me with irritation. She was heading toward a boil. Then she looked at the blind man and said, "Robert, do you have a TV?"

The blind man said, "My dear, I have two TVs. I have a color set and a black-and-white thing, an old relic. It's funny, but if I turn the TV on, and I'm always turning it on, I turn on the color set. It's funny, don't you think?"

I didn't know what to say to that. I had absolutely nothing to say to that. No opinion. So I watched the news program and tried to listen to what the announcer was saying.

"This is a color TV," the blind man said. "Don't ask me how, but I can tell."

"We traded up a while ago," I said.

The blind man had another taste of his drink. He lifted his beard, sniffed it, and let it fall. He leaned forward on the sofa. He positioned his ashtray on the coffee table, then put the lighter to his cigarette. He leaned back on the sofa and crossed his legs at the ankles.

My wife covered her mouth, and then she yawned. She stretched. She said, "I think I'll go upstairs and put on my robe. I think I'll change into something else. Robert, you make yourself comfortable," she said.

"I'm comfortable," the blind man said.

"I want you to feel comfortable in this house," she said.

"I am comfortable," the blind man said.

After she'd left the room, he and I listened to the weather report and then to the sports roundup. By that time, she'd been gone so long I didn't know if she was going to come back. I thought she might have gone to bed. I wished she'd come back downstairs. I didn't want to be left alone with a blind man. I asked him if he wanted another drink, and he said sure. Then I asked if he wanted to smoke some dope with me. I said I'd just rolled a number. I hadn't, but I planned to do so in about two shakes.

"I'll try some with you," he said.

"Damn right," I said. "That's the stuff."

I got our drinks and sat down on the sofa with him. Then I rolled us two fat numbers. I lit one and passed it. I brought it to his fingers. He took it and inhaled.

"Hold it as long as you can," I said. I could tell he didn't know the first thing.

My wife came back downstairs wearing her pink robe and her pink slippers.

"What do I smell?" she said.

"We thought we'd have us some cannabis," I said.

My wife gave me a savage look. Then she looked at the blind man and said, "Robert, I didn't know you smoked."

He said, "I do now, my dear. There's a first time for everything. But I don't feel anything yet."

"This stuff is pretty mellow," I said. "This stuff is mild. It's dope you can reason with," I said. "It doesn't mess you up."

"Not much it doesn't, bub," he said, and laughed.

My wife sat on the sofa between the blind man and me. I passed her the number. She took it and toked and then passed it back to me. "Which way is this going?" she said. Then she said, "I shouldn't be smoking this. I can hardly keep my eyes open as it is. That dinner did me in. I shouldn't have eaten so much."

"It was the strawberry pie," the blind man said. "That's what did it," he said, and he laughed his big laugh. Then he shook his head.

"There's more strawberry pie," I said.

"Do you want some more, Robert?" my wife said.

"Maybe in a little while," he said.

We gave our attention to the TV. My wife yawned again. She said, "Your bed is made up when you feel like going to bed, Robert. I know you must have had a long day. When you're ready to go to bed, say so." She pulled his arm. "Robert?"

He came to and said, "I've had a real nice time. This beats tapes, doesn't it?"

I said, "Coming at you," and I put the number between his fingers. He inhaled, held the smoke, and then let it go. It was like he'd been doing it since he was nine years old.

"Thanks, bub," he said. "But I think this is all for me. I think I'm beginning to feel it," he said. He held the burning roach out for my wife.

"Same here," she said. "Ditto. Me, too." She took the roach and passed it to me. "I may just sit here for a while between you two guys with my eyes closed. But don't let me bother you, okay? Either one of you. If it bothers you, say so. Otherwise, I may just sit here with my eyes closed until you're ready to go to bed," she said. "Your bed's made up, Robert, when you're ready. It's right next to our room at the top of the stairs. We'll show you up when you're ready. You wake me up now, you guys, if I fall asleep." She said that and then she closed her eyes and went to sleep.

The news program ended. I got up and changed the channel. I sat back down on the sofa. I wished my wife hadn't pooped out. Her head lay across the back of the sofa, her mouth open. She'd turned so that her robe slipped away from her legs, exposing a juicy thigh. I reached to draw her robe back over her, and it was then that I glanced at the blind man. What the hell! I flipped the robe open again.

"You say when you want some strawberry pie," I said.

"I will," he said.

I said, "Are you tired? Do you want me to take you up to your bed? Are you ready to hit the hay?"

"Not yet," he said. "No, I'll stay up with you, bub. If that's all right. I'll stay up until you're ready to turn in. We haven't had a chance to talk. Know what I mean? I feel like me and her monopolized the evening." He lifted his beard and he let it fall. He picked up his cigarettes and his lighter.

"That's all right," I said. Then I said, "I'm glad for the company."

And I guess I was. Every night I smoked dope and stayed up as long as I could before I fell asleep. My wife and I hardly ever went to bed at the same time. When I did go to sleep, I had these dreams. Sometimes I'd wake up from one of them, my heart going crazy.

Something about the church and the Middle Ages was on the TV. Not your run-of-the-mill TV fare. I wanted to watch something else. I turned to the other channels. But there was nothing on them, either. So I turned back to the first channel and apologized.

"Bub, it's all right," the blind man said. "It's fine with me. Whatever you want to watch is okay, I'm always learning something. Learning never ends. It won't hurt me to learn something tonight. I got ears," he said.

We didn't say anything for a time. He was leaning forward with his head turned at me, his right ear aimed in the direction of the set. Very disconcerting. Now and then his eyelids drooped and then they snapped open again. Now and then he put his fingers into his beard and tugged, like he was thinking about something he was hearing on the television.

On the screen, a group of men wearing cowls was being set upon and tormented by men dressed in skeleton costumes and men dressed as devils. The men dressed as devils wore devil masks, horns, and long tails. This pageant was part of a procession. The Englishman who was narrating the thing said it took place in Spain once a year. I tried to explain to the blind man what was happening.

"Skeletons," he said. "I know about skeletons," he said, and he nodded.

The TV showed this one cathedral. Then there was a long, slow look at another one. Finally, the picture switched to the famous one in Paris, with its flying buttresses and its spires reaching up to the clouds. The camera pulled away to show the whole of the cathedral rising above the skyline.

There were times when the Englishman who was telling the thing would shut up, would simply let the camera move around the cathedrals. Or else the camera would tour the countryside, men in fields walking behind oxen. I waited as long as I could. Then I felt I had to say something. I said, "They're showing the outside of this cathedral now. Gargoyles. Little statues carved to look like monsters. Now I guess they're in Italy. Yeah, they're in Italy. There's paintings on the walls of this one church."

"Are those fresco paintings, bub?" he asked, and he sipped from his drink.

I reached for my glass. But it was empty. I tried to remember what I could remember. "You're asking me are those frescoes?" I said. "That's a good question. I don't know."

The camera moved to a cathedral outside Lisbon. The differences in the Portuguese cathedral compared with the French and Italian were not that great. But they were there. Mostly the interior stuff. Then something occurred to me, and I said, "Something has occurred to me. Do you have any idea what a cathedral is? What they look like, that is? Do you follow me? If somebody says cathedral to you, do you have any notion what they're talking about? Do you know the difference between that and a Baptist church, say?"

He let the smoke dribble from his mouth. "I know they took hundreds of workers fifty or a hundred years to build," he said. "I just heard the man say that, of course. I know generations of the same families worked on a cathedral. I heard him say that, too. The men who began their life's work on them, they never lived to see the completion of their work. In that wise, bub, they're no different from the rest of us, right?" He laughed. Then his eyelids drooped again. His head nodded. He seemed to be snoozing. Maybe he was imagining himself in Portugal. The TV was showing another cathedral now. This one was in Germany. The Englishman's voice droned on. "Cathedrals," the blind man said. He sat up and rolled his head back and forth. "If you want the truth, bub, that's about all I know. What I just said. What I heard him say. But maybe you could describe one to me? I wish you'd do it. I'd like that. If you want to know. I really don't have a good idea."

I stared hard at the shot of the cathedral on the TV. How could I even begin to describe it? But say my life depended on it. Say my life was being threatened by an insane guy who said I had to do it or else.

I stared some more at the cathedral before the picture flipped off into the countryside. There was no use. I turned to the blind man and said, "To begin with, they're very tall." I was looking around the room for clues. "They reach way up. Up and up. Toward the sky. They're so big, some of them, they have to have these supports. To help hold them up, so to speak. These supports are called buttresses. They remind me of viaducts, for some reason. But maybe you don't know viaducts, either? Sometimes the cathedrals have devils and such carved into the front. Sometimes lords and ladies. Don't ask me why this is," I said.

He was nodding. The whole upper part of his body seemed to be moving back and forth.

"I'm not doing so good, am I?" I said.

He stopped nodding and leaned forward on the edge of the sofa. As he listened to me, he was running his fingers through his beard. I wasn't getting through to him, I could see that. But he waited for me to go on just the same. He nodded, like he was trying to encourage me. I tried to think what else to say. "They're really big," I said. "They're massive. They're built of stone. Marble, too, sometimes. In those olden days, when they built cathedrals, men wanted to be close to God. In those olden days, God was an important part of every-one's life. You could tell this from their cathedral-building. I'm sorry," I said, "but it looks like that's the best I can do for you. I'm just no good at it."

"That's all right, bub," the blind man said. "Hey, listen. I hope you don't mind my asking you. Can I ask you something? Let me ask you a simple question, yes or no. I'm just curious and there's no offense. You're my host. But let me ask if you are in any way religious? You don't mind my asking?"

I shook my head. He couldn't see that, though. A wink is the same as a nod to a blind man. "I guess I don't believe in it. In anything. Sometimes it's hard. You know what I'm saying?"

"Sure, I do," he said.

"Right," I said.

The Englishman was still holding forth. My wife sighed in her sleep. She drew a long breath and went on with her sleeping.

"You'll have to forgive me," I said. "But I can't tell you what a cathedral looks like. It just isn't in me to do it. I can't do any more than I've done."

The blind man sat very still, his head down, as he listened to me.

I said, "The truth is, cathedrals don't mean anything special to me. Nothing. Cathedrals. They're something to look at on late-night TV. That's all they are."

It was then that the blind man cleared his throat. He brought something up. He took a handkerchief from his back pocket. Then he said, "I get it, bub. It's okay. It happens. Don't worry about it," he said. "Hey, listen to me. Will you do me a favor? I got an idea. Why don't you find us some heavy paper? And a pen. We'll do something. We'll draw one together. Get us a pen and some heavy paper. Go on, bub, get the stuff," he said.

So I went upstairs. My legs felt like they didn't have any strength in them. They felt like they did after I'd done some running. In my wife's room, I looked around. I found some ballpoints in a little basket on her table. And then I tried to think where to look for the kind of paper he was talking about.

Downstairs, in the kitchen. I found a shopping bag with onion skins in the bottom of the bag. I emptied the bag and shook it. I brought it into the living room and sat down with it near his legs. I moved some things, smoothed the wrinkles from the bag, spread it out on the coffee table.

The blind man got down from the sofa and sat next to me on the carpet.

He ran his fingers over the paper. He went up and down the sides of the paper. The edges, even the edges. He fingered the corners.

"All right," he said. "All right, let's do her."

He found my hand, the hand with the pen. He closed his hand over my hand. "Go ahead, bub, draw," he said. "Draw. You'll see. I'll follow along with you. It'll be okay. Just begin now like I'm telling you. You'll see. Draw," the blind man said.

So I began. First I drew a box that looked like a house. It could have been the house I lived in. Then I put a roof on it. At either end of the roof. I drew spires. Crazy.

"Swell," he said, "Terrific. You're doing fine," he said. "Never thought anything like this could happen in your lifetime, did you, bub? Well, it's a strange life, we all know that. Go on now. Keep it up."

I put in windows with arches. I drew flying buttresses. I hung great doors. I couldn't stop. The TV station went off the air. I put down the pen and closed and opened my fingers. The blind man felt around over the paper. He moved the tips of his fingers over the paper, all over what I had drawn, and he nodded.

"Doing fine," the blind man said.

I took up the pen again, and he found my hand. I kept at it. I'm no artist. But I kept drawing just the same.

My wife opened up her eyes and gazed at us. She sat up on the sofa, her robe hanging open. She said, "What are you doing? Tell me, I want to know."

I didn't answer her.

The blind man said, "We're drawing a cathedral. Me and him are working on it. Press hard," he said to me. "That's right. That's good," he said. "Sure. You got it, bub, I can tell. You didn't think you could. But you can, can't you? You're cooking with gas now. You know what I'm saying? We're going to really have us something here in a minute. How's the old arm?" he said. "Put some people in there now. What's a cathedral without people?"

My wife said, "What's going on? Robert, what are you doing? What's going on?"

"It's all right," he said to her. "Close your eyes now," the blind man said to me.

I did it. I closed them just like he said.

"Are they closed?" he said. "Don't fudge."

"They're closed," I said.

"Keep them that way," he said. He said, "Don't stop now. Draw."

So we kept on with it. His fingers rode my fingers as my hand went over the paper. It was like nothing else in my life up to now.

Then he said, "I think that's it. I think you got it," he said. "Take a look. What do you think?"

But I had my eyes closed. I thought I'd keep them that way for a little longer. I thought it was something I ought to do.

"Well?" he said. "Are you looking?"

My eyes were still closed. I was in my house. I knew that. But I didn't feel like I was inside anything.

"It's really something," I said.

Sandra Cisneros

Sandra Cisneros, born in 1954 to a Mexican father and Chicana mother, was raised in working class neighborhoods in Chicago. She began writing poetry at an early age and developed her craft at the University of Iowa Writers' Workshop, where she found herself "determined to fill a literary void . . . trying to write the stories that haven't been written." Her first book, The House on Mango Street, *was published to wide critical acclaim in 1983 and combined prose with poetry in short interconnected chapters. Cisneros has also published two books of poetry and, most recently, the novel* Caramelo (2002). *In a 2002 interview with PBS' NewsHour, Cisneros said about her role as the writer in the family: "Generally if you're a daughter in a Mexican family, no one wants to tell you anything, they tell you the healthy lies about your family. But the older I got and the more people recognized me as the writer, family stories started getting passed to me, memoirs, a little bit of gossip, this and that. And I found myself drawing from families' memorias, their memoirs, as well as doing some research by doing interviews with the real people, the 'walking Smithsonians' as I like to put it, sitting down and talking to people, and then doing the research to add to that."*

The House on
Mango Street

We didn't always live on Mango Street. Before that we lived on Loomis on the third floor, and before that we lived on Keeler. Before Keeler it was Paulina, and before that I can't remember. But what I remember most is moving a lot. Each time it seemed there'd be one more of us. By the time we got to Mango Street we were six—Mama, Papa, Carlos, Kiki, my sister Nenny, and me.

The house on Mango Street is ours, and we don't have to pay rent to anybody, or share the yard with the people downstairs, or be careful not to make too much noise, and there isn't a landlord banging on the ceiling with a broom. But even so, it's not the house we'd thought we'd get.

We had to leave the flat on Loomis quick. The water pipes broke and the landlord wouldn't fix them because the house was too old. We had to leave fast. We were using the washroom next door and carrying water over in empty milk gallons. That's why Mama and Papa looked for a house, and that's why we moved into the house on Mango Street, far away, on the other side of town.

They always told us that one day we would move into a house, a real house that would be ours for always so we wouldn't have to move each year. And our house would have running water and pipes that worked. And inside it would have real stairs, not hallway stairs, but stairs inside like the houses on T.V. And we'd have a basement and at least three washrooms so when we took a bath we wouldn't have to tell everybody. Our house would be white with trees around it, a great big yard and grass growing without a fence. This was the house Papa talked about when he held a lottery ticket and this was the house Mama dreamed up in the stories she told us before we went to bed.

But the house on Mango Street is not the way they told it at all. It's small and red with tight steps in front and windows so small you'd think they were holding their breath. Bricks are crumbling in places, and the front door is so swollen you have to push hard to get in. There is no front yard, only four little elms the city planted by the curb. Out back is a small garage for the car we don't own yet and a small yard that looks smaller between the two buildings on either side. There are stairs in our house, but they're ordinary hallway stairs, and the house has only one washroom. Everybody has to share a bedroom—Mama and Papa, Carlos and Kiki, me and Nenny.

Once when we were living on Loomis, a nun from my school passed by and saw me playing out front. The laundromat downstairs had been boarded up because it had been robbed two days before and the owner had painted on the wood YES WE'RE OPEN so as not to lose business.

Where do you live? she asked.

There, I said pointing up to the third floor.

You live *there*?

There, I had to look to where she pointed—the third floor, the paint peeling, wooden bars Papa had nailed on the windows so we wouldn't fall out. You live *there*? The way she said it made me feel like nothing. *There*, I lived *there*. I nodded.

I knew then I had to have a house. A real house. One I could point to. But this isn't it. The house on Mango Street isn't it. For the time being, Mama says. Temporary, says Papa. But I know how those things go.

Lydia Davis

*Lydia Davis was born in 1947 in Northampton, Massachusetts. A gradu-
ate of Barnard College, she has translated over 20 works of French
literature. Davis's work is known for its experimentation and wordplay, its
humor and irony, and its unique rendering of human consciousness and relationships. She is the author of the novel* The End of the Story *(1995),
and five short story collections:* The Thirteenth Woman *(1976),* Sketches
for a Life of Wassily *(1981),* Story and Other Stories *(1983),* Break It
Down *(1986), and* Samuel Johnson Is Indignant *(2001). In a 1997 interview with* Salon, *Davis discussed how she begins a story: "I don't write
something unless I feel impelled to write it. In other words, I don't have a
regular schedule and sit down every day and say, 'Well, what do I do today?' It's more that an idea or a sentence will come to me like 'What was
he really feeling yesterday while he was walking through my yard and saying nice things about my flowers? Maybe underneath he was really distressed by the overgrown garden.' And that will make me go on from
there. And so the beginnings of the stories come to me from somewhere
else. They sort of pop into my mind while I'm doing something else, usually."*

Story

I get home from work and there is a message from him: that he is not
coming, that he is busy. He will call again. I wait to hear from him,
then at nine o'clock I go to where he lives, find his car, but he's not
home. I knock at his apartment door and then at the garage doors, not
knowing which garage door is his—no answer. I write a note read it
over, write a new note, and stick it in his door. At home I am restless
and all can do, though I have a lot to do, since I'm going on a trip in
the morning, is play the piano. I call again at 10:45 and he's home, he
has been to the movies with his girlfriend, and she's still there. He says
he'll call back. I wait. Finally I sit down and write in my notebook that
when he calls me either he will then come to me, or he will not and I
will be angry, and so I will have either him or my own anger, and this
might be all right, since anger is always a great comfort, as I found
with my husband. And then I go on to write, in the third person and
the past tense, that clearly she always needed to have a love even if it
was a complicated love. He calls back before I have time to finish writing all this down. When he calls, it is a little after 11:30. We argue until
nearly twelve. Everything he says is contradiction: for example, he says

he did not want to see me because he wanted to work and even more because he wanted to be alone, but he has not worked and he has not been alone. There is no way I can get him to reconcile any of his contradictions and when this conversation begins to sound too much like many I had with my husband I say goodbye and hang up. I finish writing down what I started to write down even though by now it no longer seems true that anger is any great comfort.

I call him back five minutes later to tell him that I am sorry about all this arguing, and that I love him, but there is no answer. I call again five minutes later, thinking he might have walked out to his garage and walked back, but again there is no answer. I think of driving to where he lives again and looking for his garage to see if he is in there working, because he keeps his desk there and his books and that is where he goes to read and write. I am in my nightgown, it is after twelve and I have to leave the next morning at five. Even so, I get dressed and drive the mile or so to his place. I am afraid that when I get there I will see other cars by his house that I did not see earlier and that one of them will belong to his old girlfriend. When I drive down the driveway I see two cars that weren't there before, and one of them is parked as close as possible to his door, and I think that she is there. I walk around the small building to the back where his apartment is, and look in the window: the light is on, but I can't see anything clearly because of the half closed venetian blinds and the steam on the glass. But things inside the room are not the same as they were earlier in the evening, and before there was no steam. I open the outer screen door and knock. I wait. No answer. I let the screen door fall shut and I walk away to check the garages. Now the door opens behind me as I am walking away and he comes out. I can't see him very well because it is dark in the narrow lane beside his door and he is wearing dark clothes and whatever light there is is behind him. He comes up to me and puts his arms around me without speaking, and I think he is not speaking not because he is feeling so much but because he is preparing what he will say. He lets go of me and walks around me and ahead of me out to where the cars are parked by the garage doors.

As we walk out there he says "Look," and my name, and I am waiting for him to say that she is here and also that it's all over between us. But he doesn't, and I have the feeling he did intend to say something like that, at least say that she was here, and that he then thought better of it for some reason. Instead, he says that everything that went wrong tonight was his fault and he's sorry. He stands with his back against a garage door and his face in the light and I stand in front of him with my back to the light. At one point he hugs me so suddenly that the fire of my cigarette crumbles against the garage door behind him. I know why we're out here and not in his room, but I don't ask him until everything is all right between us. Then he says, "She wasn't here when I called you. She came back later." He says the only reason she is there is that something is troubling her and he is the only one she can talk to about it. Then he says, "You don't understand, do you."

I try to figure it out.

So when they went to the movies and then came back to his place and then I called and then she left and he called back and we argued and then I called back twice but he had gone out to get a beer (he says) and then I drove over and in the meantime he had returned from buying beer and she had also come back and she was in his room so we talked by the garage doors. But what is the truth? Could he and she both really have come back in that short interval between my last phone call and my arrival at his place? Or is the truth really that during his call to me she waited outside or in his garage or in her car and that he then brought her in again, and that when the phone rang with my second and third calls he let it ring without answering, because he was fed up with me and with arguing? Or is the truth that she did leave and did come back later but that he remained and let the phone ring without answering? Or did he perhaps bring her in and then go out for the beer while she waited there and listened to the phone ring? The last is the least likely. I don't believe anyway that there was any trip out for beer.

The fact that he does not tell me the truth all the time makes me not sure of his truth at certain times, and then I work to figure out for myself if what he is telling me is the truth or not, and sometimes I can figure out that it's not the truth and sometimes I don't know and never know, and sometimes just because he says it to me over and over again I am convinced it is the truth because I don't believe he would repeat a lie so often. Maybe the truth does not matter, but I want to know it if only so that I can come to some conclusions about such questions as: whether he is angry at me or not; if he is, then how angry; whether he still loves her or not; if he does, then how much; whether he loves me or not; how much; how capable he is of deceiving me in the act and after the act in the telling.

Junot Díaz

Junot Díaz was born in 1968 in Santo Domingo, Dominican Republic. When he was seven his family immigrated to the United States, settling in an African-American and Latino neighborhood in central New Jersey. The life of immigrants struggling to define and redefine their identity is a major theme in Díaz's short story collection, Drown, *which was published in 1996 to great critical praise. Besides his unique subject matter that negotiates the borders of cultural difference, Díaz's stories are notable for their striking, original, and immediate voice and their melding of language and dialect. In 1999* The New Yorker *named Díaz one of the best fiction writers in America under 40. He has continued to publish short stories in* The New Yorker *and is frequently anthologized in the* Best American Short Stories. *He graduated from Rutgers University and earned an M.F.A. in creative writing from Cornell University. Discussing his experience as a first-generation immigrant, Díaz has said, "The moment my family set foot in Kennedy Airport, a world ended for me. You'd think that sort of cataclysm would make itself apparent quickly and with umbrage, but in actuality it took me years to notice. The end was not so much an apocalypse as it was a fading, a merging, and, ultimately, a metamorphosis."*

Fiesta, 1980

Mami's youngest sister—my tía Yrma—finally made it to the United States that year. She and tío Miguel got themselves an apartment in the Bronx, off the Grand Concourse and everybody decided that we should have a party. Actually, my pops decided, but everybody—meaning Mami, tía Yrma, tío Miguel and their neighbors—thought it a dope idea. On the afternoon of the party Papi came back from work around six. Right on time. We were all dressed by then, which was a smart move on our part. If Papi had walked in and caught us lounging around in our underwear, he would have kicked our asses something serious.

He didn't say nothing to nobody, not even my moms. He just pushed past her, held up his hand when she tried to talk to him and headed right into the shower. Rafa gave me the look and I gave it back to him; we both knew Papi had been with that Puerto Rican woman he was seeing and wanted to wash off the evidence quick.

Mami looked really nice that day. The United States had finally put some meat on her; she was no longer the same flaca who had arrived here three years before. She had cut her hair short and was wearing tons of cheapass jewelry which on her didn't look too lousy. She smelled like herself, like the wind through a tree. She always waited until the last possible minute to put on her perfume because she said it was a waste to spray it on early and then have to spray it on again once you got to the party.

We—meaning me, my brother, my little sister and Mami—waited for Papi to finish his shower. Mami seemed anxious, in her usual dispassionate way. Her hands adjusted the buckle of her belt over and over again. That morning, when she had gotten us up for school, Mami told us that she wanted to have a good time at the party. I want to dance, she said, but now, with the sun sliding out of the sky like spit off a wall, she seemed ready just to get this over with.

Rafa didn't much want to go to no party either, and me, I never wanted to go anywhere with my family. There was a baseball game in the parking lot outside and we could hear our friends, yelling, Hey, and, Cabrón, to one another. We heard the pop of a ball as it sailed over the cars, the clatter of an aluminum bat dropping to the concrete. Not that me or Rafa loved baseball; we just liked playing with the local kids, thrashing them at anything they were doing. By the sounds of the shouting, we both knew the game was close, either of us could have made a difference. Rafa frowned and when I frowned back, he put up his fist. Don't you mirror me, he said.

Don't you mirror me, I said.

He punched me—I would have hit him back but Papi marched into the living room with his towel around his waist, looking a lot smaller than he did when he was dressed. He had a few strands of hair around his nipples and a surly closed-mouth expression, like maybe he'd scalded his tongue or something.

Have they eaten? he asked Mami.

She nodded. I made you something.

You didn't let him eat, did you?

Ay, Dios mío, she said, letting her arms fall to her side.

Ay, Dios mío is right, Papi said.

I was never supposed to eat before our car trips, but earlier, when she had put out our dinner of rice, beans and sweet platanos, guess who had been the first one to clean his plate? You couldn't blame Mami really, she had been busy—cooking, getting ready, dressing my sister Madai. I should have reminded her not to feed me but I wasn't that sort of son.

Papi turned to me. Coño, muchacho, why did you eat?

Rafa had already started inching away from me. I'd once told him I considered him a low-down chickenshit for moving out of the way every time Papi was going to smack me.

Collateral damage, Rafa had said. Ever heard of it?

No.

Look it up.

Chickenshit or not, I didn't dare glance at him. Papi was old-fashioned; he expected your undivided attention when you were getting your ass whupped. You couldn't look him in the eye either—that wasn't allowed. Better to stare at his belly button, which was perfectly round and immaculate. Papi pulled me to my feet by my ear.

If you throw up—

I won't, I cried, tears in my eyes, more out of reflex than pain.

Ya, Ramón, ya. It's not his fault, Mami said.

They've known about this party forever. How did they think we were going to get there? Fly?

He finally let go of my ear and I sat back down. Madai was too scared to open her eyes. Being around Papi all her life had turned her into a major-league wuss. Anytime Papi raised his voice her lip would start trembling, like some specialized tuning fork. Rafa pretended that he had knuckles to crack and when I shoved him, he gave me a *Don't start* look. But even that little bit of recognition made me feel better.

I was the one who was always in trouble with my dad. It was like my God-given duty to piss him off, to do everything the way he hated. Our fights didn't bother me too much. I still wanted him to love me, something that never seemed strange or contradictory until years later, when he was out of our lives.

By the time my ear stopped stinging Papi was dressed and Mami was crossing each one of us, solemnly, like we were heading off to war. We said, in turn, Bendición, Mami, and she poked us in our five cardinal spots while saying, Que Dios te bendiga.

This was how all our trips began, the words that followed me every time I left the house.

None of us spoke until we were inside Papi's Volkswagen van. Brand-new, lime-green and bought to impress. Oh, we were impressed, but me, every time I was in that VW and Papi went above twenty miles an hour, I vomited. I'd never had trouble with cars before—that van was like my curse. Mami suspected it was the upholstery. In her mind, American things—appliances, mouthwash, funny-looking upholstery— all seemed to have an intrinsic badness about them. Papi was careful about taking me anywhere in the VW, but when he had to, I rode up front in Mami's usual seat so I could throw up out a window.

¿Cómo te sientes? Mami asked over my shoulder when Papi pulled onto the turnpike. She had her hand on the base of my neck. One thing about Mami, her palms never sweated.

I'm OK, I said, keeping my eyes straight ahead. I definitely didn't want to trade glances with Papi. He had this one look, furious and sharp, that always left me feeling bruised.

Toma. Mami handed me four mentas. She had thrown three out her window at the beginning of our trip, an offering to Eshú; the rest were for me.

I took one and sucked it slowly, my tongue knocking it up against my teeth. We passed Newark Airport without any incident. If Madai had been awake she would have cried because the planes flew so close to the cars.

How's he feeling? Papi asked.

Fine, I said. I glanced back at Rafa and he pretended like he didn't see me. That was the way he was, at school and at home. When I was in trouble, he didn't know me. Madai was solidly asleep, but even with her face all wrinkled up and drooling she looked cute, her hair all separated into twists.

I turned around and concentrated on the candy. Papi even started to joke that we might not have to scrub the van out tonight. He was beginning to loosen up, not checking his watch too much. Maybe he was thinking about that Puerto Rican woman or maybe he was just happy that we were all together. I could never tell. At the toll, he was feeling positive enough to actually get out of the van and search around under the basket for dropped coins. It was something he had once done to amuse Madai, but now it was habit. Cars behind us honked their horns and I slid down in my seat. Rafa didn't care; he grinned back at the other cars and waved. His actual job was to make sure no cops were coming. Mami shook Madai awake and as soon as she saw Papi stooping for a couple of quarters she let out this screech of delight that almost took off the top of my head.

That was the end of the good times. Just outside the Washington Bridge, I started feeling woozy. The smell of the upholstery got all up inside my head and I found myself with a mouthful of saliva. Mami's hand tensed on my shoulder and when I caught Papi's eye, he was like, No way. Don't do it.

The first time I got sick in the van Papi was taking me to the library. Rafa was with us and he couldn't believe I threw up. I was famous for my steel-lined stomach. A third-world childhood could give you that. Papi was worried enough that just as quick as Rafa could drop off the books we were on our way home. Mami fixed me one of her honey-and-onion concoctions and that made my stomach feel better. A week later we tried the library again and on this go-around I couldn't get the window open in time. When Papi got me home, he went and cleaned out the van himself, an expression of askho on his face. This was a big deal, since Papi almost never cleaned anything himself. He came back inside and found me sitting on the couch feeling like hell.

It's the car, he said to Mami. It's making him sick.

This time the damage was pretty minimal, nothing Papi couldn't wash off the door with a blast of the hose. He was pissed, though; he jammed his finger into my cheek, a nice solid thrust. That was the way he was with his punishments: imaginative. Earlier that year I'd written an essay in school called "My Father the Torturer," but the teacher made me write a new one. She thought I was kidding.

We drove the rest of the way to the Bronx in silence. We only stopped once, so I could brush my teeth. Mami had brought along my toothbrush and a tube of toothpaste and while every car known to man sped by us she stood outside with me so I wouldn't feel alone.

Tío Miguel was about seven feet tall and had his hair combed up and out, into a demi-fro. He gave me and Rafa big spleen-crushing hugs and then kissed Mami and finally ended up with Madai on his shoulder. The last time I'd seen Tío was at the airport, his first day in the United States. I remembered how he hadn't seemed all that troubled to be in another country.

He looked down at me. Carajo, Yunior, you look horrible!

He threw up, my brother explained.

I pushed Rafa. Thanks a lot, ass-face.

Hey, he said. Tío asked.

Tío clapped a bricklayer's hand on my shoulder. Everybody gets sick sometimes, he said. You should have seen me on the plane over here. Dios mio! He rolled his Asian-looking eyes for emphasis. I thought we were all going to die.

Everybody could tell he was lying. I smiled like he was making me feel better.

Do you want me to get you a drink? Tío asked. We got beer and rum.

Miguel, Mami said. He's young.

Young? Back in Santo Domingo, he'd be getting laid by now.

Mami thinned her lips, which took some doing.

Well, it's true, Tío said.

So, Mami, I said. When do I get to go visit the D.R.?

That's enough, Yunior.

It's the only pussy you'll ever get, Rafa said to me in English.

Not counting your girlfriend, of course.

Rafa smiled. He had to give me that one.

Papi came in from parking the van. He and Miguel gave each other the sort of handshakes that would have turned my fingers into Wonder bread.

Coño, compa'i, ¿cómo va todo? they said to each other.

Tía came out then, with an apron on and maybe the longest Lee Press-On Nails I've ever seen in my life. There was this one guru motherfucker in the *Guinness Book of World Records* who had longer nails, but I tell you, it was close. She gave everybody kisses, told me and Rafa how guapo we were—Rafa, of course, believed her—told Madai how bella she was, but when she got to Papi, she froze a little, like maybe she'd seen a wasp on the tip of his nose, but then kissed him all the same.

Mami told us to join the other kids in the living room. Tío said, Wait a minute, I want to show you the apartment. I was glad Tía said, Hold on, because from what I'd seen so far, the place had been furnished in Contemporary Dominican Tacky. The less I saw, the better. I mean, I liked plastic sofa covers but damn, Tío and Tía had taken it to another level. They had a disco ball hanging in the living room and the type of stucco ceilings that looked like stalactite heaven. The sofas all had golden tassels dangling from their edges. Tía came out of the kitchen with some people I didn't know and by the time she got done introducing everybody, only Papi and Mami were given the guided tour of the four-room third-floor apartment. Me and Rafa joined the kids in the living room. They'd already started eating. We were hungry, one of the girls explained, a pastelito in hand. The boy was about three years younger than me but the girl who'd spoken, Leti, was my age. She and another girl were on the sofa together and they were cute as hell.

Leti introduced them: the boy was her brother Wilquins and the other girl was her neighbor Mari. Leti had some serious tetas and I could tell that my brother was going to gun for her. His taste in girls was predictable. He sat down right between Leti and Mari and by the way they were smiling at him I knew he'd do fine. Neither of the girls gave me more than a cursory one-two, which didn't bother me. Sure, I liked girls but I was always too terrified to speak to them unless we were arguing or I was calling them stupidos, which was one of my favorite words that year. I turned to Wilquins and asked him what there was to do around here. Mari, who had the lowest voice I'd ever heard, said, He can't speak.

What does that mean?

He's mute.

I looked at Wilquins incredulously. He smiled and nodded, as if he'd won a prize or something.

Does he understand? I asked.

Of course he understands, Rafa said. He's not dumb.

I could tell Rafa had said that just to score points with the girls. Both of them nodded. Low-voice Mari said, He's the best student in his grade.

I thought, Not bad for a mute. I sat next to Wilquins. After about two seconds of TV Wilquins whipped out a bag of dominos and motioned to me. Did I want to play? Sure. Me and him played Rafa and Leti and we whupped their collective asses twice, which put Rafa in a real bad mood. He looked at me like maybe he wanted to take a swing, just one to make him feel better. Leti kept whispering into Rafa's ear, telling him it was OK.

In the kitchen I could hear my parents slipping into their usual modes. Papi's voice was loud and argumentative; you didn't have to be anywhere near him to catch his drift. And Mami, you had to put cups to your ears to hear hers. I went into the kitchen a few times—once so the tíos could show off how much bullshit I'd been able to cram in my head the last few years; another time for a bucket-sized cup of soda. Mami and Tía were frying tostones and the last of the pastelitos. She appeared happier now and the way her hands worked on our dinner you would think she had a life somewhere else making rare and precious things. She nudged Tia every now and then, shit they must have been doing all their lives. As soon as Mami saw me though, she gave me the eye. Don't stay long, that eye said. Don't piss your old man off.

Papi was too busy arguing about Elvis to notice me. Then somebody mentioned María Montez and Papi barked, María Montez? Let me tell *you* about María Montez, compa'i.

Maybe I was used to him. His voice—louder than most adults'—didn't bother me none, though the other kids shifted uneasily in their seats. Wilquins was about to raise the volume on the TV, but Rafa said, I wouldn't do that. Muteboy had balls, though. He did it anyway and then sat down. Wilquins's pop came into the living room a second later, a bottle of Presidente in hand. That dude must have had Spider-senses or something. Did you raise that? he asked Wilquins and Wilquins nodded.

Is this your house? his pops asked. He looked ready to beat Wilquins silly but he lowered the volume instead.

See, Rafa said. You nearly got your ass *kicked*.

I met the Puerto Rican woman right after Papi had gotten the van. He was taking me on short trips, trying to cure me of my vomiting. It wasn't really working but I looked forward to our trips, even though at the end of each one I'd be sick. These were the only times me and Papi did anything together. When we were alone he treated me much better, like maybe I was his son or something.

Before each drive Mami would cross me.

Bendición, Mami, I'd say.

She'd kiss my forehead. Que Dios te bendiga. And then she would give me a handful of mentas because she wanted me to be OK. Mami didn't think these excursions would cure anything, but the one time she had brought it up to Papi he had told her to shut up, what did she know about anything anyway?

Me and Papi didn't talk much. We just drove around our neighborhood. Occasionally he'd ask, How is it?

And I'd nod, no matter how I felt.

One day I was sick outside of Perth Amboy. Instead of taking me home he went the other way on Industrial Avenue, stopping a few minutes later in front of a light blue house I didn't recognize. It reminded me of the Easter eggs we colored at school, the ones we threw out the bus windows at other cars.

The Puerto Rican woman was there and she helped me clean up. She had dry papery hands and when she rubbed the towel on my chest, she did it hard, like I was a bumper she was waxing. She was very thin and had a cloud of brown hair rising above her narrow face and the sharpest blackest eyes you've ever seen.

He's cute, she said to Papi.

Not when he's throwing up, Papi said.

What's your name? she asked me. Are you Rafa?

I shook my head.

Then it's Yunior, right?

I nodded.

You're the smart one, she said, suddenly happy with herself. Maybe you want to see my books?

They weren't hers. I recognized them as ones my father must have left in her house. Papi was a voracious reader, couldn't even go cheating without a paperback in his pocket.

Why don't you go watch TV? Papi suggested. He was looking at her like she was the last piece of chicken on earth.

We got plenty of channels, she said. Use the remote if you want.

The two of them went upstairs and I was too scared of what was happening to poke around. I just sat there, ashamed, expecting something big and fiery to crash down on our heads. I watched a whole hour of the news before Papi came downstairs and said, Let's go.

About two hours later the women laid out the food and like always nobody but the kids thanked them. It must be some Dominican tradition or something. There was everything I liked—chicharrones, fried chicken, tostones, sancocho, rice, fried cheese, yuca, avocado, potato salad, a meteor-sized hunk of pernil, even a tossed salad which I could do without—but when I joined the other kids around the serving table, Papi said, Oh no you don't, and took the paper plate out of my hand. His fingers weren't gentle.

What's wrong now? Tia asked, handing me another plate.

He ain't eating, Papi said. Mami pretended to help Rafa with the pernil.

Why can't he eat?

Because I said so.

The adults who didn't know us made like they hadn't heard a thing and Tio just smiled sheepishly and told everybody to go ahead and eat. All the kids—about ten of them now—trooped back into the living room with their plates a-heaping and all the adults ducked into the kitchen and the dining room, where the radio was playing loud-ass bachatas. I was the only one without a plate. Papi stopped me before I could get away from him. He kept his voice nice and low so nobody else could hear him.

If you eat anything, I'm going to beat you. ¿Entiendes?

I nodded.

And if your brother gives you any food, I'll beat him too. Right here in front of everybody. ¿Entiendes?

I nodded again. I wanted to kill him and he must have sensed it because he gave my head a little shove.

All the kids watched me come in and sit down in front of the TV.

What's wrong with your dad? Leti asked.

He's a dick, I said.

Rafa shook his head. Don't say that shit in front of people.

Easy for you to be nice when you're eating, I said.

Hey, if I was a pukey little baby, I wouldn't get no food either.

I almost said something back but I concentrated on the TV. I wasn't going to start it. No fucking way. So I watched Bruce Lee beat Chuck Norris into the floor of the Colosseum and tried to pretend that there was no food anywhere in the house. It was Tia who finally saved me. She came into the living room and said, Since you ain't eating, Yunior, you can at least help me get some ice.

I didn't want to, but she mistook my reluctance for something else. I already asked your father.

She held my hand while we walked; Tia didn't have any kids but I could tell she wanted them. She was the sort of relative who always remembered your birthday but who you only went to visit because you had to. We didn't get past the first-floor landing before she opened her pocketbook and handed me the first of three pastelitos she had smuggled out of the apartment.

Go ahead, she said. And as soon as you get inside make sure you brush your teeth.

Thanks a lot, Tia, I said.

Those pastelitos didn't stand a chance.

She sat next to me on the stairs and smoked her cigarette. All the way down on the first floor and we could still hear the music and the adults and the television. Tía looked a ton like Mami; the two of them were both short and light-skinned. Tía smiled a lot and that was what set them apart the most.

How is it at home, Yunior?

What do you mean?

How's it going in the apartment? Are you kids OK?

I knew an interrogation when I heard one, no matter how sugar-coated it was. I didn't say anything. Don't get me wrong, I loved my tía, but something told me to keep my mouth shut. Maybe it was family loyalty, maybe I just wanted to protect Mami or I was afraid that Papi would find out—it could have been anything really.

Is your mom all right?

I shrugged.

Have there been lots of fights?

None, I said. Too many shrugs would have been just as bad as an answer. Papi's at work too much.

Work, Tía said, like it was somebody's name she didn't like.

Me and Rafa, we didn't talk much about the Puerto Rican woman. When we ate dinner at her house, the few times Papi had taken us over there, we still acted like nothing was out of the ordinary. Pass the ketchup, man. No sweat, bro. The affair was like a hole in our living room floor, one we'd gotten so used to circumnavigating that we sometimes forgot it was there.

By midnight all the adults were crazy dancing. I was sitting outside Tía's bedroom—where Madai was sleeping—trying not to attract attention. Rafa had me guarding the door; he and Leti were in there too, with some of the other kids, getting busy no doubt. Wilquins had gone across the hall to bed so I had me and the roaches to mess around with.

Whenever I peered into the main room I saw about twenty moms and dads dancing and drinking beers. Every now and then somebody yelled, ¡Quisqueya! And then everybody else would yell and stomp their feet. From what I could see my parents seemed to be enjoying themselves.

Mami and Tía spent a lot of time side by side, whispering, and I kept expecting something to come of this, a brawl maybe. I'd never once been out with my family when it hadn't turned to shit. We weren't even theatrical or straight crazy like other families. We fought like sixth-graders, without any real dignity. I guess the whole night I'd been waiting for a blowup, something between Papi and Mami. This was how I always figured Papi would be exposed, out in public, where everybody would know.

You're a cheater!

But everything was calmer than usual. And Mami didn't look like she was about to say anything to Papi. The two of them danced every now and then but they never lasted more than a song before Mami joined Tía again in whatever conversation they were having.

I tried to imagine Mami before Papi. Maybe I was tired, or just sad, thinking about the way my family was. Maybe I already knew how it would all end up in a few years, Mami without Papi, and that was why I did it. Picturing her alone wasn't easy. It seemed like Papi had always been with her, even when we were waiting in Santo Domingo for him to send for us.

The only photograph our family had of Mami as a young woman, before she married Papi, was the one that somebody took of her at an election party that I found one day while rummaging for money to go to the arcade. Mami had it tucked into her immigration papers. In the photo, she's surrounded by laughing cousins I will never meet, who are all shiny from dancing, whose clothes are rumpled and loose. You can tell it's night and hot and that the mosquitos have been biting. She sits straight and even in a crowd she stands out, smiling quietly like maybe she's the one everybody's celebrating. You can't see her hands but I imagined they're knotting a straw or a bit of thread. This was the woman my father met a year later on the Malecón, the woman Mami thought she'd always be.

Mami must have caught me studying her because she stopped what she was doing and gave me a smile, maybe her first one of the night. Suddenly I wanted to go over and hug her, for no other reason than I loved her, but there were about eleven fat jiggling bodies between us. So I sat down on the tiled floor and waited.

I must have fallen asleep because the next thing I knew Rafa was kicking me and saying, Let's go. He looked like he'd been hitting those girls off; he was all smiles. I got to my feet in time to kiss Tía and Tío good-bye. Mami was holding the serving dish she had brought with her.

Where's Papi? I asked.

He's downstairs, bringing the van around. Mami leaned down to kiss me.

You were good today, she said.

And then Papi burst in and told us to get the hell downstairs before some pendejo cop gave him a ticket. More kisses, more handshakes and then we were gone.

I don't remember being out of sorts after I met the Puerto Rican woman, but I must have been because Mami only asked me questions when she thought something was wrong in my life. It took her about ten passes but finally she cornered me one afternoon when we were alone in the apartment. Our upstairs neighbors were beating the crap out of their kids, and me and her had been listening to it all afternoon. She put her hand on mine and said, Is everything OK, Yunior? Have you been fighting with your brother?

Me and Rafa had already talked. We'd been in the basement, where our parents couldn't hear us. He told me that yeah, he knew about her.

Papi's taken me there twice now, he said.

Why didn't you tell me? I asked.

What the hell was I going to say? *Hey, Yunior, guess what happened yesterday? I met Papi's sucia!*

I didn't say anything to Mami either. She watched me, very very closely. Later I would think, maybe if I had told her, she would have confronted him, would have done something, but who can know these things? I said I'd been having trouble in school and like that everything was back to normal between us. She put her hand on my shoulder and squeezed and that was that.

We were on the turnpike, just past Exit 11, when I started feeling it again. I sat up from leaning against Rafa. His fingers smelled and he'd gone to sleep almost as soon as he got into the van. Madai was out too but at least she wasn't snoring.

In the darkness, I saw that Papi had a hand on Mami's knee and that the two of them were quiet and still. They weren't slumped back or anything; they were both wide awake, bolted into their seats. I couldn't see either of their faces and no matter how hard I tried I could not imagine their expressions. Neither of them moved. Every now and then the van was filled with the bright rush of somebody else's headlights. Finally I said, Mami, and they both looked back, already knowing what was happening.

Stuart Dybek

Stuart Dybek was born in 1942 in Chicago. His upbringing in a Catholic household in working-class Slavic and Mexican neighborhoods of Chicago influenced his writing, as seen in the poetry collection Brass Knuckles *(1979) and the short story collections* Childhood and Other Neighborhoods *(1980),* The Coast of Chicago *(1990), and* I Sailed with Magellan *(2003). Widely published in magazines such as* Harper's, The Atlantic, *and* The New Yorker, *Dybek has received numerous awards and honors, including a PEN/Malamud Award for excellence in the short story. Dybek is particularly known for his stories of adolescent yearning, his lyricism, and for blurring the lines between the real and the magical. In a profile in* Ploughshares, *Dybek explained how music continues to influence his work: "When I first started writing I thought it would be about saying something. I don't think that now. I think of writing as making something. What's come to fascinate me more and more is trying to use language the way that the mediums of other arts—music in particular—are used, so that they lead you to nonverbal places. I don't know if it's a paradox or just foggy thinking to believe language can do the same thing, that language can in some way or another lead you to something unsayable."*

We Didn't

> We did it in front of the mirror
> And in the light. We did it in darkness,
> In water, and in the high grass.
>> —*Yehuda Amichai, "We Did It"*

We didn't in the light; we didn't in darkness. We didn't in the fresh-cut summer grass or in the mounds of autumn leaves or on the snow where moonlight threw down our shadows. We didn't in your room on the canopy bed you slept in, the bed you'd slept in as a child, or in the backseat of my father's rusted Rambler, which smelled of the smoked chubs and kielbasa he delivered on weekends from my uncle Vincent's meat market. We didn't in your mother's Buick Eight, where a rosary twined the rearview mirror like a beaded, black snake with silver, cruciform fangs.

At the dead end of our lovers' lane—a side street of abandoned factories—where I perfected the pinch that springs open a bra; behind the lilac bushes in Marquette Park, where you first touched me through my jeans and your nipples, swollen against transparent cotton, seemed the shade of lilacs; in the balcony of the now defunct Clark Theater, where I wiped popcorn salt from my palms and slid them up your thighs and you whispered, "I feel like Doris Day is watching us," we didn't.

How adept we were at fumbling, how perfectly mistimed our timing, how utterly we confused energy with ecstasy.

Remember that night becalmed by heat, and the two of us, fused by sweat, trembling as if a wind from outer space that only we could feel was gusting across Oak Street Beach? Entwined in your faded Navajo blanket, we lay soul-kissing until you wept with wanting.

We'd been kissing all day—all summer—kisses tasting of different shades of lip gloss and too many Cokes. The lake had turned hot pink, rose rapture, pearl amethyst with dusk, then washed in night black with a ruff of silver foam. Beyond a momentary horizon, silent bolts of heat lightning throbbed, perhaps setting barns on fire somewhere in Indiana. The beach that had been so crowded was deserted as if there was a curfew. Only the bodies of lovers remained, visible in lightning flashes, scattered like the fallen on a battlefield, a few of them moaning, waiting for the gulls to pick them clean.

On my fingers your slick scent mixed with the coconut musk of the suntan lotion we'd repeatedly smeared over each other's bodies. When your bikini top fell away, my hands caught your breasts, memorizing their delicate weight, my palms cupped as if bringing water to parched lips.

Along the Gold Coast, high-rises began to glow, window added to window, against the dark. In every lighted bedroom, couples home from work were stripping off their business suits, falling to the bed, and doing it. They did it before mirrors and pressed against the glass in streaming shower stalls; they did it against walls and on the furniture in ways that required previously unimagined gymnastics, which they invented on the spot. They did it in honor of man and woman, in honor of beast, in honor of God. They did it because they'd been released, because they were home free, alive, and private, because they couldn't wait any longer, couldn't wait for the appointed hour, for the right time or temperature, couldn't wait for the future, for Messiahs, for peace on earth and justice for all. They did it because of the Bomb, because of pollution, because of the Four Horsemen of the Apocalypse, because extinction might be just a blink away. They did it because it was Friday night. It was Friday night and somewhere delirious music was playing—flutter-tongued flutes, muted trumpets meowing like cats in heat, feverish plucking and twanging, tom-toms, congas, and gongs all pounding the same pulsebeat.

I stripped your bikini bottom down the skinny rails of your legs, and you tugged my swimsuit past my tan. Swimsuits at our ankles, we kicked like swimmers to free our legs, almost expecting a tide to wash over us the way the tide rushes in on Burt Lancaster and Deborah Kerr in *From Here to Eternity*—a love scene so famous that although neither of us had seen the movie, our bodies assumed the exact position of movie stars on the sand and you whispered to me softly, "I'm afraid of getting pregnant," and I whispered back, "Don't worry, I have protection," then, still kissing you, felt for my discarded cutoffs and the wallet in which for the last several months I had carried a Trojan as if it was a talisman. Still kissing, I tore its flattened, dried-out wrapper, and it sprang through my fingers like a spring from a clock and dropped to the sand between our legs. My hands were shaking. In a panic, I groped for it, found it, tried to dust it off, tried as Burt Lancaster never had to, to slip it on without breaking the mood, felt the grains of sand inside it, a throb of lightning, and the Great Lake behind us became, for all practical purposes, the Pacific, and your skin tasted of salt and to the insistent question that my hips were asking your body answered yes, your thighs opened like wings from my waist as we surfaced panting from a kiss that left you pleading *Oh, Christ yes,* a *yes* gasped sharply as a cry of pain so that for a moment I thought that we *were* already doing it and that somehow I had missed the instant when I entered you, entered you in the bloodless way in which a young man discards his own virginity, entered you as if passing through a gateway into the rest of my life, into a life as I wanted it to be lived *yes* but Oh then I realized that we were still floundering unconnected in the slick between us and there was sand in the Trojan as we slammed together still feeling for that perfect fit, still in the *Here* groping for an *Eternity* that was only a fine adjustment away, just a millimeter to the left or a fraction of an inch farther south though with all the adjusting the sandy Trojan was slipping off and then it was gone but *yes* you kept repeating although your head was shaking *no-not-quite-almost* and our hearts were going like mad and you said, *Yes. Yes wait. . . Stop!*

"What?" I asked, still futilely thrusting as if I hadn't quite heard you.

"Oh. God!" You gasped, pushing yourself up. "What's coming?"

"Gin, what's the matter?" I asked, confused, and then the beam of a spotlight swept over us and I glanced into its blinding eye.

All around us lights were coming, speeding across the sand. Blinking blindness away, I rolled from your body to my knees, feeling utterly defenseless in the way that only nakedness can leave one feeling. Headlights bounded toward us, spotlights crisscrossing, blue dome lights revolving as squad cars converged. I could see other lovers, caught in the beams, fleeing bare-assed through the litter of garbage that daytime hordes had left behind and that night had deceptively concealed. You were crying, clutching the Navajo blanket to your breasts with one hand and clawing for your bikini with the other, and I was trying to calm your terror with reassuring phrases such as "Holy shit! I don't fucking believe this!"

Swerving and fishtailing in the sand, police calls pouring from their radios, the squad cars were on us, and then they were by us while we struggled to pull on our clothes.

They braked at the water's edge, and cops slammed out, brandishing huge flashlights, their beams deflecting over the dark water. Beyond the darting of those beams, the far-off throbs of lightning seemed faint by comparison.

"Over there, goddamn it!" one of them hollered, and two cops sloshed out into the shallow water without even pausing to kick off their shoes, huffing aloud for breath, their leather cartridge belts creaking against their bellies.

"Grab the sonofabitch! It ain't gonna bite!" one of them yelled, then they came sloshing back to shore with a body slung between them.

It was a woman—young, naked, her body limp and bluish beneath the play of flashlight beams. They set her on the sand just past the ring of drying, washed-up alewives. Her face was almost totally concealed by her hair. Her hair was brown and tangled in a way that even wind or sleep can't tangle hair, tangled as if it had absorbed the ripples of water—thick strands, slimy looking like dead seaweed.

"She's been in there awhile, that's for sure," a cop with a beer belly said to a younger, crew-cut cop, who had knelt beside the body and removed his hat as if he might be considering the kiss of life.

The crew-cut officer brushed the hair away from her face, and the flashlight beams settled there. Her eyes were closed. A bruise or a birthmark stained the side of one eye. Her features appeared swollen, her lower lip protruding as if she was pouting.

An ambulance siren echoed across the sand, its revolving red light rapidly approaching.

"Might as well take their sweet-ass time," the beer-bellied cop said.

We had joined the circle of police surrounding the drowned woman almost without realizing that we had. You were back in your bikini, robed in the Navajo blanket, and I had slipped on my cutoffs, my underwear dangling out of a back pocket.

Their flashlight beams explored her body, causing its whiteness to gleam. Her breasts were floppy; her nipples looked shriveled. Her belly appeared inflated by gallons of water. For a moment, a beam focused on her mound of pubic hair, which was overlapped by the swell of her belly, and then moved almost shyly away down her legs, and the cops all glanced at us—at you, especially—above their lights, and you hugged your blanket closer as if they might confiscate it as evidence or to use as a shroud.

When the ambulance pulled up, one of the black attendants immediately put a stethoscope to the drowned woman's swollen belly and announced, "Drowned the baby, too."

Without saying anything, we turned from the group, as unconsciously as we'd joined them, and walked off across the sand, stopping only long enough at the spot where we had lain together like lovers, in order to stuff the rest of our gear into a beach bag, to gather our shoes, and for me to find my wallet and kick sand over the forlorn, deflated Trojan that you pretended not to notice. I was grateful for that.

Behind us, the police were snapping photos, flashbulbs throbbing like lightning flashes, and the lightning itself, still distant but moving in closer, rumbling audibly now, driving a lake wind before it so that gusts of sand tingled against the metal sides of the ambulance.

Squinting, we walked toward the lighted windows of the Gold Coast, while the shadows of gapers attracted by the whirling emergency lights hurried past us toward the shore.

"What happened? What's going on?" they asked without waiting for an answer, and we didn't offer one, just continued walking silently in the dark.

It was only later that we talked about it, and once we began talking about the drowned woman it seemed we couldn't stop.

"She was pregnant," you said. "I mean, I don't want to sound morbid, but I can't help thinking how the whole time we were, we almost—you know—there was this poor, dead woman and her unborn child washing in and out behind us."

"It's not like we could have done anything for her even if we had known she was there."

"But what if we *had* found her? What if after we had—you know," you said, your eyes glancing away from mine and your voice tailing into a whisper, "what if after we did it, we went for a night swim and found her in the water?"

"But, Gin, we didn't," I tried to reason, though it was no more a matter of reason than anything else between us had ever been.

It began to seem as if each time we went somewhere to make out—on the back porch of your half-deaf, whiskery Italian grandmother, who sat in the front of the apartment cackling at *I Love Lucy* reruns; or in your girlfriend Tina's basement rec room when her parents were away on bowling league nights and Tina was upstairs with her current crush, Brad; or way off in the burbs, at the Giant Twin Drive-In during the weekend they called Elvis Fest—the drowned woman was with us.

We would kiss, your mouth would open, and when your tongue flicked repeatedly after mine, I would unbutton the first button of your blouse, revealing the beauty spot at the base of your throat, which matched a smaller spot I loved above a corner of your lips, and then the second button, which opened on a delicate gold cross—which I had always tried to regard as merely a fashion statement—dangling above the cleft of your breasts. The third button exposed the lacy swell of your bra, and I would slide my hand over the patterned mesh, feeling for the firmness of your nipple rising to my fingertip, but you would pull slightly away, and behind your rapid breath your kiss would grow distant, and I would kiss harder, trying to lure you back from wherever you had gone, and finally, holding you as if only consoling a friend, I'd ask, "What are you thinking?" although of course I knew.

"I don't want to think about her but I can't help it. I mean, it seems like some kind of weird omen or something, you know?"

"No, I don't know," I said. "It was just a coincidence."

"Maybe if she'd been farther away down the beach, but she was so close to us. A good wave could have washed her up right beside us."

"Great, then we could have had a ménage à trois."

"Gross! I don't believe you just said that! Just because you said it in French doesn't make it less disgusting."

"You're driving me to it. Come on, Gin, I'm sorry," I said. "I was just making a dumb joke to get a little different perspective on things."

"What's so goddamn funny about a woman who drowned herself and her baby?"

"We don't even know for sure she did."

"Yeah, right, it was just an accident. Like she just happened to be going for a walk pregnant and naked, and she fell in."

"She could have been on a sailboat or something. Accidents happen; so do murders."

"Oh, like murder makes it less horrible? Don't think that hasn't occurred to me. Maybe the bastard who knocked her up killed her, huh?"

"How should I know? You're the one who says you don't want to talk about it and then gets obsessed with all kinds of theories and scenarios. Why are we arguing about a woman we don't even know, who doesn't have the slightest thing to do with us?"

"I *do* know about her," you said. "I dream about her."

"You dream about her?" I repeated, surprised. "Dreams you remember?"

"Sometimes they wake me up. In one I'm at my *nonna*'s cottage in Michigan, swimming for a raft that keeps drifting farther away, until I'm too tired to turn back. Then I notice there's a naked person sunning on the raft and start yelling, 'Help!' and she looks up and offers me a hand, but I'm too afraid to take it even though I'm drowning because it's her."

"God! Gin, that's creepy."

"I dreamed you and I are at the beach and you bring us a couple hot dogs but forget the mustard, so you have to go all the way back to the stand for it."

"Hot dogs, no mustard—a little too Freudian, isn't it?"

"Honest to God, I dreamed it. You go back for mustard and I'm wondering why you're gone so long, then a woman screams that a kid has drowned and everyone stampedes for the water. I'm swept in by the mob and forced under, and I think, This is it, I'm going to drown, but I'm able to hold my breath longer than could ever be possible. It feels like a flying dream—flying under water—and then I see this baby down there flying, too, and realize it's the kid everyone thinks has drowned, but he's no more drowned than I am. He looks like Cupid or one of those baby angels that cluster around the face of God."

"Pretty weird. What do you think all the symbols mean?— hot dogs, water, drowning . . ."

"It means the baby who drowned inside her that night was a love child—a boy—and his soul was released there to wander through the water."

"You don't really believe that?"

We argued about the interpretation of dreams, about whether dreams are symbolic or psychic, prophetic or just plain nonsense, until you said, "Look, Dr. Freud, you can believe what you want about your dreams, but keep your nose out of mine, okay?"

We argued about the drowned woman, about whether her death was a suicide or a murder, about whether her appearance that night was an omen or a coincidence which, you argued, is what an omen is anyway: a coincidence that means something. By the end of summer, even if we were no longer arguing about the woman, we had acquired the habit of arguing about everything else. What was better: dogs or cats, rock or jazz, Cubs or Sox, tacos or egg rolls, right or left, night or day?—we could argue about anything.

It no longer required arguing or necking to summon the drowned woman; everywhere we went she surfaced by her own volition: at Rocky's Italian Beef, at Lindo Mexico, at the House of Dong, our favorite Chinese restaurant, a place we still frequented because when we'd first started seeing each other they had let us sit and talk until late over tiny cups of jasmine tea and broken fortune cookies. We would always kid about going there. "Are you in the mood for Dong tonight?" I'd whisper conspiratorially. It was a dopey joke, meant for you to roll your eyes at its repeated dopiness. Back then, in winter, if one of us ordered the garlic shrimp we would both be sure to eat them so that later our mouths tasted the same when we kissed.

Even when she wasn't mentioned, she was there with her drowned body—so dumpy next to yours—and her sad breasts, with their wrinkled nipples and sour milk—so saggy beside yours, which were still budding—with her swollen belly and her pubic bush colorless in the glare of electric light, with her tangled, slimy hair and her pouting, placid face—so lifeless beside yours—and her skin a pallid white, lightning-flash white, flash-bulb white, a whiteness that couldn't be duplicated in daylight—how I'd come to hate that pallor, so cold beside the flush of your skin.

There wasn't a particular night when we finally broke up, just as there wasn't a particular night when we began going together, but it was a night in fall when I guessed that it was over. We were parked in the Rambler at the dead end of the street of factories that had been our lovers' lane, listening to a drizzle of rain and dry leaves sprinkle the hood. As always, rain revitalized the smells of smoked fish and kielbasa in the upholstery. The radio was on too low to hear, the windshield wipers swished at intervals as if we were driving, and the windows were steamed as if we'd been making out. But we'd been arguing, as usual, this time about a woman poet who had committed suicide, whose work you were reading. We were sitting, no longer talking or touching, and I remember thinking that I didn't want to argue with you anymore. I didn't want to sit like this in hurt silence; I wanted to talk excitedly all night as we once had. I wanted to find some way that wasn't corny sounding to tell you how much fun I'd had in your company, how much knowing you had meant to me, and how I had suddenly realized that I'd been so intent on becoming lovers that I'd overlooked how close we'd been as friends. I wanted you to know that. I wanted you to like me again.

"It's sad," I started to say, meaning that I was sorry we had reached the point of silence, but before I could continue you challenged the statement.

"What makes you so sure it's sad?"

"What do you mean, what makes me so sure?" I asked, confused by your question.

You looked at me as if what was sad was that I would never understand. "For all either one of us knows," you said, "death could have been her triumph!"

Maybe when it really ended was the night I felt we had just reached the beginning, that one time on the beach in the summer when our bodies rammed so desperately together that for a moment I thought we did it, and maybe in our hearts we did, although for me, then, doing it in one's heart didn't quite count. If it did, I supposed we'd all be Casanovas.

We rode home together on the El train that night, and I felt sick and defeated in a way I was embarrassed to mention. Our mute reflections emerged like negative exposures on the dark, greasy window of the train. Lightning branched over the city, and when the train entered the subway tunnel, the lights inside flickered as if the power was disrupted, though the train continued rocketing beneath the Loop.

When the train emerged again we were on the South Side of the city and it was pouring, a deluge as if the sky had opened to drown the innocent and guilty alike. We hurried from the El station to your house, holding the Navajo blanket over our heads until, soaked, it collapsed. In the dripping doorway of your apartment building, we said good night. You were shivering. Your bikini top showed through the thin blouse plastered to your skin. I swept the wet hair away from your face and kissed you lightly on the lips, then you turned and went inside. I stepped into the rain, and you came back out, calling after me.

"What?" I asked, feeling a surge of gladness to be summoned back into the doorway with you.

"Want an umbrella?"

I didn't. The downpour was letting up. It felt better to walk back to the station feeling the rain rinse the sand out of my hair, off my legs, until the only places where I could still feel its grit were in the crotch of my cutoffs and each squish of my shoes. A block down the street, I passed a pair of jockey shorts lying in a puddle and realized they were mine, dropped from my back pocket as we ran to your house. I left them behind, wondering if you'd see them and recognize them the next day.

By the time I had climbed the stairs back to the El platform, the rain had stopped. Your scent still hadn't washed from my fingers. The station—the entire city it seemed—dripped and steamed. The summer sound of crickets and nighthawks echoed from the drenched neighborhood. Alone, I could admit how sick I felt. For you, it was a night that would haunt your dreams. For me, it was another night when I waited, swollen and aching, for what I had secretly nicknamed the Blue Ball Express.

Literally lovesick, groaning inwardly with each lurch of the train and worried that I was damaged for good, I peered out at the passing yellow-lit stations, where lonely men stood posted before giant advertisements, pictures of glamorous models defaced by graffiti—the same old scrawled insults and pleas: fuck you, eat me. At this late hour the world seemed given over to men without women, men waiting in abject patience for something indeterminate, the way I waited for our next times. I avoided their eyes so that they wouldn't see the pity in mine, pity for them because I'd just been with you, your scent was still on my hands, and there seemed to be so much future ahead.

For me it was another night like that, and by the time I reached my stop I knew I would be feeling better, recovered enough to walk the dark street home making up poems of longing that I never wrote down. I was the D. H. Lawrence of not doing it, the voice of all the would-be lovers who ached and squirmed. From our contortions in doorways, on stairwells, and in the bucket seats of cars we could have composed a Kama Sutra of interrupted bliss. It must have been that night when I recalled all the other times of walking home after seeing you, so that it seemed as if I was falling into step behind a parade of my former selves—myself walking home on the night we first kissed, myself on the night when I unbuttoned your blouse and kissed your breasts, myself on the night when I lifted your skirt above your thighs and dropped to my knees—each succeeding self another step closer to that irrevocable moment for which our lives seemed poised.

But we didn't, not in the moonlight, or by the phosphorescent lanterns of lightning bugs in your back yard, not beneath the constellations we couldn't see, let alone decipher, or in the dark glow that replaced the real darkness of night, a darkness already stolen from us, not with the skyline rising behind us while a city gradually decayed, not in the heat of summer while a Cold War raged, despite the freedom of youth and the license of first love—because of fate, karma, luck, what does it matter?—we made not doing it a wonder, and yet we didn't, we didn't, we never did.

Louise Erdrich

Louise Erdrich was born in 1954. Of German and Chippewa Indian descent, she grew up on a North Dakota reservation and attended Dartmouth College, where she later taught. In 1984 Erdrich published a book of poems, Jacklight, *and her first work of fiction,* Love Medicine, *which won the National Book Critics Circle Award.* Love Medicine *straddles the line between short story and novel; each section can stand alone as a self-contained story, as with "Saint Marie," yet the narratives also interconnect as a whole. The Kashpaws, Lamartines, and other characters in their lives also appear in Erdrich's subsequent novels* The Beet Queen *(1986),* Tracks *(1988),* The Bingo Palace *(1994), and* Four Souls *(2004). Erdrich's other novels are* The Last Report on the Miracles at Little No Horse *(2001) and* The Master Butchers Singing Club *(2003). In an interview with* The Atlantic Monthly, *Erdrich discussed the extent to which she retells traditional Native American narratives: "I love stories whether they function to reclaim old narratives or occur spontaneously. Often, to my surprise, they do both. I'll follow an inner thread of a plot and find that I am actually retelling a very old story, often in a contemporary setting. I usually can't recall whether it is something I remember hearing, or something I dreamed, or read, or imagined on the spot."*

Saint Marie

So when I went there, I knew the dark fish must rise. Plumes of radiance had soldered on me. No reservation girl had ever prayed so hard. There was no use in trying to ignore me any longer. I was going up there on the hill with the black robe women. They were not any lighter than me. I was going up there to pray as good as they could. Because I don't have that much Indian blood. And they never thought they'd have a girl from this reservation as a saint they'd have to kneel to. But they'd have me. And I'd be carved in pure gold. With ruby lips. And my toenails would be little pink ocean shells, which they would have to stoop down off their high horse to kiss.

I was ignorant. I was near age fourteen. The length of sky is just about the size of my ignorance. Pure and wide. And it was just that— the pure and wideness of my ignorance—that got me up the hill to Sacred Heart Convent and brought me back down alive. For maybe Jesus did not take my bait, but them Sisters tried to cram me right down whole.

You ever see a walleye strike so bad the lure is practically out its back end before you reel it in? That is what they done with me. I don't like to make that low comparison, but I have seen a walleye do that once. And it's the same attempt as Sister Leopolda made to get me in her clutch.

I had the mail-order Catholic soul you get in a girl raised out in the bush, whose only thought is getting into town. For Sunday Mass is the only time my father brought his children in except for school, when we were harnessed. Our soul went cheap. We were so anxious to get there we would have walked in on our hands and knees. We just craved going to the store, slinging bottle caps in the dust, making fool eyes at each other. And of course we went to church.

Where they have the convent is on top of the highest hill, so that from its windows the Sisters can be looking into the marrow of the town. Recently a windbreak was planted before the bar "for the purposes of tornado insurance." Don't tell me that. That poplar stand was put up to hide the drinkers as they get the transformation. As they are served into the beast of their burden. While they're drinking, that body comes upon them and then they stagger or crawl out the bar door, pulling a weight they can't move past the poplars. They don't want no holy witness to their fall.

Anyway, I climbed. That was a long-ago day. There was a road then for wagons that wound in ruts to the top of the hill where they had their buildings of painted brick. Gleaming white. So white the sun glanced off in dazzling display to set forms whirling behind your eyelids. The face of God you could hardly look at. But that day it drizzled, so I could look all I wanted. I saw the homelier side. The cracked whitewash and swallows nesting in the busted ends of eaves. I saw the boards sawed the size of broken windowpanes and the fruit trees, stripped. Only the tough wild rhubarb flourished. Goldenrod rubbed up their walls. It was a poor convent. I didn't see that then but I know that now. Compared to others it was humble, ragtag, out in the middle of no place. It was the end of the world to some. Where the maps stopped. Where God had only half a hand in the creation. Where the Dark One had put in thick bush, liquor, wild dogs, and Indians.

I heard later that the Sacred Heart Convent was a catchall place for nuns that don't get along elsewhere. Nuns that complain too much or lose their mind. I'll always wonder now, after hearing that, where they picked up Sister Leopolda. Perhaps she had scarred someone else, the way she left a mark on me. Perhaps she was just sent around to test her Sisters' faith, here and there, like the spot-checker in a factory. For she was the definite most-hard trial to anyone's endurance, even when they started out with veils of wretched love upon their eyes.

I was that girl who thought the black hem of her garment would help me rise. Veils of love which was only hate petrified by longing— that was me. I was like those bush Indians who stole the holy black hat of a Jesuit and swallowed little scraps of it to cure their fevers. But the hat itself carried smallpox and was killing them with belief. Veils of faith! I had this confidence in Leopolda. She was different. The other Sisters had long ago gone blank and given up on Satan. He slept for them. They never noticed his comings and goings. But Leopolda kept track of him and knew his habits, minds he burrowed in, deep spaces where he hid. She knew as much about him as my grandma, who called him by other names and was not afraid.

In her class, Sister Leopolda carried a long oak pole for opening high windows. It had a hook made of iron on one end that could jerk a patch of your hair out or throttle you by the collar—all from a distance. She used this deadly hook-pole for catching Satan by surprise. He could have entered without your knowing it—through your lips or your nose or any one of your seven openings—and gained your mind. But she would see him. That pole would brain you from behind. And he would gasp, dazzled, and take the first thing she offered, which was pain.

She had a stringer of children who could only breathe if she said the word. I was the worst of them. She always said the Dark One wanted me most of all, and I believed this. I stood out. Evil was a common thing I trusted. Before sleep sometimes he came and whispered conversation in the old language of the bush. I listened. He told me things he never told anyone but Indians. I was privy to both worlds of his knowledge. I listened to him, but I had confidence in Leopolda. She was the only one of the bunch he even noticed.

There came a day, though, when Leopolda turned the tide with her hook-pole.

It was a quiet day with everyone working at their desks, when I heard him. He had sneaked into the closets in the back of the room. He was scratching around, tasting crumbs in our pockets, stealing buttons, squirting his dark juice in the linings and the boots. I was the only one who heard him, and I got bold. I smiled. I glanced back and smiled and looked up at her sly to see if she had noticed. My heart jumped. For she was looking straight at me. And she sniffed. She had a big stark bony nose stuck to the front of her face for smelling out brimstone and evil thoughts. She had smelled him on me. She stood up. Tall, pale, a blackness leading into the deeper blackness of the slate wall behind her. Her oak pole had flown into her grip. She had seen me glance at the closet. Oh, she knew. She knew just where he was. I watched her watch him in her mind's eye. The whole class was watching now. She was staring, sizing, following his scuffle. And all of a sudden she tensed down, posed on her bent kneesprings, cocked her arm back. She threw the oak pole singing over my head, through my braincloud. It cracked through the thin wood door of the back closet, and the heavy pointed hook drove through his heart. I turned. She'd speared her own black rubber overboot where he'd taken refuge in the tip of her darkest toe.

Something howled in my mind. Loss and darkness. I understood. I was to suffer for my smile.

He rose up hard in my heart. I didn't blink when the pole cracked. My skull was tough. I didn't flinch when she shrieked in my ear. I only shrugged at the flowers of hell. He wanted me. More than anything he craved me. But then she did the worst. She did what broke my mind to her. She grabbed me by the collar and dragged me, feet flying, through the room and threw me in the closet with her dead black overboot. And I was there. The only light was a crack beneath the door. I asked the Dark One to enter into me and boost my mind. I asked him to restrain my tears, for they was pushing behind my eyes. But he was afraid to come back there. He was afraid of her sharp pole. And I was afraid of Leopolda's pole for the first time, too. I felt the cold hook in my heart. How it could crack through the door at any minute and drag me out, like a dead fish on a gaff, drop me on the floor like a gutshot squirrel.

I was nothing. I edged back to the wall as far as I could. I breathed the chalk dust. The hem of her full black cloak cut against my cheek. He had left me. Her spear could find me any time. Her keen ears would aim the hook into the beat of my heart.

What was that sound?

It filled the closet, filled it up until it spilled over, but I did not recognize the crying wailing voice as mine until the door cracked open, brightness, and she hoisted me to her camphor-smelling lips.

"He *wants* you," she said. "That's the difference. I give you love."

Love. The black hook. The spear singing through the mind. I saw that she had tracked the Dark One to my heart and flushed him out into the open. So now my heart was an empty nest where she could lurk.

Well, I was weak. I was weak when I let her in, but she got a foothold there. Hard to dislodge as the year passed. Sometimes I felt him—the brush of dim wings—but only rarely did his voice compel. It was between Marie and Leopolda now, and the struggle changed. I began to realize I had been on the wrong track with the fruits of hell. The real way to overcome Leopolda was this: I'd get to heaven first. And then, when I saw her coming, I'd shut the gate. She'd be out! That is why, besides the bowing and the scraping I'd be dealt, I wanted to sit on the altar as a saint.

To this end, I went up on the hill. Sister Leopolda was the consecrated nun who had sponsored me to come there.

"You're not vain," she said. "You're too honest, looking into the mirror, for that. You're not smart. You don't have the ambition to get clear. You have two choices. One, you can marry a no-good Indian, bear his brats, die like a dog. Or two, you can give yourself to God."

"I'll come up there," I said, "but not because of what you think."

I could have had any damn man on the reservation at the time. And I could have made him treat me like his own life. I looked good. And I looked white. But I wanted Sister Leopolda's heart. And here was the thing: sometimes I wanted her heart in love and admiration. Sometimes. And sometimes I wanted her heart to roast on a black stick.

She answered the back door where they had instructed me to call. I stood there with my bundle. She looked me up and down.

"All right," she said finally. "Come in."

She took my hand. Her fingers were like a bundle of broom straws, so thin and dry, but the strength of them was unnatural. I couldn't have tugged loose if she was leading me into rooms of white-hot coal. Her strength was a kind of perverse miracle, for she got it from fasting herself thin. Because of this hunger practice her lips were a wounded brown and her skin deadly pale. Her eye sockets were two deep lashless hollows in a taut skull. I told you about the nose already. It stuck out far and made the place her eyes moved even deeper, as if she stared out the wrong end of a gun barrel. She took the bundle from my hands and threw it in the corner.

"You'll be sleeping behind the stove, child."

It was immense, like a great furnace. There was a small cot close behind it.

"Looks like it could get warm there," I said.

"Hot. It does."

"Do I get a habit?"

I wanted something like the thing she wore. Flowing black cotton. Her face was strapped in white bandages, and a sharp crest of starched white cardboard hung over her forehead like a glaring beak. If possible, I wanted a bigger, longer, whiter beak than hers.

"No," she said, grinning her great skull grin. "You don't get one yet. Who knows, you might not like us. Or we might not like you."

But she had loved me, or offered me love. And she had tried to hunt the Dark One down. So I had this confidence.

"I'll inherit your keys from you," I said.

She looked at me sharply, and her grin turned strange. She hissed, taking in her breath. Then she turned to the door and took a key from her belt. It was a giant key, and it unlocked the larder where the food was stored.

Inside there was all kinds of good stuff. Things I'd tasted only once or twice in my life. I saw sticks of dried fruit, jars of orange peel, spice like cinnamon. I saw tins of crackers with ships painted on the side. I saw pickles. Jars of herring and the rind of pigs. There was cheese, a big brown block of it from the thick milk of goats. And besides that there was the everyday stuff, in great quantities, the flour and the coffee.

It was the cheese that got to me. When I saw it my stomach hollowed. My tongue dripped. I loved that goat-milk cheese better than anything I'd ever ate. I stared at it. The rich curve in the buttery cloth.

"When you inherit my keys," she said sourly, slamming the door in my face, "you can eat all you want of the priest's cheese."

Then she seemed to consider what she'd done. She looked at me. She took the key from her belt and went back, sliced a hunk off, and put it in my hand.

"If you're good you'll taste this cheese again. When I'm dead and gone," she said.

Then she dragged out the big sack of flour. When I finished that heaven stuff she told me to roll my sleeves up and begin doing God's labor. For a while we worked in silence, mixing up the dough and pounding it out on stone slabs.

"God's work," I said after a while. "If this is God's work, I've done it all my life."

"Well, you've done it with the Devil in your heart then," she said. "Not God."

"How do you know?" I asked. But I knew she did. And wished I had not brought up the subject.

"I see right into you like a clear glass," she said. "I always did."

"You don't know it," she continued after a while, "but he's come around here sulking. He's come around here brooding. You brought him in. He knows the smell of me, and he's going to make a last ditch try to get you back. Don't let him." She glared over at me. Her eyes were cold and lighted. "Don't let him touch you. We'll be a long time getting rid of him."

So I was careful. I was careful not to give him an inch. I said a rosary, two rosaries, three, underneath my breath. I said the Creed. I said every scrap of Latin I knew while we punched the dough with our fists. And still, I dropped the cup. It rolled under that monstrous iron stove, which was getting fired up for baking.

And she was on me. She saw he'd entered my distraction.

"Our good cup," she said. "Get it out of there, Marie."

I reached for the poker to snag it out from beneath the stove. But I had a sinking feel in my stomach as I did this. Sure enough, her long arm darted past me like a whip. The poker lighted in her hand.

"Reach," she said. "Reach with your arm for that cup. And when your flesh is hot, remember that the flames you feel are only one fraction of the heat you will feel in his hellish embrace."

She always did things this way, to teach you lessons. So I wasn't surprised. It was playacting, anyway, because a stove isn't very hot underneath right along the floor. They aren't made that way. Otherwise a wood floor would burn. So I said yes and got down on my stomach and reached under. I meant to grab it quick and jump up again, before she could think up another lesson, but here it happened. Although I groped for the cup, my hand closed on nothing. That cup was nowhere to be found. I heard her step toward me, a slow step. I heard the creak of thick shoe leather, the little *plat* as the folds of her heavy skirts met, a trickle of fine sand sifting, somewhere, perhaps in the bowels of her, and I was afraid. I tried to scramble up, but her foot came down lightly behind my ear, and I was lowered. The foot came down more firmly at the base of my neck, and I was held.

"You're like I was," she said. "He wants you very much."

"He doesn't want me no more," I said. "He had his fill. I got the cup!"

I heard the valve opening the hissed intake of breath, and knew that I should not have spoke.

"You lie," she said. "You're cold. There is a wicked ice forming in your blood. You don't have a shred of devotion for God. Only wild cold dark lust. I know it. I know how you feel. I see the beast . . . the beast watches me out of your eyes sometimes. Cold."

The urgent scrape of metal. It took a moment to know from where. Top of the stove. Kettle. Lessons. She was steadying herself with the iron poker. I could feel it like pure certainty, driving into the wood floor. I would not remind her of pokers. I heard the water as it came, tipped from the spout, cooling as it fell but still scalding as it struck. I must have twitched beneath her foot, because she steadied me, and then the poker nudged up beside my arm as if to guide. "To warm your cold ash heart," she said. I felt how patient she would be. The water came. My mind went dead blank. Again. I could only think the kettle would be cooling slowly in her hand. I could not stand it. I bit my lip so as not to satisfy her with a sound. She gave me more reason to keep still.

"I will boil him from your mind if you make a peep," she said, "by filling up your ear."

Any sensible fool would have run back down the hill the minute Leopolda let them up from under her heel. But I was snared in her black intelligence by then. I could not think straight. I had prayed so hard I think I broke a cog in my mind. I prayed while her foot squeezed my throat. While my skin burst. I prayed even when I heard the wind come through, shrieking in the busted bird nests. I didn't stop when pure light fell, turning slowly behind my eyelids. God's face. Even that did not disrupt my continued praise. Words came. Words came from nowhere and flooded my mind.

Now I could pray much better than any one of them. Than all of them full force. This was proved. I turned to her in a daze when she let me up. My thoughts were gone, and yet I remember how surprised I was. Tears glittered in her eyes, deep down, like the sinking reflection in a well.

"It was so hard, Marie," she gasped. Her hands were shaking. The kettle clattered against the stove. "But I have used all the water up now. I think he is gone."

"I prayed," I said foolishly. "I prayed very hard."

"Yes," she said. "My dear one, I know."

We sat together quietly because we had no more words. We let the dough rise and punched it down once. She gave me a bowl of mush, unlocked the sausage from a special cupboard, and took that in to the

Sisters. They sat down the hall, chewing their sausage, and I could hear them. I could hear their teeth bite through their bread and meat. I couldn't move. My shirt was dry but the cloth stuck to my back, and I couldn't think straight. I was losing the sense to understand how her mind worked. She'd gotten past me with her poker and I would never be a saint. I despaired. I felt I had no inside voice, nothing to direct me, no darkness, no Marie. I was about to throw that cornmeal mush out to the birds and make a run for it, when the vision rose up blazing in my mind.

I was rippling gold. My breasts were bare and my nipples flashed and winked. Diamonds tipped them. I could walk through panes of glass. I could walk through windows. She was at my feet, swallowing the glass after each step I took. I broke through another and another. The glass she swallowed ground and cut until her starved insides were only a subtle dust. She coughed. She coughed a cloud of dust. And then she was only a black rag that flapped off, snagged in bob wire, hung there for an age, and finally rotted into the breeze.

I saw this, mouth hanging open, gazing off into the flagged boughs of trees.

"Get up!" she cried. "Stop dreaming. It is time to bake."

Two other Sisters had come in with her, wide women with hands like paddles. They were evening and smoothing out the firebox beneath the great jaws of the oven.

"Who is this one?" they asked Leopolda. "Is she yours?"

"She is mine," said Leopolda. "A very good girl."

"What is your name?" one asked me.

"Marie."

"Marie. Star of the Sea."

"She will shine," said Leopolda, "when we have burned off the dark corrosion."

The others laughed, but uncertainly. They were mild and sturdy French, who did not understand Leopolda's twisted jokes, although they muttered respectfully at things she said. I knew they wouldn't believe what she had done with the kettle. There was no question. So I kept quiet.

"*Elle est docile,*" they said approvingly as they left to starch the linens.

"Does it pain?" Leopolda asked me as soon as they were out the door.

I did not answer. I felt sick with the hurt.

"Come along," she said.

The building was wholly quiet now. I followed her up the narrow staircase into a hall of little rooms, many doors. Her cell was the quietest, at the very end. Inside, the air smelled stale, as if the door had not been opened for years. There was a crude straw mattress, a tiny bookcase with a picture of Saint Francis hanging over it, a ragged palm, a stool for sitting on, a crucifix. She told me to remove my blouse and sit on the stool. I did so. She took a pot of salve from the bookcase and began to smooth it upon my burns. Her hands made slow, wide circles, stopping the pain. I closed my eyes. I expected to see blackness. Peace. But instead the vision reared up again. My chest was still tipped with diamonds. I was walking through windows. She was chewing up the broken litter I left behind.

"I am going," I said. "Let me go."

But she held me down.

"Don't go," she said quickly. "Don't. We have just begun."

I was weakening. My thoughts were whirling pitifully. The pain had kept me strong, and as it left me I began to forget it; I couldn't hold on. I began to wonder if she'd really scalded me with the kettle. I could not remember. To remember this seemed the most important thing in the world. But I was losing the memory. The scalding. The pouring. It began to vanish. I felt like my mind was coming off its hinge, flapping in the breeze, hanging by the hair of my own pain. I wrenched out of her grip.

"He was always in you," I said. "Even more than in me. He wanted you even more. And now he's got you. Get thee behind me!"

I shouted that, grabbed my shirt, and ran through the door throwing it on my body. I got down the stairs and into the kitchen, even, but no matter what I told myself, I couldn't get out the door. It wasn't finished. And she knew I would not leave. Her quiet step was immediately behind me.

"We must take the bread from the oven now," she said.

She was pretending nothing happened. But for the first time I had gotten through some chink she'd left in her darkness. Touched some doubt. Her voice was so low and brittle it cracked off at the end of her sentence.

"Help me, Marie," she said slowly.

But I was not going to help her, even though she had calmly buttoned the back of my shirt up and put the big cloth mittens in my hands for taking out the loaves. I could have bolted for it then. But I didn't. I knew that something was nearing completion. Something was about to happen. My back was a wall of singing flame. I was turning. I watched her take the long fork in one hand, to tap the loaves. In the other hand she gripped the black poker to hook the pans.

"Help me," she said again, and I thought, Yes, this is part of it. I put the mittens on my hands and swung the door open on its hinges. The oven gaped. She stood back a moment, letting the first blast of heat rush by. I moved behind her. I could feel the heat at my front and at my back. Before, behind. My skin was turning to beaten gold. It was coming quicker than I thought. The oven was like the gate of a personal hell. Just big enough and hot enough for one person, and that was her. One kick and Leopolda would fly in headfirst. And that would be one-millionth of the heat she would feel when she finally collapsed in his hellish embrace.

Saints know these numbers.

She bent forward with her fork held out. I kicked her with all my might. She flew in. But the outstretched poker hit the back wall first, so she rebounded. The oven was not so deep as I had thought.

There was a moment when I felt a sort of thin, hot disappointment, as when a fish slips off the line. Only I was the one going to be lost. She was fearfully silent. She whirled. Her veil had cutting edges. She had the poker in one hand. In the other she held that long sharp fork she used to tap the delicate crusts of loaves. Her face turned upside down on her shoulders. Her face turned blue. But saints are used to miracles. I felt no trace of fear.

If I was going to be lost, let the diamonds cut! Let her eat ground glass!

"Bitch of Jesus Christ!" I shouted. "Kneel and beg! Lick the floor!"

That was when she stabbed me through the hand with the fork, then took the poker up alongside my head, and knocked me out.

It must have been a half an hour later when I came around. Things were so strange. So strange I can hardly tell it for delight at the remembrance. For when I came around this was actually taking place. I was being worshiped. I had somehow gained the altar of a saint.

I was laying back on the stiff couch in the Mother Superior's office. I looked around me. It was as though my deepest dream had come to life. The Sisters of the convent were kneeling to me. Sister Bonaventure. Sister Dympna. Sister Cecilia Saint-Claire. The two French with hands like paddles. They were down on their knees. Black capes were slung over some of their heads. My name was buzzing up and down the room, like a far autumn fly lighting on the tips of their tongues between Latin, humming up the heavy blood-dark curtains, circling their little cosseted heads. Marie! Marie! A girl thrown in a closet. Who was afraid of a rubber overboot. Who was half overcome. A girl who came in the back door where they threw their garbage. Marie! Who never found the cup. Who had to eat their cold mush. Marie! Leopolda had her face buried in her knuckles. Saint Marie of the Holy Slops! Saint Marie of the Bread Fork! Saint Marie of the Burnt Back and Scalded Butt!

I broke out and laughed.

They looked up. All holy hell burst loose when they saw I'd woke. I still did not understand what was happening. They were watching, talking, but not to me.

"The marks . . ."

"She has her hand closed."

"*Je ne peux pas voir.*"

I was not stupid enough to ask what they were talking about. I couldn't tell why I was laying in white sheets. I couldn't tell why they were praying to me. But I'll tell you this: it seemed entirely natural. It was me. I lifted up my hand as in my dream. It was completely limp with sacredness.

"Peace be with you."

My arm was dried blood from the wrist down to the elbow. And it hurt. Their faces turned like flat flowers of adoration to follow that hand's movements. I let it swing through the air, imparting a saint's blessing. I had practiced. I knew exactly how to act.

They murmured. I heaved a sigh, and a golden beam of light suddenly broke through the clouded window and flooded down directly on my face. A stroke of perfect luck! They had to be convinced.

Leopolda still knelt in the back of the room. Her knuckles were crammed halfway down her throat. Let me tell you, a saint has senses honed keen as a wolf. I knew that she was over my barrel now. How it happened did not matter. The last thing I remembered was how she flew from the oven and stabbed me. That one thing was most certainly true.

"Come forward, Sister Leopolda." I gestured with my heavenly wound. Oh, it hurt. It bled when I reopened the slight heal. "Kneel beside me," I said.

She kneeled, but her voice box evidently did not work, for her mouth opened, shut, opened, but no sound came out. My throat clenched in noble delight I had read of as befitting a saint. She could not speak. But she was beaten. It was in her eyes. She stared at me now with all the deep hate of the wheel of devilish dust that rolled wild within her emptiness.

"What is it you want to tell me?" I asked. And at last she spoke.

"I have told my Sisters of your passion," she managed to choke out. "How the stigmata . . . the marks of the nails . . . appeared in your palm and you swooned at the holy vision. . . ."

"Yes," I said curiously.

And then, after a moment, I understood.

Leopolda had saved herself with her quick brain. She had witnessed a miracle. She had hid the fork and told this to the others. And of course they believed her, because they never knew how Satan came and went or where he took refuge.

"I saw it from the first," said the large one who put the bread in the oven. "Humility of the spirit. So rare in these girls."

"I saw it too," said the other one with great satisfaction. She sighed quietly. "If only it was me."

Leopolda was kneeling bolt upright, face blazing and twitching, a barely held fountain of blasting poison.

"Christ has marked me," I agreed.

I smiled the saint's smirk into her face. And then I looked at her. That was my mistake.

For I saw her kneeling there. Leopolda with her soul like a rubber overboot. With her face of a starved rat. With the desperate eyes drowning in the deep wells of her wrongness. There would be no one else after me. And I would leave. I saw Leopolda kneeling within the shambles of her love.

My heart had been about to surge from my chest with the blackness of my joyous heat. Now it dropped. I pitied her. I pitied her. Pity twisted in my stomach like that hook-pole was driven through me. I was caught. It was a feeling more terrible than any amount of boiling water and worse than being forked. Still, still, I could not help what I did. I had already smiled in a saint's mealy forgiveness. I heard myself speaking gently.

"Receive the dispensation of my sacred blood," I whispered.

But there was no heart in it. No joy when she bent to touch the floor. No dark leaping. I fell back into the white pillows. Blank dust was whirling through the light shafts. My skin was dust. Dust my lips. Dust the dirty spoons on the ends of my feet.

Rise up! I thought. Rise up and walk! There is no limit to this dust!

Percival Everett

Percival Everett was born in 1956 in Fort Gordon, Georgia, and grew up in Columbia, South Carolina. He is known for his inventive, often surrealistic stories and novels that range in location from ancient Greece to the American West, and in tone from satiric to philosophical. Everett resists the label of "African-American writer." "When I see my books in the Black Fiction or Black Studies section, I feel baffled," he said in an interview with The Guardian. *"I really don't know what those terms mean. Especially, when I look around the store and there is no corresponding White Fiction section." A prolific author, Everett's seventeen works of short fiction and novels include* Suder *(1983),* Zulus *(1989),* God's Country *(1994),* Big Picture *(1996),* Glyph *(1999),* Grand Canyon, Inc. *(2001),* Erasure *(2002),* American Desert *(2004),* Damned If I Do *(2004), and* A History of the African-American People (Proposed) by Strom Thurmond, as told to Percival Everett & James Kincaid *(2004). Asked if he writes every day, Everett has said, "No. I read every day. I think every day. I tend to my horses every day. I talk to my wife all day long every day. I write when I think I might understand something. Ironically, I spend less time writing now, but get more done."*

The Fix

Douglas Langley owned a little sandwich shop at the intersection of Fourteenth and T streets in the District. Beside his shop was a seldom used alley and above his shop lived a man by the name of Sherman Olney whom Douglas had seen beaten to near extinction one night by a couple of silky-looking men who seemed to know Sherman and wanted something in particular from him. Douglas had been drawn outside from cleaning up the storeroom by a rhythmic thumping sound, like someone dropping a telephone book onto a table over and over. He stepped out into the November chill and discovered that the sound was actually that of the larger man's fists finding again and again the belly of Sherman Olney, who was being kept on his feet by the second assailant. Douglas ran back inside and grabbed the pistol he kept in the roll-top desk in his business office. He returned to the scene with the powerful flashlight his son had given him and shone the light into the faces of the two villains.

The men were not overly impressed by the light, the bigger one saying, "Hey, man, you better get that light out my face!"

They did however show proper respect for the discharging of the .32 by running away. Sherman Olney crumpled to the ground, moaning and clutching at his middle, saying he didn't have it anymore.

"Are you all right?" Douglas asked, realizing how stupid the question was before it was fully out.

But Sherman's response was equally insipid as he said, "Yes."

"Come, let's get you inside." Douglas helped the man to his feet and into the shop. He locked the glass door behind them, then took Sherman over to the counter and helped him onto a stool.

"Thanks," Sherman said.

"You want me to call the cops?" Douglas asked.

Sherman Olney shook his head. "They're long gone by now."

"I'll make you a sandwich," Douglas said, as he stepped behind the counter.

"Really, that's not necessary."

"You'll like it. I don't know first aid, but I can make a sandwich." Douglas made the man a pastrami and Muenster on rye and poured him a glass of barely cold milk, then took him to sit in one of the three booths in the shop. Douglas sat across the table from the man, watched him take a bite of sandwich.

"What did they want?" Douglas put to him.

"To hurt me," Sherman said, his mouth working on the tough bread. He picked a seed from his teeth and put it on his plate. "They wanted to hurt me."

"My name is Douglas Langley."

"Sherman Olney."

"What were they after, Sherman?" Douglas asked, but he didn't get an answer.

As they sat there, the quiet of the room was disturbed by the loud refrigerator motor kicking on. Douglas felt the vibration of it through the soles of his shoes.

"Your compressor is a little shot," Sherman said.

Douglas looked at him, not knowing what he was talking about.

"Your fridge. The compressor is bad."

"Oh, yes," Douglas said. "It's loud."

"I can fix it."

Douglas just looked at him.

"You want me to fix it?"

Douglas didn't know what to say. Certainly he wanted the machine fixed, but what if this man just liked to take things apart? What if he made it worse? Douglas imagined the kitchen floor strewn with refrigerator parts. But he said, "Sure."

With that, Sherman got up and walked back into the kitchen, Douglas on his heels. The skinny man removed the plate from the bottom of the big and embarrassingly old machine and looked around. "Do you have any chewing gum?" Sherman asked.

As it turned out, Douglas had, in his pocket, the last stick of a pack of Juicy Fruit, which he promptly handed over. Sherman unwrapped the stick, folded it in his mouth, then lay there on the floor chewing.

"What are you doing?" Douglas asked.

Sherman paused him with a finger, then as if feeling the texture of the gum with his tongue, he took it from his mouth and stuck it into the workings of the refrigerator. And just like that the machine ran with a quiet steady hum, just like it had when it was new.

"How'd you do that?" Douglas asked.

Sherman, now on his feet, shrugged.

"Thank you, this is terrific. All you used was chewing gum. Can you fix other things?"

Sherman nodded.

"What are you? Are you a repairman or an electrician?" Douglas asked.

"I can fix things."

"Would you like another sandwich?"

Sherman shook his head, and said, "I should be going. Thanks for the food and all your help."

"These men might be waiting for you," Douglas said. He suddenly remembered his pistol. He could feel the weight of it in his pocket. "Just sit in here a while." Douglas felt a great deal of sympathy for the underfed man who had just repaired his refrigerator. "Where do you live? I could drive you."

"Actually, I don't have a place to live." Sherman stared down at the floor.

"Come over here." Douglas led the man to the big metal sink across the kitchen. He turned the ancient lever and the pipes started with a thin whistle and then screeched as the water came out. "Tell me, can you fix that?"

"Do you want me to?"

"Yes." Douglas turned off the water.

"Do you have a wrench?"

Douglas stepped away and into his business office, where he dug through a pile of sweaters and newspapers until he found a twelve-inch crescent wrench and a pipe wrench. He took them back to Sherman. "Will these do?"

"Yes." Sherman took a wrench and got down under the sink.

Douglas bent low to try and see what the man was doing, but before he could figure anything out, Sherman was getting up.

"There you go," Sherman said.

Incredulously, Douglas reached over to the faucet and turned on the water. The water came out smoothly and quietly. He turned it off, then tried it again. "You did it. You know, I could really use somebody like you around here. I mean, do you want a job? I can't pay much, just minimum wage, but I can let you stay in the apartment upstairs. Actually, it's just a room. Are you interested?"

"You don't even know me," Sherman said.

Douglas stopped. Of course, the man was right. He didn't know anything about him. But he had a strong feeling that Sherman Olney was an honest man. An honest man who could fix things. "You're right," Douglas admitted. "But I'm a good judge of character."

"I don't know," Sherman said.

"You said you don't have a place to go. You can live here and work until you find another job." Douglas was unsure why he was pleading so with the stranger, and, in fact, had a terribly uneasy feeling about the whole business, but, for some reason, he really wanted him to stay.

"Okay," Sherman said.

Douglas took the man up the back stairs and showed him the little room. The single bulb hung from a cord in the middle of the ceiling, and its dim light revealed the single bed made up with a yellow chenille spread. Douglas had taken many naps there.

"This is it," Douglas said. "The bathroom is down the hall. There's a narrow shower stall in it."

"I'm sure I'll be comfortable. Thank you."

Douglas stood in awkward silence for a while wondering what else there was to say. Then he said. "Well, I guess I should go on home to my wife."

"And I should get some sleep."

Douglas nodded and left the shop.

Douglas's wife said. "Are you crazy?"

Douglas sat at the kitchen table and held his face in his hands. He could smell the ham, salami, turkey, Muenster, Cheddar, and Swiss from his day's work. He peeked through his fingers and watched his short, plump wife reach over and turn down the volume of the television on the counter. The muted mouths of the news anchors still moved.

"I asked you a question," she said.

"It sounded more like an assertion." He looked at her eyes, which were narrowed and burning into him. "He's a fine fellow. Just a little down on his luck, Sheila."

Sheila laughed, then stopped cold. "And he's in the shop all alone." She shook her head, her lips tightening across her teeth. "You have lost your mind. Now, you go right back down there and you get rid of that guy."

"I don't feel like driving," Douglas said.

"I'll drive you."

He sighed. Sheila was obviously right. Even he hadn't understood his impulse to offer the man a job and invite him to use the room above the shop. So he would let her drive him back down there, and he'd tell Sherman Olney he'd have to go.

So they got into the old, forest green Buick Le Sabre, Sheila behind the wheel and Douglas sunk down into the passenger seat that Sheila's concentrated weight had through the years mashed so flat. He usually hated when she drove, but especially right at that moment, as she was angry and with a mission. She took their corner at Underwood on two wheels and sped through the city and moderately heavy traffic back toward the shop.

"You really should slow down," Douglas said. He watched a man in a blue suit toss his briefcase between two parked cars and dive after it out of the way.

"You're one to give advice. You? An old fool who takes in a stray human being and leaves him alone in his place of business is giving advice? He's probably cleaned us out already."

Douglas considered the situation and felt incredibly stupid. He could not, in fact, assure Sheila that she was wrong. Sherman might be halfway to Philadelphia with twelve pounds of Genoa salami. For all he knew Sherman Olney had turned on the gas of the oven and grilled and blown the restaurant to smithereens. He rolled down his window just a crack and listened for sirens.

"If anything bad has happened, I'm having you committed," Sheila said. She let out a brief scream and rattled the steering wheel. "Then I'll sell what little we have left and spend the rest of my life in Bermuda. That's what I'll do."

When Sheila made marks on the street braking to a stop, the store was still there and not ablaze. All the lights were off and the only people on the street were a couple of hookers on the far corner. Douglas unlocked and opened the front door of the shop, then followed Sheila inside. They walked past the tables and counter and into the kitchen where Douglas switched on the bright overhead lights. The fluorescent tubes flickered, then filled the place with a steady buzz.

"Go check the safe," Sheila said.

"There was no money in it," Douglas said. "There never is." She knew that. He had taken the money home and was going to drop it off by the bank on his way to work the next day. He always did that.

"Check it anyway."

He walked into his business office and switched on the standing lamp by the door. He looked across the room to see that the safe was still closed and that the stack of newspapers was still in front of it. "Hasn't been touched," he said.

"What's his name?" Sheila asked.

"Sherman."

"Sherman!" she called up the stairs. "Sherman!"

In short order, Sherman came walking down the stairs in his trousers and sleeveless undershirt. He was rubbing his eyes, trying to adjust to the bright light.

"Sherman," Douglas said, "it's me, Douglas."

"Douglas? What are you doing back?" He stood in front of them in his stocking feet. "By the way, I fixed the toilet and also that funny massager thing."

"You mean my foot massager?" Sheila asked.

"If you say so."

"I told you, Sherman can fix things," Douglas said to Sheila. "That's why I hired him." Sheila had purchased the foot massager from a fancy store in Georgetown. On the days when she worked in the shop she used to disappear every couple of hours for about fifteen minutes and then return happy and refreshed. She would be upstairs in the bathroom, sitting on the closed toilet with her feet stationed on her machine. Then the thing stopped working. Sheila loved the machine.

"The man at the store said my foot massager couldn't be repaired," Sheila said.

Sherman shrugged. "Well, it works now."

"I'll be right back," Sheila said, and she walked away from the men and up the stairs.

Sherman watched her, then turned to Douglas. "Why did you come back?"

"Well, you see, Sheila doesn't think it's a good idea that you stay here. You know, alone and everything. Since we don't know you or anything about you." Douglas blew out a long slow breath. "I'm really sorry."

Upstairs, Sheila screamed, then came running back to the top of the stairs. "It works! It works! He did fix it." She came down, smiling at Sherman. "Thank you so much."

"You're welcome," Sherman said.

"I was just telling Sherman that we're sorry, but he's going to have to leave."

"Don't be silly," Sheila said.

Douglas stared at her and rubbed a hand over his face. He gave Sheila a baffled look.

"No, no, it's certainly all right if Sherman sleeps here. And tomorrow, he can get to work." She grabbed Sherman's arm and turned him toward the stairs. "Now, you get on back up there and get some rest."

Sherman said nothing, but followed her directions. Douglas and Sheila watched him disappear upstairs.

Douglas looked at his wife. "What happened to you?"

"He fixed my foot rubber."

"So that makes him a good guy? Just like that?"

"I don't know," she said, uncertainly. She seemed to reconsider for a second. "I guess. Come on, let's go home."

Two weeks later, Sherman had said nothing more about himself, responding only to trivial questions put to him. He did, however, repair or make better every machine in the restaurant. He had fixed the toaster oven, the gas lines of the big griddle, the dishwasher, the phone, the neon open sign, the electric-eye buzzer on the front door, the meat slicer, the coffee machine, the manual mustard dispenser, and the cash register. Douglas found the man's skills invaluable and wondered how he had ever managed without him. Still, his presence was disconcerting as he never spoke of his past nor family nor friends and he never went out, not even to the store, his food being already there, and so Douglas began to worry that he might be a fugitive from the law.

"He never leaves the shop," Sheila complained. She was sitting in the passenger seat while Douglas drove them to the movie theater.

"That's where he lives," Douglas said. "All the food he needs is right there. I'm hardly paying him anything."

"You pay him plenty. He doesn't have to pay rent and he doesn't have to buy food."

"I don't see what the trouble is," he said. "After all, he's fixed your massage thingamajig. And he fixed your curling iron and your VCR and your watch and he even got the squeak out of your shoes."

"I know. I know." Sheila sighed. "Still, just what do we know about this man?"

"He's honest, I know that. He never even glances at the till. I've never seen anyone who cares less about money." Douglas turned right onto Connecticut.

"That's exactly how a crook wants to come across."

"Well, Sherman's no crook. Why, I'd trust the man with my life. There are very few people I can say that about."

Sheila laughed softly and disbelievingly. "Well, don't you sound melodramatic."

Douglas really couldn't argue with her. Everything she had said was correct and he was at a loss to explain his tenacious defense of a man who was, after all, a relative stranger. He pulled the car into a parallel space and killed the engine.

"The car didn't do that thing," Sheila said. She was referring to the way the car usually refused to shut off, the stubborn engine firing a couple of extra times.

Douglas glanced over at her.

"Sherman," she said.

"This morning. He opened the hood, grabbed this and jiggled that, and then slammed it shut."

The fact of the matter was finally that Sherman hadn't stolen anything and hadn't come across in any way threatening and so Douglas kept his fears and suspicions in check and counted his savings. No more electricians. No more plumbers. No more repairmen of any kind. Sherman's handiness, however, did not remain a secret in spite of Douglas's best efforts.

It began when Sherman offered and then repaired a small radio-controlled automobile owned by a fat boy named Loomis Rump. Fat Loomis Rump and his skinny pals told their friends and they brought in their broken toys. Sherman fixed them. The fat boy's friends told their parents and Douglas found his shop increasingly crowded with customers and their small appliances.

"The Rump boy told me that you fixed his toy car and the Johnson woman told me that you repaired her radio," the short man who wore the waterworks uniform said.

Sherman was wiping down the counter.

"Is that true?"

Sherman nodded.

"Well, you see these cuts on my face?"

Douglas could see the cuts under the man's three-day growth of stubble from the door to the kitchen. Sherman leaned forward and studied the wound.

"They seem to be healing nicely," Sherman said.

"It's this damn razor," the man said, and he pulled the small unit from his trouser pocket. "It cuts me bad every time I try to shave."

"You'd like me to fix your razor?"

"If you wouldn't mind. But I don't have any money."

"That's okay." Sherman took the razor and began taking it apart. Douglas as always moved closer and tried to see. He smiled at the waterworks man, who smiled back. Other people gathered around and watched Sherman's hands. Then they watched him hand the reassembled little machine back to the waterworks man. The man turned on the shaver and put it to his face.

"Hey," he said. "This is wonderful. It works just like it did when it was new. This is wonderful. Thank you. Can I bring you some money tomorrow?"

"Not necessary," Sherman said.

"This is wonderful."

Everyone in the restaurant oohed and aahed.

"Look," the waterworks man said. "I'm not bleeding from my face."

Sherman sat quietly at the end of the counter and fixed whatever was put in front of him. He repaired hair dryers and calculators and watches and cellular phones and carburetors. And while people waited for the repairs to be done, they ate sandwiches, and this appealed to Sherman, though he didn't like his handyman's time so consumed. But the fact of the matter was that there was little more to fix in the shop.

One day a woman who believed her husband was having an affair came in and complained over a turkey and provolone on wheat. Sherman sat next to her at the counter and listened as she finished. ". . . and then he comes home hours after he's gotten off from work, smelling of beer and perfume and he doesn't want to talk or anything and says he has a sinus headache and I'm wondering if I ought to follow him or check the mileage on his car before he leaves in the morning. What should I do?"

"Tell him it's his turn to cook and that you'll be late and don't tell him where you're going," Sherman said.

Everyone in the shop nodded, more in shared confusion than in agreement.

"Where should I go?" the woman asked.

"Go to the library and read about the praying mantis," Sherman said.

Douglas came up to Sherman after the woman had left, and asked, "Do you think that was a good idea?"

Sherman shrugged.

The woman came in the next week, her face full with a smile and announced that her home life was now perfect.

"Everything at home is perfect now," she said. "Thanks to Sherman."

Customers slapped Sherman on the back.

So began a new dimension of fixing in the shop as people brought in with their electric pencil sharpeners, pacemakers and microwaves, their relationship woes and their tax problems. Sherman saved the man who owned the automotive supply business across the street twelve thousand dollars and got him some fifty-seven dollars in refund.

One night after the shop was closed, Douglas and Sherman sat at the counter and ate the stale leftover doughnuts and drank coffee. Douglas looked at his handyman and shook his head. "That was really something the way you straightened the Rhinehart boy's teeth."

"Physics," Sherman said.

Douglas washed down a dry bite and set his cup on the counter. "I know I've asked you before, but we've known each other longer now. How did you learn to fix things?"

"Fixing things is easy. You just have to know how things work."

"That's it," Douglas said more than asked.

Sherman nodded.

"Doesn't it make you happy to do it?"

Sherman looked at Douglas, questioning.

"I ask because you never smile."

"Oh," Sherman said, and took another bite of doughnut.

The next day Sherman fixed a chain saw and a laptop computer and thirty-two parking tickets. Sherman, who had always been quiet, became increasingly more so. He would listen, nod, and fix it. That evening, a few minutes before closing, just after Sherman had solved the Morado woman's sexual identity problem, two paramedics came in with a patient on a stretcher.

"This is my wife," the more distressed of the ambulance men said of the supine woman. "She's been hit by a car, and she died in our rig on the way to the hospital," he cried.

Sherman looked at the woman, pulling back the blanket.

"She had massive internal—"

Sherman stopped the man with a raised hand, pulled the blanket off and then over himself and the dead woman. Douglas stepped over to stand with the paramedics.

Sherman worked under the blanket, moving this way and that way, and then he and the woman emerged, alive and well. The paramedic hugged her.

"You're alive," the man said to his wife.

The other paramedic shook Sherman's hand. Douglas just stared at his handyman.

"Thank you, thank you," the husband said, crying.

The woman was confused, but she too offered Sherman thanks.

Sherman nodded and walked quietly away, disappearing into the kitchen.

The paramedics and the restored woman left. Douglas locked the shop and walked into the kitchen, where he found Sherman sitting on the floor with his back against the refrigerator.

"I don't know what to say," Douglas said. His head was swimming. "You just brought that woman back to life."

Sherman's face looked lifeless. He seemed drained of all energy. He lifted his sad face up to look at Douglas.

"How did you do that?" Douglas asked.

Sherman shrugged.

"You just brought a woman back to life and you give me a shrug?" Douglas could hear the fear in his voice. "Who are you? What are you? Are you from outer space or something?"

"No," Sherman said.

"Then what's going on?"

"I can fix things."

"That wasn't a thing," Douglas pointed out. "That was a human being."

"Yeah, I know."

Douglas ran a hand over his face and just stared down at Sherman. "I wonder what Sheila will say."

"Please don't tell anyone about this," Sherman said.

Douglas snorted out a laugh. "Don't tell anyone. I don't have to tell anyone. Everyone probably knows by now. What do you think those paramedics are out there doing right now? They're telling anybody and everybody that there's some freak in Langley's Sandwich Shop who can revive the dead."

Sherman held his face in his hands.

"Who are you?"

News spread. Television news trucks and teams camped outside the front door of the sandwich shop. They were waiting with cameras ready when Douglas showed up to open for business the day following the resurrection.

"Yes, this is my shop," he said. "No, I don't know how it was done," he said. "No, you can't come in just yet," he said.

Sherman was sitting at the counter waiting, his face long, his eyes red as if from crying.

"This is crazy," Douglas said.

Sherman nodded.

"They want to talk to you." Douglas looked closely at Sherman. "Are you all right?"

But Sherman was looking past Douglas and through the front window where the crowd was growing ever larger.

"Are you going to talk to them?" Douglas asked.

Sherman shook his sad face. "I have to run away," he said. "Everyone knows where I am now."

Douglas at first thought Sherman was making cryptic reference to the men who had been beating him that night long ago, but then realized that Sherman meant simply everyone.

Sherman stood and walked into the back of the shop. Douglas followed him, not knowing why, unable to stop himself. He in fact followed the man out of the store and down the alley, away from the shop and the horde of people.

They ran up this street and across that avenue, crossed bridges and scurried through tunnels. Douglas finally asked where they were going and confessed that he was afraid. They were sitting on a bench in the park and it was by now just after sundown.

"You don't have to come with me," Sherman said. "I need only to get away from all of them." He shook his head, and said, more to himself, "I knew this would happen."

"If you knew this would happen, why did you fix all of those things?"

"Because I can. Because I was asked."

Douglas gave nervous glances this way and that across the park. "This has something to do with why the men were beating you that night, doesn't it?"

"They were from the government or some businesses, I'm not completely sure," Sherman said. "They wanted me to fix a bunch of things and I said no."

"But they asked you," Douglas said. "You just told me—"

"You have to be careful about what you fix. If you fix the valves in an engine, but the bearings are shot, you'll get more compression, but the engine will still burn up." Sherman looked at Douglas's puzzled face. "If you irrigate a desert, you might empty a sea. It's a complicated business, fixing things."

Douglas said, "So, what do we do now?"

Sherman was now weeping, tears streaming down his face and curving just under his chin before falling to the open collar of his light blue shirt. Douglas watched him, not believing that he was seeing the same man who had fixed so many machines and so many relationships and so many businesses and concerns and even fixed a dead woman.

Sherman raised his tear-filled eyes to Douglas. "I am the empty sea," he said.

Douglas turned to see the night dotted with yellow-orange torches.

The two men ran, Douglas pushing Sherman, as he was now so engaged in sobbing that he had trouble keeping his feet. They made it to the big bridge that crossed the bay and stopped in the middle, discovering that at either end thousands of people waited.

"Fix us!" they shouted. "Fix us! Fix us!"

Sherman looked down at the peaceful water below. It was a long drop, which no one could hope to survive. He looked at Douglas.

Douglas nodded.

The masses of people pressed in from either side.

Sherman stepped over the railing and stood on the brink, the toes of his shoes pushed well over the edge.

"Don't!" they all screamed. "Fix us! Fix us!"

Mary Gaitskill

Mary Gaitskill was born in 1954 in Lexington, Kentucky. She is known mostly for her short stories, many of which deal with sex, sexual marginality, abuse, and human isolation. Regarding her first short story collection, Bad Behavior *(1988), Gaitskill told* Contemporary Authors, *"My characters' apparent interest in sadomasochistic sex is more a confusion of violation with closeness than a desire to be hurt." Gaitskill also works with these themes in her first novel,* Two Girls, Fat and Thin *(1991) and her second short story collection,* Because They Wanted To *(1997). Her story "Secretary" was made into a critically acclaimed film. In an essay in* Salon *about her favorite writer, Vladimir Nabokov, Gaitskill discussed her own process: "Sometimes I write from the point of view of characters whom I would dislike as people, not as a perverse exercise, but because this cracks the story open and makes me see it in a way I would not see it naturally. Not being locked into one set of feelings which you run the risk of mistaking for the Truth, you have greater and more intense access to all feeling states, including those you would never choose to act out. Such an accepting and at times dispassionate approach to feeling allows for an understanding of both tenderness and cruelty."*

Tiny, Smiling Daddy

The phone rang five times before he got up to answer it. It was his friend Norm. They greeted each other and then Norm, his voice strangely weighted, said, "I saw the issue of *Self* with Kitty in it."

He waited for an explanation. None came so he said, "What? Issue of *Self*? What's *Self*?"

"Good grief, Stew, I thought for sure you'd of seen it. Now I feel awkward."

"So do I. Do you want to tell me what this is about?"

"My daughter's got a subscription to this magazine, *Self*. And they printed an article that Kitty wrote about fathers and daughters talking to each other, and she well, she wrote about you. Laurel showed it to me."

"My God."

"It's ridiculous that I'm the one to tell you. I just thought—"

"It was bad?"

"No. No, she didn't say anything bad. I just didn't understand the whole idea of it. And I wondered what you thought."

He got off the phone and walked back into the living room, shocked. His daughter Kitty was living in South Carolina working in a record store and making pots, vases, and statuettes which she sold on commission. She had never written anything that he knew of, yet she'd apparently published an article in a national magazine about him without telling him. He lifted his arms and put them on the window sill; the air from the open window cooled his underarms. Outside, the Starlings' tiny dog marched officiously up and down the pavement, looking for someone to bark at. Maybe she had written an article about how wonderful he was, and she was too shy to show him right away. This was doubtful. Kitty was quiet but she wasn't shy. She was untactful and she could be aggressive. Uncertainty only made her doubly aggressive.

He turned the edge of one nostril over with his thumb and nervously stroked his nose-hairs with one finger. He knew it was a nasty habit but it soothed him. When Kitty was a little girl he would do it to make her laugh: "Well," he'd say, "do you think it's time we played with the hairs in our nose?" And she would giggle, holding her hands against her face, eyes sparkling over her knuckles.

Then she was fourteen, and as scornful and rejecting as any girl he had ever thrown a spitball at when he was that age. They didn't get along so well any more. Once, they were sitting in the rec room watching TV, he on the couch, she on the footstool. There was a Charlie Chan movie on TV, but he was mostly watching her back and her long, thick brown hair, which she had just washed and was brushing. She dropped her head forward from the neck to let the hair fall between her spread legs, and began slowly stroking it with a pink nylon brush.

"Say, don't you think it's time we played with the hairs in our nose?"

No reaction from bent back and hair.

"Who wants to play with the hairs in their nose?"

Nothing.

"Hairs in the nose, hairs in the nose," he sang.

She bolted violently up from the stool. "You are so gross you disgust me!" She stormed from the room, shoulders in a tailored jacket of indignation.

Sometimes he said it just to see her exasperation, to feel the adorable, futile outrage of her violated girl delicacy.

He wished that his wife would come home with the car so that he could drive to the store and buy a copy of *Self*. His car was being repaired and he could not walk to the little cluster of stores and parking lots that constituted "town" in this heat. It would take a good twenty minutes and he would be completely worn out when he got there. He would find the magazine and stand there in the drugstore and read it and if it was something bad, he might not have the strength to walk back.

He went into the kitchen, opened a beer and brought it into the living room. His wife had been gone for over an hour, and God knows how much longer she would be. She could spend literally all day driving around the county doing nothing but buying a jar of honey or a bag of apples. Of course, he could call Kitty, but he'd probably just get her answering machine, and besides, he didn't want to talk to her before he understood the situation. He felt helplessness move through his body like a swimmer feels a large sea creature pass beneath him. How could she have done this to him? She knew how he dreaded exposure of any kind, she knew the way he guarded himself against strangers, the way he carefully drew all the curtains when twilight approached so that no one could see them walking through the house. She knew how ashamed he had been when, at sixteen, she had announced that she was lesbian.

The Starling dog was now across the street, yapping at the heels of a bow-legged old lady in a blue dress who was trying to walk down the street. "Dammit," he said. He left the window and got the afternoon opera station on the radio. They were in the final act of *La Bohème*.

He did not remember precisely when it had happened, but Kitty, his beautiful, happy little girl, turned into a glum, weird teenager that other kids picked on. She got skinny and ugly. Her blue eyes, which had been so sensitive and bright, turned filmy, as if the real Kitty had retreated so far from the surface that her eyes existed to shield rather than reflect her. It was as if she deliberately held her beauty away from them, only showing glimpses of it during unavoidable lapses, like the time she sat before the TV, daydreaming and lazily brushing her hair. At moments like this, her dormant charm broke his heart. It also annoyed him. What did she have to retreat from? They had both loved her. When she was little, and she couldn't sleep at night, Marsha would sit with her in bed for hours. She praised her stories and her drawings as if she were a genius. When Kitty was seven, she and her mother had special times, during which they went off together and talked about whatever Kitty wanted to talk about.

He tried to compare the sullen, morbid Kitty of sixteen with the slender, self-possessed twenty-eight-year-old lesbian who wrote articles for *Self*. He pictured himself in court, waving a copy of *Self* before a shocked jury. The case would be taken up by the press. He saw the headlines: Dad Sues Mag—Dyke Daughter Reveals . . . reveals what?

What had Kitty found to say about him that was of interest to the entire country that she didn't want him to know about?

Anger overrode his helplessness. Kitty could be vicious. He hadn't seen her vicious side in years, but he knew it was there. He remembered the time he'd stood behind the half-open front door when fifteen-year-old Kitty sat hunched on the front steps with one of her few friends, a homely blond who wore white lipstick and a white leather jacket. He had come to the door to view the weather and say something to the girls, but they were muttering so intently that curiosity got the better of him, and he hung back a moment to listen. "Well, at least your mom's smart," said Kitty. "My mom's not only a bitch, she's stupid."

This after the lullabies and special times! It wasn't just an isolated incident either; every time he'd come home from work, his wife had something bad to say about Kitty. She hadn't set the table until she had been asked four times. She'd gone to Lois's house instead of coming straight home like she'd been told to do. She'd worn a dress to school that was short enough to show the tops of her panty hose.

By the time Kitty came to dinner, looking as if she'd been doing slave labor all day, he would be mad at her. He couldn't help it. Here was his wife doing her damnedest to raise a family and cook dinner and here was this awful kid looking ugly, acting mean and not setting the table. It seemed unreasonable that she should turn out so badly after taking up so much time. Her afflicted expression made him angry too. What had anybody ever done to her?

He sat forward and gently gnawed the insides of his mouth as he listened to the dying girl in *La Bohème*. He saw his wife's car pull into the driveway. He walked to the back door, almost wringing his hands, and waited for her to come through the door. When she did, he snatched the grocery bag from her arms and said, "Give me the keys." She stood open-mouthed in the stairwell, looking at him with idiotic consternation. "Give me the keys!"

"What is it, Stew? What's happened?"

"I'll tell you when I get back."

He got in the car and became part of it, this panting, mobile case propelling him through the incredibly complex and fast-moving world of other people, their houses, their children, their dogs, their lives. He wasn't usually so aware of this unpleasant sense of disconnection between him and everyone else, but he had the feeling that it had been there all along, underneath what he thought of most of the time. It was ironic that it should rear up so visibly at a time when there was in fact a mundane yet invasive and horribly real connection between him and everyone else in Wayne County: the hundreds of copies of *Self* magazine sitting in countless drugstores, bookstores, groceries, and libraries. It was as if there was a tentacle plugged into the side of the car, linking him with the random humans who picked up the magazine, possibly his very neighbors. He stopped at a crowded intersection, feeling like an ant in an enemy swarm.

Kitty had projected herself out of the house and into this swarm very early, ostensibly because life with him and Marsha had been so awful. Well, it had been awful, but because of Kitty, not them. As if it wasn't enough to be sullen and dull, she turned into a lesbian. Kids followed her down the street jeering at her. Somebody dropped her books in a toilet. She got into a fistfight. Their neighbors gave them looks. This reaction seemed only to steel Kitty's grip on her new identity; it made her romanticize herself like the kid she was. She wrote poems about heroic women warriors, she brought home strange books and magazines which, among other things, seemed to glorify prostitutes. Marsha looked for them and threw them away. Kitty screamed at her, the tendons leaping out on her slender neck. He hit Kitty, Marsha tried to stop him and he yelled at her. Kitty leapt between them, as if to defend her mother. He grabbed her and shook her but he could not shake the conviction off her face.

Most of the time though, they continued as always, eating dinner together, watching TV, making jokes. That was the worse thing; he would look at Kitty and see his daughter, now familiar in her withdrawn sullenness, and feel comfort and affection. Then he would remember that she was a lesbian and a morass of complication and wrongness would come down between them, making it impossible for him to see her. Then she would be just Kitty again. He hated it.

She ran away at sixteen and the police found her in the apartment of an eighteen-year-old body builder named Dolores who had a naked woman tattooed on her sinister bicep. Marsha made them put her in a mental hospital so psychiatrists could observe her, but he hated the psychiatrists—mean, supercilious sons of bitches who delighted in the trick question—so he took her back out. She finished school and they told her if she wanted to leave it was all right with them. She didn't waste any time getting out of the house.

She moved into an apartment near Detroit with a girl named George and took a job at a home for retarded kids. She would appear for visits with a huge bag of laundry every few weeks. She was thin and neurotically muscular, her body having the look of a fighting dog on a leash. She wore her hair like a boy's and wore black sunglasses, black leather half-gloves and leather belts. The only remnant of her beauty was her erect martial carriage and her efficient movements; she walked through a room like the commander of a guerrilla force. She would sit at the dining room table with Marsha, drinking tea and having a laconic verbal conversation, her body speaking its precise martial language while the washing machine droned from the utility room and he wandered in and out trying to make sense of what she said. Sometimes she would stay into the evening to eat dinner and watch *All in the Family*. Then Marsha would send her home with a jar of homemade tapioca pudding or a bag of apples and oranges.

One day instead of a visit they got a letter postmarked San Francisco. She had left George, she said. She listed strange details about her current environment and was vague about how she was supporting herself. He had nightmares about Kitty, with her brave, proudly muscular little body, lost among big fleshy women who danced naked in go-go bars and took drugs with needles, terrible women who his confused romantic daughter invested with oppressed heroism and intensely female glamour. He got up at night and stumbled into the bathroom for stomach medicine, the familiar darkness of the house heavy with menacing images that pressed about him, images that he saw reflected in his own expression when he turned on the bathroom light over the mirror.

Then one year she came home for Christmas. She came into the house with her luggage and a shopping bag of gifts for them and he saw that she was beautiful again. It was a beauty that both offended and titillated his senses. Her short spiky hair was streaked with purple, her dainty mouth was lipsticked, her nose and ears were pierced with amethyst and dangling silver. Her face had opened in thousands of petals. Her eyes shone with quick perception as she put down her bag and he knew that she had seen him see her beauty. She moved towards him with fluid hips, she embraced him for the first time in years. He felt her live, lithe body against him and his heart pulsed a message of blood and love. "Merry Christmas, Daddy," she said.

Her voice was husky and coarse, it reeked of knowledge and confidence. Her T-shirt said "Chicks With Balls." She was twenty-two years old.

She stayed for a week, discharging her strange jangling beauty into the house and changing the molecules of its air. She talked about the girls she shared an apartment with, her job at a coffee shop, how Californians were different from Michiganders. She talked about her friends: Lorraine, who was so pretty men fell off their bicycles as they twisted their bodies for a better look at her; Judy, a martial arts expert; and Meredith, who was raising a child with her husband, Angela. She talked of poetry readings, ceramics classes, celebrations of spring.

He realized, as he watched her, that she was now doing things that were as bad as or worse than the things that had made him angry at her five years before, yet they didn't quarrel. It seemed that a large white space existed between him and her, and that it was impossible to enter this space or to argue across it. Besides, she might never come back if he yelled at her.

Instead, he watched her, puzzling at the metamorphosis she had undergone. First she had been a beautiful, happy child turned homely, snotty, miserable adolescent. From there she had become a martinet girl with the eyes of a stifled pervert. Now she was a vibrant imp living, it seemed, in a world constructed of topsy-turvy junk pasted with rhinestones. Where had these three different people come from? Not even Marsha, who had spent so much time with her as a child, could trace the genesis of the new Kitty from the old one. Sometimes he bitterly reflected that he and Marsha weren't even real parents anymore, but bereft old people rattling around in a house, connected not to a real child who was going to college, or who at least had some kind of understandable life, but a changeling who was the product of only their most obscure quirks, a being who came from recesses that neither of them suspected they'd had.

There were only a few cars in the parking lot. He wheeled through it with pointless deliberation before parking near the drugstore. He spent irritating seconds searching for *Self* until he realized that its airbrushed cover girl was grinning right at him. He stormed the table of contents, then headed for the back of the magazine. "Speak Easy" was written sideways across the top of the appointed page in round turquoise letters. At the bottom was his daughter's name in a little box. "Kitty Thorne is a ceramic artist living in South Carolina." His hands were trembling.

It was hard for him to rationally ingest the beginning paragraphs which seemed, incredibly, to be about a phone conversation they'd had some time ago about the emptiness and selfishness of people who have sex but don't get married and have children. A few phrases that stood out clearly: ". . . my father may love me but he doesn't love the way I live." ". . . even more complicated because I'm gay." "Because it still hurts me."

For reasons he didn't understand, he felt a nervous smile tremble under his skin. He suppressed it.

"This hurt has its roots deep in our relationship, starting, I think, when I was a teenager."

He had a horrible sensation of being in public so he paid for the thing and took it out to the car with him. He slowly drove to another spot in the lot, as far away from the drugstore as possible, picked up the magazine, and began again. She described "the terrible difficulties" between him and her. She recounted, briefly and with hieroglyphic politeness, the fighting, the running away, the return, the tacit reconciliation.

"There is an emotional distance that we have both accepted and chosen to work around, hoping the occasional contact—love, anger, something—will get through."

He put the magazine down and looked out the window. It was near dusk; most of the stores in the little mall were closed. There were only two other cars in the parking lot, and a big, slow, frowning woman with two grocery bags was getting ready to drive one away. He was parked before a weedy piece of land at the edge of the parking lot. In it were rough, picky weeds spread out like big green tarantulas, young yellow dandelions, frail old dandelions, and bunches of tough blue chickweed. Even in his distress he vaguely appreciated the beauty of the blue weeds against the cool white and grey sky. For a moment the sound of insects comforted him. Images of Kitty passed through his memory with terrible speed: her nine-year-old forehead bent over her dish of ice cream, her tiny nightgowned form ran up the stairs, her ringed hand brushed her face, the keys on her belt jiggled as she walked her slow blue-jeaned walk away from the house. Gone, all gone.

The article went on to describe how Kitty hung up the phone feeling frustrated and then listed all the things she could've said to him to let him know how hurt she was, paving the way for "real communication," all in ghastly talk-show language. He was unable to put these words together with the Kitty he had last seen lounging around the house. She was twenty-eight now and she no longer dyed her hair or wore jewels in her nose. Her demeanor was serious, bookish, almost old-maidish. Once he'd overheard her talking to Marsha and heard her say, "So then this Italian girl gives me the once-over and says to Joanne, 'You 'ang around with too many Wasp.' And I said, 'I'm not a Wasp, I'm white trash.' "

"Speak for yourself," he'd said.

"If the worst occurred and my father was unable to respond to me in kind, I still would have done a good thing. I would have acknowledged my own needs and created the possibility to connect with what therapists call 'the good parent' in myself."

Well, if that was the kind of thing she was going to say to him, he was relieved she hadn't said it. But if she hadn't said it to him, why was she saying it to the rest of the country?

He turned on the radio. It sang: "Try to remember, and if you remember, then follow, follow." He turned it off. He closed his eyes. When he was nine or ten an uncle of his had told him, "Everybody makes his own world. You see what you want to see and hear what you want to hear. You can do it right now. If you blink ten times and then close your eyes real tight, you can see anything you want to see in front of you." He'd tried it rather half-heartedly and hadn't seen anything but the vague suggestion of a yellowish-white ball moving creepily through the dark. At the time, he'd thought it was perhaps because he hadn't tried hard enough.

He had told Kitty to do the same thing, or something like it, when she was eight or nine. They were on the back porch sitting in striped lawn chairs, holding hands and watching the fire-flies turn off and on. She closed her eyes for a long time. Then very seriously, she said, "I see big balls of color, like shaggy flowers. They're pink and red and turquoise. I see an island with palm trees and pink rocks. There's dolphins and mermaids swimming in the water around it." He'd been almost awed by her belief in this impossible vision. Then he was sad because she would never see what she wanted to see.

His memory floated back to his boyhood; he was walking down the middle of the street at dusk, sweating lightly after a basketball game. There were crickets and the muted barks of dogs and the low, affirming mumble of people on their front porches. He felt securely held by the warm light and its sounds, he felt an exquisite blend of happiness and sorrow that life could contain this perfect moment, and sadness that he would soon arrive home, walk into bright light and be on his way into the next day, with its loud noise and alarming possibility. He resolved to hold this evening walk in his mind forever, to imprint all the sensations that occurred to him as he walked by the Oatlander's house in a permanent place, so that he could always take it out and look at it. He dimly recalled feeling that if he could successfully do that, he could stop time and hold it.

He knew he had to go home soon. He didn't want to talk about the article with Marsha, but the idea of sitting in the house with her and not talking about it was hard to bear. He imagined the conversation grinding into being, a future conversation with Kitty gestating within it. The conversation was a vast, complex machine like those that occasionally appeared in his dreams; if he could only pull the switch everything would be all right, but he felt too stupefied by the weight and complexity of the thing to do so. Besides, in this case, everything might not be all right. He put the magazine under his seat and started the car.

Marsha was in her armchair reading. She looked up and the expression on her face seemed like the result of internal conflict as complicated and strong as his own, but cross-pulled in different directions, uncomprehending of him and what he knew. In his mind he withdrew from her so quickly that for a moment the familiar room was fraught with the inexplicable horror of a banal nightmare. Then the ordinariness of the scene threw the extraordinary event of the day into relief and he felt so angry and bewildered he could've howled.

"Everything all right, Stew?" asked Marsha.

"No, nothing is all right. I'm a tired old man in a shitty world I don't want to be in. I go out there, it's like walking on knives. Everything is an attack, the ugliness, the cheapness, the rudeness, everything." He sensed her withdrawing from him into her own world of disgruntlement, her lips drawn together in that look of exasperated perseverance she'd gotten from her mother. Like Kitty, like everyone, she was leaving him. "I don't have a real daughter and I don't have a real wife who's here with me because she's too busy running around on some—"

"We've been through this before. We agreed I could—"

"That was different! That was when we had two cars!" His voice tore through his throat in a jagged whiplash and came out a cracked half-scream. "I don't have a car, remember? That means I'm stranded, all alone for hours and Norm Pisarro can just call me up and casually tell me that my lesbian daughter has just betrayed me in a national magazine and what do I think about that?" He wanted to punch the wall until his hand was bloody. He wanted Kitty to see the blood. Marsha's expression broke into soft open-mouthed consternation. The helplessness of it made his anger seem huge and terrible, then impotent and helpless itself. He sat down on the couch and instead of anger felt pain.

"What did Kitty do? What happened? What does Norm have—"

"She wrote an article in *Self* magazine about being a lesbian and her problems and something to do with me. I don't know, I could barely read the crap."

Marsha looked down at her nails.

He looked at her and saw the aged beauty of her ivory skin, sagging under the weight of her years and her cock-eyed bifocals, the emotional receptivity of her face, the dark down on her upper lip, the childish pearl buttons of her sweater, only the top button done.

"I'm surprised at Norm, that he would call you like that."

"Oh, who the hell knows what he thought." His heart was soothed and slowed by her words, even if they didn't address its real unhappiness.

"Here," she said, "let me rub your shoulders."

He allowed her to approach him and they sat sideways on the couch, his weight balanced on the edge by his awkwardly planted legs, she sitting primly on one hip with her legs tightly crossed. The discomfort of the position negated the practical value of the massage, but he welcomed her touch. Marsha had strong, intelligent hands that spoke to his muscles of deep safety and love and delight of physical life. In her effort, she leaned close and her sweatered breast touched him, releasing his tension almost against his will. Through half-closed eyes he observed her sneakers on the floor—he could not quite get over this phenomenon of adult women wearing what had been boys' shoes—in the dim light, one toe atop the other as though cuddling, their laces in pretty disorganization.

Poor Kitty. It hadn't really been so bad that she hadn't set the table on time. He couldn't remember why he and Marsha had been so angry over the table. Unless it was Kitty's coldness, her always turning away, her sarcastic voice. But she was a teenager and that's what teenagers did. Well, it was too bad, but it couldn't be helped now.

He thought of his father. That was too bad too, and nobody was writing articles about that. There had been a distance between them too, so great and so absolute that the word "distance" seemed inadequate to describe it. But that was probably because he had only known his father when he was a very young child; if his father had lived longer, perhaps they would've become closer. He could recall his father's face clearly only at the breakfast table, where it appeared silent and still except for lip and jaw motions, comforting in its constancy. His father ate his oatmeal with one hand working the spoon, one elbow on the table, eyes down, sometimes his other hand holding a cold rag to his head, which always hurt with what seemed to be a noble pain, willingly taken on with his duties as a husband and father. He had loved to stare at the big face with its deep lines and long earlobes, its thin lips and loose, loopily chewing jaws. Its almost godlike stillness and expressionlessness filled him with admiration and reassurance, until one day, his father slowly looked up from his cereal, met his eyes and said, "Stop staring at me, you little shit."

In the other memories, his father was a large, heavy body with a vague oblong face. He saw him sleeping in the armchair in the living room, his large, hairy-knuckled hands grazing the floor. He saw him walking up the front walk with the quick, clipped steps that he always used coming home from work, the straight-backed choppy gait that gave the big body an awesome mechanicalness. His shirt was wet under the arms, his head down, the eyes abstracted but alert, as though keeping careful watch on the outside world in case something nasty came at him, while he attended to the more important business inside.

"The good parent in yourself."

What did the well-meaning idiots who thought of these phrases mean by them? When a father dies, he is gone, there is no tiny, smiling daddy who appears, waving happily, in a secret pocket in your chest. Some kinds of loss are absolute. And no amount of self-realization or self-expression will change that.

As if she heard him, Marsha urgently pressed her weight into her hands and applied all her strength to relaxing his muscles. Her sweat and scented deodorant filtered through her sweater, which added its muted woolliness to her smell. "All righty!" She rubbed his shoulders and briskly patted him. He reached back and touched her hand in thanks.

Across from where they sat had once been a red chair, and in it had once sat Kitty, gripping her face in her hand, her expression mottled by tears. "And if you ever try to come back here I'm going to spit in your face. I don't care if I'm on my deathbed, I'll still have the energy to spit in your face," he had said.

Marsha's hands lingered on him for a moment. Then she moved and sat away from him on the couch.

Alekᵴandar Hemon

Aleksandar Hemon was born in 1964 in Sarajevo. He came to Chicago in 1992 for a short journalist exchange program, but when war spread in Bosnia, Hemon sought asylum in the United States. Realizing that he could no longer publish in his native Serbo-Croatian he set out to master English and began writing in the language in 1995. His short story collection, The Question of Bruno, *was published in 2000 to wide acclaim, and his novel,* Nowhere Man *(2002), was a finalist for the National Book Critics Circle Award. His work revolves around exile, violence, and the view of America from the new immigrant's perspective, and his language has been praised for its nuance, playfulness, power, and originality. In his essay "The Question of Influence," Hemon praises his favorite writers and goes on to say, "It is impossible to write without being nearly pathologically opened to influences, if you understand 'influence' as a way to be related to the world around, as a mode of perpetual, endless conversation. All I do is filter the influences through language. It's an exhilarating process. . . . I need to write books in order to come to terms with all of the influences. You can say that the world is my biggest influence, and the only important one."*

A Coin

Suppose there is a Point A and a Point B and that, if you want to get from point A to point B, you have to pass through an open space clearly visible to a skillful sniper. You have to run from Point A to Point B and the faster you run, the more likely you are to reach Point B alive. The space between Point A and Point B is littered with things that sprinting citizens dropped along the way. A black leather wallet, probably empty. A purse, agape like a mouth. A white plastic water vessel, with a bullet hole in its center. A green-red-brown shawl ornamented with snowflakes, dirty. A wet loaf of bread, with busy ants crawling all over it, as if building a pyramid. A videocassette, dismembered, several of its pieces still connected with a dark writhing tape. On days when snipers are particularly rabid, there are scattered bodies as well. Some of them may still be alive and twitching toward the distant cover, leaving a bloody trail behind, like snails. People seldom try to help them, for everybody knows that the snipers are just waiting for that. Sometimes a sniper mercifully finishes off the crawling person. Sometimes the snipers play with the body, shooting off his or her knees, feet, or elbows. They seem to have made a bet how far he or she is going to get before bleeding away.

Sarajevo is a catless city. It is so because people couldn't feed them, or couldn't take them along when they were fleeing, or their owners were killed. Hence the dogs that couldn't be fed or taken along hunt them down and devour them. One can often see, among the rubble on the streets, underneath burnt cars, or stuck in sewers, cat carcasses, or cat heads with a death grin, eye-teeth like miniature daggers. Sometimes one can see two or more dogs fighting over a cat, tearing apart a screaming loaf of fur and flesh.

Aida's letters are scarce and sudden, escaping the siege via UN convoys, foreign reporters, or refugee transports. I imagine them in a sack, in the back of a UN truck, driven by a Pakistani or Ukrainian soldier oblivious to everything but the muddy road before him and the gaze of the bearded thugs by the road, their index fingers conspicuously close to the trigger; or a letter in a reporter's bag carelessly thrown over a tattooed shoulder, sharing the bottom of the bag with a Walkman, notebooks, condoms, bread and pot crumbs, and a wallet crammed with family pictures. I imagine letters in a post office in Zagreb or Split, Amsterdam or London, in the midst of a pile of letters sent to people I know nothing about by the people who care about them. Sometimes it takes dismal months for her letters to reach me and when I open my mailbox—a long tunnel dead-ending with a dark square—and find Aida's letter, I shiver with dread. What terrifies me is that, as I rip the exhausted envelope, she may be dead. She may have vanished, may have already become a ghost, a nothing—a fictitious character, so to speak—and I'm reading her letter as if she were alive, her voice ringing in my brain, her visions projected before my eyes, her hand shaping curved letters. I fear to communicate with a creature of my memory, with a dead person. I dread the fact that life is always slower than death and I have been chosen, despite my weakness, against my will, to witness the discrepancy.

In September, Aunt Fatima passed away. She had had asthma for a long time, but in September she just asphyxiated in our apartment. They were pouring shells for weeks on end, and even when they didn't there was an eager sniper. He killed our neighbor who hadn't even left the building. He just peeked out of the door, cautiously ajar, and the bullet hit him in the forehead and he just dropped down dead. Anyway, Aunt

Fatima ran out of her asthma medicine, and she couldn't go out. The windows had been shattered long ago. She was always cold, breathing in cold air saturated with floating dust and hovering particles of rubble. She simply suffocated, producing that inhaling, sucking sound, and nothing was being inhaled. We couldn't bury her, or even take her out, because they kept shelling and sniping as if there was no tomorrow.

Kevin is an American, from Chicago. He's a cameraman. He's been around, he says. He's been in Afghanistan and Lebanon and the Persian Gulf and Africa with his camera. He's tall, his arms are little hills of muscles. His eyes are greenish, like dried turf. He has two parallel silver earrings in his left ear. His hair is short. He's balding and has a peninsula of grayish hair crawling down his forehead. He's lean. When you look closely, you can see purple ruptured blood vessels where his nose meets his face. It's from cocaine. He did it a lot in Lebanon. It was cheap and he broke down. He couldn't stand it any longer. An Arab child shot at him with what he took to be a toy gun. There is a scar-furrow on his thigh. He was new, he broke down, he did cocaine. Now he's fine, he says. I like him because he tells stories. All of those people do, all those reporters and cameramen and all those who have been around. But they're all clichés, as if they watched too many movies about foreign correspondents and war reporters. Kevin's stories are different. All those others always tell stories about other journalists. A British drunk, a German ex-Nazi, a French sissy, an American whore, are stock characters. They never tell stories about the local people, because the natives are news, they're what's to be reported. Kevin told me stories from Afghanistan, about lying in a high mountain ambush with bearded rebels. And about terrified Russian convoys crawling up a dire mountain road, knowing they're being watched. About a Russian soldier being cut in pieces alive, producing unreal shrieks, until a merciful *mullah* shot him in the head. He filmed it, even though he knew they would take the tape away from him. Even if they didn't, it would have never been broadcast.

She sent me a black-and-white picture: she is standing on a pile of debris in the midst of the Library ruins. I could see holes that used to be windows, and pillars like scorched matches. The camera looks at her from underneath: she is tall and erect, as if on the top of a mountain; she is in a bulletproof vest, wearing it detachedly, as though it were a bathing suit.

I've got this job as a liaison for the pool of foreign TV companies. Besides helping them to get by in hell, to approach and bribe government officials and find good parties, I edit footage that crews shoot in and around the city. Then I send it via satellite to London, Amsterdam, Luxembourg, or wherever. I get two–three hours of footage every day. It's mainly blood and gore and severed limbs. I cut it into fifteen–twenty minutes, which are then transmitted to the invisible people who edit it into one–two minutes of a news story, if there is one. At the beginning, I was trying to choose the most telling images, with as much blood and bowels, stumps and child corpses as possible. I was trying to induce some compassion or understanding or pain or whatever, although the one–two minutes that I would later recognize as having been cut by me would contain only mildly horrific images. I've changed my view. I stopped sifting horror after I saw footage of a dead woman being carried by four men. She was prone on their arms, as if on a hearse. As they were carrying her, her head was bent backward, hanging down. Her skull was cut open by a piece of shrapnel. There was a skull-sod with hair, hanging on a patch of skin. They put her in the back of a truck, with other heaped corpses. Her head was still open. I could see the brainless bloody cavity. Then one of the men closed the cavity, putting the sod back into its place, as if putting on a lid. He did it with a certain reluctant respect, as though he was covering her naked body, as though there was something indecent in seeing the inside of somebody's head. I cut all that out and put it on a separate tape. From then on I was cutting out everything that was as horrid. I put it all on one tape, which I hoarded underneath my pillow made of clothes. There once was that corny idiotic movie *Cinema Paradiso,* where the projectionist kept all the kisses from films censored by a priest. Hence I christened the tape *Cinema Inferno.* I haven't watched it entirely yet. Some day I will, paying particular attention to the cuts, to see how the montage of death attractions works.

I had a dream: a woman alone on the glowing screen, and a moat in front of it, and beyond the moat is a room, windowless, full of people. She is performing me, she is acting me out. I'm in the audience, sitting in a row at the end of my gaze, on the verge of darkness. She's not doing it right. This is not how I felt, this is not my pain. I want to get up and scream, and tell her that she's much too involved in myself. She's even attaining my shapes, my face, my voice. I want to help her step out of me. But I can't do anything. She's a light mirage. I can't get up, because I don't know what exactly is wrong. And then I realize—it's the language. I'm confined within the wrong language.

Purebred dogs can be seen running in packs or, seldom, alone. You can see German shepherds, Irish setters, Belgian collies, Border collies, rottweilers, poodles, chow chows, Dobermans, cocker spaniels, malamutes, Siberian huskies, everything. After years of siege, there are, naturally, many mongrels. Some of the breeding combinations would amaze, or terrify, a canine expert. In the winter, when every living creature is in the middle of starvation, dogs are more inclined to move in packs, often attacking with common strategy, like wolves. There have been occasions when an improbable mixture of dog races attacked a child or a feeble elderly person. A German shepherd would be going for the throat, a poodle would be tearing the flesh off the calves.

It is after I write her a letter with trite reminiscing that I begin wanting to tell her all about me—I have imaginary conversations with her, making real grimaces, gesturing with real hands. I think of all the things I could've told her or should've told her: how awkward and cumbersome I feel in English, sinking in syntax, my sentences flapping helplessly, like a drowning child's arms; about Bach's St. Matthew's Passion; *about hoping for the arrival of spiders—the vicious cockroach-killers—into my living space; about the lack of relationship—or contact, rather—with women; about the friendless immigrant life; about the* Headline News *I keep watching, waiting for a glimpse of Sarajevo; about my western window, looking at corny sunsets and the distant O'Hare Airport, night airplanes landing like tired firebugs; about an involuntary memory I had about my father smashing a nest of infant mice with a shovel; about the fact that almost everything I wanted to tell her is not in the letter; about the sense of loss and the damp stamp-glue taste lingering on my tongue for hours after I drop the letter in the mailbox. I used to believe that words can convey and contain everything, but not anymore, not anymore.*

I grew fond of Kevin because he never openly showed me his affection. He would just tell me stories. Even in a room full of people, I knew the stories were for me. I liked him because he was so detached. He said it was the "cameraman syndrome," always being a gaze away from the world. We're not in love, love is out of the question. Nobody's in love in this godforsaken city. We just keep learning about each other. We just share stories, becoming a story along the way. And the story may end at any moment. When we make love, in the darkness—no electricity—it's harsh and cruel, as if we were fighting, because we have to wrestle joy and flashes of love from our irked bodies. We never talk about his future departure. He has callused feet, from marching through the Afghanistan mountains.

After some grotesque obsequies, we put Aunt Fatima in my room. It soon became *her* room. None of us would go in there. When something was needed from her room—a scarf, a blanket, a photo—someone would say: "It's in Fatima's room," which meant it was irretrievable. We kept hoping that we would be able to bury her, but a week passed and she was still there—my malodorous aunt.

On Tuesday I had a sensation (a hallucination?) of cockroaches scurrying up my shins—I may be losing my mind, because of the solitude and nothingness that constitute my life. I had the sensation at a rock show, while boys and girls shook their heads like rattles. I thought that the cockroaches were my home-grown cockroaches, that I brought them with me from my apartment, unknowingly. The next day I asked Art, my janitor, to help me and he gave me those roach motels in which roaches get lured by sweet syrup and then get stuck in glue. Let's put it this way: Art provides room for abhorrent insects, Art terminates cockroaches.

I hate Kevin. He brought footage of yet another massacre: people crawling in their own blood, faceless skulls, limbs strewn, stuff like that. There was this woman, her arms were severed. You could see two frayed, blood-spurting stumps. She was raising the bloody mess of her ex-arms toward Kevin's camera. Kevin had a close-up of her face, still in shock, not feeling any pain, not being armless yet. The close-up lasted for a good five minutes, like fucking Tarkovsky. I asked Kevin why he didn't drop the goddamn camera and help the woman. He said there was nothing he could do. He's a cameraman, he said, and that is what he does and how he helps people. I told him he shouldn't have shot that close-up. He said he didn't do it. It was his camera who did it, he just held it. I cut it out anyway. I put it on the *Cinema Inferno* tape. Nobody saw the footage but me. Kevin is so detached and so protected.

I sleep in a former TV studio, next to the editing room. It is windowless, of course, safe from shelling, unless they use concrete-piercing shells. Which they seldom do, for whatever reason. I suppose that even such a shell wouldn't kill us immediately. It would just open a hole for more shells. I prefer to die immediately. The studio has a little stage where mindless folk singers used to perform their playback love pain. This is where we sleep, as if on a raft—on a stage soaked with false tears and real sweat. There are still several cameras in the studio, with their lenses turned to the floor, looking between their wheels, as if ashamed. The studio is immense and very dark. We light it with two strategically positioned candles. There is some electricity in the building, to be sure, produced by a coughing gasoline-run generator, but we need electricity to produce and broadcast images. We move around the studio as if blind, having a memory of the studio as the map in our heads. We never move cameras, lest we run into them and get hurt. But somehow they always get in our way, as if they're moving silently behind our backs, like ghosts, recording us.

I've been sending letters for her through obscure Red Cross channels—it takes months for a Red Cross convoy to reach Sarajevo and even more for my letters to reach her. When they do, they're already obsolete, they're rendering someone other than myself, someone saner—a stranger not only to her but indeed to myself. When I'm writing those letters I have to accept my helplessness, I have to admit that someone else is writing them, using my body, my Pelikan fountain pen, my cramped right hand. Whatever I write, I feel it to be untrue, because it'll be untrue in a day or two, if not in a moment or two. Whatever I say I am lying or will be lying. On the pages of the letter, the whiteness of the page stained with ink, a dismal present descends into a desolate past. That is why I tend to write her things that she already knows, tell her stories told wars ago. It is cowardly, I confess, but I'm just trying to create an illusion that our lives, however distant, may still be simultaneous.

The odor escaped Fatima's room no matter what we tried to do. We stuffed the cracks between the door and the frame with rugs. We soaked the rugs and the door with vinegar and our useless perfumes (Obsession, Magie Noir). But the stench was always there—the sweet, dense, meaty scent of decay. In the midst of a rare and brief nocturnal lull in shelling, we decided to throw her out of the window, after my mother woke up screaming, having dreamt maggots coming out of her sister's eye sockets.

Kevin and I, we get drunk over his stories, with bourbon that he keeps fetching from somewhere. He tells me then what he considers to be intimate things: about his long-time girlfriend, who was working as a real estate agent, having a dream of becoming a congresswoman. She was from a place called White Pigeon, Michigan, fifty miles south of Kalamazoo. While he was in the Gulf, she left him a message on his answering machine about leaving him because he was a "selfish dreamy idiot." He tells me how he sees everything through a viewfinder. He has confidence in the camera objective. He feels natural with his camera, because "with the camera I see nothing alone." There's always another pair of eyes, he says.

A friend of mine asked me to help her identify some damaged buildings in Sarajevo; she sent me photographs hoping that I could recognize the buildings, but they were unidentifiable as far as I was concerned. They all looked the same: they all had shattered windows— black holes, as if their eyes had been gouged; there were rings of debris around them, as if ruins were being carved out of whole buildings; there were no people in the pictures. What was in the pictures were not buildings—let alone buildings I could've come in or out of: what was in the pictures was what was not in the pictures—the pictures recorded the very end of the process of disappearing, the nothingness itself.

People stand in line at Point A, waiting for their turn to run across. When it's your turn, you cannot wait, you have to go, because the longer you wait, the readier the sniper is. Plus you don't want to share the unspeakable fear of the waiting throng. The first time I ran from Point A to Point B, the fear was unspeakable indeed. Pain in your stomach, as if a big steel ball is grinding your bowels. Blood throbbing in your neck veins. Wet heat inside your eyeballs. Numbness of your limbs, increasing as you're running. Sweat trickling down your cheeks, like a miniature avalanche of dread. You see no life unwinding before your eyes. All you see is one or two meters ahead of you and all the little things that you can trip over. You hear every tiny sound. Your feet brushing away dirt and rubble. Distant detonations. Cries of scared and wounded people. Whistling ricocheting bullets. The death rattle from the person behind you.

This is me in what's left of the Library. If you could magnify this picture sufficiently you would see motes levitating around me—cold ashes of books. This picture was made on the day I got the bulletproof vest. It was one of the happiest days of my life, this life. A bulletproof vest significantly increases your (well, mine) chances of survival. The sniper has to shoot you in the head to kill you. Which is why I cut my hair so short, to make my head smaller. Sometimes I feel like a fucking Joan of Arc, except I have no army and no voices to guide me.

Mother and Father wrapped her up in a bedsheet, and then another one, and then another one, their faces distorted by the urge to vomit. I couldn't watch when they actually pushed her over the windowsill, but I heard the thud. I thought, as if remembering a line from a movie: "Her life ended with a thud."

Since April I have received no letters from Aida. From that time on I had to make up her letters, I had to write her letters for her, I had to imagine her, because that was the only way to break the siege and stay connected with her. I'm sure she's alive, I'm sure that one of these days I'll have a bundle of her consecutive letters stowed in my mailbox, I'm sure she's writing them this very moment.

This war, my friend, is men's business. The other day I heard a "joke": "What is a woman?"—"The stuff around the pussy!" The men in the camouflage uniforms thought it was so hilarious that they kicked the floor with their rifle butts. I sensed that the joke was for me. We're expected to remain silent, spread our legs, breed more warriors, and die with motherly dignity. I think what I fear the most is rape. When a sniper bullet hits you, your body and yourself die simultaneously. Provided, naturally, that you're killed instantly; which you usually are, because they're so fucking good. But I don't want my body to be mutilated, mauled, violated. I don't want to witness that. When I'm gone I'd like to take my body with me. Have you heard about the rape camps?

When I got this job, I moved to the TV building, going home only occasionally, to check if my parents were alive and well. I'd usually go on Sunday afternoons, after the morning transmission of Friday leftovers. But then I stopped doing that because I realized that my local sniper was waiting for me. Before I ran, everything was silent, and several people ran across the parking lot without being shot at. When I started crossing it, bullets buzzed around me like rabid bees. He watched me. He knew I was coming. He waited for me and then toyed with me. Now I go to see them at different times, using different routes, trying to appear differently each time in order to be unrecognizable to the sharpshooter, who could be one of my exboyfriends for all I know.

While my head was still on the pillow, my nightmare not completely erased by the sudden awakening, I opened my eyes and saw a cockroach running from the stove, over the gray kitchen-floor tiles, getting on the carpet, running a bit slower, as if on sand, going beneath the chair, coming diagonally across, going around my slippers, trying to reach the safe space underneath my futon. I watched it, it was running fast, never stopping, going straight without hesitation. What was it running from? What was running that little engine? Desire to live? Fear of death? The instinctual—perhaps, even, molecular—awareness of the gaze of the supreme sharpshooter? What a horrible world, I thought, when every living creature lives and dies in fear. I reached for my left slipper, but the cockroach was already underneath the futon.

Snipers often kill dogs, just for fun. Sometimes they have competitions in dog-shooting, but only when there aren't any targetable people on the streets. Shooting a dog in the head gets you the most points, I suppose. One can often see a dog corpse with a shattered head, like a crushed tomato. When snipers shoot dogs, antisniping patrols refrain from confronting them, because of the constant danger of a rabies epidemic. When an unskilled, new, or careless sharpshooter only wounds a dog and the dog frantically ricochets around, bleeding, howling, biting anything that can ease the pain and fear, a member of the antisniping patrol might even shoot the dog, aiming, as always, at the head.

The other day I took Kevin to a tour of my favorite places in Sarajevo. He took his camera. What I like about Kevin is that you don't have to explain everything to him. He just sees what you want him to see. What's more, he doesn't say that he understands. You just know. We both knew, for instance, that the places on our tour were between being a memory and being reduced to nothing but a pile of rubble. The camera was recording the process of disappearing. There is a truce in place these days, which always scares me a bit. Partly because silence is often more terrifying than the familiar relentless noise of shelling. Partly because I'm afraid that Kevin might get bored and leave. Which is why, I suppose, I took him on the tour. He followed me with his camera like a shadow. I showed him our school. I stood in the wrecked window of our classroom and he shot me waving to his objective. I stood on the corner from which Princip shot those historic shots. My little feet were fitting, as always, into the concrete shapes of his feet. I took him to the few bars we used to frequent. Some of them were closed—the owner dead or something—and some of them were full of black marketers and men in uniform, their rifles conspicuous on the bar-stand before them. I took him to the park, now treeless—desperate firewood demand—where I used to take boys and make them touch my breasts, while they were being too pusillanimous to go further. I told all that to the camera, and he circled around me, his knees bent, as if genuflecting. And then I told him, as I am telling the invisible you now, that I was pregnant.

Then we watched over it, the white pile that used to be my aunt, from the window that was hidden from snipers. We watched the bundle of decomposed flesh, as if we were on a wake, but a wake for something other than Aunt Fatima, and transcendentally important nonetheless. We would take turns, we would have shifts. Father even asked me, taking his shift, if everything was all right. I said: "No, nothing will ever be all right." I'm terrified with the calmness, even if ostensible, with which I'm telling you this. I feel I might burst out into madness.

In the corners of my room, there are elaborate cobwebs, but I haven't seen any spiders. It seems that the cobwebs have a purely symbolic function—they're there to remind me that I am trapped and that, at any given moment, a tooth or a sting will inject poison into my body and then suck out my blood. The space I inhabit becomes me—the room speaks about me, as if the walls were pages of a book and I were a hero, a character, somebody.

So I had the morning shift. And right after it dawned, I saw a pack of dogs coming toward us. There was a rottweiler, a poodle, and several mongrels. They tore the sheets and I turned my head away, but I could not leave. The only thought I remember having was about skiing. I had a vision of myself coming down the slope, going very fast, and air slapping my cheeks, and the sound of the skis brushing snow away, like a speeded-up recording of waves. When I looked out again, I couldn't look at the place where the corpse was. I looked around it, as if making a compromise. I saw the rottweiler, trotting away, with a hand in his jaw. I wish I'd had a camera so I wouldn't have to remember. I'm sorry I had to tell you this.

My hair is all gray now. How is Chicago? Write, even if your letters can't reach me.

With a lightning move of my hand superbly handling the knife, I split the cockroach in two: the front half continued running for an inch

or two and then started frenetically revolving around the head; the
back half just stood in place, as if surprised, oozing pallid slime.

I woke up bleeding, in a bed soaked with blood, by the Heathrow
Airport, in an expensive bland hotel, having waited for Kevin for more
than a week. Kevin, who didn't even bother to call me. I tried to reach
him in Amsterdam, Paris, Atlanta, New York, Cyprus, even Johannes-
burg, leaving messages and curses. But then I just wiped myself off and
went back to Sarajevo, leaving a heap of bloody towels and bedsheets,
an empty refreshment bar, a broken glass in the bathroom, and an un-
paid bill, to Kevin's name, with his Cyprus address. So here I am now,
un-pregnant, as sanguine as ever, but never as sad.

I bought a Polaroid camera to explore my absence, to find out how
space and things appear when I'm not exerting my presence on them. I
took snapshots—glossy still moments with edges darker than the cen-
ter, as if everything is fading away—I took snapshots of my apartment
and the things in it: here's my ceiling fan not revolving; here's my empty
chair; here's my futon, looking like somebody's just got up; here's my
vacuous bathroom; here's a dried cockroach; here's a glass, with still
water not being drunk; here are my vacant shoes; here's my TV not be-
ing watched; here's a flash in the mirror; here's nothing.

When you get to Point B, the adrenaline rush is so strong that you
feel *too* alive. You see everything clearly, but you can't comprehend
anything. Your senses are so overloaded that you forget everything before you even register it. I've run from Point A to Point B hundreds of
times and the feeling is always the same but I've never had it before. I
suppose it is this high pressure of excitement that makes people bleed
away so quickly. I saw deluges of blood coming out of svelte bodies. A
woman holding on to her purse while her whole body is shaking with
death rattle. I saw bloodstreams spouting out of surprised children,
and they look at you as if they'd done something wrong—broken a vial
of expensive perfume or something. But once you get to Point B everything is quickly gone, as if it never happened. You pick yourself up and
walk back into your besieged life, happy to be. You move a wet curl
from your forehead, inhale deeply, and put your hand in the pocket,
where you may or may not find a worthless coin; a coin.

Gish Jen

Born in 1956 in New York, Gish Jen is the daughter of immigrants from Shanghai. She is the author of the novels Typical American *(1991),* Mona in the Promised Land *(1996), and* The Love Wife *(2004), and a short story collection* Who's Irish? *(1999). Her work addresses issues of race, community, and identity. In an interview with Powell's, Jen talked about her particular blend of humor and seriousness: "Early on in my career people would say, 'Is this supposed to be funny or is it supposed to be sad?' And I would hear voices like that and think that somehow I was supposed to resolve my work, be either funny or sad. Then at a certain point I finally decided, for better or worse, I was somebody who simultaneously sees things as happy and sad. I am the kind of person who would make a joke on someone's deathbed, tacky as it may seem. . . . It could be seen as an Asian part of my sensibility, in the sense that it's a very Asian thing to imagine that opposites go together. Yin-yang, sweet and sour. There isn't the sense that something should be sweet or sour, one or the other . . . that yin-yang quality certainly embodies a lot of [my] stories."*

Birthmates

This was what responsibility meant in a dinosaur industry, toward the end of yet another quarter of bad-to-worse news: that you called the travel agent back, and even though there was indeed an economy room in the hotel where the conference was being held, a room overlooking the cooling towers, you asked if there wasn't something still cheaper. And when Marie-the-new-girl came back with something amazingly cheap, you took it—only to discover, as Art Woo was discovering now, that the doors were locked after nine o'clock. The neighborhood had looked not great but not bad, and the building itself, regular enough. Brick, four stories, a rolled-up awning. A bright-lit hotel logo, with a raised-plastic, smiling sun. But there was a kind of crossbar rigged across the inside of the glass door, and that was not at all regular. A two-by-four, it appeared, wrapped in rust-colored carpet. Above this, inside the glass, hung a small gray sign. If the taxi had not left, Art might not have rung the buzzer, as per the instructions.

But the taxi had indeed left, and the longer Art huddled on the stoop in the clumpy December snow, the emptier and more poorly lit the street appeared. His buzz was answered by an enormous black man wearing a neck brace. The shoulder seams of the man's blue waffle-weave jacket were visibly straining; around the brace was tied a necktie, which reached only a third of the way down his chest. All the same, it was neatly fastened together with a hotel-logo tie tack about two inches from the bottom. The tie tack was smiling; the man was not. He held his smooth, round face perfectly expressionless, and he lowered his gaze at every opportunity—not so that it was rude, but so that it was clear he wasn't selling anything to anybody. Regulation tie, thought Art. Regulation jacket. He wondered if the man would turn surly soon enough.

For Art had come to few conclusions about life in his forty-nine years, but this was one of them: that men turned surly when their clothes didn't fit them. This man, though, belied the rule. He was courteous, almost formal in demeanor; and if the lobby seemed not only too small for him, like his jacket, but also too much like a bus station, what with its smoked mirror wall, and its linoleum, and its fake wood, and its vending machines, what did that matter to Art? The sitting area looked as though it was in the process of being cleaned; the sixties Scandinavian chairs and couch and coffee table had been pulled every which way, as if by someone hell-bent on the dust balls. Still Art proceeded with his check-in. He was going with his gut, here as in any business situation. Here as in any business situation, he was looking foremost at the personnel, and the man with the neck brace had put him at some ease. It wasn't until after Art had taken his credit card back that he noticed, above the checkout desk, a wooden plaque from a neighborhood association. He squinted at its brass faceplate: FEWEST CUSTOMER INJURIES, 1972–73.

What about the years since '73? Had the hotel gotten more dangerous, or had other hotels gotten safer? Maybe neither. For all he knew, the neighborhood association had dissolved and was no longer distributing plaques. Art reminded himself that in life, some signs were no signs. It's what he used to tell his ex-wife, Lisa. Lisa, who loved to read everything into everything; Lisa, who was attuned. She left him on a day when she saw a tree get split by lightning. Of course, that was an extraordinary thing to see. An event of a lifetime. Lisa said the tree had sizzled. He wished he had seen it, too. But what did it mean, except that the tree had been the tallest in the neighborhood, and was no longer? It meant nothing; ditto for the plaque. Art made his decision, which perhaps was not the right decision. Perhaps he should have looked for another hotel.

But it was late—on the way out, his plane had sat on the runway, just sat and sat, as if it were never going to take off—and God only knew what he would have ended up paying if he had relied on a cabbie simply to take him somewhere else. Forget twice—it could have been three, four times what he would have paid for that room with the view of the cooling towers, easy. At this hour, after all, and that was a conference rate.

So he double-locked his door instead. He checked behind the hollow-core doors of the closet, and under the steel-frame bed, and also in the swirly-green shower stall unit. He checked behind the seascapes to be sure there weren't any peepholes. The window opened onto a fire escape; not much he could do about that except check the window locks. Big help that those were—a sure deterrent for the subset of all burglars that was burglars too skittish to break glass. Which was what percent of intruders, probably? Ten percent? Fifteen? He closed the drapes, then decided he would be more comfortable with the drapes open. He wanted to be able to see what approached, if anything did. He unplugged the handset of his phone from the base, a calculated risk. On the one hand, he wouldn't be able to call the police if there was an intruder. On the other, he would be armed. He had read somewhere a story about a woman who threw the handset of her phone at an attacker, and killed him. Needless to say, there had been some luck involved in that eventuality. Still, Art thought that (a) surely he could throw as hard as that woman, and (b) even without the luck, his throw would most likely be hard enough to slow up an intruder at least. Especially since this was an old handset, the hefty kind that made you feel the seriousness of human communication. In a newer hotel, he probably would have had a lighter phone, with lots of buttons he would never use but which would make him feel he had many resources at his disposal. In the conference hotel, there were probably buttons for the health club, and for the concierge, and for the three restaurants, and for room service. He tried not to think about this as he went to sleep, clutching the handset.

He did not sleep well.

In the morning, he debated whether to take the handset with him into the elevator. It wasn't like a knife, say, that could be whipped out of nowhere. Even a pistol at least fit in a guy's pocket. A telephone handset did not. All the same, he took it with him. He tried to carry it casually, as if he was going out for a run and using it for a hand weight, or as if he was in the telephone business.

He strode down the hall. Victims shuffled; that's what everybody said. A lot of mugging had to do with nonverbal cues, which is why Lisa used to walk tall after dark, sending vibes. For this, he used to tease her. If she was so worried, she should lift weights and run, the way he did. That, he maintained, was the substantive way of helping oneself. She had agreed. For a while they had met after work at the gym. Then she dropped a weight on her toe and decided she preferred to sip pina coladas and watch. Naturally, he grunted on. But to what avail? Who could appreciate his pectorals through his suit and overcoat? Pectorals had no deterrent value, that was what he was thinking now. And he was, though not short, not tall. He continued striding. Sending vibes. He was definitely going to eat in the dining room of the hotel where the conference was being held, he decided. What's more, he was going to have a full American breakfast with bacon and eggs, none of this continental bullshit.

In truth, he had always considered the sight of men eating croissants slightly ridiculous, especially at the beginning, when for the first bite they had to maneuver the point of the crescent into their mouths. No matter what a person did, he ended up with an asymmetrical mouthful of pastry, which he then had to relocate with his tongue to a more central location. This made him look less purposive than he might. Also, croissants were more apt than other breakfast foods to spray little flakes all over one's clean dark suit. Art himself had accordingly never ordered a croissant in any working situation, and he believed that attention to this sort of detail was how it was that he had not lost his job like so many of his colleagues.

This was, in other words, how it happened that he was still working in a dying industry, and was now carrying a telephone handset with him into the elevator. Art braced himself as the elevator doors opened slowly, jerkily, in the low-gear manner of elevator doors in the Third World. He strode in, and was surrounded by, of all things, children. Down in the lobby, too, there were children and, here and there, women he knew to be mothers by their looks of dogged exasperation. A welfare hotel! He laughed out loud. Almost everyone was black; the white children stood out like little missed opportunities of the type that made Art's boss throw his tennis racket across the room. Of course, the racket was always in its padded protective cover and not in much danger of getting injured, though the person in whose vicinity it was aimed sometimes was. Art once suffered what he rather hoped would turn out to be a broken nose, but was only a bone bruise. There was so little skin discoloration that people had a hard time believing the incident had actually taken place. Yet it had. *Don't talk to me about fault. Bottom line, it's you Japs who are responsible for this whole fucking mess,* his boss had said. Never mind that what was the matter with minicomputers, really, was personal computers, a wholly American phenomenon. And never mind that Art could have sued over this incident if he could have proved that it had happened. Some people, most notably Lisa, thought he at least ought to have quit.

But he didn't sue and he didn't quit. He took his tennis racket on the nose, so to speak, and when his boss apologized the next day for losing control, Art said he understood. And when his boss said that Art shouldn't take what he said personally—that he knew Art was not a Jap, but a Chink, plus he had called someone else a lazy Wop that very morning, it was just his style—Art said again that he understood, and also that he hoped his boss would remember Art's great understanding come promotion time. Which his boss did, to Art's satisfaction. In Art's view, this was a victory. In Art's view, he had made a deal out of the incident. He had perceived leverage where others would only have perceived affront. He had maintained a certain perspective.

But this certain perspective was, in addition to the tree, why Lisa had left him. He thought of that now, the children underfoot, his handset in hand. So many children. It was as if he were seeing before him all the children he would never have. His heart lost muscle. A child in a red running suit ran by, almost grabbed the handset out of Art's grasp. Then another, in a brown jacket with a hood. Art looked up. A group of grade-school boys was arrayed about the seating area, watching. Art had become the object of a dare, apparently; realizing this, he felt renewed enough to want to laugh again. When a particularly small child swung by in his turn—a child of maybe five or six, small enough to be wearing snow pants—Art almost tossed the handset to him. But who wanted to be charged for a missing phone?

As it was, Art wondered if he shouldn't put the handset back in his room rather than carry it around all day. For what was he going to do at the hotel where the conference was, check it? He imagined himself running into Billy Shore—that was his counterpart at Info-Edge, and his competitor in the insurance market. A man with no management ability, and no technical background, either, but he could offer customers a personal computer option, which Art could not. What's more. Billy had been a quarterback in college. This meant he strutted around as though it still mattered that he had connected with his tight end in the final minutes of what Art could not help but think of as the Wilde-Beastie game. And it meant that Billy was sure to ask him, *What are you doing with a phone in your hand? Talking to yourself again?* Making everyone around them laugh.

Billy was that kind of guy. He had come up through sales, and was always cracking a certain type of joke—about drinking, or sex, or how much the wife shopped. Of course, he never used those words. He never called things by their plain names. He always talked in terms of *knocking back some brewskis,* or *running the triple option,* or *doing some damage.* He made assumptions as though it were a basic bodily function. Of course his knowledge was the common knowledge. Of course people understood what it was that he was referring to so delicately. *Listen, champ,* he said, putting his arm around you. If he was smug, it was in an affable kind of way. *So what do you think the poor people are doing tonight?* Billy not only spoke what Art called Mainstreamese, he spoke such a pure dialect of it that Art once asked him if he realized he was a pollster's delight. He spoke the thoughts of thousands, Art told him; he breathed their very words. Naturally, Billy did not respond, except to say, *What's that?* and turn away. He rubbed his torso as he turned, as if ruffling his chest hairs through the long-staple cotton. Primate behavior, Lisa used to call this. It was her belief that neckties evolved in order to check this very motion, uncivilized as it was. She also believed that this was the sort of thing you never saw Asian men do—at least not if they were brought up properly.

Was that true? Art wasn't so sure. Lisa had grown up on the West Coast. She was full of Asian consciousness, whereas all he knew was that no one had so much as smiled politely at his pollster remark. On the other hand, the first time Art was introduced to Billy, and Billy said, *Art Woo, how's that for a nice Pole-ack name,* everyone broke right up in great rolling guffaws. Of course, they laughed the way people laughed at conferences, which was not because something was really funny, but because it was part of being a good guy, and because they didn't want to appear to have missed their cue.

The phone, the phone. If only Art could fit it in his briefcase! But his briefcase was overstuffed; it was always overstuffed; really, it was too bad he had the slim silhouette type, and hard-side besides. Italian. That was Lisa's doing; she thought the fatter kind made him look like a salesman. Not that there was anything the matter with that, in his view. Billy Shore notwithstanding, sales were important. But she was the liberal arts type, Lisa was, the type who did not like to think about money, but only about her feelings. Money was not money to her, but support, and then a means of support much inferior to hand-holding or other forms of fingerplay. She did not believe in a modern-day economy, in which everyone played a part in a large and complex whole that introduced efficiencies that at least theoretically raised everyone's standard of living. She believed in expressing herself. Also in taking classes, and in knitting. There was nothing, she believed, like taking a walk in the autumn woods wearing a hand-knit sweater. Of course, she did look beautiful in them, especially the violet ones. That was her color—Asians are winters, she always said—and sometimes she liked to wear the smallest smidgen of matching violet eyeliner.

Little Snowpants ran at Art again, going for the knees. A tackle, thought Art as he went down. Red Running Suit snatched away the handset and went sprinting off, trimphant. Teamwork! The children chortled together. How could Art not smile, even if they had gotten his overcoat dirty? He brushed himself off, ambled over.

"Hey, guys," he said. "That was some move back there."

"Ching chong polly wolly wing wong," said Little Snowpants.

"Now, now, that's no way to talk," said Art.

"Go to hell!" said Brown Jacket, pulling at the corners of his eyes to make them slanty.

"Listen up," said Art. "I'll make you a deal." Really he only meant to get the handset back, so as to avoid getting charged for it.

But the next thing he knew, something had hit his head with a crack, and he was out.

Lisa had left in a more or less amicable way. She had not called a lawyer, or a mover. She had simply pressed his hands with both of hers and, in her most California voice, said, *Let's be nice.* Then she had asked him if he wouldn't help her move her boxes, at least the heavy ones. He had helped. He had carried the heavy boxes, and also the less heavy ones. Being a weight lifter, after all. He had sorted books and rolled glasses into pieces of newspaper, feeling all the while like a statistic. A member of the modern age, a story for their friends to rake over, and all because he had not gone with Lisa to her grieving group. Or at least that was the official beginning of the trouble. Probably the real beginning had been when Lisa—no, *they*—had trouble getting pregnant. When they decided to, as the saying went, do infertility. Or had he done the deciding, as Lisa later maintained? He had thought it was a joint decision, though it was true that he had done the analysis that led to the joint decision. He had been the one to figure the odds, to do the projections. He had drawn the decision tree according to whose branches they had nothing to lose by going ahead.

Neither one of them had realized how much would be involved— the tests, the procedures, the drugs, the ultrasounds. Lisa's arms were black and blue from having her blood drawn every day, and before long he was giving practice shots to an orange, that he might prick her some more. Then he was telling her to take a breath so that on the exhale he could poke her in the buttocks. This was nothing like poking an orange. The first time, he broke out in such a sweat that his vision blurred; he pulled the needle out slowly and crookedly, occasioning a most unorangelike cry. The second time, he wore a sweatband. Her ovaries swelled to the point where he could feel them through her jeans.

Art still had the used syringes—snapped in half and stored, as per their doctor's recommendation, in plastic soda bottles. Lisa had left him those. Bottles of medical waste, to be disposed of responsibly, meaning that he was probably stuck with them, ha-ha, for the rest of his life. This was his souvenir of their ordeal. Hers was sweeter—a little pile of knit goods. For through it all, she had knit, as if to demonstrate an alternative use of needles. Sweaters, sweaters, but also baby blankets, mostly to give away, only one or two to keep. She couldn't help herself. There was anesthesia, and egg harvesting, and anesthesia and implanting, until she finally did get pregnant, twice. The third time, she went to four and a half months before the doctors found a problem. On the amnio, it showed up, brittle-bone disease—a genetic abnormality such as could happen to anyone.

He steeled himself for another attempt; she grieved. And this was the difference between them, that he saw hope, still, some feeble, skeletal hope, where she saw loss. She called the fetus her baby, though it was not a baby, just a baby-to-be, as he tried to say; as even the grieving-group facilitator tried to say. Lisa said Art didn't understand, couldn't possibly understand. She said it was something you understood with your body, and that it was not his body, but hers, which knew the baby, loved the baby, lost the baby. In the grieving class, the women agreed. They commiserated. They bonded, subtly affirming their common biology by doing 85 percent of the talking. The room was painted mauve—a feminine color that seemed to support them in their process. At times, it seemed that the potted palms were female, too, nodding, nodding, though really their sympathy was just rising air from the heating vents. Other husbands started missing sessions—they never talked anyway, you hardly noticed their absence—and finally he missed some also. One, maybe two, for real reasons, nothing cooked up. But the truth was, as Lisa sensed, that he thought she had lost perspective. They could try again, after all. What did it help to despair? Look, they knew they could get pregnant and, what's more, sustain the

pregnancy. That was progress. But she was like an island in her grief—
a retreating island, if there was such a thing, receding toward the horizon of their marriage, and then to its vanishing point.

Of course, he had missed her terribly at first. Now he missed her still,
but more sporadically, at odd moments—for example, now, waking up
in a strange room with ice on his head. He was lying on an unmade bed
just like the bed in his room, except that everywhere around it were
heaps of what looked to be blankets and clothes. The only clothes on a
hanger were his jacket and overcoat; these hung neatly, side by side, in
the otherwise-empty closet. There was also an extra table in this room,
with a two-burner hot plate, a pan on top of that, and a pile of dishes.
A brown cube refrigerator. The drapes were closed. A chair had been
pulled up close to him; the bedside light was on. A woman was leaning
into its circle, mopping his brow.
      "Don't you move, now," she said.
      She was the shade of black Lisa used to call mochaccino, and she
was wearing a blue flowered apron. Kind eyes; a long face—the kind of
face where you could see the muscles of the jaw working alongside the
cheekbone. An upper lip like an archery bow; a graying Afro, shortish.
She smelled of smoke. Nothing unusual except that she was so very
thin, about the thinnest person he had ever seen, and yet she was cooking something—burning something, it seemed, though maybe the smell
was just a hair fallen onto the heating element. She stood up to tend the
pan. The acrid smell faded. He saw powder on the table. White; there
was a plastic bag full of it. His eyes widened. He sank back, trying to
figure out what to do. His head pulsed. Tylenol, he needed, two. Lisa
always took one because she was convinced the dosages recommended
were based on large male specimens, and though she had never said
that she thought he ought to keep it to one also, not being so tall, he
was adamant about taking two. Two, two, two. He wanted his drugs;
he wanted them now. And his own drugs, that was, not somebody
else's.
      "Those kids kind of rough," said the woman. "They getting to that
age. I told them one of these days somebody gonna get hurt, and sure
enough, they knocked you right out. You might as well been hit with a
bowling ball. I never saw anything like it. We called the Man, but they
got other things on their mind besides to come see about trouble here.
Nobody shot, so they went on down to the Dunkin' Donuts. They
know they can count on a ruckus there." She winked. "How you
feelin? That egg hurt?"

He felt his head. A lump sat right on top of it, incongruous as something left by a glacier. What were those called, those stray boulders you saw perched in hair-raising positions? On cliffs? He thought.

"I feel like I died and came back to life headfirst," he said.

"I gonna make you something nice. Make you feel a whole lot better."

"Uh," said Art. "If you don't mind, I'd rather just have a Tylenol. You got any Tylenol? I had some in my briefcase. If I still have my briefcase."

"Your what?"

"My briefcase," said Art again, with a panicky feeling. "Do you know what happened to my briefcase?"

"Oh, it's right by the door. I'll get it, don't move."

Then there it was, his briefcase, its familiar hard-sided Italian slenderness resting right on his stomach. He clutched it. "Thank you," he whispered.

"You need help with that thing?"

"No," said Art. But when he opened the case, it slid, and everything spilled out—his notes, his files, his papers. All that figuring. How strange his concerns looked on this brown shag carpet.

"Here," said the woman. And again—"I'll get it, don't move"— as gently, beautifully, she gathered up all the folders and put them in the case. There was an odd, almost practiced finesse to her movements; the files could have been cards in a card dealer's hands. "I used to be a nurse," she explained, as if reading his mind. "I picked up a few folders in my time. Here's the Tylenol."

"I'll have two."

"Course you will," she said. "Two Tylenol and some hot milk with honey. Hope you don't mind the powdered. We just got moved here, we don't have no supplies. I used to be a nurse, but I don't got no milk and I don't got no Tylenol, my guests got to bring their own. How you like that."

Art laughed as much as he could. "You got honey, though. How's that?"

"I don't know, it got left here by somebody," said the nurse. "Hope there's nothing growing in it."

Art laughed again, then let her help him sit up to take his pills. The nurse—her name was Cindy—plumped his pillows. She administered his milk. Then she sat—very close to him, it seemed—and chatted amiably about this and that. How she wasn't going to be staying at the hotel for too long, how her kids had had to switch schools, how she wasn't afraid to take in a strange, injured man. After all, she grew up in the projects; she could take care of herself. She showed him her switch-blade, which had somebody's initials carved on it, she didn't know whose. She had never used it, she said, somebody gave it to her. And that somebody didn't know whose initials those were, either, she said, at least so far as she knew. Then she lit a cigarette and smoked while he told her first about his conference and then about how he had ended up at this hotel by mistake. He told her the latter with some hesitation, hoping he wasn't offending her. She laughed with a cough, emitting a series of smoke puffs.

"Sure musta been a shock," she said. "End up in a place like this. This ain't no place for a nice boy like you."

That stung a little, being called *boy*. But more than the stinging, he felt something else. "What about you? It's no place for you, either, you and your kids."

"Maybe so," she said. "But that's how the Almighty planned it, right? You folk rise up while we set and watch." She said this with so little rancor, with something so like intimacy, that it almost seemed an invitation of sorts.

Maybe he was kidding himself. Maybe he was assuming things, just like Billy Shore, just like men throughout the ages. Projecting desire where there was none, assigning and imagining, and in juicy detail. Being Asian didn't exempt him from that. *You folk.*

Art was late, but it didn't much matter. His conference was being held in conjunction with a much larger conference, the real draw; the idea being that maybe between workshops and on breaks, the confer-ees would drift down and see what minicomputers could do for them. That mostly meant lunch, which probably would be slow at best. In the meantime, things were totally dead, allowing Art to appreciate just how much the trade-show floor had shrunk—down to a fraction of what it had been in previous years, and the booths were not what they had been, either. It used to be that the floor was crammed with the fan-ciest booths on the market. Art's was twenty by twenty; it took days to put together. Now you saw blank spots on the floor where exhibitors didn't even bother to show up, and those weren't even as demoralizing as some of the makeshift jobbies—exhibit booths that looked like high school science-fair projects. They might as well have been made out of cardboard and Magic Marker. Art himself had a booth you could buy from an airplane catalog, the kind that rolled up into Cordura bags. And people were stingy with brochures now, too. Gone were the twelve-page, four-color affairs. Now the pamphlets were four-page, two-color, with extrabold graphics for attempted pizzazz, and not everybody got one, only people who were serious.

Art set up. Then, even though he should have been manning his spot, he drifted from booth to booth, saying hello to people he should have seen at breakfast. They were happy to see him, to talk shop, to pop some grapes off the old grapevine. Really, if he hadn't been staying in a welfare hotel, he would have felt downright respected. *You folk.* What folk did Cindy mean? Maybe she was just being matter-of-fact, keeping her perspective. Although how could anyone be so matter-of-fact about something so bitter? He wondered this even as he imagined taking liberties with her. These began with a knock on her door and coursed through some hot times but finished (what a good boy he was) with him rescuing her and her children (he wondered how many there were) from their dead-end life. What was the matter with him, that he could not imagine mating without legal sanction? His libido was not what it should be, clearly, or at least it was not what Billy Shore's was. Art tried to think *game plan*, but in truth he could not even identify what a triple option would be in this case. All he knew was that, assuming, to begin with, that she was willing, he couldn't sleep with a woman like Cindy and then leave her flat. She could *you folk* him, he could never *us folk* her.

He played with some software at a neighboring booth. It appeared interesting enough but kept crashing, so he couldn't tell much. Then he dutifully returned to his own booth, where he was visited by a number of people he knew, people with whom he was friendly—the sort of people to whom he might have shown pictures of his children. He considered telling one or two of them about the events of the morning. Not about the invitation that might not have been an invitation, but about finding himself in a welfare hotel and being beaned with his own telephone. Phrases drifted through his head. *Not as bad as you'd think. You'd be surprised how friendly. And how unpretentious. Though, of course, no health club.* But in the end, the subject simply did not come up and did not come up, until he realized that he was keeping it to himself, and that he was committing more resources to this task than he had readily available. He felt invaded—as if he had been infected by a self-replicating bug. Something that was iterating and iterating, crowding the CPU. The secret was intolerable; it was bound to spill out of him sooner or later. He just hoped it wouldn't be sooner.

He just hoped it wouldn't be to Billy Shore, for whom Art had begun to search, so as to be certain to avoid him.

Art had asked about Billy at the various booths, but no one had seen him; his absence spooked Art. When finally some real live conferees stopped by to see his wares, Art had trouble concentrating. Everywhere in the conversation he was missing opportunities; he knew it. And all because his CPU was full of iterating nonsense. Not too long ago, in looking over some database software in which were loaded certain fun facts about people in the industry, Art had looked up Billy, and discovered that he had been born the same day Art was, only four years later. It just figured that Billy would be younger. That was irritating. But Art was happy for the information, too. He had made a note of it, so that when he ran into Billy at this conference, he could kid him about their birthdays. Now, he rehearsed. *Have I got a surprise for you. I always knew you were a Leo. I believe this makes us birthmates.* Anything not to mention the welfare hotel and all that had happened there.

In the end, Art did not run into Billy at all. In the end, Art wondered about Billy all day, only to learn, finally, that Billy had moved on to a new job in the Valley, with a start-up. In personal computers, naturally. A good move, no matter what kind of beating he took on his house.

"Life is about the long term," said Ernie Ford, the informant. "And let's face it, there is no long term here."

Art agreed as warmly as he could. In one way, he was delighted that his competitor had left. If nothing else, that would mean a certain amount of disarray at Info-Edge, which was good news for Art. The insurance market was, unfortunately, some 40 percent of his business, and he could use any advantage he could get. Another bonus was that Art was never going to have to see Billy again. Billy his birthmate, with his jokes and his Mainstreamese. Still, Art felt depressed.

"We should all have gotten out way before this," he said.

"Truer words were never spoke," said Ernie. Ernie had never been a particular friend of Art's, but talking about Billy was somehow making him chummier. "I'd have packed my bags by now if it weren't for the wife, the kids—they don't want to leave their friends, you know? Plus, the oldest is a junior in high school. We can't afford for him to move now. He's got to stay put and make those nice grades so he can make a nice college. That means I've got to stay, if it means pushing Mc-Muffins for Ronald McDonald. But now you . . ."

"Maybe I should go," said Art.

"Definitely, you should go," said Ernie. "What's keeping you?"

"Nothing," said Art. "I'm divorced now. And that's that, right? Sometimes people get undivorced, but you can't exactly count on it."

"Go," said Ernie. "Take my advice. If I hear of anything, I'll send it your way."

"Thanks," said Art.

But of course he did not expect that Ernie would likely turn anything up soon. It had been a long time since anyone had called Art or anybody else he knew of. Too many people had gotten stranded, and they were too desperate, everybody knew it. Also, the survivors were looked upon with suspicion. Anybody who was any good had jumped ship early, that was the conventional wisdom. There was Art, struggling to hold on to his job, only to discover that there were times you didn't want to hold on to your job—times you ought to maneuver for the golden parachute and jump. Times the goal was to get yourself fired. Who would have figured that?

A few warm-blooded conferees at the end of the day—at least they were polite. Then, as he was packing up to return to the hotel, a surprise. A headhunter approached him, a friend of Ernest's, he said.

"Ernest?" said Art. "Oh, Ernie! Ford! Of course!"

The headhunter was a round, ruddy man with a ring of hair like St. Francis of Assisi, and, sure enough, a handful of bread crumbs. A great opportunity, he said. Right now he had to run, but he knew just the guy Art had to meet, a guy who was coming in that evening. For something else, it happened, but he also needed someone like Art. Needed him yesterday, really. Should've been a priority. Might just be a match. Maybe a quick breakfast in the a.m.? Could he call in an hour or so? Art said, Of course. And when Saint Francis asked his room number, Art hesitated, but then gave the name of the welfare hotel. How would Saint Francis know what kind of hotel it was? Art gave the name out confidently, making his manner count. He almost hadn't made it to the conference at all, he said. Being so busy. It was only at the last minute that he realized he could do it. Things moved around, he found an opening and figured what the hell. But it was too late to book the conference hotel. Hence he was staying elsewhere.

Success. All day Art's mind had been churning; suddenly it seemed to empty. He might as well have been Billy, born on the same day as Art was, but in another year, under different stars. How much simpler things seemed. He did not labor on two, three, six tasks at once, multiprocessing. He knew one thing at a time, and that thing just now was that the day was a victory. He walked briskly back to the hotel. He crossed the lobby in a no-nonsense manner. An impervious man. He did not knock on Cindy's door. He was moving on, moving west. There would be a good job there, and a new life. Perhaps he would take up tennis. Perhaps he would own a Jacuzzi. Perhaps he would learn to like all those peculiar foods people ate out there, like jicama, and seaweed. Perhaps he would go macrobiotic.

It wasn't until he got to his room that he remembered that his telephone had no handset.

He sat on his bed. There was a noise at his window, followed, sure enough, by someone's shadow. He wasn't even surprised. Anyway, the fellow wasn't stopping at Art's room, at least not on this trip. That was luck. *You folk,* Cindy had said, taking back the ice bag. Art could see her perspective; he was luckier than she, by far. But just now, as the shadow crossed his window again, he thought mostly about how unarmed he was. If he had a telephone, he would probably call Lisa—that was how big a pool seemed to be forming around him, all of a sudden; an ocean, it seemed. Also, he would call the police. But first he would call Lisa, and see how she felt about his possibly moving west. *Quite possibly,* he would say, not wanting to make it sound as though he was calling her for nothing—not wanting to make it sound as though he was awash, at sea, perhaps drowning. He would not want to sound like a haunted man; he would not want to sound as though he was calling from a welfare hotel, years too late, to say *Yes, that was a baby we had together, it would have been a baby.* For he could not help now but recall the doctor explaining about that child, a boy, who had appeared so mysteriously perfect in the ultrasound. Transparent, he had looked, and gelatinous, all soft head and quick heart; but he would have, in being born, broken every bone in his body.

Jamaica Kincaid

Jamaica Kincaid, born in 1946, was raised in St. John's, Antigua, where she received a British education. At the age of 17 she immigrated to the United States and worked as an au pair before enrolling in college. She has written a story collection, At the Bottom of the River *(1983); three novels:* Annie John *(1985),* Lucy *(1990), and* Autobiography of My Mother *(1996); and five books of nonfiction, including:* A Small Place *(1988),* Talk Stories *(2000), and the memoir* My Brother *(1997). In an interview with Allan Vorda, she explained a metaphor in "Girl" that is also a controlling idea in many of her voice-driven, subtly political books: "I've come to see that I've worked through the relationship of the mother and the girl to a relationship between Europe and the place that I'm from, which is to say, a relationship between the powerful and the powerless. . . . The mother shows [the girl] how to be in the world, but at the back of her mind she never will get it. She's deeply skeptical that this child could ever grow up to be a self-possessed woman and in the end she reveals her skepticism; yet even within the skepticism is, of course, dismissal and scorn. So it's not unlike the relationship between the conquered and the conqueror."*

Girl

Wash the white clothes on Monday and put them on the stone heap; wash the color clothes on Tuesday and put them on the clothes-line to dry; don't walk barehead in the hot sun; cook pumpkin fritters in very hot sweet oil; soak your little cloths right after you take them off; when buying cotton to make yourself a nice blouse, be sure that it doesn't have gum on it, because that way it won't hold up well after a wash; soak salt fish overnight before you cook it; is it true that you sing benna in Sunday school?; always eat your food in such a way that it won't turn someone else's stomach; on Sundays try to walk like a lady and not like the slut you are so bent on becoming; don't sing benna in Sunday school; you mustn't speak to wharf-rat boys, not even to give directions; don't eat fruits on the street—flies will follow you; *but I don't sing benna on Sundays at all and never in Sunday school;* this is how to sew on a button; this is how to make a buttonhole for the button you have just sewed on; this is how to hem a dress when you see the hem coming down and so to prevent yourself from looking like the slut I know you are so bent on becoming; this is how you iron your father's khaki shirt so that it doesn't have a crease; this is how you iron your father's khaki pants so that they don't have a crease; this is how you grow okra—far from the house, because okra tree harbors red ants; when you are growing dasheen, make sure it gets plenty of water or else it makes your throat itch when you are eating it; this is how you sweep a corner; this is how you sweep a whole house; this is how you sweep a yard; this is how you smile to someone you don't like too much; this is how you smile to someone you don't like at all; this is how you smile to someone you like completely; this is how you set a table for tea; this is how you set a table for dinner; this is how you set a table for dinner with an important guest; this is how you set a table for lunch; this is how you set a table for breakfast; this is how to behave in the presence of men who don't know you very well, and this way they won't recognize immediately the slut I have warned you against becoming; be sure to wash every day, even if it is with your own spit; don't squat down to play marbles—you are not a boy, you know; don't pick people's flowers—you might catch something; don't throw stones at blackbirds, because it might not be a blackbird at all; this is how to make a bread pudding; this is how to make doukona; this is how to make pepper pot; this is how to make a good medicine for a cold; this is how to make a good medicine to throw away a child before it even becomes a child; this is how to catch a fish; this is how to throw back a fish you don't like, and that way something bad won't fall on you; this is how to bully a man; this is how a man bullies you; this is how to love a man, and if this doesn't work there are other ways, and if they don't work don't feel too bad about giving up; this is how to spit up in the air if you feel like it, and this is how to move quick so that it doesn't fall on you; this is how to make ends meet; always squeeze bread to make sure it's fresh; *but what if the baker won't let me feel the bread?*; you mean to say that after all you are really going to be the kind of woman who the baker won't let near the bread?

Jhumpa Lahiri

Jhumpa Lahiri was born in 1967 in London and grew up in Rhode Island. She received her MFA in Creative Writing and Ph.D. in Renaissance Studies from Boston University. Her first collection of stories, Interpreter of Maladies, *won the 2000 Pulitzer Prize for Fiction. She has also published a novel,* The Namesake *(2003). Discussing the role of setting in her work, Lahiri has said: "When I began writing fiction seriously, my first attempts were, for some reason, always set in Calcutta, which is a city I know quite well as a result of repeated visits with my family, sometimes for several months at a time. These trips, to a vast, unruly, fascinating city so different from the small New England town where I was raised, shaped my perceptions of the world and of people from a very early age. I went to Calcutta neither as a tourist nor as a former resident—a valuable position, I think, for a writer. The reason my first stories were set in Calcutta is due partly to that perspective—that necessary combination of distance and intimacy with a place. . . . As most of my characters have an Indian background, India keeps cropping up as a setting, sometimes literally, sometimes more figuratively, in the memory of the characters."*

Interpreter of Maladies

At the tea stall Mr. and Mrs. Das bickered about who should take Tina to the toilet. Eventually Mrs. Das relented when Mr. Das pointed out that he had given the girl her bath the night before. In the rearview mirror Mr. Kapasi watched as Mrs. Das emerged slowly from his bulky white Ambassador, dragging her shaved, largely bare legs across the back seat. She did not hold the little girl's hand as they walked to the rest room.

They were on their way to see the Sun Temple at Konarak. It was a dry, bright Saturday, the mid-July heat tempered by a steady ocean breeze, ideal weather for sightseeing. Ordinarily Mr. Kapasi would not have stopped so soon along the way, but less than five minutes after he'd picked up the family that morning in front of Hotel Sandy Villa, the little girl had complained. The first thing Mr. Kapasi had noticed when he saw Mr. and Mrs. Das, standing with their children under the portico of the hotel, was that they were very young, perhaps not even thirty. In addition to Tina they had two boys, Ronny and Bobby, who appeared very close in age and had teeth covered in a network of flashing silver wires. The family looked Indian but dressed as foreigners did, the children in stiff, brightly colored clothing and caps with translucent visors. Mr. Kapasi was accustomed to foreign tourists; he was assigned to them regularly because he could speak English. Yesterday he had driven an elderly couple from Scotland, both with spotted faces and fluffy white hair so thin it exposed their sunburnt scalps. In comparison, the tanned, youthful faces of Mr. and Mrs. Das were all the more striking. When he'd introduced himself, Mr. Kapasi had pressed his palms together in greeting, but Mr. Das squeezed hands like an American so that Mr. Kapasi felt it in his elbow. Mrs. Das, for her part, had flexed one side of her mouth, smiling dutifully at Mr. Kapasi, without displaying any interest in him.

As they waited at the tea stall, Ronny, who looked like the older of the two boys, clambered suddenly out of the back seat, intrigued by a goat tied to a stake in the ground.

"Don't touch it," Mr. Das said. He glanced up from his paperback tour book, which said "INDIA" in yellow letters and looked as if it had been published abroad. His voice, somehow tentative and a little shrill, sounded as though it had not yet settled into maturity.

"I want to give it a piece of gum," the boy called back as he trotted ahead.

Mr. Das stepped out of the car and stretched his legs by squatting briefly to the ground. A clean-shaven man, he looked exactly like a magnified version of Ronny. He had a sapphire blue visor, and was dressed in shorts, sneakers, and a T-shirt. The camera slung around his neck, with an impressive telephoto lens and numerous buttons and markings, was the only complicated thing he wore. He frowned, watching as Ronny rushed toward the goat, but appeared to have no intention of intervening. "Bobby, make sure that your brother doesn't do anything stupid."

"I don't feel like it," Bobby said, not moving. He was sitting in the front seat beside Mr. Kapasi, studying a picture of the elephant god taped to the glove compartment.

"No need to worry," Mr. Kapasi said. "They are quite tame." Mr. Kapasi was forty-six years old, with receding hair that had gone completely silver, but his butterscotch complexion and his unlined brow, which he treated in spare moments to dabs of lotus-oil balm, made it easy to imagine what he must have looked like at an earlier age. He wore gray trousers and a matching jacket-style shirt, tapered at the waist, with short sleeves and a large pointed collar, made of a thin but durable synthetic material. He had specified both the cut and the fabric to his tailor—it was his preferred uniform for giving tours because it did not get crushed during his long hours behind the wheel. Through the windshield he watched as Ronny circled around the goat, touched it quickly on its side, then trotted back to the car.

"You left India as a child?" Mr. Kapasi asked when Mr. Das had settled once again into the passenger seat.

"Oh, Mina and I were both born in America," Mr. Das announced with an air of sudden confidence. "Born and raised. Our parents live here now, in Assansol. They retired. We visit them every couple years." He turned to watch as the little girl ran toward the car, the wide purple bows of her sundress flopping on her narrow brown shoulders. She was holding to her chest a doll with yellow hair that looked as if it had been chopped, as a punitive measure, with a pair of dull scissors. "This is Tina's first trip to India, isn't it, Tina?"

"I don't have to go to the bathroom anymore," Tina announced.

"Where's Mina?" Mr. Das asked.

Mr. Kapasi found it strange that Mr. Das should refer to his wife by her first name when speaking to the little girl. Tina pointed to where Mrs. Das was purchasing something from one of the shirtless men who worked at the tea stall. Mr. Kapasi heard one of the shirtless men sing a phrase from a popular Hindi love song as Mrs. Das walked back to the car, but she did not appear to understand the words of the song, for she did not express irritation, or embarrassment, or react in any other way to the man's declarations.

He observed her. She wore a red-and-white-checkered skirt that stopped above her knees, slip-on shoes with a square wooden heel, and a close-fitting blouse styled like a man's undershirt. The blouse was decorated at chest-level with a calico appliqué in the shape of a strawberry. She was a short woman, with small hands like paws, her frosty pink fingernails painted to match her lips, and was slightly plump in her figure. Her hair, shorn only a little longer than her husband's, was parted far to one side. She was wearing large dark brown sunglasses with a pinkish tint to them, and carried a big straw bag, almost as big as her torso, shaped like a bowl, with a water bottle poking out of it. She walked slowly, carrying some puffed rice tossed with peanuts and chili peppers in a large packet made from newspapers. Mr. Kapasi turned to Mr. Das.

"Where in America do you live?"

"New Brunswick, New Jersey."

"Next to New York?"

"Exactly. I teach middle school there."

"What subject?"

"Science. In fact, every year I take my students on a trip to the Museum of Natural History in New York City. In a way we have a lot in common, you could say, you and I. How long have you been a tour guide, Mr. Kapasi?"

"Five years."

Mrs. Das reached the car. "How long's the trip?" she asked, shutting the door.

"About two and a half hours," Mr. Kapasi replied.

At this Mrs. Das gave an impatient sigh, as if she had been traveling her whole life without pause. She fanned herself with a folded Bombay film magazine written in English.

"I thought that the Sun Temple is only eighteen miles north of Puri," Mr. Das said, tapping on the tour book.

"The roads to Konarak are poor. Actually it is a distance of fifty-two miles," Mr. Kapasi explained.

Mr. Das nodded, readjusting the camera strap where it had begun to chafe the back of his neck.

Before starting the ignition, Mr. Kapasi reached back to make sure the cranklike locks on the inside of each of the back doors were secured. As soon as the car began to move the little girl began to play with the lock on her side, clicking it with some effort forward and backward, but Mrs. Das said nothing to stop her. She sat a bit slouched at one end of the back seat, not offering her puffed rice to anyone. Ronny and Tina sat on either side of her, both snapping bright green gum.

"Look," Bobby said as the car began to gather speed. He pointed with his finger to the tall trees that lined the road. "Look."

"Monkeys!" Ronny shrieked. "Wow!"

They were seated in groups along the branches, with shining black faces, silver bodies, horizontal eyebrows, and crested heads. Their long gray tails dangled like a series of ropes among the leaves. A few scratched themselves with black leathery hands, or swung their feet, staring as the car passed.

"We call them the hanuman," Mr. Kapasi said. "They are quite common in the area."

As soon as he spoke, one of the monkeys leaped into the middle of the road, causing Mr. Kapasi to brake suddenly. Another bounced onto the hood of the car, then sprang away, Mr. Kapasi beeped his horn. The children began to get excited, sucking in their breath and covering their faces partly with their hands. They had never seen monkeys outside of a zoo, Mr. Das explained. He asked Mr. Kapasi to stop the car so that he could take a picture.

While Mr. Das adjusted his telephoto lens, Mrs. Das reached into her straw bag and pulled out a bottle of colorless nail polish, which she proceeded to stroke on the tip of her index finger.

The little girl stuck out a hand. "Mine too. Mommy, do mine too."

"Leave me alone," Mrs. Das said, blowing on her nail and turning her body slightly. "You're making me mess up."

The little girl occupied herself by buttoning and unbuttoning a pinafore on the doll's plastic body.

"All set," Mr. Das said, replacing the lens cap.

The car rattled considerably as it raced along the dusty road, causing them all to pop up from their seats every now and then, but Mrs. Das continued to polish her nails. Mr. Kapasi eased up on the accelerator, hoping to produce a smoother ride. When he reached for the gearshift the boy in front accommodated him by swinging his hairless knees out of the way. Mr. Kapasi noted that this boy was slightly paler than the other children. "Daddy, why is the driver sitting on the wrong side in this car, too?" the boy asked.

"They all do that here, dummy," Ronny said.

"Don't call your brother a dummy," Mr. Das said. He turned to Mr. Kapasi. "In America, you know . . . it confuses them."

"Oh yes, I am well aware," Mr. Kapasi said. As delicately as he could, he shifted gears again, accelerating as they approached a hill in the road. "I see it on *Dallas,* the steering wheels are on the left-hand side."

"What's *Dallas?*" Tina asked, banging her now naked doll on the seat behind Mr. Kapasi.

"It went off the air," Mr. Das explained. "It's a television show."

They were all like siblings, Mr. Kapasi thought as they passed a row of date trees. Mr. and Mrs. Das behaved like an older brother and sister, not parents. It seemed that they were in charge of the children only for the day; it was hard to believe they were regularly responsible for anything other than themselves. Mr. Das tapped on his lens cap, and his tour book, dragging his thumbnail occasionally across the pages so that they made a scraping sound. Mrs. Das continued to polish her nails. She had still not removed her sunglasses. Every now and then Tina renewed her plea that she wanted her nails done, too, and so at one point Mrs. Das flicked a drop of polish on the little girl's finger before depositing the bottle back inside her straw bag.

"Isn't this an air-conditioned car?" she asked, still blowing on her hand. The window on Tina's side was broken and could not be rolled down.

"Quit complaining," Mr. Das said. "It isn't so hot."

"I told you to get a car with air-conditioning," Mrs. Das continued. "Why do you do this, Raj, just to save a few stupid rupees. What are you saving us, fifty cents?"

Their accents sounded just like the ones Mr. Kapasi heard on American television programs, though not like the ones on *Dallas*.

"Doesn't it get tiresome, Mr. Kapasi, showing people the same thing every day?" Mr. Das asked, rolling down his own window all the way. "Hey, do you mind stopping the car. I just want to get a shot of this guy."

Mr. Kapasi pulled over to the side of the road as Mr. Das took a picture of a barefoot man, his head wrapped in a dirty turban, seated on top of a cart of grain sacks pulled by a pair of bullocks. Both the man and the bullocks were emaciated. In the back seat Mrs. Das gazed out another window, at the sky, where nearly transparent clouds passed quickly in front of one another.

"I look forward to it, actually," Mr. Kapasi said as they continued on their way. "The Sun Temple is one of my favorite places. In that way it is a reward for me. I give tours on Fridays and Saturdays only. I have another job during the week."

"Oh? Where?" Mr. Das asked.

"I work in a doctor's office."

"You're a doctor?"

"I am not a doctor. I work with one. As an interpreter."

"What does a doctor need an interpreter for?"

"He has a number of Gujarati patients. My father was Gujarati, but many people do not speak Gujarati in this area, including the doctor. And so the doctor asked me to work in his office, interpreting what the patients say."

"Interesting. I've never heard of anything like that," Mr. Das said.

Mr. Kapasi shrugged. "It is a job like any other."

"But so romantic," Mrs. Das said dreamily, breaking her extended silence. She lifted her pinkish brown sunglasses and arranged them on top of her head like a tiara. For the first time, her eyes met Mr. Kapasi's in the rearview mirror: pale, a bit small, their gaze fixed but drowsy.

Mr. Das craned to look at her. "What's so romantic about it?"

"I don't know. Something." She shrugged, knitting her brows together for an instant. "Would you like a piece of gum, Mr. Kapasi?" she asked brightly. She reached into her straw bag and handed him a small square wrapped in green-and-white-striped paper. As soon as Mr. Kapasi put the gum in his mouth a thick sweet liquid burst onto his tongue.

"Tell us more about your job, Mr. Kapasi," Mrs. Das said.

"What would you like to know, madame?"

"I don't know," she shrugged, munching on some puffed rice and licking the mustard oil from the corners of her mouth. "Tell us a typical situation." She settled back in her seat, her head tilted in a patch of sun, and closed her eyes. "I want to picture what happens."

"Very well. The other day a man came in with a pain in his throat."

"Did he smoke cigarettes?"

"No. It was very curious. He complained that he felt as if there were long pieces of straw stuck in his throat. When I told the doctor he was able to prescribe the proper medication."

"That's so neat."

"Yes," Mr. Kapasi agreed after some hesitation.

"So these patients are totally dependent on you," Mrs. Das said. She spoke slowly, as if she were thinking aloud. "In a way, more dependent on you than the doctor."

"How do you mean? How could it be?"

"Well, for example, you could tell the doctor that the pain felt like a burning, not straw. The patient would never know what you had told the doctor, and the doctor wouldn't know that you had told the wrong thing. It's a big responsibility."

"Yes, a big responsibility you have there, Mr. Kapasi," Mr. Das agreed.

Mr. Kapasi had never thought of his job in such complimentary terms. To him it was a thankless occupation. He found nothing noble in interpreting people's maladies, assiduously translating the symptoms of so many swollen bones, countless cramps of bellies and bowels, spots on people's palms that changed color, shape, or size. The doctor, nearly half his age, had an affinity for bell-bottom trousers and made humorless jokes about the Congress party. Together they worked in a stale little infirmary where Mr. Kapasi's smartly tailored clothes clung to him in the heat, in spite of the blackened blades of a ceiling fan churning over their heads.

The job was a sign of his failings. In his youth he'd been a devoted scholar of foreign languages, the owner of an impressive collection of dictionaries. He had dreamed of being an interpreter for diplomats and dignitaries, resolving conflicts between people and nations, settling disputes of which he alone could understand both sides. He was a self-educated man. In a series of notebooks, in the evenings before his parents settled his marriage, he had listed the common etymologies of words, and at one point in his life he was confident that he could converse, if given the opportunity, in English, French, Russian, Portuguese, and Italian, not to mention Hindi, Bengali, Orissi, and Gujarati. Now only a handful of European phrases remained in his memory, scattered words for things like saucers and chairs. English was the only non-Indian language he spoke fluently anymore. Mr. Kapasi knew it was not a remarkable talent. Sometimes he feared that his children knew better English than he did, just from watching television. Still, it came in handy for the tours.

He had taken the job as an interpreter after his first son, at the age of seven, contracted typhoid—that was how he had first made the acquaintance of the doctor. At the time Mr. Kapasi had been teaching English in a grammar school, and he bartered his skills as an interpreter to pay the increasingly exorbitant medical bills. In the end the boy had died one evening in his mother's arms, his limbs burning with fever, but then there was the funeral to pay for, and the other children who were born soon enough, and the newer, bigger house, and the good schools and tutors, and the fine shoes and the television, and the countless other ways he tried to console his wife and to keep her from crying in her sleep, and so when the doctor offered to pay him twice as much as he earned at the grammar school, he accepted. Mr. Kapasi knew that his wife had little regard for his career as an interpreter. He knew it reminded her of the son she'd lost, and that she resented the other lives he helped, in his own small way, to save. If ever she referred to his position, she used the phrase "doctor's assistant," as if the process of interpretation were equal to taking someone's temperature, or changing a bedpan. She never asked him about the patients who came to the doctor's office, or said that his job was a big responsibility.

For this reason it flattered Mr. Kapasi that Mrs. Das was so intrigued by his job. Unlike his wife, she had reminded him of its intellectual challenges. She had also used the word "romantic." She did not behave in a romantic way toward her husband, and yet she had used the word to describe him. He wondered if Mr. and Mrs. Das were a bad match, just as he and his wife were. Perhaps they, too, had little in common apart from three children and a decade of their lives. The signs he recognized from his own marriage were there—the bickering, the indifference, the protracted silences. Her sudden interest in him, an interest she did not express in either her husband or her children, was mildly intoxicating. When Mr. Kapasi thought once again about how she had said "romantic," the feeling of intoxication grew.

He began to check his reflection in the rearview mirror as he drove, feeling grateful that he had chosen the gray suit that morning and not the brown one, which tended to sag a little in the knees. From time to time he glanced through the mirror at Mrs. Das. In addition to glancing at her face he glanced at the strawberry between her breasts, and the golden brown hollow in her throat. He decided to tell Mrs. Das about another patient, and another: the young woman who had complained of a sensation of raindrops in her spine, the gentleman whose birthmark had begun to sprout hairs. Mrs. Das listened attentively, stroking her hair with a small plastic brush that resembled an oval bed of nails, asking more questions, for yet another example. The children were quiet, intent on spotting more monkeys in the trees, and Mr. Das was absorbed by his tour book, so it seemed like a private conversation between Mr. Kapasi and Mrs. Das. In this manner the next half hour passed, and when they stopped for lunch at a roadside restaurant that sold fritters and omelette sandwiches, usually something Mr. Kapasi looked forward to on his tours so that he could sit in peace and enjoy some hot tea, he was disappointed. As the Das family settled together under a magenta umbrella fringed with white and orange tassels, and placed their orders with one of the waiters who marched about in tricornered caps, Mr. Kapasi reluctantly headed toward a neighboring table.

"Mr. Kapasi, wait. There's room here," Mrs. Das called out. She gathered Tina onto her lap, insisting that he accompany them. And so, together, they had bottled mango juice and sandwiches and plates of onions and potatoes deep-fried in graham-flour batter. After finishing two omelette sandwiches Mr. Das took more pictures of the group as they ate.

"How much longer?" he asked Mr. Kapasi as he paused to load a new roll of film in the camera.

"About half an hour more."

By now the children had gotten up from the table to look at more monkeys perched in a nearby tree, so there was a considerable space between Mrs. Das and Mr. Kapasi. Mr. Das placed the camera to his face and squeezed one eye shut, his tongue exposed at one corner of his mouth. "This looks funny. Mina, you need to lean in closer to Mr. Kapasi."

She did. He could smell a scent on her skin, like a mixture of whiskey and rosewater. He worried suddenly that she could smell his perspiration, which he knew had collected beneath the synthetic material of his shirt. He polished off his mango juice in one gulp and smoothed his silver hair with his hands. A bit of the juice dripped onto his chin. He wondered if Mrs. Das had noticed.

She had not. "What's your address, Mr. Kapasi?" she inquired, fishing for something inside her straw bag.

"You would like my address?"

"So we can send you copies," she said. "Of the pictures." She handed him a scrap of paper which she had hastily ripped from a page of her film magazine. The blank portion was limited, for the narrow strip was crowded by lines of text and a tiny picture of a hero and heroine embracing under a eucalyptus tree.

The paper curled as Mr. Kapasi wrote his address in clear, careful letters. She would write to him, asking about his days interpreting at the doctor's office, and he would respond eloquently, choosing only the most entertaining anecdotes, ones that would make her laugh out loud as she read them in her house in New Jersey. In time she would reveal the disappointment of her marriage, and he his. In this way their friendship would grow, and flourish. He would possess a picture of the two of them, eating fried onions under a magenta umbrella, which he would keep, he decided, safely tucked between the pages of his Russian grammar. As his mind raced, Mr. Kapasi experienced a mild and pleasant shock. It was similar to a feeling he used to experience long ago when, after months of translating with the aid of a dictionary, he would finally read a passage from a French novel, or an Italian sonnet, and understand the words, one after another, unencumbered by his own efforts. In those moments Mr. Kapasi used to believe that all was right with the world, that all struggles were rewarded, that all of life's mistakes made sense in the end. The promise that he would hear from Mrs. Das now filled him with the same belief.

When he finished writing his address Mr. Kapasi handed her the paper, but as soon as he did so he worried that he had either misspelled his name, or accidentally reversed the numbers of his postal code. He dreaded the possibility of a lost letter, the photograph never reaching him, hovering somewhere in Orissa, close but ultimately unattainable. He thought of asking for the slip of paper again, just to make sure he had written his address accurately, but Mrs. Das had already dropped it into the jumble of her bag.

They reached Konarak at two-thirty. The temple, made of sandstone, was a massive pyramid-like structure in the shape of a chariot. It was dedicated to the great master of life, the sun, which struck three sides of the edifice as it made its journey each day across the sky. Twenty-four giant wheels were carved on the north and south sides of the plinth. The whole thing was drawn by a team of seven horses, speeding as if through the heavens. As they approached, Mr. Kapasi explained that the temple had been built between A.D. 1243 and 1255, with the efforts of twelve hundred artisans, by the great ruler of the Ganga dynasty, King Narasimhadeva the First, to commemorate his victory against the Muslim army.

"It says the temple occupies about a hundred and seventy acres of land," Mr. Das said, reading from his book.

"It's like a desert," Ronny said, his eyes wandering across the sand that stretched on all sides beyond the temple.

"The Chandrabhaga River once flowed one mile north of here. It is dry now," Mr. Kapasi said, turning off the engine.

They got out and walked toward the temple, posing first for pictures by the pair of lions that flanked the steps. Mr. Kapasi led them next to one of the wheels of the chariot, higher than any human being, nine feet in diameter.

"'The wheels are supposed to symbolize the wheel of life,'" Mr. Das read. "'They depict the cycle of creation, preservation, and achievement of realization.' Cool." He turned the page of his book. "'Each wheel is divided into eight thick and thin spokes, dividing the day into eight equal parts. The rims are carved with designs of birds and animals, whereas the medallions in the spokes are carved with women in luxurious poses, largely erotic in nature.'"

What he referred to were the countless friezes of entwined naked bodies, making love in various positions, women clinging to the necks of men, their knees wrapped eternally around their lovers' thighs. In addition to these were assorted scenes from daily life, of hunting and trading, of deer being killed with bows and arrows and marching warriors holding swords in their hands.

It was no longer possible to enter the temple, for it had filled with rubble years ago, but they admired the exterior, as did all the tourists Mr. Kapasi brought there, slowly strolling along each of its sides. Mr. Das trailed behind, taking pictures. The children ran ahead, pointing to figures of naked people, intrigued in particular by the Nagamithunas, the half-human, half-serpentine couples who were said, Mr. Kapasi told them, to live in the deepest waters of the sea. Mr. Kapasi was pleased that they liked the temple, pleased especially that it appealed to Mrs. Das. She stopped every three or four paces, staring silently at the carved lovers, and the processions of elephants, and the topless female musicians beating on two-sided drums.

Though Mr. Kapasi had been to the temple countless times, it occurred to him, as he, too, gazed at the topless women, that he had never seen his own wife fully naked. Even when they had made love she kept the panels of her blouse hooked together, the string of her petticoat knotted around her waist. He had never admired the backs of his wife's legs the way he now admired those of Mrs. Das, walking as if for his benefit alone. He had, of course, seen plenty of bare limbs before, belonging to the American and European ladies who took his tours. But Mrs. Das was different. Unlike the other women, who had an interest only in the temple, and kept their noses buried in a guidebook, or their eyes behind the lens of a camera, Mrs. Das had taken an interest in him.

Mr. Kapasi was anxious to be alone with her, to continue their private conversation, yet he felt nervous to walk at her side. She was lost behind her sunglasses, ignoring her husband's requests that she pose for another picture, walking past her children as if they were strangers. Worried that he might disturb her, Mr. Kapasi walked ahead, to admire, as he always did, the three life-sized bronze avatars of Surya, the sun god, each emerging from its own niche on the temple facade to greet the sun at dawn, noon, and evening. They wore elaborate headdresses, their languid, elongated eyes closed, their bare chests draped with carved chains and amulets. Hibiscus petals, offerings from previous visitors, were strewn at their gray-green feet. The last statue, on the northern wall of the temple, was Mr. Kapasi's favorite. This Surya had a tired expression, weary after a hard day of work, sitting astride a horse with folded legs. Even his horse's eyes were drowsy. Around his body were smaller sculptures of women in pairs, their hips thrust to one side.

"Who's that?" Mrs. Das asked. He was startled to see that she was standing beside him.

"He is the Astachala-Surya," Mr. Kapasi said. "The setting sun."

"So in a couple of hours the sun will set right here?" She slipped a foot out of one of her square-heeled shoes, rubbed her toes on the back of her other leg.

"That is correct."

She raised her sunglasses for a moment, then put them back on again. "Neat."

Mr. Kapasi was not certain exactly what the word suggested, but he had a feeling it was a favorable response. He hoped that Mrs. Das had understood Surya's beauty, his power. Perhaps they would discuss it further in their letters. He would explain things to her, things about India, and she would explain things to him about America. In its own way this correspondence would fulfill his dream, of serving as an interpreter between nations. He looked at her straw bag, delighted that his address lay nestled among its contents. When he pictured her so many thousands of miles away he plummeted, so much so that he had an overwhelming urge to wrap his arms around her, to freeze with her, even for an instant, in an embrace witnessed by his favorite Surya. But Mrs. Das had already started walking.

"When do you return to America?" he asked, trying to sound placid.

"In ten days."

He calculated: A week to settle in, a week to develop the pictures, a few days to compose her letter, two weeks to get to India by air. According to his schedule, allowing room for delays, he would hear from Mrs. Das in approximately six weeks' time.

The family was silent as Mr. Kapasi drove them back, a little past four-thirty, to Hotel Sandy Villa. The children had bought miniature granite versions of the chariot's wheels at a souvenir stand, and they turned them round in their hands. Mr. Das continued to read his book. Mrs. Das untangled Tina's hair with her brush and divided it into two little ponytails.

Mr. Kapasi was beginning to dread the thought of dropping them off. He was not prepared to begin his six-week wait to hear from Mrs. Das. As he stole glances at her in the rearview mirror, wrapping elastic bands around Tina's hair, he wondered how he might make the tour last a little longer. Ordinarily he sped back to Puri using a shortcut, eager to return home, scrub his feet and hands with sandalwood soap, and enjoy the evening newspaper and a cup of tea that his wife would serve him in silence. The thought of that silence, something to which he'd long been resigned, now oppressed him. It was then that he suggested visiting the hills at Udayagiri and Khandagiri, where a number of monastic dwellings were hewn out of the ground, facing one another across a defile. It was some miles away, but well worth seeing, Mr. Kapasi told them.

"Oh yeah, there's something mentioned about it in this book," Mr. Das said. "Built by a Jain king or something."

"Shall we go then?" Mr. Kapasi asked. He paused at a turn in the road. "It's to the left."

Mr. Das turned to look at Mrs. Das. Both of them shrugged.

"Left, left," the children chanted.

Mr. Kapasi turned the wheel, almost delirious with relief. He did not know what he would do or say to Mrs. Das once they arrived at the hills. Perhaps he would tell her what a pleasing smile she had. Perhaps he would compliment her strawberry shirt, which he found irresistibly becoming. Perhaps, when Mr. Das was busy taking a picture, he would take her hand.

He did not have to worry. When they got to the hills, divided by a steep path thick with trees, Mrs. Das refused to get out of the car. All along the path, dozens of monkeys were seated on stones, as well as on the branches of the trees. Their hind legs were stretched out in front and raised to shoulder level, their arms resting on their knees.

"My legs are tired," she said, sinking low in her seat. "I'll stay here."

"Why did you have to wear those stupid shoes?" Mr. Das said. "You won't be in the pictures."

"Pretend I'm there."

"But we could use one of these pictures for our Christmas card this year. We didn't get one of all five of us at the Sun Temple. Mr. Kapasi could take it."

"I'm not coming. Anyway, those monkeys give me the creeps."

"But they're harmless," Mr. Das said. He turned to Mr. Kapasi. "Aren't they?"

"They are more hungry than dangerous," Mr. Kapasi said. "Do not provoke them with food, and they will not bother you."

Mr. Das headed up the defile with the children, the boys at his side, the little girl on his shoulders. Mr. Kapasi watched as they crossed paths with a Japanese man and woman, the only other tourists there, who paused for a final photograph, then stepped into a nearby car and drove away. As the car disappeared out of view some of the monkeys called out, emitting soft whooping sounds, and then walked on their flat black hands and feet up the path. At one point a group of them formed a little ring around Mr. Das and the children. Tina screamed in delight. Ronny ran in circles around his father. Bobby bent down and picked up a fat stick on the ground. When he extended it, one of the monkeys approached him and snatched it, then briefly beat the ground.

"I'll join them," Mr. Kapasi said, unlocking the door on his side. "There is much to explain about the caves."

"No. Stay a minute," Mrs. Das said. She got out of the back seat and slipped in beside Mr. Kapasi. "Raj has his dumb book anyway." Together, through the windshield, Mrs. Das and Mr. Kapasi watched as Bobby and the monkey passed the stick back and forth between them.

"A brave little boy," Mr. Kapasi commented.

"It's not so surprising," Mrs. Das said.

"No?"

"He's not his."

"I beg your pardon?"

"Raj's. He's not Raj's son."

Mr. Kapasi felt a prickle on his skin. He reached into his shirt pocket for the small tin of lotus-oil balm he carried with him at all times, and applied it to three spots on his forehead. He knew that Mrs. Das was watching him, but he did not turn to face her. Instead he watched as the figures of Mr. Das and the children grew smaller, climbing up the steep path, pausing every now and then for a picture, surrounded by a growing number of monkeys.

"Are you surprised?" The way she put it made him choose his words with care.

"It's not the type of thing one assumes," Mr. Kapasi replied slowly. He put the tin of lotus-oil balm back in his pocket.

"No, of course not. And no one knows, of course. No one at all. I've kept it a secret for eight whole years." She looked at Mr. Kapasi, tilting her chin as if to gain a fresh perspective. "But now I've told you."

Mr. Kapasi nodded. He felt suddenly parched, and his forehead was warm and slightly numb from the balm. He considered asking Mrs. Das for a sip of water, then decided against it.

"We met when we were very young," she said. She reached into her straw bag in search of something, then pulled out a packet of puffed rice. "Want some?"

"No, thank you."

She put a fistful in her mouth, sank into the seat a little, and looked away from Mr. Kapasi, out the window on her side of the car. "We married when we were still in college. We were in high school when he proposed. We went to the same college, of course. Back then we couldn't stand the thought of being separated, not for a day, not for a minute. Our parents were best friends who lived in the same town. My entire life I saw him every weekend, either at our house or theirs. We were sent upstairs to play together while our parents joked about our marriage. Imagine! They never caught us at anything, though in a way I think it was all more or less a setup. The things we did those Friday and Saturday nights, while our parents sat downstairs drinking tea . . . I could tell you stories, Mr. Kapasi."

As a result of spending all her time in college with Raj, she continued, she did not make many close friends. There was no one to confide in about him at the end of a difficult day, or to share a passing thought or a worry. Her parents now lived on the other side of the world, but she had never been very close to them, anyway. After marrying so young she was overwhelmed by it all, having a child so quickly, and nursing, and warming up bottles of milk and testing their temperature against her wrist while Raj was at work, dressed in sweaters and corduroy pants, teaching his students about rocks and dinosaurs. Raj never looked cross or harried, or plump as she had become after the first baby.

Always tired, she declined invitations from her one or two college girlfriends, to have lunch or shop in Manhattan. Eventually the friends stopped calling her, so that she was left at home all day with the baby, surrounded by toys that made her trip when she walked or wince when she sat, always cross and tired. Only occasionally did they go out after Ronny was born, and even more rarely did they entertain. Raj didn't mind; he looked forward to coming home from teaching and watching television and bouncing Ronny on his knee. She had been outraged when Raj told her that a Punjabi friend, someone whom she had once met but did not remember, would be staying with them for a week for some job interviews in the New Brunswick area.

Bobby was conceived in the afternoon, on a sofa littered with rubber teething toys, after the friend learned that a London pharmaceutical company had hired him, while Ronny cried to be freed from his playpen. She made no protest when the friend touched the small of her back as she was about to make a pot of coffee, then pulled her against his crisp navy suit. He made love to her swiftly, in silence, with an expertise she had never known, without the meaningful expressions and smiles Raj always insisted on afterward. The next day Raj drove the friend to JFK. He was married now, to a Punjabi girl, and they lived in London still, and every year they exchanged Christmas cards with Raj and Mina, each couple tucking photos of their families into the envelopes. He did not know that he was Bobby's father. He never would.

"I beg your pardon, Mrs. Das, but why have you told me this information?" Mr. Kapasi asked when she had finally finished speaking, and had turned to face him once again.

"For God's sake, stop calling me Mrs. Das. I'm twenty-eight. You probably have children my age."

"Not quite." It disturbed Mr. Kapasi to learn that she thought of him as a parent. The feeling he had had toward her, that had made him check his reflection in the rearview mirror as they drove, evaporated a little.

"I told you because of your talents." She put the packet of puffed rice back into her bag without folding over the top.

"I don't understand," Mr. Kapasi said.

"Don't you see? For eight years I haven't been able to express this to anybody, not to friends, certainly not to Raj. He doesn't even suspect it. He thinks I'm still in love with him. Well, don't you have anything to say?"

"About what?"

"About what I've just told you. About my secret, and about how terrible it makes me feel. I feel terrible looking at my children, and at Raj, always terrible. I have terrible urges, Mr. Kapasi, to throw things away. One day I had the urge to throw everything I own out the window, the television, the children, everything. Don't you think it's unhealthy?"

He was silent.

"Mr. Kapasi, don't you have anything to say? I thought that was your job."

"My job is to give tours, Mrs. Das."

"Not that. Your other job. As an interpreter."

"But we do not face a language barrier. What need is there for an interpreter?"

"That's not what I mean. I would never have told you otherwise. Don't you realize what it means for me to tell you?"

"What does it mean?"

"It means that I'm tired of feeling so terrible all the time. Eight years, Mr. Kapasi, I've been in pain eight years. I was hoping you could help me feel better, say the right thing. Suggest some kind of remedy."

He looked at her, in her red plaid skirt and strawberry T-shirt, a woman not yet thirty, who loved neither her husband nor her children, who had already fallen out of love with life. Her confession depressed him, depressed him all the more when he thought of Mr. Das at the top of the path, Tina clinging to his shoulders, taking pictures of ancient monastic cells cut into the hills to show his students in America, unsuspecting and unaware that one of his sons was not his own. Mr. Kapasi felt insulted that Mrs. Das should ask him to interpret her common, trivial little secret. She did not resemble the patients in the doctor's office, those who came glassy-eyed and desperate, unable to sleep or breathe or urinate with ease, unable, above all, to give words to their pains. Still, Mr. Kapasi believed it was his duty to assist Mrs. Das. Perhaps he ought to tell her to confess the truth to Mr. Das. He would explain that honesty was the best policy. Honesty, surely, would help her feel better, as she'd put it. Perhaps he would offer to preside over the discussion, as a mediator. He decided to begin with the most obvious question, to get to the heart of the matter, and so he asked. "Is it really pain you feel, Mrs. Das, or is it guilt?"

She turned to him and glared, mustard oil thick on her frosty pink lips. She opened her mouth to say something, but as she glared at Mr. Kapasi some certain knowledge seemed to pass before her eyes, and she stopped. It crushed him; he knew at that moment that he was not even important enough to be properly insulted. She opened the car door and began walking up the path, wobbling a little on her square wooden heels, reaching into her straw bag to eat handfuls of puffed rice. It fell through her fingers, leaving a zigzagging trail, causing a monkey to leap down from a tree and devour the little white grains. In search of more, the monkey began to follow Mrs. Das. Others joined him, so that she was soon being followed by about half a dozen of them, their velvety tails dragging behind.

Mr. Kapasi stepped out of the car. He wanted to holler, to alert her in some way, but he worried that if she knew they were behind her, she would grow nervous. Perhaps she would lose her balance. Perhaps they would pull at her bag or her hair. He began to jog up the path, taking a fallen branch in his hand to scare away the monkeys. Mrs. Das continued walking, oblivious, trailing grains of puffed rice. Near the top of the incline, before a group of cells fronted by a row of squat stone pillars, Mr. Das was kneeling on the ground, focusing the lens of his camera. The children stood under the arcade, now hiding, now emerging from view.

"Wait for me," Mrs. Das called out. "I'm coming."

Tina jumped up and down. "Here comes Mommy!"

"Great," Mr. Das said without looking up. "Just in time. We'll get Mr. Kapasi to take a picture of the five of us."

Mr. Kapasi quickened his pace, waving his branch so that the monkeys scampered away, distracted, in another direction.

"Where's Bobby?" Mrs. Das asked when she stopped.

Mr. Das looked up from the camera. "I don't know. Ronny, where's Bobby?"

Ronny shrugged. "I thought he was right here."

"Where is he?" Mrs. Das repeated sharply. "What's wrong with all of you?"

They began calling his name, wandering up and down the path a bit. Because they were calling, they did not initially hear the boy's screams. When they found him, a little farther down the path under a tree, he was surrounded by a group of monkeys, over a dozen of them, pulling at his T-shirt with their long black fingers. The puffed rice Mrs. Das had spilled was scattered at his feet, raked over by the monkeys' hands. The boy was silent, his body frozen, swift tears running down his startled face. His bare legs were dusty and red with welts from where one of the monkeys struck him repeatedly with the stick he had given to it earlier.

"Daddy, the monkey's hurting Bobby," Tina said.

Mr. Das wiped his palms on the front of his shorts. In his nervousness he accidentally pressed the shutter on his camera; the whirring noise of the advancing film excited the monkeys, and the one with the stick began to beat Bobby more intently. "What are we supposed to do? What if they start attacking?"

"Mr. Kapasi," Mrs. Das shrieked, noticing him standing to one side. "Do something, for God's sake, do something!"

Mr. Kapasi took his branch and shooed them away, hissing at the ones that remained, stomping his feet to scare them. The animals retreated slowly, with a measured gait, obedient but unintimidated. Mr. Kapasi gathered Bobby in his arms and brought him back to where his parents and siblings were standing. As he carried him he was tempted to whisper a secret into the boy's ear. But Bobby was stunned, and shivering with fright, his legs bleeding slightly where the stick had broken the skin. When Mr. Kapasi delivered him to his parents, Mr. Das brushed some dirt off the boy's T-shirt and put the visor on him the right way. Mrs. Das reached into her straw bag to find a bandage which she taped over the cut on his knee. Ronny offered his brother a fresh piece of gum. "He's fine. Just a little scared, right, Bobby?" Mr. Das said, patting the top of his head.

"God, let's get out of here," Mrs. Das said. She folded her arms across the strawberry on her chest. "This place gives me the creeps."

"Yeah. Back to the hotel, definitely," Mr. Das agreed.

"Poor Bobby," Mrs. Das said. "Come here a second. Let Mommy fix your hair." Again she reached into her straw bag, this time for her hairbrush, and began to run it around the edges of the translucent visor. When she whipped out the hairbrush, the slip of paper with Mr. Kapasi's address on it fluttered away in the wind. No one but Mr. Kapasi noticed. He watched as it rose, carried higher and higher by the breeze, into the trees where the monkeys now sat, solemnly observing the scene below. Mr. Kapasi observed it too, knowing that this was the picture of the Das family he would preserve forever in his mind.

David Leavitt

David Leavitt was born in 1961 in Pittsburgh and grew up in Northern California. He attended Yale University and had his first New Yorker story published when he was twenty-one. His story collections are the National Book Critics Circle Finalist Family Dancing (1984); A Place I've Never Been (1990), from which "Gravity," a story about a man with AIDS, is taken; and The Marble Quilt (2001). He has written a book of novellas, Arkansas (1997), and six novels: The Lost Language of Cranes (1986), Equal Affections (1989), While England Sleeps (1993), The Page Turner (1998), Martin Bauman; or a Sure Thing (2000), and The Body of Jonah Boyd (2004). Coeditor of The Penguin Book of Gay Short Stories, Leavitt has received fellowships from the Guggenheim Foundation and the National Endowment for the Arts. In a 1984 profile in the New York Times, Leavitt spoke of writing and his generation's lack of social concern: "We are concerned with politics only when it touches our immediate needs. Ours is a generation that is more interested in achieving stability. I believe the phenomenon of Yuppieism stems from that. Yet I consider myself political in my own way. I'm not an activist like my mother, but I do have my own political consciousness."

Gravity

Theo had a choice between a drug that would save his sight and a drug that would keep him alive, so he chose not to go blind. He stopped the pills and started the injections—these required the implantation of an unpleasant and painful catheter just above his heart—and within a few days the clouds in his eyes started to clear up; he could see again. He remembered going into New York City to a show with his mother, when he was twelve and didn't want to admit he needed glasses. "Can you read that?" she'd shouted, pointing to a Broadway marquee, and when he'd squinted, making out only one or two letters, she'd taken off her own glasses—harlequins with tiny rhinestones in the corners—and shoved them onto his face. The world came into focus, and he gasped, astonished at the precision around the edges of things, the legibility, the hard, sharp, colorful landscape. Sylvia had to squint through *Fiddler on the Roof* that day, but for Theo, his face masked by his mother's huge glasses, everything was as bright and vivid as a comic book. Even though people stared at him, and muttered things, Sylvia didn't care; he could *see*.

Because he was dying again, Theo moved back to his mother's house in New Jersey. The DHPG injections she took in stride—she'd seen her own mother through *her* dying, after all. Four times a day, with the equanimity of a nurse, she cleaned out the plastic tube implanted in his chest, inserted a sterilized hypodermic and slowly dripped the bag of sight-giving liquid into his veins. They endured this procedure silently, Sylvia sitting on the side of the hospital bed she'd rented for the duration of Theo's stay—his life, he sometimes thought—watching reruns of *I Love Lucy* or the news, while he tried not to think about the hard piece of pipe stuck into him, even though it was a constant reminder of how wide and unswimmable the gulf was becoming between him and the ever-receding shoreline of the well. And Sylvia was intricately cheerful. Each day she urged him to go out with her somewhere—to the library, or the little museum with the dinosaur replicas he'd been fond of as a child—and when his thinness and the cane drew stares, she'd maneuver him around the people who were staring, determined to shield him from whatever they might say or do. It had been the same that afternoon so many years ago, when she'd pushed him through a lobbyful of curious and laughing faces, determined that nothing should interfere with the spectacle of his seeing. What a pair they must have made, a boy in ugly glasses and a mother daring the world to say a word about it!

This warm, breezy afternoon in May they were shopping for revenge. "Your cousin Howard's engagement party is next month," Sylvia explained in the car. "A very nice girl from Livingston. I met her a few weeks ago, and really, she's a superior person."

"I'm glad," Theo said. "Congratulate Howie for me."

"Do you think you'll be up to going to the party?"

"I'm not sure. Would it be okay for me just to give him a gift?"

"You already have. A lovely silver tray, if I say so myself. The thank-you note's in the living room."

"Mom," Theo said, "why do you always have to—"

Sylvia honked her horn at a truck making an illegal left turn. "Better they should get something than no present at all, is what I say," she said. "But now, the problem is, *I* have to give Howie something, to be from me, and it better be good. It better be very, very good."

"Why?"

"Don't you remember that cheap little nothing Bibi gave you for your graduation? It was disgusting."

"I can't remember what she gave me."

"Of course you can't. It was a tacky pen-and-pencil set. Not even a real leather box. So naturally, it stands to reason that I have to get something truly spectacular for Howard's engagement. Something that will make Bibi blanch. Anyway, I think I've found just the thing, but I need your advice."

"Advice? Well, when my old roommate Nick got married, I gave him a garlic press. It cost five dollars and reflected exactly how much I felt, at that moment, our friendship was worth."

Sylvia laughed. "Clever. But my idea is much more brilliant, because it makes it possible for me to get back at Bibi *and* give Howard the nice gift he and his girl deserve." She smiled, clearly pleased with herself. "Ah, you live and learn."

"You live," Theo said.

Sylvia blinked. "Well, look, here we are." She pulled the car into a handicapped-parking place on Morris Avenue and got out to help Theo, but he was already hoisting himself up out of his seat, using the door handle for leverage. "I can manage myself," he said with some irritation. Sylvia stepped back.

"Clearly one advantage to all this for you," Theo said, balancing on his cane, "is that it's suddenly so much easier to get a parking place."

"Oh Theo, please," Sylvia said. "Look, here's where we're going."

She leaned him into a gift shop filled with porcelain statuettes of Snow White and all seven of the dwarves, music boxes which, when you opened them, played "The Shadow of Your Smile," complicated-smelling potpourris in purple wallpapered boxes, and stuffed snakes you were supposed to push up against drafty windows and doors.

"Mrs. Greenman," said an expansive, gray-haired man in a cream-colored cardigan sweater. "Look who's here, Archie, it's Mrs. Greenman."

Another man, this one thinner and balding, but dressed in an identical cardigan, peered out from the back of the shop. "Hello there!" he said, smiling. He looked at Theo, and his expression changed.

"Mr. Sherman, Mr. Baker. This is my son, Theo."

"Hello," Mr. Sherman and Mr. Baker said. They didn't offer to shake hands.

"Are you here for that item we discussed last week?" Mr. Sherman asked.

"Yes," Sylvia said. "I want advice from my son here." She walked over to a large ridged crystal bowl, a very fifties sort of bowl, stalwart and square-jawed. "What do you think? Beautiful, isn't it?"

"Mom, to tell the truth, I think it's kind of ugly."

"Four hundred and twenty-five dollars," Sylvia said admiringly. "You have to feel it."

Then she picked up the big bowl and tossed it to Theo, like a football.

The gentlemen in the cardigan sweaters gasped and did not exhale. When Theo caught it, it sank his hands. His cane rattled as it hit the floor.

"That's heavy," Sylvia said, observing with satisfaction how the bowl had weighted Theo's arms down. "And where crystal is concerned, heavy is impressive."

She took the bowl back from him and carried it to the counter. Mr. Sherman was mopping his brow. Theo looked at the floor, still surprised not to see shards of glass around his feet.

Since no one else seemed to be volunteering, he bent over and picked up the cane.

"Four hundred and fifty-nine, with tax," Mr. Sherman said, his voice still a bit shaky, and a look of relish came over Sylvia's face as she pulled out her checkbook to pay. Behind the counter, Theo could see Mr. Baker put his hand on his forehead and cast his eyes to the ceiling.

It seemed Sylvia had been looking a long time for something like this, something heavy enough to leave an impression, yet so fragile it could make you sorry.

They headed back out to the car.

"Where can we go now?" Sylvia asked, as she got in. "There must be someplace else to go."

"Home," Theo said. "It's almost time for my medicine."

"Really? Oh. All right." She pulled on her seat belt, inserted the car key in the ignition and sat there.

For just a moment, but perceptibly, her face broke. She squeezed her eyes shut so tight the blue shadow on the lids cracked.

Almost as quickly she was back to normal again, and they were driving. "It's getting hotter," Sylvia said. "Shall I put on the air?"

"Sure." Theo said. He was thinking about the bowl, or more specifically, about how surprising its weight had been, pulling his hands down. For a while now he'd been worried about his mother, worried about what damage his illness might secretly be doing to her that of course she would never admit. On the surface things seemed all right. She still broiled herself a skinned chicken breast for dinner every night, still swam a mile and a half a day, still kept used teabags wrapped in foil in the refrigerator. Yet she had also, at about three o'clock one morning, woken him up to tell him she was going to the twenty-four-hour supermarket, and was there anything he wanted. Then there was the gift shop: She had literally pitched that bowl toward him, pitched it like a ball, and as that great gleam of flight and potential regret came sailing in his direction, it had occurred to him that she was trusting his two feeble hands, out of the whole world, to keep it from shattering. What was she trying to test? Was it his newly regained vision? Was it the assurance that he was there, alive, that he hadn't yet slipped past all her caring, a little lost boy in rhinestone-studded glasses? There are certain things you've already done before you even think how to do them—a child pulled from in front of a car, for instance, or the bowl, which Theo was holding before he could even begin to calculate its brief trajectory. It had pulled his arms down, and from that apish posture he'd looked at his mother, who smiled broadly, as if, in the war between heaviness and shattering, he'd just helped her win some small but sustaining victory.

Ursula K. Le Guin

Ursula K. Le Guin was born in 1929 in Berkeley, California. Best known for her literary science fiction, Le Guin has published many novels, short stories, poems, and essays, and in 1995 received a Lifetime Achievement Award at the World Fantasy Convention. Her short story collections include The Wind's Twelve Quarters *(1975),* The Water Is Wide *(1976),* The Compass Rose *(1982), and* Unlocking the Air *(1996). She is an editor of* The Norton Book of Science Fiction, *and lives in Portland, Oregon. As a writer of science fiction and fantasy, Le Guin recognizes the particular importance of communicating her ideas to a broad audience. In her essay "Where Do You Get Your Ideas From?" she discusses the unique relationship between writer and reader: "When I, the writer, reread my work and settle down to reconsider it, reshape it, revise it, then my consciousness of the reader, of collaborating with the reader, is appropriate and, I think, necessary. Indeed I may have to make an act of faith and declare that they will exist, those unknown, perhaps unborn people, my dear readers. . . . Because the writer cannot do it alone. The unread story is not a story; it is little black marks on wood pulp. The reader, reading it, makes it live: a live thing, a story."*

The Ones Who Walk Away from Omelas

(Variations on a Theme by William James)

With a clamor of bells that set the swallows soaring, the Festival of Summer came to the city Omelas, bright-towered by the sea. The rigging of the boats in harbor sparkled with flags. In the streets between houses with red roofs and painted walls, between old moss-grown gardens and under avenues of trees, past great parks and public buildings, processions moved. Some were decorous: old people in long stiff robes of mauve and grey, grave master workmen, quiet, merry women carrying their babies and chatting as they walked. In other streets the music beat faster, a shimmering of gong and tambourine, and the people went dancing, the procession was a dance. Children dodged in and out, their high calls rising like the swallows' crossing flights over the music and the singing. All the processions wound towards the north side of the city, where on the great water-meadow called the Green Fields boys and girls, naked in the bright air, with mud-stained feet and ankles and long, lithe arms, exercised their restive horses before the race. The horses wore no gear at all but a halter without bit. Their manes were braided with streamers of silver, gold, and green. They flared their nostrils and pranced and boasted to one another; they were vastly excited, the horse being the only animal who has adopted our ceremonies as his own. Far off to the north and west the mountains stood up half encircling Omelas on her bay. The air of morning was so clear that the snow still crowning the Eighteen Peaks burned with white-gold fire across the miles of sunlit air, under the dark blue of the sky. There was just enough wind to make the banners that marked the racecourse snap and flutter now and then. In the silence of the broad green meadows one could hear the music winding through the city streets, farther and nearer and ever approaching, a cheerful faint sweetness of the air that from time to time trembled and gathered together and broke out into the great joyous clanging of the bells.

Joyous! How is one to tell about joy? How describe the citizens of Omelas?

They were not simple folk, you see, though they were happy. But we do not say the words of cheer much any more. All smiles have become archaic. Given a description such as this one tends to make certain assumptions. Given a description such as this one tends to look next for the King, mounted on a splendid stallion and surrounded by his noble knights, or perhaps in a golden litter borne by great-muscled slaves. But there was no king. They did not use swords, or keep slaves. They were not barbarians. I do not know the rules and laws of their society, but I suspect that they were singularly few. As they did without monarchy and slavery, so they also got on without the stock exchange, the advertisement, the secret police, and the bomb. Yet I repeat that these were not simple folk, not dulcet shepherds, noble savages, bland utopians. They were not less complex than us. The trouble is that we have a bad habit, encouraged by pedants and sophisticates, of considering happiness as something rather stupid. Only pain is intellectual, only evil interesting. This is the treason of the artist: a refusal to admit the banality of evil and the terrible boredom of pain. If you can't lick 'em, join 'em. If it hurts, repeat it. But to praise despair is to condemn delight, to embrace violence is to lose hold of everything else. We have almost lost hold, we can no longer describe a happy man, nor make any celebration of joy. How can I tell you about the people of Omelas? They were not naïve and happy children—though their children were, in fact, happy. They were mature, intelligent, passionate adults whose lives were not wretched. O miracle! but I wish I could describe it better. I wish I could convince you. Omelas sounds in my words like a city in a fairy tale, long ago and far away, once upon a time. Perhaps it would be best if you imagined it as your own fancy bids, assuming it will rise to the occasion, for certainly I cannot suit you all. For instance, how about technology? I think that there would be no cars or helicopters in and above the streets; this follows from the fact that the people of Omelas are happy people. Happiness is based on a just discrimination of what is necessary, what is neither necessary nor destructive, and what is destructive. In the middle category, however—that of the unnecessary but undestructive, that of comfort, luxury, exuberance, etc.—they could perfectly well have central heating, subway trains, washing machines, and all kinds of marvelous devices not yet invented here, floating light-sources, fuelless power, a cure for the common cold. Or they could have none of that: it doesn't matter. As you like it. I incline to think that people from towns up and down the coast have been coming in to Omelas during the last days before the Festival on very fast little trains and double-decked trams, and that the train station of Omelas is actually the handsomest building in town, though plainer than the magnificent Farmers' Market. But even granted trains, I fear that Omelas so far strikes some of you as goody-goody. Smiles, bells, parades, horses, bleh. If so, please add an orgy. If an orgy would help, don't hesitate. Let us not, however, have temples from which issue beautiful nude priests and priestesses already half in ecstasy and ready to copulate with any man or woman, lover or stranger, who desires union with the deep godhead of the blood, although that was my first idea. But really it would be better not to have any temples in Omelas—at least, not manned temples. Religion yes, clergy no. Surely the beautiful nudes can just wander about, offering themselves like divine souffles to the hunger of the needy and the rapture of the flesh. Let them join the processions. Let tambourines be struck above the copulations, and the glory of desire be proclaimed upon the gongs, and (a not unimportant point) let the offspring of these delightful rituals be beloved and looked after by all. One thing I know there is none of in Omelas is guilt. But what else should there be? I thought at first there were no drugs, but that is puritanical. For those who like it, the faint insistent sweetness of *drooz* may perfume the ways of the city, *drooz* which first brings a great lightness and brilliance to the mind and limbs, and then after some hours a dreamy languor, and wonderful visions at last of the very arcana and inmost secrets of the Universe, as well as exciting the pleasure of sex beyond all belief; and it is not habit-forming. For more modest tastes I think there ought to be beer. What else, what else belongs in the joyous city? The sense of victory, surely, the celebration of courage. But as we did without clergy, let us do without soldiers. The joy built upon successful slaughter is not the right kind of joy; it will not do; it is fearful and it is trivial. A boundless and generous contentment, a magnanimous triumph felt not against some outer enemy but in communion with the finest and fairest in the souls of all men everywhere and the splendor of the world's summer: this is what swells the hearts of the people of Omelas, and the victory they celebrate is that of life. I really don't think many of them need to take *drooz*.

Most of the procession have reached the Green Fields by now. A marvelous smell of cooking goes forth from the red and blue tents of the provisioners. The faces of small children are amiably sticky; in the benign grey beard of a man a couple of crumbs of rich pastry are entangled. The youths and girls have mounted their horses and are beginning to group around the starting line of the course. An old woman, small, fat, and laughing, is passing out flowers from a basket, and tall young men wear her flowers in their shining hair. A child of nine or ten sits at the edge of the crowd, alone, playing on a wooden flute. People pause to listen, and they smile, but they do not speak to him, for he never ceases playing and never sees them, his dark eyes wholly rapt in the sweet, thin magic of the tune.

He finishes, and slowly lowers his hands holding the wooden flute.

As if that little private silence were the signal, all at once a trumpet sounds from the pavilion near the starting line: imperious, melancholy, piercing. The horses rear on their slender legs, and some of them neigh in answer. Sober-faced, the young riders stroke the horses' necks and soothe them, whispering, "Quiet, quiet, there my beauty, my hope. . . ." They begin to form in rank along the starting line. The crowds along the racecourse are like a field of grass and flowers in the wind. The Festival of Summer has begun.

Do you believe? Do you accept the festival, the city, the joy? No? Then let me describe one more thing.

In a basement under one of the beautiful public buildings of Omelas, or perhaps in the cellar of one of its more spacious private homes, there is a room. It has one locked door, and no window. A little light seeps in dustily between cracks in the boards, secondhand from a cobwebbed window somewhere across the cellar. In one corner of the little room a couple of mops, with stiff, clotted, foul-smelling heads, stand near a rusty bucket. The floor is dirt, a little damp to the touch, as cellar dirt usually is. The room is about three paces long and two wide: a mere broom closet or disused tool room. In the room a child is sitting. It could be a boy or a girl. It looks about six, but actually is nearly ten. It is feeble-minded. Perhaps it was born defective, or perhaps it has become imbecile through fear, malnutrition, and neglect. It picks its nose and occasionally fumbles vaguely with its toes or genitals, as it sits hunched in the corner farthest from the bucket and the two mops. It is afraid of the mops. It finds them horrible. It shuts its eyes, but it knows the mops are still standing there; and the door is locked; and nobody will come. The door is always locked; and nobody ever comes, except that sometimes—the child has no understanding of time or interval—sometimes the door rattles terribly and opens, and a person, or several people, are there. One of them may come in and kick the child to make it stand up. The others never come close, but peer in at it with frightened, disgusted eyes. The food bowl and the water jug are hastily filled, the door is locked, the eyes disappear. The people at the door never say anything, but the child, who has not always lived in the tool room, and can remember sunlight and its mother's voice, sometimes speaks. "I will be good," it says. "Please let me out. I will be good!" They never answer. The child used to scream for help at night, and cry a good deal, but now it only makes a kind of whining, "eh-haa, eh-haa," and it speaks less and less often. It is so thin there are no calves to its legs; its belly protrudes; it lives on a half-bowl of corn meal and grease a day. It is naked. Its buttocks and thighs are a mass of festered sores, as it sits in its own excrement continually.

They all know it is there, all the people of Omelas. Some of them have come to see it, others are content merely to know it is there. They all know that it has to be there. Some of them understand why, and some do not, but they all understand that their happiness, the beauty of their city, the tenderness of their friendships, the health of their children, the wisdom of their scholars, the skill of their makers, even the abundance of their harvest and the kindly weathers of their skies, depend wholly on this child's abominable misery.

This is usually explained to children when they are between eight and twelve, whenever they seem capable of understanding; and most of those who come to see the child are young people, though often enough an adult comes, or comes back, to see the child. No matter how well the matter has been explained to them, these young spectators are always shocked and sickened at the sight. They feel disgust, which they had thought themselves superior to. They feel anger, outrage, impotence, despise all the explanations. They would like to do something for the child. But there is nothing they can do. If the child were brought up into the sunlight out of the vile place, if it were cleaned and fed and comforted, that would be a good thing, indeed; but if it were done, in that day and hour all the prosperity and beauty and delight of Omelas would wither and be destroyed. Those are the terms. To exchange all the goodness and grace of every life in Omelas for that single, small improvement: to throw away the happiness of thousands for the chance of the happiness of one: that would be to let guilt within the walls indeed.

The terms are strict and absolute; there may not even be a kind word spoken to the child.

Often the young people go home in tears, or in a tearless rage, when they have seen the child and faced this terrible paradox. They may brood over it for weeks or years. But as time goes on they begin to realize that even if the child could be released, it would not get much good of its freedom: a little vague pleasure of warmth and food, no doubt, but little more. It is too degraded and imbecile to know any real joy. It has been afraid too long ever to be free of fear. Its habits are too uncouth for it to respond to humane treatment. Indeed, after so long it would probably be wretched without walls about it to protect it, and darkness for its eyes, and its own excrement to sit in. Their tears at the bitter injustice dry when they begin to perceive the terrible justice of reality, and to accept it. Yet it is their tears and anger, the trying of their generosity and the acceptance of their helplessness, which are perhaps the true source of the splendor of their lives. Theirs is no vapid, irresponsible happiness. They know that they, like the child, are not free. They know compassion. It is the existence of the child, and their knowledge of its existence, that makes possible the nobility of their architecture, the poignancy of their music, the profundity of their science. It is because of the child that they are so gentle with children. They know that if the wretched one were not there snivelling in the dark, the other one, the flute-player, could make no joyful music as the young riders line up in their beauty for the race in the sunlight of the first morning of summer.

Now do you believe in them? Are they not more credible? But there is one more thing to tell, and this is quite incredible.

At times one of the adolescent girls or boys who go to see the child does not go home to weep or rage, does not, in fact, go home at all. Sometimes also a man or woman much older falls silent for a day or two, and then leaves home. These people go out into the street, and walk down the street alone. They keep walking, and walk straight out of the city of Omelas, through the beautiful gates. They keep walking across the farmlands of Omelas. Each one goes alone, youth or girl, man or woman. Night falls; the traveler must pass down village streets, between the houses with yellow-lit windows, and on out into the darkness of the fields. Each alone, they go west or north, towards the mountains. They go on. They leave Omelas, they walk ahead into the darkness, and they do not come back. The place they go towards is a place even less imaginable to most of us than the city of happiness. I cannot describe it at all. It is possible that it does not exist. But they seem to know where they are going, the ones who walk away from Omelas.

David Wong Louie

David Wong Louie was born in 1954 on Long Island, New York. He received degrees from Vassar College and The University of Iowa Writers Workshop, worked briefly in advertising in New York, and currently teaches in the Department of English and the Asian American Studies Center at UCLA. He is the author of two acclaimed books of fiction: the short story collection Pangs of Love *(1991) and the novel* The Barbarians Are Coming *(2000). His work combines pathos and humor in dealing with complex issues of Chinese American identity, immigration, and alienation. In an interview with 30/30 Louie discussed his childhood and some of the symbols at work in his story "Cold-Hearted": "I grew up in a home full of symbols. Nothing was the thing itself. As a kid I constantly thought in terms of similes, translating the world to myself: 'Object A is like. . . .' The two refrigerators [in 'Cold-Hearted'] are found symbols. The mother—another symbol—keeps their shelves and drawers crammed with food products hidden in brown paper bags. In a parallel universe she is [the artist] Christo. No one can discern one lumpy mass from another, but she seems to see through to its treasure. Even after her enlightened offspring introduce her to cellophane wrap—but the bags are plentiful and free!—she adheres to her old practice, which, of course, isn't Chinese, but feels that way."*

Cold-Hearted

His father had disappeared. Opened the freezer, pulled out two steaks, and was gone. His mother had said so. A woman incapable of lies. Driving south across the Sound, Lawrence Lung remembered how Genius used to run his seashell-thick thumbnail along the plastic wrap that covered the supermarket steaks, tracing the T-shaped bones. "Best money can buy," he would say. This was nothing but a father imparting the facts of life to his son. So when his mother called him, the youngest of four, only boy, and closest to home, the fact of the steaks did not faze him. What did though was the suit. She said he was wearing his suit. And where could he be going in his suit, she wanted to know? It was the only one he owned, a decades-old, double-breasted number straight off the set of *The Untouchables*, with lapels as broad as shark fins, raspberry and navy pinstripes on dark gray wool cloth. There were the photos of Genius, taken in his early days in the U.S.: suit, white hat, cigarette, a mischievous light in his eyes. This was the man he sent across seas to the wife he left in Hong Kong. He wore it on special occasions, weddings, banquets, funerals, the day Lawrence was born. He seemed taller in the suit, more substantial, even though he had obviously bought it a size or two too big, expecting to grow into the wide shoulders and waist, the long sleeves and pant legs, and from an early age Lawrence knew it would one day be his by default, the three sisters posing no competition, his inheritance, and that was just fine, he thought, as long as it did not come with the man inside.

■ ■ ■

As soon as he got home Lawrence went straight for the refrigerators. It was his habit, how it was to be at home. One refrigerator, then the next, opening the doors and looking, but knowing there was nothing in there he'd want to eat. As his mother repeated the story of the vanishing husband, the very same one she had told him, almost to the word, over the phone, he moved busily back and forth between these obese twins, set side by side, one's motor whirring on, then the other's. On a good day, if he were lucky, he might find a bottle of Coke stuffed among the paper bags of oranges, greens, and roots; the bundles of medicinal herbs, twigs, bark, berries, and what looked like worms bound with pink cellophane ribbon; there were see-through packages of black mushrooms and funky salted fish; wrappers of duck sausage and waxy pork bellies; take-out boxes with scraps of roast pig, roast liver, roast ribs; jars of oysters, shrimp, wood ears, lily buds; and dishes and bowls, of metal and porcelain, stacked one on top of the other, holding left-overs that had been reheated and re-served so many times not a trace of nutrients or flavor lingered in their pale cells. It was barefoot food, food eaten with sticks, under harvest moons. Rinse off the maggots, slice, and steam. It was squatting in still water food, water snake around your ankle food. Pole across your shoulders, hooves in the house food.

It was among the embarrassments of his youth. Thanks to his oldest sister, Lucy, the family flirted from time to time with real food. What real people ate. With forks and knives, your own plate, your own portions, no more dipping into the communal soup bowl. Food from boxes and cans. The best were Swanson TV dinners. Meat loaf, Salisbury steak. He was convinced Salisbury steak was served in the White House every night. Meat in one compartment, vegetable medley in another, apple crisp next door. What a concept! Everything had its own house or its own room. That was how real people lived. By the time Lawrence was eleven, he had cooked his first meal: roast beef, Green Giant canned corn, Betty Crocker instant mashed potatoes, Pillsbury Pop 'n' Fresh rolls. Call it the march of generations.

They were not a family of big eaters. Lily and Patty pecked. Lucy consistently left half her rice. Lawrence and his parents were the family jaws, though since his operation his father had slacked off from his usual two-bowl pace. Consider this then: as the household was presently constituted there was a three-to-two diner-to-refrigerator ratio.

Lawrence was partly responsible for the excess. He had helped his father bring the second refrigerator home. It happened one New Year's Eve, Lawrence returning from school to find his sisters already pressed into service of the new year, scrubbing and dusting and vacuuming every inch of the store for that clean start, just as they would for the same reason wash their feet and hair later that night. In the kitchen his mother was frying the New Year's fish, a porgy for the ancestors, while his father sat like an ancestor himself, stolid, in a nimbus of smoke, his hand serving his Lucky Strikes up to his lips, the cigarette like a thick stick of incense, the action like a prayer to his own spirit.

"Where have you been?" his father asked, pouring a cup of hot water into a bowl of broken saltines and evaporated milk. He had been awaiting his return and motioned for Lawrence to eat.

When he finished they went out to the backyard, the parking lot, and Pop handed Lawrence the keys to the family car. Pop did not drive and Lawrence only had a learner's permit. Lawrence turned the ignition, the engine churned, started, and stalled. Ma stuck her head out the metal door; the expression on her face was a hybrid of hurt and confusion, and before she could utter a word the engine turned over and Lawrence gave her the gas and she roared at Ma, and Pop yanked down on the bill of his orange hunting cap and tapped the gearshift, signaling Lawrence to go.

Lawrence was a good driver even without a license. He liked the idea he and his father might get into trouble together. Bad boys. He didn't see how he could lose: "He made me do it, Officer," he would say, his finger like a gun at the earflap on Pop's cap. And now he got to drive without the encumbrance of his nervous driver's ed teacher or his bossy sisters. For the briefest instant Lawrence wondered why his father had not enlisted one of his sisters, and that way kept things legal, instead of waiting for him to come home from school. But hadn't Pop always waited for Lawrence? Waited for a son as his wife delivered girl after girl after girl; waited for the son to mature into a second pair of hands to help him with his chores; waited for him to turn into a set of wheels. He knew that was all there was to it. He knew that he wasn't singled out as someone special, someone necessary.

Lawrence played with the radio dial and he was pleased, impressed even, by how adept he was at the maneuver. He switched on the heater, the blower on *high* then *lo,* and tried the wipers and upped the volume on the radio. When somebody honked he honked back; long blasts, as if to say, "YOU'RE WELCOME. I LIKE THE WAY YOU DRIVE TOO!" After the rush of that first honk, he clutched the steering wheel at the ten o'clock and two o'clock positions and braced for his father's fierce bark or flying hand or both. But there was no reprimand, no thwack to the back of his head. For a split second he felt cheated. He glanced over at Pop. He was sitting on the edge of the vinyl seat, gripping the dash with both hands, his body so rigid one high-pitched screech and he'd shatter like glass. It was then Lawrence realized that in the car the rules that governed their life together had changed. Their common ground had shifted, a tremor enough to make you stop and reevaluate your days. As illegal as he was in the car it looked far worse for his father. Whatever advantage Pop might have claimed by virtue of his age he had forfeited when he slid in next to Lawrence and told him to go.

Then he told him to stop. They were in the middle of a tree-lined street of brick houses and, up ahead at the intersection, businesses, including a laundry run by a family friend. Lawrence eased off the brake, letting the car roll; it only stood to reason that "stop" meant at the corner. "Stop," Pop said. "We've arrived."

"What do you mean? Arrived where?"

Pop looked over his shoulder, out the rear window, and Lawrence put the car in reverse, driving to meet his father's gaze.

"We've arrived," Pop said excitedly, once, twice. He bounded from the car, circled past the front end, crossed the street. Lawrence had never seen him so frisky. There on the curb he grabbed the handle of a discarded refrigerator, as if he were shaking its hand.

It was colder outside than it could ever be inside a refrigerator.

"How do you like it?" his father asked.

Lawrence had never thought of a refrigerator as something you liked. It was just there, like your arms or your teeth. He shrugged.

"I won it," he said. "It's all mine."

Lawrence wasn't sure but he thought he heard bragging in Pop's voice. And why shouldn't he brag, he reasoned, a refrigerator is—if nothing else—impressive for its size. Then he quickly recognized that this particular refrigerator was no prize from *Let's Make a Deal*. It was nothing more than a big piece of junk. What had he won but hundreds of pounds of garbage? It was an old Frigidaire with rounded corners like a bar of soap and a dent where its heart would be if this were the body of a man.

His father removed a homemade dolly from the trunk of the car. Double-thick plywood and black supermarket carriage wheels. Then a length of coarse rope. "Two are always better than one," Pop said. "Has to be that way, except maybe in the case of children." He was pleased with himself, making a joke at others' expense, as the cigar-smoking men in tuxedos did on television. Then he said in English, "I have two kit, I feed two mouth. I have four kit, I feed four mouth. I have two refrigerator, we have more food to eat. Hey, *goong hee faht toy.*" He chuckled. "This way New Year start off in very good style."

Snow started falling, large heavy flakes. Lawrence and his father inched the refrigerator off the curb and onto the dolly positioned in the gutter, the icy snow acting as a lubricant. "Does this thing work?" Lawrence asked.

"It has to work," he said. "It's all mine now! Good machine better than money. Money you spend; no more; all gone. Paper turn into air. But a machine like this refrigerator is different. If I keep it full up, it always give you plenty good food to eat."

Following his father's directions Lawrence backed the car inches shy of the Frigidaire. Pop lashed the refrigerator to the car's bumper, then twined a draped bedsheet over it. "Chinese people don't like to show off," his father said, addressing the look of disapprobation Lawrence wore. "We don't want to call attention to ourselves. I don't want people to say, Oh look at that big shot, he must have won that nice refrigerator."

Even from his sixteen-year-old's perspective Lawrence was dubious about his father's scheme. Such an opinion was fully consistent with others he held for whatever his father did or whatever he put his mind to doing. Pop's intentions and deeds arrived in Lawrence's brain like the sight of a man who tips his hat and reveals a head of blue hair; the man is a whole human being, bearing all the requisite parts, but at the same time everything about him feels wrong, patently untrustworthy.

Lawrence put the car in drive. The tug at his rear made him feel suddenly important, heroic. The enormous weight, the mystery beneath the white sheet, his father's winnings and how he would not brag on it to the world, the big snow and hard wind, the wipers barely keeping pace with the storm, the wheels' flimsy contact with the road.

His father was smoking, more relaxed now than he was before, and when his son reached for a cigarette fully expecting his hand would be slapped away Pop tilted the package to facilitate the maneuver.

"One time," his father said, flicking his steel lighter in his son's direction, as if it were a cigar in celebration of the birth of a son, the sheet-swathed baby riding in back.

When Lawrence turned his head to catch the light, when his eyes momentarily left the road, when he sucked in the first big smoke and coughed into his hand, the traffic light changed from yellow to red without his notice, and the snow-slick road itself seemed to move, as he honked his horn and slammed on the brakes in this winter world with its white cars and white roads and white headlight beams. All he could see in his panic was the black word "STOP!" like soot stamped on his mind's eye and all he could feel was shame building like a fire under his collar, a heat as mean as hardware on a burning door, and all around him he could smell it: the tobacco, the metal, the vinyl, the heater, the sudden aging of the man and the boy within the compartment.

Cars everywhere were honking. Theirs had skidded nearly perpendicular to the traffic flow. He could have killed them both, they came that close to crashing. And before his heart stopped racing and the pulse in his temples calmed, once that slow wave of relief and gratitude had passed, he saw how the worst could have just happened, and how he couldn't even blame Pop for it, and how Pop couldn't really pin this one on him.

When he started the car again he felt a lightness. A release, your opponent in a tug-of-war letting go. In the rearview the Frigidaire was free between lanes of traffic. A snowman adrift on wheels. A car swerved to avoid it. The car's driver sped up until their cars were rolling side by side and the driver honked his horn impatiently and Lawrence motioned for Pop to lower his window and he did and the driver and his buddy stared into their car, two men with blue eyes who seemed to own the road, and the driver sneered, "Oh, it's just some crazy chinks," and as they laughed at his father—they couldn't have been laughing at Lawrence—Lawrence came to the quick conclusion that these two thugs were right, there was something unerringly Chinese about hauling this useless machine, a won-at-cards slant-eyed prize, garbage-picker special, tethered to the car like Gregory Peck on the back of the Great White Whale; he could not imagine his friends and their dads doing likewise in their Electras or Continentals. Then as the other car peeled away in the slickness his father stuck his orange-hunting-capped head out the window, bracing himself with his Lucky Strike hand, and shouted, "Fuck you!" without a trace of accent, and flipped them off with his free hand, the right one, the one that lit the matches and in anger struck the blows. It was all too much for Lawrence. If Pop had a hold of that car he would have torn loose the hood, tossed the engine into their laps. Instead he had a hold of Lawrence, his hot words ripping a hole in his chest as fresh and smoky as the one those men just shot through his boy soul.

They parked and curbed the refrigerator. Pop told him to telephone one of his road-legal sisters. He brought out a palmful of change and let Lawrence pick his own coins for the call. This was unexpected, something new, dipping into his personal till, like drawing blood, and he didn't flinch. Lawrence could smell the metal warmed by the heat of his leg. Drawing twice, two nickels.

Through the storm Lawrence walked to a pay phone, called home, and when he returned to his father he was standing beside the Frigidaire, both covered with snow. He wondered why he had not taken shelter inside the car but decided not to ask. He wanted to remember his father's imitation of a real man, the man with the dangerous voice, the man with a palm of silver.

They sat in the car. Lawrence suggested they wait at Uncle Law's place, Pop's friend's laundry up the block. Warm and steamy, fragrant with pressed cotton. Maybe even score a cup of hot tea. But Pop wouldn't bite. He had lost face, his only son having failed him.

When Patty arrived, Pop stuffed a five-dollar bill in Lawrence's jacket and zipped the pocket. A surprise reward. Perhaps he wasn't so disappointed after all. Then his father and sister drove home. Lawrence was left guarding the refrigerator, and even as day darkened, and cold cut crosswise against his cheeks he did not stray from his post.

When Pop returned with the upholstery man neighbor and his truck he said Lawrence was *saw-saw* for waiting outside by the refrigerator rather than waiting in the car. "Did you think it was going to run away?" he asked. After a protracted struggle they loaded the refrigerator onto the truck. As he was about to climb into the cab, his father grabbed Lawrence by his jacket sleeve. Pop would give thanks now,

Lawrence thought, for a job well done, mission accomplished. Pin a medal on his chest, plant a kiss on his cheek, shake his hand firmly, tousle his hair. Robert Young and Fred MacMurray, slippered and piped, their depthless compassion and broad streaks of sanity, as white as their starched shirts. Right then, in the exhilarating moment of anticipation, the upholstery truck's idling motor was music, its blue-burning oil perfume. But what Pop did was unzip Lawrence's pocket and filch the five-dollar bill—a tip for the upholstery man.

Later that night after the New Year's Eve feast and the chores and the homework, when everyone was washing their feet before sleeping into the next year and all the sinks and pails were occupied, Pop filled his refrigerator's vegetable drawers with hot soapy water and rolled up his pants and plunged his blue-white feet in and said, "Who said it's good for nothing?" He had cleaned his prize with Comet cleanser, scrubbing away dirt as well as paint, and defended it against the girls' wisecracks, and by now had shed whatever diffidence he felt when he first introduced this newest member of the clan. Then he plugged the Frigidaire in and sat there, with the door open, soaking his feet, wiping down its insides, using a rag and soapy water from the vegetable bin. No one could see his face but Lawrence was on to him. Cut off from the rest of the family, his father basked in the refrigerator's chilled air, in its silvery vapors, and the glow of its measly light. What Lawrence saw in his father's gentle cleaning of each egg holder's deep dimple was kindness, and the pang Lawrence felt, like fingers fanning in his throat, was envy, and the motor's hum were murmurings of love. And he wondered then, if he'd ever be so brave as to love like that. A machine or the man.

Reginald McKnight

Reginald McKnight was born in 1951 in Fürstenfeldbruck, Germany. After receiving a degree from Colorado College he won a fellowship to study and write in Senegal, which became a focal point in several of his works. He has published the short story collections Moustapha's Eclipse *(1988),* The Kind of Light That Shines on Texas *(1992), and* White Boys and Other Stories *(1998); and the novels* I Get on the Bus *(1990) and* He Sleeps *(2001). Discussing themes and characters in his work, McKnight has said: "I think that very generally my work deals with the deracinated African-Americans who came of age after the civil rights struggle. . . . They're part of the struggle whether they want to be or not, for they are in the thick of the white world, daily being judged by their employers, peers, et cetera as to the depths of their intellects and souls. They're the ones who, like other ethnic peoples in this nation's history, often lose their culture in exchange for the material and intellectual fruits that the dominant culture has for so long been heir to. They lose the culture sometimes, but not their color. That color, in the eyes of many non-African-Americans, calls up fear, rage, and derision, whether deserved or not. And often in these rootless blacks a self-hatred takes hold, or a pathological passiveness, an emptiness."*

The Kind of Light That Shines on Texas

I never liked Marvin Pruitt. Never liked him, never knew him, even though there were only three of us in the class. Three black kids. In our school there were fourteen classrooms of thirty-odd white kids (in '66, they considered Chicanos provisionally white) and three or four black kids. Primary school in primary colors. Neat division. Alphabetized. They didn't stick us in the back, or arrange us by degrees of hue, apartheidlike. This was real integration, a ten-to-one ratio as tidy as upper-class landscaping. If it all worked, you could have ten white kids all to yourself. They could talk to you, get the feel of you, scrutinize you bone deep if they wanted to. They seldom wanted to, and that was fine with me for two reasons. The first was that their scrutiny was irritating. How do you comb your hair—why do you comb your hair— may I please touch your hair—were the kinds of questions they asked. This is no way to feel at home. The second reason was Marvin. He embarrassed me. He smelled bad, was at least two grades behind, was hostile, dark skinned, homely, close-mouthed. I feared him for his size, pitied him for his dress, watched him all the time. Marveled at him, mystified, astonished, uneasy.

He had the habit of spitting on his right arm, juicing it down till it would glisten. He would start in immediately after taking his seat when we'd finished with the Pledge of Allegiance, "The Yellow Rose of Texas," "The Eyes of Texas Are upon You," and "Mistress Shady." Marvin would rub his spitflecked arm with his left hand, rub and roll as if polishing an ebony pool cue. Then he would rest his head in the crook of his arm, sniffing, huffing deep like black-jacket boys huff bagsful of acrylics. After ten minutes or so, his eyes would close, heavy. He would sleep till recess. Mrs. Wickham would let him.

There was one other black kid in our class. A girl they called Ah-so. I never learned what she did to earn this name. There was nothing Asian about this big-shouldered girl. She was the tallest, heaviest kid in school. She was quiet, but I don't think any one of us was subtle or so-phisticated enough to nickname our classmates according to any but physical attributes. Fat kids were called Porky or Butterball, skinny ones were called Stick or Ichabod. Ah-so was big, thick, and African. She would impassively sit, sullen, silent as Marvin. She wore the same dark blue pleated skirt every day, the same ruffled white blouse every day. Her skin always shone as if worked by Marvin's palms and fingers. I never spoke one word to her, nor she to me.

Of the three of us, Mrs. Wickham called only on Ah-so and me. Ah-so never answered one question, correctly or incorrectly, so far as I can recall. She wasn't stupid. When asked to read aloud she read well, sel-dom stumbling over long words, reading with humor and expression. But when Wickham asked her about Farmer Brown and how many cows, or the capital of Vermont, or the date of this war or that, Ah-so never spoke. Not one word. But you always felt she could have an-swered those questions if she'd wanted to. I sensed no tension, embar-rassment, or anger in Ah-so's reticence. She simply refused to speak. There was something unshakable about her, some core so impenetrably solid, you got the feeling that if you stood too close to her she could eat your thoughts like a black star eats light. I didn't despise Ah-so as I de-spised Marvin. There was nothing malevolent about her. She sat like a great icon in the back of the classroom, tranquil, guarded, sealed up, watchful. She was close to sixteen, and it was my guess she'd given up on school. Perhaps she was just obliging the wishes of her family, stick-ing it out till the law could no longer reach her.

There were at least half a dozen older kids in our class. Besides Marvin and Ah-so there was Oakley, who sat behind me, whispering threats into my ear; Varna Willard with the large breasts; Eddie Limon, who played bass for a high school rock band; and Lawrence Ridderbeck, who everyone said had a kid and a wife. You couldn't expect me to know anything about Texan educational practices of the 1960s, so I never knew why there were so many older kids in my sixth-grade class. After all, I was just a boy and had transferred into the school around midyear. My father, an Air Force sergeant, had been sent to Viet Nam. The Air Force sent my mother, my sister, Claire, and me to Connolly Air Force Base, which during the war housed "unaccompanied wives." I'd been to so many different schools in my short life that I ceased wondering about their differences. All I knew about the Texas schools is that they weren't afraid to flunk you.

Yet though I was only twelve then, I had a good idea why Wickham never once called on Marvin, why she let him snooze in the crook of his polished arm. I knew why she would press her lips together, and narrow her eyes at me whenever I correctly answered a question, rare as that was. I know why she badgered Ah-so with questions everyone knew Ah-so would never even consider answering. Wickham didn't like us. She wasn't gross about it, but it was clear she didn't want us around. She would prove her dislike day after day with little stories and jokes. "I just want to share with you all," she would say, "a little riddle my daughter told me at the supper table th'other day. Now, where do you go when you injure your knee?" Then one, two, or all three of her pets would say for the rest of us, "We don't know, Miz Wickham," in that skin-chilling way suck-asses speak, "where?" "Why, to Africa," Wickham would say, "where the knee grows."

The thirty-odd white kids would laugh, and I would look across the room at Marvin. He'd be asleep. I would glance back at Ah-so. She'd be sitting still as a projected image, staring down at her desk. I, myself, would smile at Wickham's stupid jokes, sometimes fake a laugh. I tried to show her that at least one of us was alive and alert, even though her jokes hurt. I sucked ass, too, I suppose. But I wanted her to understand more than anything that I was not like her other nigra children, that I was worthy of more than the non-attention and the negative attention she paid Marvin and Ah-so. I hated her, but never showed it. No one could safely contradict that woman. She knew all kinds of tricks to demean, control, and punish you. And she could swing her two-foot paddle as fluidly as a big-league slugger swings a bat. You didn't speak in Wickham's class unless she spoke to you first. You didn't chew gum, or wear "hood" hair. You didn't drag your feet, curse, pass notes, hold hands with the opposite sex. Most especially, you didn't say anything bad about the Aggies, Governor Connolly, LBJ, Sam Houston, or Waco. You did the forbidden and she would get you. It was that simple.

She never got me, though. Never gave her reason to. But she could have invented reasons. She did a lot of that. I can't be sure, but I used to think she pitied me because my father was in Viet Nam and my uncle A.J. had recently died there. Whenever she would tell one of her racist jokes, she would always glance at me, preface the joke with, "Now don't you nigra children take offense. This is all in fun, you know. I just want to share with you all something Coach Gilchrest told me th'other day." She would tell her joke, and glance at me again. I'd giggle, feeling a little queasy. "I'm half Irish," she would chuckle, "and you should hear some of those Irish jokes." She never told any, and I never really expected her to. I just did my Tom-thing. I kept my shoes shined, my desk neat, answered her questions as best I could, never brought gum to school, never cursed, never slept in class. I wanted to show her we were not all the same.

I tried to show them all, all thirty-odd, that I was different. It worked to some degree, but not very well. When some article was stolen from someone's locker or desk, Marvin, not I, was the first accused. I'd be second. Neither Marvin, nor Ah-so nor I were ever chosen for certain classroom honors—"Pledge leader," "flag holder," "noise monitor," "paper passer outer," but Mrs. Wickham once let me be "eraser duster." I was proud. I didn't even care about the cracks my fellow students made about my finally having turned the right color. I had done something that Marvin, in the deeps of his never-ending sleep, couldn't even dream of doing. Jack Preston, a kid who sat in front of me, asked me one day at recess whether I was embarrassed about Marvin. "Can you believe that guy?" I said. "He's like a pig or something. Makes me sick."

"Does it make you ashamed to be colored?"

"No," I said, but I meant yes. Yes, if you insist on thinking us all the same. Yes, if his faults are mine, his weaknesses inherent in me.

"I'd be," said Jack.

I made no reply. I was ashamed. Ashamed for not defending Marvin and ashamed that Marvin even existed. But if it had occurred to me, I would have asked Jack whether he was ashamed of being white because of Oakley. Oakley, "Oak Tree," Kelvin "Oak Tree" Oakley. He was sixteen and proud of it. He made it clear to everyone, including Wickham, that his life's ambition was to stay in school one more year, till he'd be old enough to enlist in the army. "Them slopes got my brother," he would say. "I'mna sign up and git me a few slopes. Gonna kill them bastards deader'n shit." Oakley, so far as anyone knew, was and always had been the oldest kid in his family. But no one contradicted him. He would, as anyone would tell you, "snap yet neck jest as soon as look at you." Not a boy in class, excepting Marvin and myself, had been able to avoid Oakley's pink bellies, Texas titty twisters, moon pie punches, or worse. He didn't bother Marvin, I suppose, because Marvin was closer to his size and age, and because Marvin spent five-sixths of the school day asleep. Marvin probably never crossed Oakley's mind. And to say that Oakley hadn't bothered me is not to say he had no intention of ever doing so. In fact, this haphazard sketch of hairy fingers, slash of eyebrow, explosion of acne, elbows, and crooked teeth, swore almost daily that he'd like to kill me.

Naturally, I feared him. Though we were about the same height, he out-weighed me by no less than forty pounds. He talked, stood, smoked, and swore like a man. No one, except for Mrs. Wickham, the principal, and the coach, ever laid a finger on him. And even Wickham knew that the hot lines she laid on him merely amused him. He would smile out at the classroom, goofy and bashful, as she laid down the two, five, or maximum ten strokes on him. Often he would wink, or surreptitiously flash us the thumb as Wickham worked on him. When she was finished, Oakley would walk so cool back to his seat you'd think he was on wheels. He'd slide into his chair, sniff the air, and say, "Somethin's burnin. Do y'all smell smoke? I swanee, I smell smoke and fahr back heie." If he had made these cracks and never threatened me, I might have grown to admire Oakley, even liked him a little. But he hated me, and took every opportunity during the six-hour school day to make me aware of this. "Some Sambo's gittin his ass broke open one of these days," he'd mumble. "I wanna fight somebody. Need to keep in shape till I git to Nam."

I never said anything to him for the longest time. I pretended not to hear him, pretended not to notice his sour breath on my neck and ear. "Yep," he'd whisper. "Coonies keep y' in good shape for slope killin." Day in, day out, that's the kind of thing I'd pretend not to hear. But one day when the rain dropped down like lead balls, and the cold air made your skin look plucked, Oakley whispered to me, "My brother tells me it rains like this in Nam. Maybe I oughta go out at recess and break your ass open today. Nice and cool so you don't sweat. Nice and wet to clean up the blood." I said nothing for at least half a minute, then I turned half right and said, "Thought you said your brother was dead."

Oakley, silent himself, for a time, poked me in the back with his pencil and hissed, "*Yer* dead." Wickham cut her eyes our way, and it was over.

It was hardest avoiding him in gym class. Especially when we played murderball. Oakley always aimed his throws at me. He threw with unblinking intensity, his teeth gritting, his neck veining, his face flushing, his black hair sweeping over one eye. He could throw hard, but the balls were squishy and harmless. In fact, I found his misses more intimidating than his hits. The balls would whizz by, thunder against the folded bleachers. They rattled as though a locomotive were passing through them. I would duck, dodge, leap as if he were throwing grenades. But he always hit me, sooner or later. And after a while I noticed that the other boys would avoid throwing at me, as if I belonged to Oakley.

One day, however, I was surprised to see that Oakley was throwing at everyone else but me. He was uncommonly accurate, too; kids were falling like tin cans. Since no one was throwing at me, I spent most of the game watching Oakley cut this one and that one down. Finally, he and I were the only ones left on the court. Try as he would, he couldn't hit me, nor I him. Coach Gilchrest blew his whistle and told Oakley and me to bring the red rubber balls to the equipment locker. I was relieved I'd escaped Oakley's stinging throws for once. I was feeling triumphant, full of myself. As Oakley and I approached Gilchrest, I thought about saying something friendly to Oakley: Good game, Oak Tree, I would say. Before I could speak, though, Gilchrest said, "All right boys, there's five minutes left in the period. Y'all are so good, looks like, you're gonna have to play like men. No boundaries, no catch outs, and you gotta hit your opponent three times in order to win. Got me?"

We nodded.

"And you're gonna use these," said Gilchrest, pointing to three volleyballs at his feet. "And you better believe they're pumped full. Oates, you start at that end of the court. Oak Tree, you're at th'other end. Just like usual, I'll set the balls at mid-court, and when I blow my whistle I want y'all to haul your cheeks to the middle and th'ow for all you're worth. Got me?" Gilchrest nodded at our nods, then added, "Remember, no boundaries, right?"

I at my end, Oakley at his, Gilchrest blew his whistle. I was faster than Oakley and scooped up a ball before he'd covered three quarters of his side. I aimed, threw, and popped him right on the knee. "One-zip!" I heard Gilchrest shout. The ball bounced off his knee and shot right back into my hands. I hurried my throw and missed. Oakley bent

down, clutched the two remaining balls. I remember being amazed that
he could palm each ball, run full out, and throw left-handed or right-
handed without a shade of awkwardness. I spun, ran, but one of Oakley's throws glanced off the back of my head. "One-one!" hollered
Gilchrest. I fell and spun on my ass as the other ball came sailing at me.
I caught it. "He's out!" I yelled. Gilchrest's voice boomed, "No catch
outs. Three hits. Three hits." I leapt to my feet as Oakley scrambled
across the floor for another ball. I chased him down, leapt, and heaved
the ball hard as he drew himself erect. The ball hit him dead in the face,
and he went down flat. He rolled around, cupping his hands over his
nose. Gilchrest sped to his side, helped him to his feet, asked him
whether he was OK. Blood flowed from Oakley's nose, dripped in star-
tlingly bright spots on the floor, his shoes, Gilchrest's shirt. The coach
removed Oakley's T-shirt and pressed it against the big kid's nose to
stanch the bleeding. As they walked past me toward the office I mumbled an apology to Oakley, but couldn't catch his reply. "You watch
your filthy mouth, boy," said Gilchrest to Oakley.

The locker room was unnaturally quiet as I stepped into its steamy
atmosphere. Eyes clicked in my direction, looked away. After I was out
of my shorts, had my towel wrapped around me, my shower kit in
hand, Jack Preston and Brian Nailor approached me. Preston's hair
was combed slick and plastic looking. Nailor's stood up like frozen
flames. Nailor smiled at me with his big teeth and pale eyes. He poked
my arm with a finger. "You fucked up," he said.

"I tried to apologize."

"Won't do you no good," said Preston.

"I swanee," said Nailor.

"It's part of the game," I said. "It was an accident. Wasn't my idea
to use volleyballs."

"Don't matter," Preston said. "He's jest lookin for an excuse to
fight you."

"I never done nothing to him."

"Don't matter," said Nailor. "He don't like you."

"Brian's right, Clint. He'd jest as soon kill you as look at you."

"I never done nothing to him."

"Look," said Preston, "I know him pretty good. And jest between
you and me, it's 'cause you're a city boy—"

"Whadda you mean? I've never—"

"He don't like your clothes—"

"And he don't like the fancy way you talk in class."

"What fancy—"

"I'm tellin him, if you don't mind, Brian."

"Tell him then."

"He don't like the way you say 'tennis shoes' instead of sneakers. He don't like coloreds. A whole bunch a things, really."

"I never done nothing to him. He's got no reason—"

"*And,*" said Nailor, grinning, "*and,* he says you're a stuck-up rich kid." Nailor's eyes had crow's-feet, bags beneath them. They were a man's eyes.

"My dad's a sergeant," I said.

"You chicken to fight him?" said Nailor.

"Yeah. Clint, don't be chicken. Jest go on and git it over with. He's whupped pert near ever'body else in the class. It ain't so bad."

"Might as well, Oates."

"Yeah, yer pretty skinny, but yer jest about his height. Jest git 'im in a head-lock and don't let go."

"Goddamn," I said, "he's got no reason to—"

Their eyes shot right and I looked over my shoulder. Oakley stood at his locker, turning its tumblers. From where I stood I could see that a piece of cotton was wedged up one of his nostrils, and he already had the makings of a good shiner. His acne burned red like a fresh abrasion. He snapped the locker open and kicked his shoes off without sitting. Then he pulled off his shorts, revealing two paddle stripes on his ass. They were fresh red bars speckled with white, the white speckles being the reverse impression of the paddle's suction holes. He must not have watched his filthy mouth while in Gilchrest's presence. Behind me, I heard Preston and Nailor pad to their lockers.

Oakley spoke without turning around. "Somebody's gonna git his skinny black ass kicked, right today, right after school." He said it softly. He slipped his jock off, turned around. I looked away. Out the corner of my eye I saw him stride off, his hairy nakedness a weapon clearing the younger boys from his path. Just before he rounded the corner of the shower stalls, I threw my toilet kit to the floor and stammered, "I—I never did nothing to you, Oakley." He stopped, turned, stepped closer to me, wrapping his towel around himself. Sweat streamed down my rib cage. It felt like ice water. "You wanna go at it right now, boy?"

"I never did nothing to you." I felt tears in my eyes. I couldn't stop them even though I was blinking like mad. "Never."

He laughed. "You busted my nose, asshole."

"What about before? What'd I ever do to you?"

"See you after school, Coonie." Then he turned away, flashing his acne-spotted back like a semaphore. "Why?" I shouted, "Why you wanna fight me?" Oakley stopped and turned, folded his arms, leaned against a toilet stall. "Why you wanna fight *me*, Oakley?" I stepped over the bench. "What'd I do? Why me?" And then unconsciously, as if scratching, as if breathing, I walked toward Marvin, who stood a few feet from Oakley, combing his hair at the mirror. "Why not him?" I said. "How come you're after *me* and not *him*?" The room froze. Froze for a moment that was both evanescent and eternal, somewhere between an eye blink and a week in hell. No one moved, nothing happened; there was no sound at all. And then it was as if all of us at the same moment looked at Marvin. He just stood there, combing away, the only body in motion, I think. He combed his hair and combed it, as if seeing only his image, hearing only his comb scraping his scalp. I knew he'd heard me. There's no way he could not have heard me. But all he did was slide the comb into his pocket and walk out the door.

"I got no quarrel with Marvin," I heard Oakley say. I turned toward his voice, but he was already in the shower.

I was able to avoid Oakley at the end of the school day. I made my escape by asking Mrs. Wickham if I could go to the rest room.

"'Rest room,'" Oakley mumbled. "It's a damn toilet, sissy."

"Clinton," said Mrs. Wickham. "Can you *not* wait till the bell rings? It's almost three o'clock."

"No ma'am," I said. "I won't make it."

"Well I should make you wait just to teach you to be more mindful about . . . hygiene . . . uh things." She sucked in her cheeks, squinted. "But I'm feeling charitable today. You may go." I immediately left the building, and got on the bus. "Ain't you a little early?" said the bus driver, swinging the door shut. "Just left the office," I said. The driver nodded, apparently not giving me a second thought. I had no idea why I'd told her I'd come from the office, or why she found it a satisfactory answer. Two minutes later the bus filled, rolled, and shook its way to Connolly Air Base. When I got home, my mother was sitting in the living room, smoking her Slims, watching her soap opera. She absently asked me how my day had gone and I told her fine. "Hear from Dad?" I said.

"No, but I'm sure he's fine." She always said that when we hadn't heard from him in a while. I suppose she thought I was worried about him, or that I felt vulnerable without him. It was neither. I just wanted to discuss something with my mother that we both cared about. If I spoke with her about things that happened at school, or on my weekends, she'd listen with half an ear, say something like, "Is that so?" or "You don't say?" I couldn't stand that sort of thing. But when I mentioned my father, she treated me a bit more like an adult, or at least someone who was worth listening to. I didn't want to feel like a boy that afternoon. As I turned from my mother and walked down the hall I thought about the day my father left for Viet Nam. Sharp in his uniform, sure behind his aviator specs, he slipped a cigar from his pocket and stuck it in mine. "Not till I get back," he said. "We'll have us one when we go fishing. Just you and me, out on the lake all day, smoking and casting and sitting. Don't let Mama see it. Put it in y'back pocket." He hugged me, shook my hand, and told me I was the man of the house now. He told me he was depending on me to take good care of my mother and sister. "Don't you let me down, now, hear?" And he tapped his thick finger on my chest. "You almost as big as me. Boy, you something else." I believed him when he told me those things. My heart swelled big enough to swallow my father, my mother, Claire. I loved, feared, and respected myself, my manhood. That day I could have put all of Waco, Texas, in my heart. And it wasn't till about three months later that I discovered I really wasn't the man of the house, that my mother and sister, as they always had, were taking care of me.

For a brief moment I considered telling my mother about what had happened at school that day, but for one thing, she was deep down in the halls of *General Hospital,* and never paid you much mind till it was over. For another thing, I just wasn't the kind of person—I'm still not, really—to discuss my problems with anyone. Like my father I kept things to myself, talked about my problems only in retrospect. Since my father wasn't around I consciously wanted to be like him, doubly like him, I could say. I wanted to be the man of the house in some respect, even if it had to be in an inward way. I went to my room, changed my clothes, and laid out my homework. I couldn't focus on it. I thought about Marvin, what I'd said about him or done to him—I couldn't tell which. I'd done something to him, said something about him; said something about and done something to myself. *How come you're after me and not him?* I kept trying to tell myself I hadn't meant it that way. *That* way. I thought about approaching Marvin, telling him what I really meant was that he was more Oakley's age and weight than I. I would tell him I meant I was no match for Oakley. *See, Marvin, what I meant was that he wants to fight a colored guy, but is afraid to fight you 'cause you could beat him.* But try as I did, I couldn't for a moment convince myself that Marvin would believe me. I meant it *that* way and no other. Everybody heard. Everybody knew. That afternoon I forced myself to confront the notion that tomorrow I would probably have to fight both Oakley and Marvin. I'd have to be two men.

I rose from my desk and walked to the window. The light made my skin look orange, and I started thinking about what Wickham had told us once about light. She said that oranges and apples, leaves and flowers, the whole multicolored world, was not what it appeared to be. The colors we see, she said, look like they do only because of the light or ray that shines on them. "The color of the thing isn't what you see, but the light that's reflected off it." Then she shut out the lights and shone a white light lamp on a prism. We watched the pale splay of colors on the projector screen; some people oohed and aahed. Suddenly, she switched on a black light and the color of everything changed. The prism colors vanished, Wickham's arms were purple, the buttons of her dress were as orange as hot coals, rather than the blue they had been only seconds before. We were all very quiet. "Nothing," she said, after a while, "is really what it appears to be." I didn't really understand then. But as I stood at the window, gazing at my orange skin, I wondered what kind of light I could shine on Marvin, Oakley, and me that would reveal us as the same.

I sat down and stared at my arms. They were dark brown again. I worked up a bit of saliva under my tongue and spat on my left arm. I spat again, then rubbed the spittle into it, polishing, working till my arm grew warm. As I spat, and rubbed, I wondered why Marvin did this weird, nasty thing to himself, day after day. Was he trying to rub away the black, or deepen it, doll it up? And if he did this weird nasty thing for a hundred years, would he spitshine himself invisible, rolling away the eggplant skin, revealing the scarlet muscle, blue vein, pink and yellow tendon, white bone? Then disappear? Seen through, all colors, no colors. Spitting and rubbing. Is this the way you do it? I leaned forward, sniffed the arm. It smelled vaguely of mayonnaise. After an hour or so, I fell asleep.

I saw Oakley the second I stepped off the bus the next morning. He stood outside the gym in his usual black penny loafers, white socks, high-water jeans, T-shirt, and black jacket. Nailor stood with him, his big teeth spread across his bottom lip like playing cards. If there was anyone I felt like fighting, that day, it was Nailor. But I wanted to put off fighting for as long as I could. I stepped toward the gymnasium, thinking that I shouldn't run, but if I hurried I could beat Oakley to the door and secure myself near Gilchrest's office. But the moment I stepped into the gym, I felt Oakley's broad palm clap down on my shoulder. "Might as well stay out here, Coonie," he said. "I need me a little target practice." I turned to face him and he slapped me, one-two, with the back, then the palm of his hand, as I'd seen Bogart do to Peter Lorre in *The Maltese Falcon*. My heart went wild. I could scarcely breathe. I couldn't swallow.

"Call me a nigger," I said. I have no idea what made me say this. All I know is that it kept me from crying. "Call me a nigger, Oakley."

"Fuck you, ya black-ass slope." He slapped me again, scratching my eye. "I don't do what coonies tell me."

"Call me a nigger."

"Outside, Coonie."

"Call me one. Go ahead!"

He lifted his hand to slap me again, but before his arm could swing my way, Marvin Pruitt came from behind me and calmly pushed me aside. "Git out my way, boy," he said. And he slugged Oakley on the side of his head. Oakley stumbled back, stiff-legged. His eyes were big. Marvin hit him twice more, once again to the side of the head, once to the nose. Oakley went down and stayed down. Though blood was drawn, whistles blowing, fingers pointing, kids hollering, Marvin just stood there, staring at me with cool eyes. He spat on the ground, licked his lips, and just stared at me, till Coach Gilchrest and Mr. Calderon tackled him and violently carried him away. He never struggled, never took his eyes off me.

Nailor and Mrs. Wickham helped Oakley to his feet. His already fattened nose bled and swelled so that I had to look away. He looked around, bemused, walleyed, maybe scared. It was apparent he had no idea how bad he was hurt. He didn't blink. He didn't even touch his nose. He didn't look like he knew much of anything. He looked at me, looked me dead in the eye, in fact, but didn't seem to recognize me.

That morning, like all other mornings, we said the Pledge of Allegiance, sang "The Yellow Rose of Texas," "The Eyes of Texas Are upon You," and "Mistress Shady." The room stood strangely empty without Oakley, and without Marvin, but at the same time you could feel their presence more intensely somehow. I felt like I did when I'd walk into my mother's room and could smell my father's cigars or cologne. He was more palpable, in certain respects, than when there in actual flesh. For some reason, I turned to look at Ah-so, and just this once I let my eyes linger on her face. She had a very gentle-looking face, really. That surprised me. She must have felt my eyes on her because she glanced up at me for a second and smiled, white teeth, downcast eyes. Such a pretty smile. That surprised me too. She held it for a few seconds, then let it fade. She looked down at her desk, and sat still as a photograph.

Rick Moody

Rick Moody was born in 1961 in New York City and grew up in suburban Connecticut. He is the author of the novels Garden State *(1991),* Purple America *(1997), and* The Ice Storm *(1994), which was made into a critically acclaimed film by director Ang Lee. Moody's two short story collections are* The Ring of Brightest Angels Around Heaven *(1995) and* Demonology *(2001). He has also published a work of nonfiction,* The Black Veil: A Memoir with Digressions *(2002). His fiction and essays have been published in* The New Yorker, Esquire, Paris Review, *and* Harper's, *and have been cited for their humor, impressionistic style, and interest in popular culture. Since* Purple America, *his writing has become increasingly experimental, to the delight and occasional disdain of critics. In the* 2001 Best American Short Stories *anthology, Moody writes, "I got the idea for 'Boys' after hearing a reading by the great southern writer Max Steele. Max read a long, lyrical, realistic story that had in it the words 'Then the boys entered the house.' It was really just a connective image in his story, getting those boys from one sequence to another, but for some reason I became preoccupied with this ligament of his story, deciding that it was perhaps the most essential gesture in a boy's life. Entering the house."*

Boys

Boys enter the house, boys enter the house. Boys, and with them the ideas of boys (ideas leaden, reductive, inflexible), enter the house. Boys, two of them, wound into hospital packaging, boys with infant-pattern baldness, slung in the arms of parents, boys dreaming of breasts, enter the house. Twin boys, kettles on the boil, boys in hideous vinyl knapsacks that young couples from Edison, N.J., wear on their shirt fronts, knapsacks coated with baby saliva and staphylococcus and milk vomit, enter the house. Two boys, one striking the other with a rubberized hot dog, enter the house. Two boys, one of them striking the other with a willow switch about the head and shoulders, the other crying, enter the house. Boys enter the house speaking nonsense. Boys enter the house calling for mother. On a Sunday, in May, a day one might nearly describe as perfect, an ice cream truck comes slowly down the lane, chimes inducing salivation, and children run after it, not long after which boys dig a hole in the back yard and bury their younger sister's dolls two feet down, so that she will never find these dolls and these dolls will rot in hell, after which boys enter the house. Boys, trailing after their father like he is the Second Goddamned Coming of Christ Goddamned Almighty, enter the house, repair to the basement to watch baseball. Boys enter the house, site of devastation, and repair immediately to the kitchen, where they mix lighter fluid, vanilla pudding, drain-opening lye, balsamic vinegar, blue food coloring, calamine lotion, cottage cheese, ants, a plastic lizard one of them received in his Christmas stocking, tacks, leftover mashed potatoes, Spam, frozen lima beans, and chocolate syrup in a medium-sized saucepan and heat over a low flame until thick, afterward transferring the contents of this saucepan into a Pyrex lasagna dish, baking the Pyrex lasagna dish in the oven for nineteen minutes before attempting to persuade their sister that she should eat the mixture; later they smash three family heirlooms (the last, a glass egg, intentionally) in a two-and-a-half-hour stretch, where-upon they are sent to their bedroom until freed, in each case thirteen minutes after. Boys enter the house, starchy in pressed shirts and flannel pants that itch so bad, fresh from Sunday school instruction, blond and brown locks (respectively) plastered down but even so with a number of cowlicks protruding at odd angles, disconsolate and humbled, uncertain if boyish things—such as shooting at the neighbor's dog with a pump-action BB gun and gagging the fat boy up the street with a bandanna and showing their shriveled boy-penises to their younger sister—are exempted from the commandment to *Love the Lord thy God with all thy heart and with all thy soul and with all thy mind, and thy neighbor as thy-self.* Boys enter the house in baseball gear (only one of the boys can hit): in their spikes, in mismatched tube socks that smell like Stilton cheese. Boys enter the house in soccer gear. Boys enter the house carrying skates. Boys enter the house with lacrosse sticks, and soon after, tossing a lacrosse ball lightly in the living room, they destroy a lamp. One boy enters the house sporting basketball clothes, the other wearing jeans and a sweatshirt. One boy enters the house bleeding profusely and is taken out to get stitches, the other watches. Boys enter the house at the end of term carrying report cards, sneak around the house like spies of foreign nationality, looking for a place to hide the report cards for the time being (under a toaster? in a medicine cabinet?). One boy with a black eye enters the house, one boy without. Boys with acne enter the house and squeeze and prod large skin blemishes in front of their sister. Boys with acne-treatment products hidden about their persons enter the house. Boys, standing just up the street, sneak cigarettes behind a willow in the Elys' yard, wave smoke away from their natural fibers, hack terribly, experience nausea, then enter the house. Boys call each other *Retard, Homo,*

Geek, and, later, *Neckless Thug, Theater Fag,* and enter the house exchanging further epithets. Boys enter house with nose-hair clippers, chase sister around house threatening to depilate her eyebrows. She cries. Boys attempt to induce girls to whom they would not have spoken only six or eight months prior to enter the house with them. Boys enter the house with girls efflorescent and homely and attempt to induce girls to sneak into their bedroom, as they still share a single bedroom; girls refuse. Boys enter the house, go to separate bedrooms. Boys, with their father (an arm around each of them), enter the house, but of the monologue preceding and succeeding this entrance, not a syllable is preserved. Boys enter the house having masturbated in a variety of locales. Boys enter the house having masturbated in train-station bathrooms, in forests, in beach houses, in football bleachers at night under the stars, in cars (under a blanket), in the shower, backstage, on a plane, the boys masturbate constantly, identically, three times a day in some cases, desire like a madness upon them, at the mere sound of certain words, words that sound like other words, *interrogative* reminding them of *intercourse, beast* reminding them of *breast, sects* reminding them of *sex,* and so forth, the boys are not very smart yet, and as they enter the house they feel, as always, immense shame at the scale of this self-abusive cogitation, seeing a classmate, seeing a billboard, seeing a fire hydrant, seeing things that should not induce thoughts of masturbation (their sister, e.g.) and then thinking of masturbation anyway. Boys enter the house, go to their rooms, remove sexually explicit magazines from hidden stashes, put on loud music, feel despair. Boys enter the house worried; they argue. The boys are ugly, they are failures, they will never be loved, they enter the house. Boys enter the house and kiss their mother, who feels differently now they have outgrown her. Boys enter the house, kiss their mother, she explains the seriousness of their sister's difficulty, her diagnosis. Boys enter the house, having attempted to locate the spot in their yard where the dolls were buried, eight or nine years prior, without success; they go to their sister's room, sit by her bed. Boys enter the house and tell their completely bald sister jokes about baldness. Boys hold either hand of their sister, laying aside differences, having trudged grimly into the house. Boys skip school, enter house, hold vigil. Boys enter the house after their parents have both gone off to work, sit with their sister and with their sister's nurse. Boys enter the house carrying cases of beer. Boys enter the house, very worried now, didn't know more worry was possible. Boys enter the house carrying controlled substances, neither having told the other that he is carrying a controlled substance, though an intoxicated posture seems appropriate under the circumstances. Boys enter the house weeping and hear weeping around them. Boys enter the house embarrassed, silent, anguished, keening, afflicted, angry, woeful, grief-stricken. Boys enter the house on vacation, each clasps the hand of the other with genuine warmth, the one wearing dark colors and having shaved a portion of his head, the other having grown his hair out longish and wearing, uncharacteristically, a tie-dyed shirt. Boys enter the house on vacation and argue bitterly about politics (other subjects are no longer discussed), one boy supporting the Maoist insurgency in a certain Southeast Asian country, one believing that to change the system you need to work inside it; one boy threatens to beat the living shit out of the other, refuses crème brûlée, though it is created by his mother in order to keep the peace. One boy writes home and thereby enters the house only through a mail slot he argues that the other boy is crypto-fascist, believing that the market can seek its own level on questions of ethics and morals; boys enter the house on vacation and announce future professions; boys enter the house on vacation and change their minds about professions; boys enter the house on vacation, and one boy brings home a sweetheart but throws a tantrum when it is suggested that the sweetheart will have to retire on the folding bed in the basement; the other boy, having no sweetheart, is distant and withdrawn, preferring to talk late into the night about family members gone from this world. Boys enter the house several weeks apart. Boys enter the house on days of heavy rain. Boys enter the house, in different calendar years, and upon entering, the boys seem to do nothing but compose manifestos, for the benefit of parents; they follow their mother around the place, having fashioned these manifestos in celebration of brand-new independence: *Mom, I like to lie in bed late into the morning watching game shows,* or, *I'm never going to date anyone but artists from now on, mad girls, dreamers, practicers of black magic,* or, *A man should eat bologna, sliced meals are important,* or, *An American should bowl at least once a year,* but these manifestos apply only for brief spells, after which they are reversed or discarded. Boys don't enter the house at all, except as ghostly afterimages of younger selves, fleeting images of sneakers dashing up a staircase; soggy towels on the floor of the bathroom; blue jeans coiled like asps in the basin of the washing machine; boys as an absence of boys, blissful at first, you put a thing down on a spot, put this book down, come back later, it's still there; you buy a box of cookies, eat three, later three are missing. Nevertheless, when boys next enter the house, which they ultimately must do, it's a relief, even if it's only in preparation for weddings of acquaintances from boyhood, one boy has a beard, neatly trimmed, the other has rakish sideburns, one boy wears a hat, the other boy thinks hats are ridiculous, one boy wears khakis pleated at the waist, the other wears denim, but each changes into his suit (one suit fits well, one is a little tight), as though suits are the liminary marker of adulthood. Boys enter the house after the wedding and they are slapping each other on the back and yelling at anyone who will listen, *It's a party?* One boy enters the house, carried by friends, having been arrested (after the wedding) for driving while intoxicated, complexion ashen; the other boy tries to keep his mouth shut: the car is on its side in a ditch, the car has the top half of a tree broken over its bonnet, the car has struck another car, which has in turn struck a third, *Everyone will have seen.* One boy misses his brother horribly, misses the past, misses a time worth being nostalgic over, a time that never existed, back when they set their sister's playhouse on fire; the other boy avoids all mention of that time; each of them is once the boy who enters the house alone, missing the other, each is devoted and each callous, and each plays his part on the telephone, over the course of months. Boys enter the house with fishing gear, according to prearranged date and time, arguing about whether to use lures or live bait, in order to meet their father for the fishing adventure, after which boys enter the house again, almost immediately, with live bait, having settled the question; boys boast of having caught fish in the past, though no fish has ever been caught: *Remember when the blues were biting?* Boys enter the house carrying their father, slumped. Happens so fast. Boys rush into the house leading EMTs to the couch in the living room where the body lies, boys enter the house, boys enter the house, boys enter the house. Boys hold open the threshold, awesome threshold that has welcomed them when they haven't even been able to welcome themselves, that threshold which welcomed them when they had to be taken in, here is its tarnished knocker, here is its euphonious bell, here's where the boys had to sand the door down because it never would hang right in the frame, here are the scuff marks from when boys were on the wrong side of the door demanding, here's where there were once milk bottles for the milkman, here's where the newspaper always landed, here's the mail slot, here's the light on the front step, illuminated, here's where the boys are standing, as that beloved man is carried out. Boys, no longer boys, exit.

Lorrie Moore

Lorrie Moore was born in 1957 in Glens Falls, New York. She received an MFA from Cornell University. She has published two novels, Anagrams *(1987) and* Who Will Run the Frog Hospital? *(1994), and the story collections* Self-Help *(1985),* Like Life *(1990), and the National Book Critics Circle finalist* Birds of America *(1998), which the* New York Times *said "will stand by itself as one of our funniest, most telling anatomies of human love and vulnerability." Moore's work is known for its language and word play, but beneath the hilarious dialogue and biting wit lie an arresting gravity and emotion. In an interview with CNN, Moore discussed how she uses humor as a stay against "nightmarish facts": "I'm interested in . . . those little moments of generosity, where someone really does want to make someone laugh . . . vis-à-vis this horrible stuff that is out there in the world that we all have to deal with. But those moments where we help each other out are . . . theatrical. And some of them are possessed of great silliness, but they are connected to an impulse that is interesting to me. So, it's also not just the awkwardness that creates the humor, but sometimes it's generosity."*

How to Talk to Your Mother (Notes)

1982.   Without her, for years now, murmur at the defrosting refrigerator, "What?" "Huh?" "Shush now," as it creaks, aches, groans, until the final ice block drops from the ceiling of the freezer like something vanquished.

Dream, and in your dreams babies with the personalities of dachshunds, fat as Macy balloons, float by the treetops.

The first permanent polyurethane heart is surgically implanted.

Someone upstairs is playing "You'll Never Walk Alone" on the recorder. Now it's "Oklahoma!" They must have a Rodgers and Hammerstein book.

1981.   On public transportation, mothers with soft, soapy, corduroyed seraphs glance at you, their faces dominoes of compassion. Their seraphs are small and quiet or else restlessly counting bus-seat colors: "Blue-blue-blue, red-red-red, lullow-lullow-lullow." The mothers see you eyeing their children. They smile sympathetically. They believe you envy them. They believe you are childless. They believe they know why. Look quickly away, out the smudge of the window.

1980. The hum, rush, clack of things in the kitchen. These are some of the sounds that organize your life. The clink of the silverware inside the drawer, piled like bones in a mass grave. Your similes grow grim, grow tired.

Reagan is elected President, though you distributed donuts and brochures for Carter.

Date an Italian. He rubs your stomach and says, "These are marks of stretch, no? Marks of stretch?" and in your dizzy mind you think: Marks of Harpo, Ideas of Marx, Ides of March, Beware. He plants kisses on the sloping ramp of your neck, and you fall asleep against him, your underpants peeled and rolled around one thigh like a bride's garter.

1979. Once in a while take evening trips past the old unsold house you grew up in, that haunted rural crossroads two hours from where you now live. It is like Halloween: the raked, moonlit lawn, the mammoth, tumid trees, arms and fingers raised into the starless wipe of sky like burns, cracks, map rivers. Their black shadows rock against the side of the east porch. There are dream shadows, other lives here. Turn the corner slowly but continue to stare from the car window. This house is embedded in you deep, something still here you know, you think you know, a voice at the top of those stairs, perhaps, a figure on the porch, an odd apron caught high in the twigs, in the too-warm-for-a-fall-night breeze, something not right, that turret window you can still see from here, from outside, but which can't be reached from within. (The ghostly brag of your childhood: "We have a mystery room. The window shows from the front, but you can't go in, there's no door. A doctor lived there years ago and gave secret operations, and now it's blocked off.") The window sits like a dead eye in the turret.

You see a ghost, something like a spinning statue by a shrub.

1978. Bury her in the cold south sideyard of that Halloweenish house. Your brother and his kids are there. Hug. The minister in a tweed sportscoat, the neighborless fields, the crossroads, are all like some stark Kansas. There is praying, then someone shoveling. People walk toward the cars and hug again. Get inside your car with your niece. Wait. Look up through the windshield. In the November sky a wedge of wrens moves south, the lines of their formation, the very sides and vertices mysteriously choreographed, shifting, flowing, crossing like a skater's legs. "They'll descend instinctively upon a tree somewhere," you say, "but not for miles yet." You marvel, watch, until, amoeba-slow, they are dark, faraway stitches in the horizon. You do not start the car. The quiet niece next to you finally speaks: "Aunt Ginnie, are we going to the restaurant with the others?" Look at her. Recognize her: nine in a pile parka. Smile and start the car.

1977.   She ages, rocks in your rocker, noiseless as wind. The front strands of her white hair dangle yellow at her eyes from too many cigarettes. She smokes even now, her voice husky with phlegm. Sometimes at dinner in your tiny kitchen she will simply stare, rheumy-eyed, at you, then burst into a fit of coughing that wracks her small old man's body like a storm.

Stop eating your baked potato. Ask if she is all right.

She will croak: "Do you remember, Ginnie, your father used to say that one day, with these cigarettes, I was going to have to 'face the mucus'?" At this she chuckles, chokes, gasps again.

Make her stand up.

Lean her against you.

Slap her lightly on the curved mound of her back.

Ask her for chrissakes to stop smoking.

She will smile and say: "For chrissakes? Is that any way to talk to your mother?"

At night go in and check on her. She lies there awake, her lips apart, open and drying. Bring her some juice. She murmurs, "Thank you, honey." Her mouth smells, swells like a grave.

1976.   The Bicentennial. In the laundromat, you wait for the time on your coins to run out. Through the porthole of the dryer, you watch your bedeviled towels and sheets leap and fall. The radio station piped in from the ceiling plays slow, sad Motown; it encircles you with the desperate hopefulness of a boy at a dance, and it makes you cry. When you get back to your apartment, dump everything on your bed. Your mother is knitting crookedly: red, white, and blue. Kiss her hello. Say: "Sure was warm in that place." She will seem not to hear you.

1975.   Attend poetry readings alone at the local library. Find you don't really listen well. Stare at your crossed thighs. Think about your mother. Sometimes you confuse her with the first man you ever loved, who ever loved you, who buried his head in the pills of your sweater and said magnificent things like "Oh god, oh god," who loved you unconditionally, terrifically, like a mother.

The poet loses his nerve for a second, a red flush through his neck and ears, but he regains his composure. When he is finished, people clap. There is wine and cheese.

Leave alone, walk home alone. The downtown streets are corridors of light holding you, holding you, past the church, past the community center. March, like Stella Dallas, spine straight, through the melodrama of street lamps, phone posts, toward the green house past Borealis Avenue, toward the rear apartment with the tilt and the squash on the stove.

Your horoscope says: Be kind, be brief.

You are pregnant again. Decide what you must do.

1974. She will have bouts with a mad sort of senility. She calls you at work. "There's no food here! Help me! I'm starving!" although you just bought forty dollars' worth of groceries yesterday. "Mom, there is too food there!"

When you get home the refrigerator is mostly empty. "Mom, where did you put all the milk and cheese and stuff?" Your mother stares at you from where she is sitting in front of the TV set. She has tears leaking out of her eyes. "There's no food here, Ginnie."

There is a rustling, scratching noise in the dishwasher. You open it up, and the eyes of a small rodent glint back at you. It scrambles out, off to the baseboards behind the refrigerator. Your mother, apparently, has put all the groceries inside the dishwasher. The milk is spilled, a white pool against blue, and things like cheese and bologna and apples have been nibbled at.

1973. At a party when a woman tells you where she bought some wonderful pair of shoes, say that you believe shopping for clothes is like masturbation—everyone does it, but it isn't very interesting and therefore should be done alone, in an embarrassed fashion, and never be the topic of party conversation. The woman will tighten her lips and eyebrows and say, "Oh, I suppose you have something more fascinating to talk about." Grow clumsy and uneasy. Say, "No," and head for the ginger ale. Tell the person next to you that your insides feel sort of sinking and vinyl like a Claes Oldenburg toilet. They will say, "Oh?" and point out that the print on your dress is one of paisleys impregnating paisleys. Pour yourself more ginger ale.

1972. Nixon wins by a landslide.

Sometimes your mother calls you by her sister's name. Say, "No, Mom, it's me. Virginia." Learn to repeat things. Learn that you have a way of knowing each other which somehow slips out and beyond the ways you have of not knowing each other at all.

Make apple crisp for the first time.

1971. Go for long walks to get away from her. Walk through wooded areas; there is a life there you have forgotten. The smells and sounds seem sudden, unchanged, exact, the papery crunch of the leaves, the mouldering sachet of the mud. The trees are crooked as backs, the fence posts splintered, trusting and precarious in their solid grasp of arms, the asters spindly, dry, white, havishammed (Havishammed!) by frost. Find a beautiful reddish stone and bring it home for your mother. Kiss her. Say: "This is for you." She grasps it and smiles. "You were always such a sensitive child," she says.

Say: "Yeah, I know."

1970. You are pregnant again. Try to decide what you should do. Get your hair chopped, short as a boy's.

1969. Mankind leaps upon the moon.

Disposable diapers are first sold in supermarkets.

Have occasional affairs with absurd, silly men who tell you to grow your hair to your waist and who, when you are sad, tickle your ribs to cheer you up. Moonlight through the blinds stripes you like zebras. You laugh. You never marry.

1968. Do not resent her. Think about the situation, for instance, when you take the last trash bag from its box: you must throw out the box by putting it in that very trash bag. What was once contained, now must contain. The container, then, becomes the contained, the enveloped, the held. Find more and more that you like to muse over things like this.

1967. Your mother is sick and comes to live with you. There is no place else for her to go. You feel many different emptinesses.

The first successful heart transplant is performed in South Africa.

1966. You confuse lovers, mix up who had what scar, what car, what mother.

1965. Smoke marijuana. Try to figure out what has made your life go wrong. It is like trying to figure out what is stinking up the refrigerator. It could be anything. The lid off the mayonnaise, Uncle Ron's honey wine four years in the left corner. Broccoli yellowing, flowering fast. They are all metaphors. They are all problems. Your horoscope says: Speak gently to a loved one.

1964. Your mother calls long distance and asks whether you are coming home for Thanksgiving, your brother and the baby will be there. Make excuses.

"As a mother gets older," your mother says, "these sorts of holidays become increasingly important."

Say: "I'm sorry, Mom."

1963. Wake up one morning with a man you had thought you'd spend your life with, and realize, a rock in your gut, that you don't even like him. Spend a weepy afternoon in his bathroom, not coming out when he knocks. You can no longer trust your affections. People and places you think you love may be people and places you hate.

Kennedy is shot.

Someone invents a temporary artificial heart, for use during operations.

1962. Eat Chinese food for the first time, with a lawyer from California. He will show you how to hold the chopsticks. He will pat your leg. Attack his profession. Ask him whether he feels the law makes large spokes out of the short stakes of men.

1961. Grandma Moses dies.

You are a zoo of insecurities. You take to putting brandy in your morning coffee and to falling in love too easily. You have an abortion.

1960. There is money from your father's will and his life insurance. You buy a car and a green velvet dress you don't need. You drive two hours to meet your mother for lunch on Saturdays. She suggests things for you to write about, things she's heard on the radio: a woman with telepathic twins, a woman with no feet.

1959. At the funeral she says: "He had his problems, but he was a generous man," though you know he was tight as a scout knot, couldn't listen to anyone, the only time you remember loving him being that once when he got the punchline of one of your jokes before your mom did and looked up from his science journal and guffawed loud as a giant, the two of you, for one split moment, communing like angels in the middle of that room, in that warm, shared light of mind.

Say: "He was okay."

"You shouldn't be bitter," your mother snaps. "He financed you and your brother's college educations." She buttons her coat. "He was also the first man to isolate a particular isotope of helium, I forget the name, but he should have won the Nobel Prize." She dabs at her nose.

Say: "Yeah, Mom."

1958.   At your brother's wedding, your father is taken away in an ambulance. A tiny cousin whispers loudly to her mother, "Did Uncle Will have a hard attack?" For seven straight days say things to your mother like: "I'm sure it'll be okay," and "I'll stay here, why don't you go home and get some sleep."

1957.   Dance the calypso with boys from a different college. Get looped on New York State burgundy, lose your virginity, and buy one of the first portable electric typewriters.

1956.   Tell your mother about all the books you are reading at college. This will please her.

1955.   Do a paint-by-numbers of Elvis Presley. Tell your mother you are in love with him. She will shake her head.

1954.   Shoplift a cashmere sweater.

1953.   Smoke a cigarette with Hillary Swedelson. Tell each other your crushes. Become blood sisters.

1952.   When your mother asks you if there are any nice boys in junior high, ask her how on earth would you ever know, having to come in at nine! every night. Her eyebrows will lift like theater curtains. "You poor, abused thing," she will say.

Say, "Don't I know it," and slam the door.

1951.   Your mother tells you about menstruation. The following day you promptly menstruate, your body only waiting for permission, for a signal. You wake up in the morning and feel embarrassed.

1949. You learn how to blow gum bubbles and to add negative numbers.

1947. The Dead Sea Scrolls are discovered.

You have seen too many Hollywood musicals. You have seen too many people singing in public places and you assume you can do it, too. Practice. Your teacher asks you a question. You warble back: "The answer to number two is twelve." Most of the class laughs at you, though some stare, eyes jewel-still, fascinated. At home your mother asks you to dust your dresser. Work up a vibrato you could drive a truck through. Sing: "Why do I have to do it now?" and tap your way through the dining room. Your mother requests that you calm down and go take a nap. Shout: "You don't care about me! You don't care about me at all!"

1946. Your brother plays "Shoofly Pie" all day long on the Victrola.

Ask your mother if you can go to Ellen's for supper. She will say, "Go ask your father," and you, pulling at your fingers, walk out to the living room and whimper by his chair. He is reading. Tap his arm. "Dad? Daddy? Dad?" He continues reading his science journal. Pull harder on your fingers and run back to the kitchen to tell your mother, who storms into the living room, saying, "Why don't you ever listen to your children when they try to talk to you?" You hear them arguing. Press your face into a kitchen towel, ashamed, the hum of the refrigerator motor, the drip in the sink scaring you.

1945. Your father comes home from his war work. He gives you a piggyback ride around the broad yellow thatch of your yard, the dead window in the turret, dark as a wound, watching you. He gives you wordless pushes on the swing.

Your brother has new friends, acts older and distant, even while you wait for the school bus together.

You spend too much time alone. You tell your mother that when you grow up you will bring your babies to Australia to see the kangaroos.

Forty thousand people are killed in Nagasaki.

1944. Dress and cuddle a tiny babydoll you have named "the Sue." Bring her everywhere. Get lost in the Wilson Creek fruit market, and call softly, "Mom, where are you?" Watch other children picking grapes, but never dare yourself. Your eyes are small, dark throats, your hand clutches the Sue.

1943. Ask your mother about babies. Have her read to you only the stories about babies. Ask her if she is going to have a baby. Ask her about the baby that died. Cry into her arm.

1940. Clutch her hair in your fist. Rub it against your cheek.

1939. As through a helix, as through an ear, it is here you are nearer the dream flashes, the other lives.

There is a tent of legs, a sundering of selves, as you both gasp blindly for breath. Across the bright and cold, she knows it when you try to talk to her, though this is something you never really manage to understand.

Germany invades Poland.

The year's big song is "Three Little Fishies" and someone, somewhere, is playing it.

Tim O'Brien

Tim O'Brien was born in 1946 in Austin, Minnesota. Shortly after graduating from Macalester College he was drafted into the U.S. Army. He arrived in Vietnam in 1969 and eventually earned a Purple Heart for wounds sustained during the war. Upon his return to the United States, O'Brien worked as a journalist for the Washington Post, *and in 1973 published his first book,* If I Die in a Combat Zone, Box Me Up and Ship Me Home. *This nonfiction account was followed by a novel,* Northern Lights, *in 1975. O'Brien received much acclaim for his National Book Award-winning novel* Going after Cacciato *(1978) and the story cycle* The Things They Carried *(1990). Many critics consider these two works to be among the definitive fictional books about the war. O'Brien's subsequent novels include* In the Lake of the Woods *(1994),* Tomcat in Love *(1998), and* July, July *(2002). In an interview in the* Chicago Review, *O'Brien discussed the confluence of dream and reality that lies at the heart of his work: "In war, the rational faculty begins to diminish . . . and what takes over is surrealism, the life of the imagination. The mind of the soldier becomes part of the experience—the brain seems to flow out of your head, joining the elements around you on the battlefield. It's like stepping outside yourself."*

The Things They Carried

First Lieutenant Jimmy Cross carried letters from a girl named Martha, a junior at Mount Sebastian College in New Jersey. They were not love letters, but Lieutenant Cross was hoping, so he kept them folded in plastic at the bottom of his rucksack. In the late afternoon, after a day's march, he would dig his foxhole, wash his hands under a canteen, unwrap the letters, hold them with the tips of his fingers, and spend the last hour of light pretending. He would imagine romantic camping trips into the White Mountains in New Hampshire. He would sometimes taste the envelope flaps, knowing her tongue had been there. More than anything, he wanted Martha to love him as he loved her, but the letters were mostly chatty, elusive on the matter of love. She was a virgin, he was almost sure. She was an English major at Mount Sebastian, and she wrote beautifully about her professors and roommates and midterm exams, about her respect for Chaucer and her great affection for Virginia Woolf. She often quoted lines of poetry; she never mentioned the war, except to say, Jimmy, take care of yourself. The letters weighed 10 ounces. They were signed Love, Martha, but

Lieutenant Cross understood that Love was only a way of signing and did not mean what he sometimes pretended it meant. At dusk, he would carefully return the letters to his rucksack. Slowly, a bit distracted, he would get up and move among his men, checking the perimeter, then at full dark he would return to his hole and watch the night and wonder if Martha was a virgin.

The things they carried were largely determined by necessity. Among the necessities or near-necessities were P-38 can openers, pocket knives, heat tabs, wristwatches, dog tags, mosquito repellent, chewing gum, candy, cigarettes, salt tablets, packets of Kool-Aid, lighters, matches, sewing kits, Military Payment Certificates, C rations, and two or three canteens of water. Together, these items weighed between 15 and 20 pounds, depending upon a man's habits or rate of metabolism. Henry Dobbins, who was a big man, carried extra rations; he was especially fond of canned peaches in heavy syrup over pound cake. Dave Jensen, who practiced field hygiene, carried a toothbrush, dental floss, and several hotel-sized bars of soap he'd stolen on R&R in Sydney, Australia. Ted Lavender, who was scared, carried tranquilizers until he was shot in the head outside the village of Than Khe in mid-April. By necessity, and because it was SOP, they all carried steel helmets that weighed 5 pounds including the liner and camouflage cover. They carried the standard fatigue jackets and trousers. Very few carried underwear. On their feet they carried jungle boots—2.1 pounds—and Dave Jensen carried three pairs of socks and a can of Dr. Scholl's foot powder as a precaution against trench foot. Until he was shot, Ted Lavender carried six or seven ounces of premium dope, which for him was a necessity. Mitchell Sanders, the RTO, carried condoms. Norman Bowker carried a diary. Rat Kiley carried comic books. Kiowa, a devout Baptist, carried an illustrated New Testament that had been presented to him by his father, who taught Sunday school in Oklahoma City, Oklahoma. As a hedge against bad times, however, Kiowa also carried his grandmother's distrust of the white man, his grandfather's old hunting hatchet. Necessity dictated. Because the land was mined and booby-trapped, it was SOP for each man to carry a steel-centered, nylon-covered flak jacket, which weighed 6.7 pounds, but which on hot days seemed much heavier. Because you could die so quickly, each man carried at least one large compress bandage, usually in the helmet band for easy access. Because the nights were cold, and because the monsoons were wet, each carried a green plastic poncho that could be used as a raincoat or groundsheet or makeshift tent. With its quilted liner, the poncho weighed almost two pounds, but it was worth every ounce. In April, for instance, when Ted Lavender was shot, they used his poncho to wrap him up, then to carry him across the paddy, then to lift him into the chopper that took him away.

They were called legs or grunts.

To carry something was to hump it, as when Lieutenant Jimmy Cross humped his love for Martha up the hills and through the swamps. In its intransitive form, to hump meant to walk, or to march, but it implied burdens far beyond the intransitive.

Almost everyone humped photographs. In his wallet, Lieutenant Cross carried two photographs of Martha. The first was a Kodacolor snapshot signed Love, though he knew better. She stood against a brick wall. Her eyes were gray and neutral, her lips slightly open as she stared straight-on at the camera. At night, sometimes, Lieutenant Cross wondered who had taken the picture, because he knew she had boyfriends, because he loved her so much, and because he could see the shadow of the picture-taker spreading out against the brick wall. The second photograph had been clipped from the 1968 Mount Sebastian yearbook. It was an action shot—women's volleyball—and Martha was bent horizontal to the floor, reaching, the palms of her hands in sharp focus, the tongue taut, the expression frank and competitive. There was no visible sweat. She wore white gym shorts. Her legs, he thought, were almost certainly the legs of a virgin, dry and without hair, the left knee cocked and carrying her entire weight, which was just over one hundred pounds. Lieutenant Cross remembered touching that left knee. A dark theater, he remembered, and the movie was *Bonnie and Clyde*, and Martha wore a tweed skirt, and during the final scene, when he touched her knee, she turned and looked at him in a sad, sober way that made him pull his hand back, but he would always remember the feel of the tweed skirt and the knee beneath it and the sound of the gunfire that killed Bonnie and Clyde, how embarrassing it was, how slow and oppressive. He remembered kissing her good night at the dorm door. Right then, he thought, he should've done something brave. He should've carried her up the stairs to her room and tied her to the bed and touched that left knee all night long. He should've risked it. Whenever he looked at the photographs, he thought of new things he should've done.

What they carried was partly a function of rank, partly of field specialty.

As a first lieutenant and platoon leader, Jimmy Cross carried a compass, maps, code books, binoculars, and a .45-caliber pistol that weighed 2.9 pounds fully loaded. He carried a strobe light and the responsibility for the lives of his men.

As an RTO, Mitchell Sanders carried the PRC-25 radio, a killer, 26 pounds with its battery.

As a medic, Rat Kiley carried a canvas satchel filled with morphine and plasma and malaria tablets and surgical tape and comic books and all the things a medic must carry, including M&M's for especially bad wounds, for a total weight of nearly 20 pounds.

As a big man, therefore a machine gunner, Henry Dobbins carried the M-60, which weighed 23 pounds unloaded, but which was almost always loaded. In addition, Dobbins carried between 10 and 15 pounds of ammunition draped in belts across his chest and shoulders.

As PFCs or Spec 4s, most of them were common grunts and carried the standard M-16 gas-operated assault rifle. The weapon weighed 7.5 pounds unloaded, 8.2 pounds with its full 20-round magazine. Depending on numerous factors, such as topography and psychology, the riflemen carried anywhere from 12 to 20 magazines, usually in cloth bandoliers, adding on another 8.4 pounds at minimum, 14 pounds at maximum. When it was available, they also carried M-16 maintenance gear—rods and steel brushes and swabs and tubes of LSA oil—all of which weighed about a pound. Among the grunts, some carried the M-79 grenade launcher, 5.9 pounds unloaded, a reasonably light weapon except for the ammunition, which was heavy. A single round weighed 10 ounces. The typical load was 25 rounds. But Ted Lavender, who was scared, carried 34 rounds when he was shot and killed outside Than Khe, and he went down under an exceptional burden, more than 20 pounds of ammunition, plus the flak jacket and helmet and rations and water and toilet paper and tranquilizers and all the rest, plus the unweighed fear. He was dead weight. There was no twitching or flopping. Kiowa, who saw it happen, said it was like watching a rock fall, or a big sandbag or something—just boom, then down—not like the movies where the dead guy rolls around and does fancy spins and goes ass over teakettle—not like that, Kiowa said, the poor bastard just flat-fuck fell. Boom. Down. Nothing else. It was a bright morning in mid-April. Lieutenant Cross felt the pain. He blamed himself. They stripped off Lavender's canteens and ammo, all the heavy things, and Rat Kiley said the obvious, the guy's dead, and Mitchell Sanders used his radio to report one U.S. KIA and to request a chopper. Then they wrapped Lavender in his poncho. They carried him out to a dry paddy, established security, and sat smoking the dead man's dope until the chopper came. Lieutenant Cross kept to himself. He pictured Martha's smooth young face, thinking he loved her more than anything, more than his men, and now Ted Lavender was dead because he loved her so much and could not stop thinking about her. When the dustoff arrived, they carried Lavender aboard. Afterward they burned Than Khe. They marched until dusk, then dug their holes, and that night Kiowa kept explaining how you had to be there, how fast it was, how the poor guy just dropped like so much concrete. Boom-down, he said. Like cement.

In addition to the three standard weapons—the M-60, M-16, and M-79—they carried whatever presented itself, or whatever seemed appropriate as a means of killing or staying alive. They carried catch-as-catch-can. At various times, in various situations, they carried M-14s and CAR-15s and Swedish Ks and grease guns and captured AK-47s and Chi-Coms and RPGs and Simonov carbines and black market Uzis and .38-caliber Smith & Wesson handguns and 66 mm LAWs and shotguns and silencers and blackjacks and bayonets and C-4 plastic explosives. Lee Strunk carried a slingshot; a weapon of last resort, he called it. Mitchell Sanders carried brass knuckles. Kiowa carried his grandfather's feathered hatchet. Every third or fourth man carried a Claymore antipersonnel mine—3.5 pounds with its firing device. They all carried fragmentation grenades—14 ounces each. They all carried at least one M-18 colored smoke grenade—24 ounces. Some carried CS or tear gas grenades. Some carried white phosphorus grenades. They carried all they could bear, and then some, including a silent awe for the terrible power of the things they carried.

In the first week of April, before Lavender died, Lieutenant Jimmy Cross received a good-luck charm from Martha. It was a simple pebble, an ounce at most. Smooth to the touch, it was a milky white color with flecks of orange and violet, oval-shaped, like a miniature egg. In the accompanying letter, Martha wrote that she had found the pebble on the Jersey shoreline, precisely where the land touched water at high tide, where things came together but also separated. It was this separate-but-together quality, she wrote, that had inspired her to pick up the pebble and to carry it in her breast pocket for several days, where it seemed weightless, and then to send it through the mail, by air, as a token of her truest feelings for him. Lieutenant Cross found this romantic. But he wondered what her truest feelings were, exactly, and what she meant by separate-but-together. He wondered how the tides and waves had come into play on that afternoon along the Jersey shoreline when Martha saw the pebble and bent down to rescue it from geology. He imagined bare feet. Martha was a poet, with the poet's sensibilities, and her feet would be brown and bare, the toenails unpainted, the eyes chilly and somber like the ocean in March, and though it was painful, he wondered who had been with her that afternoon. He imagined a pair of shadows moving along the strip of sand where things came together but also separated. It was phantom jealousy, he knew, but he couldn't help himself. He loved her so much. On the march, through the hot days of early April, he carried the pebble in his mouth, turning it with his tongue, tasting sea salt and moisture. His mind wandered. He had difficulty keeping his attention on the war. On occasion he would yell at his men to spread out the column, to keep their eyes open, but then he would slip away into daydreams, just pretending, walking barefoot along the Jersey shore, with Martha, carrying nothing. He would feel himself rising. Sun and waves and gentle winds, all love and lightness.

What they carried varied by mission.

When a mission took them to the mountains, they carried mosquito netting, machetes, canvas tarps, and extra bug juice.

If a mission seemed especially hazardous, or if it involved a place they knew to be bad, they carried everything they could. In certain heavily mined AOs, where the land was dense with Toe Poppers and Bouncing Betties, they took turns humping a 28-pound mine detector. With its head-phones and big sensing plate, the equipment was a stress on the lower back and shoulders, awkward to handle, often useless because of the shrapnel in the earth, but they carried it anyway, partly for safety, partly for the illusion of safety.

On ambush, or other night missions, they carried peculiar little odds and ends. Kiowa always took along his New Testament and a pair of moccasins for silence. Dave Jensen carried night-sight vitamins high in carotene. Lee Strunk carried his slingshot; ammo, he claimed, would never be a problem. Rat Kiley carried brandy and M&M's candy. Until he was shot, Ted Lavender carried the starlight scope, which weighed 6.3 pounds with its aluminum carrying case. Henry Dobbins carried his girlfriend's pantyhose wrapped around his neck as a comforter. They all carried ghosts. When dark came, they would move out single file across the meadows and paddies to their ambush coordinates, where they would quietly set up the Claymores and lie down and spend the night waiting.

Other missions were more complicated and required special equipment. In mid-April, it was their mission to search out and destroy the elaborate tunnel complexes in the Than Khe area south of Chu Lai. To blow the tunnels, they carried one-pound blocks of pentrite high explosives, four blocks to a man, 68 pounds in all. They carried wiring, detonators, and battery-powered clackers. Dave Jensen carried earplugs. Most often, before blowing the tunnels, they were ordered by higher command to search them, which was considered bad news, but by and large they just shrugged and carried out orders. Because he was a big man, Henry Dobbins was excused from tunnel duty. The others would draw numbers. Before Lavender died there were 17 men in the platoon, and whoever drew the number 17 would strip off his gear and crawl in headfirst with a flashlight and Lieutenant Cross's .45-caliber pistol. The rest of them would fan out as security. They would sit down or kneel, not facing the hole, listening to the ground beneath them, imagining cobwebs and ghosts, whatever was down there—the tunnel walls squeezing in—how the flashlight seemed impossibly heavy in the hand and how it was tunnel vision in the very strictest sense, compression in all ways, even time, and how you had to wiggle in—ass and elbows—a swallowed-up feeling—and how you found yourself worrying about odd things: Will your flashlight go dead? Do rats carry rabies? If you screamed, how far would the sound carry? Would your buddies hear it? Would they have the courage to drag you out? In some respects, though not many, the waiting was worse than the tunnel itself. Imagination was a killer.

On April 16, when Lee Strunk drew the number 17, he laughed and muttered something and went down quickly. The morning was hot and very still. Not good, Kiowa said. He looked at the tunnel opening, then out across a dry paddy toward the village of Than Khe. Nothing moved. No clouds or birds or people. As they waited, the men smoked and drank Kool-Aid, not talking much, feeling sympathy for Lee Strunk but also feeling the luck of the draw. You win some, you lose some, said Mitchell Sanders, and sometimes you settle for a rain check. It was a tired line and no one laughed.

Henry Dobbins ate a tropical chocolate bar. Ted Lavender popped a tranquilizer and went off to pee.

After five minutes, Lieutenant Jimmy Cross moved to the tunnel, leaned down, and examined the darkness. Trouble, he thought—a cave-in maybe. And then suddenly, without willing it, he was thinking about Martha. The stresses and fractures, the quick collapse, the two of them buried alive under all that weight. Dense, crushing love. Kneeling, watching the hole, he tried to concentrate on Lee Strunk and the war, all the dangers, but his love was too much for him, he felt paralyzed, he wanted to sleep inside her lungs and breathe her blood and be smothered. He wanted her to be a virgin and not a virgin, all at once. He wanted to know her. Intimate secrets: Why poetry? Why so sad? Why that grayness in her eyes? Why so alone? Not lonely, just alone—riding her bike across campus or sitting off by herself in the cafeteria—even dancing, she danced alone—and it was the aloneness that filled him with love. He remembered telling her that one evening. How she nodded and looked away. And how, later, when he kissed her, she received the kiss without returning it, her eyes wide open, not afraid, not a virgin's eyes, just flat and uninvolved.

Lieutenant Cross gazed at the tunnel. But he was not there. He was buried with Martha under the white sand at the Jersey shore. They were pressed together, and the pebble in his mouth was her tongue. He was smiling. Vaguely, he was aware of how quiet the day was, the sullen paddies, yet he could not bring himself to worry about matters of security. He was beyond that. He was just a kid at war, in love. He was twenty-four years old. He couldn't help it.

A few moments later Lee Strunk crawled out of the tunnel. He came up grinning, filthy but alive. Lieutenant Cross nodded and closed his eyes while the others clapped Strunk on the back and made jokes about rising from the dead.

Worms, Rat Kiley said. Right out of the grave. Fuckin' zombie.

The men laughed. They all felt great relief.

Spook city, said Mitchell Sanders.

Lee Strunk made a funny ghost sound, a kind of moaning, yet very happy, and right then, when Strunk made that high happy moaning sound, when he went *Ahhooooo,* right then Ted Lavender was shot in the head on his way back from peeing. He lay with his mouth open. The teeth were broken. There was a swollen black bruise under his left eye. The cheekbone was gone. Oh shit, Rat Kiley said, the guy's dead. The guy's dead, he kept saying, which seemed profound—the guy's dead. I mean really.

The things they carried were determined to some extent by superstition. Lieutenant Cross carried his good-luck pebble. Dave Jensen carried a rabbit's foot. Norman Bowker, otherwise a very gentle person, carried a thumb that had been presented to him as a gift by Mitchell Sanders. The thumb was dark brown, rubbery to the touch, and weighed four ounces at most. It had been cut from a VC corpse, a boy of fifteen or sixteen. They'd found him at the bottom of an irrigation ditch, badly burned, flies in his mouth and eyes. The boy wore black shorts and sandals. At the time of his death he had been carrying a pouch of rice, a rifle, and three magazines of ammunition.

You want my opinion, Mitchell Sanders said, there's a definite moral here.

He put his hand on the dead boy's wrist. He was quiet for a time, as if counting a pulse, then he patted the stomach, almost affectionately, and used Kiowa's hunting hatchet to remove the thumb.

Henry Dobbins asked what the moral was.

Moral?

You know. *Moral.*

Sanders wrapped the thumb in toilet paper and handed it across to Norman Bowker. There was no blood. Smiling, he kicked the boy's head, watched the flies scatter, and said, It's like with that old TV show—Paladin. Have gun, will travel.

Henry Dobbins thought about it.

Yeah, well, he finally said. I don't see no moral.

There it *is,* man.

Fuck off.

They carried USO stationery and pencils and pens. They carried Sterno, safety pins, trip flares, signal flares, spools of wire, razor blades, chewing tobacco, liberated joss sticks and statuettes of the smiling Buddha, candles, grease pencils, *The Stars and Stripes,* fingernail clippers, Psy Ops leaflets, bush hats, bolos, and much more. Twice a week, when the resupply choppers came in, they carried hot chow in green mermite cans and large canvas bags filled with iced beer and soda pop. They carried plastic water containers, each with a two-gallon capacity. Mitchell Sanders carried a set of starched tiger fatigues for special occasions. Henry Dobbins carried Black Flag insecticide. Dave Jensen carried empty sandbags that could be filled at night for added protection. Lee Strunk carried tanning lotion. Some things they carried in common. Taking turns, they carried the big PRC-77 scrambler radio, which weighed 30 pounds with its battery. They shared the weight of memory. They took up what others could no longer bear. Often, they carried each other, the wounded or weak. They carried infections. They carried chess sets, basketballs, Vietnamese-English dictionaries, insignia of rank, Bronze Stars and Purple Hearts, plastic cards imprinted with the Code of Conduct. They carried diseases; among them malaria and dysentery. They carried lice and ringworm and leeches and paddy algae and various rots and molds. They carried the land itself—Vietnam, the place, the soil—a powdery orange-red dust that covered their boots and fatigues and faces. They carried the sky. The whole atmosphere, they carried it, the humidity, the monsoons, the stink of fungus and decay, all of it, they carried gravity. They moved like mules. By daylight they took sniper fire, at night they were mortared, but it was not battle, it was just the endless march, village to village, without purpose, nothing won or lost. They marched for the sake of the march. They plodded along slowly, dumbly, leaning forward against the heat, unthinking, all blood and bone, simple grunts, soldiering with their legs, toiling up the hills and down into the paddies and across the rivers and up again and down, just humping, one step and then the next and then another, but no volition, no will, because it was automatic, it was anatomy, and the war was entirely a matter of posture and carriage, the hump was everything, a kind of inertia, a kind of emptiness, a dullness of desire and intellect and conscience and hope and human sensibility. Their principles were in their feet. Their calculations were biological. They had no sense of strategy or mission. They searched the villages without knowing what to look for, not caring, kicking over jars of rice, frisking children and old men, blowing tunnels, sometimes setting fires and sometimes not, then forming up and moving on to the next village, then other villages, where it would always be the same. They carried their own lives. The pressures were enormous. In the heat of early afternoon, they would remove their helmets and flak jackets, walking bare, which was dangerous but which helped ease the strain. They would often discard things along the route of march. Purely for comfort, they would throw away rations, blow their Claymores and grenades, no matter, because by nightfall the resupply choppers would arrive with more of the same, then a day or two later still more, fresh watermelons and crates of ammunition and sunglasses and woolen sweaters—the resources were stunning—sparklers for the Fourth of July, colored eggs for Easter—it was the great American war chest—the fruits of science, the smokestacks, the canneries, the arsenals at Hartford, the Minnesota forests, the machine shops, the vast fields of corn and wheat—they carried like freight trains; they carried it on their backs and shoulders—and for all the ambiguities of Vietnam, all the mysteries and unknowns, there was at least the single abiding certainty that they would never be at a loss for things to carry.

After the chopper took Lavender away, Lieutenant Jimmy Cross led his men into the village of Than Khe. They burned everything. They shot chickens and dogs, they trashed the village well, they called in artillery and watched the wreckage, then they marched for several hours through the hot afternoon, and then at dusk, while Kiowa explained how Lavender died, Lieutenant Cross found himself trembling.

He tried not to cry. With his entrenching tool, which weighed five pounds, he began digging a hole in the earth.

He felt shame. He hated himself. He had loved Martha more than his men, and as a consequence Lavender was now dead, and this was something he would have to carry like a stone in his stomach for the rest of the war.

All he could do was dig. He used his entrenching tool like an ax, slashing, feeling both love and hate, and then later, when it was full dark, he sat at the bottom of his foxhole and wept. It went on for a long while. In part, he was grieving for Ted Lavender, but mostly it was for Martha, and for himself, because she belonged to another world, which was not quite real, and because she was a junior at Mount Sebastian College in New Jersey, a poet and a virgin and uninvolved, and because he realized she did not love him and never would.

Like cement, Kiowa whispered in the dark. I swear to God—boom, down. Not a word.

I've heard this, said Norman Bowker.

A pisser, you know? Still zipping himself up. Zapped while zipping.

All right, fine. That's enough.

Yeah, but you had to see it, the guy just—

I *heard,* man. Cement. So why not shut the fuck *up?*

Kiowa shook his head sadly and glanced over at the hole where Lieutenant Jimmy Cross sat watching the night. The air was thick and wet. A warm dense fog had settled over the paddies and there was the stillness that precedes rain.

After a time Kiowa sighed.

One thing for sure, he said. The lieutenant's in some deep hurt. I mean that crying jag—the way he was carrying on—it wasn't fake or anything, it was real heavy-duty hurt. The man cares.

Sure, Norman Bowker said.

Say what you want, the man does care.

We all got problems.

Not Lavender.

No, I guess not, Bowker said. Do me a favor, though.

Shut up?

That's a smart Indian. Shut up.

Shrugging, Kiowa pulled off his boots. He wanted to say more, just to lighten up his sleep, but instead he opened his New Testament and arranged it beneath his head as a pillow. The fog made things seem hollow and unattached. He tried not to think about Ted Lavender, but then he was thinking how fast it was, no drama, down and dead, and how it was hard to feel anything except surprise. It seemed unchristian. He wished he could find some great sadness, or even anger, but the emotion wasn't there and he couldn't make it happen. Mostly he felt pleased to be alive. He liked the smell of the New Testament under his cheek, the leather and ink and paper and glue, whatever the chemicals were. He liked hearing the sounds of night. Even his fatigue, it felt fine, the stiff muscles and the prickly awareness of his own body, a floating feeling. He enjoyed not being dead. Lying there, Kiowa admired Lieutenant Jimmy Cross's capacity for grief. He wanted to share the man's pain, he wanted to care as Jimmy Cross cared. And yet when he closed his eyes, all he could think was Boom-down, and all he could feel was the pleasure of having his boots off and the fog curling in around him and the damp soil and the Bible smells and the plush comfort of night.

After a moment Norman Bowker sat up in the dark.

What the hell, he said. You want to talk, *talk*. Tell it to me.

Forget it.

No, man, go on. One thing I hate, it's a silent Indian.

For the most part they carried themselves with poise, a kind of dignity. Now and then, however, there were times of panic, when they squealed or wanted to squeal but couldn't, when they twitched and made moaning sounds and covered their heads and said Dear Jesus and flopped around on the earth and fired their weapons blindly and cringed and sobbed and begged for the noise to stop and went wild and made stupid promises to themselves and to God and to their mothers and fathers, hoping not to die. In different ways, it happened to all of them. Afterward, when the firing ended, they would blink and peek up. They would touch their bodies, feeling shame, then quickly hiding it. They would force themselves to stand. As if in slow motion, frame by frame, the world would take on the old logic—absolute silence, then the wind, then sunlight, then voices. It was the burden of being alive. Awkwardly, the men would reassemble themselves, first in private, then in groups, becoming soldiers again. They would repair the leaks in their eyes. They would check for casualties, call in dustoffs, light cigarettes, try to smile, clear their throats and spit and begin cleaning their weapons. After a time someone would shake his head and say, No lie, I almost shit my pants, and someone else would laugh, which meant it was bad, yes, but the guy had obviously not shit his pants, it wasn't that bad, and in any case nobody would ever do such a thing and then go ahead and talk about it. They would squint into the dense, oppressive sunlight. For a few moments, perhaps, they would fall silent, lighting a joint and tracking its passage from man to man, inhaling, holding in the humiliation. Scary stuff, one of them might say. But then someone else would grin or flick his eyebrows and say, Roger-dodger, almost cut me a new asshole, *almost.*

There were numerous such poses. Some carried themselves with a sort of wistful resignation, others with pride or stiff soldierly discipline or good humor or macho zeal. They were afraid of dying but they were even more afraid to show it.

They found jokes to tell.

They used a hard vocabulary to contain the terrible softness. *Greased* they'd say. *Offed, lit up, zapped while zipping.* It wasn't cruelty, just stage presence. They were actors. When someone died, it wasn't quite dying, because in a curious way it seemed scripted, and because they had their lines mostly memorized, irony mixed with tragedy, and because they called it by other names, as if to encyst and destroy the reality of death itself. They kicked corpses. They cut off thumbs. They talked grunt lingo. They told stories about Ted Lavender's supply of tranquilizers, how the poor guy didn't feel a thing, how incredibly tranquil he was.

There's a moral here, said Mitchell Sanders.

They were waiting for Lavender's chopper, smoking the dead man's dope.

The moral's pretty obvious, Sanders said, and winked. Stay away from drugs. No joke, they'll ruin your day every time.

Cute, said Henry Dobbins.

Mind blower, get it? Talk about wiggy. Nothing left, just blood and brains.

They made themselves laugh.

There it is, they'd say. Over and over—there it is, my friend, there it is—as if the repetition itself were an act of poise, a balance between crazy and almost crazy, knowing without going, there it is, which meant be cool, let it ride, because Oh yeah, man, you can't change what can't be changed, there it is, there it absolutely and positively and fucking well *is.*

They were tough.

They carried all the emotional baggage of men who might die. Grief, terror, love, longing—these were intangibles, but the intangibles had their own mass and specific gravity, they had tangible weight. They carried shameful memories. They carried the common secret of cowardice barely restrained, the instinct to run or freeze or hide, and in many respects this was the heaviest burden of all, for it could never be put down, it required perfect balance and perfect posture. They carried their reputations. They carried the soldier's greatest fear, which was the fear of blushing. Men killed, and died, because they were embarrassed not to. It was what had brought them to the war in the first place, nothing positive, no dreams of glory or honor, just to avoid the blush of dishonor. They died so as not to die of embarrassment. They crawled into tunnels and walked point and advanced under fire. Each morning, despite the unknowns, they made their legs move. They endured. They kept humping. They did not submit to the obvious alternative, which was simply to close the eyes and fall. So easy, really. Go limp and tumble to the ground and let the muscles unwind and not speak and not budge until your buddies picked you up and lifted you into the chopper that would roar and dip its nose and carry you off to the world. A mere matter of falling, yet no one ever fell. It was not courage, exactly; the object was not valor. Rather, they were too frightened to be cowards.

By and large they carried these things inside, maintaining the masks of composure. They sneered at sick call. They spoke bitterly about guys who had found release by shooting off their own toes or fingers. Pussies, they'd say. Candyasses. It was fierce, mocking talk, with only a trace of envy or awe, but even so the image played itself out behind their eyes.

They imagined the muzzle against flesh. So easy: squeeze the trigger and blow away a toe. They imagined it. They imagined the quick, sweet pain, then the evacuation to Japan, then a hospital with warm beds and cute geisha nurses.

And they dreamed of freedom birds.

At night, on guard, staring into the dark, they were carried away by jumbo jets. They felt the rush of takeoff. *Gone!* they yelled. And then velocity—wings and engines—a smiling stewardess—but it was more than a plane, it was a real bird, a big sleek silver bird with feathers and talons and high screeching. They were flying. The weights fell off; there was nothing to bear. They laughed and held on tight, feeling the cold slap of wind and altitude, soaring, thinking *It's over, I'm gone!*—they were naked, they were light and free—it was all lightness, bright and fast and buoyant, light as light, a helium buzz in the brain, a giddy bubbling in the lungs as they were taken up over the clouds and the war, beyond duty, beyond gravity and mortification and global entanglements—*Sin loi!* they yelled. *I'm sorry, motherfuckers, but I'm out of it, I'm goofed, I'm on a space cruise, I'm gone!*—and it was a restful, unencumbered sensation, just riding the light waves, sailing that big silver freedom bird over the mountains and oceans, over America, over the farms and great sleeping cities and cemeteries and highways and the golden arches of McDonald's, it was flight, a kind of fleeing, a kind of falling, falling higher and higher, spinning off the edge of the earth and beyond the sun and through the vast, silent vacuum where there were no burdens and where everything weighed exactly nothing—*Gone!* they screamed. *I'm sorry but I'm gone!*—and so at night, not quite dreaming, they gave themselves over to lightness, they were carried, they were purely borne.

On the morning after Ted Lavender died, First Lieutenant Jimmy Cross crouched at the bottom of his foxhole and burned Martha's letters. Then he burned the two photographs. There was a steady rain falling, which made it difficult, but he used heat tabs and Sterno to build a small fire, screening it with his body, holding the photographs over the tight blue flame with the tips of his fingers.

He realized it was only a gesture. Stupid, he thought. Sentimental, too, but mostly just stupid.

Lavender was dead. You couldn't burn the blame.

Besides, the letters were in his head. And even now, without photographs, Lieutenant Cross could see Martha playing volleyball in her white gym shorts and yellow T-shirt. He could see her moving in the rain.

When the fire died out, Lieutenant Cross pulled his poncho over his shoulders and ate breakfast from a can.

There was no great mystery, he decided.

In those burned letters Martha had never mentioned the war, except to say, Jimmy, take care of yourself. She wasn't involved. She signed the letters Love, but it wasn't love, and all the fine lines and technicalities did not matter. Virginity was no longer an issue. He hated her. Yes, he did. He hated her. Love, too, but it was a hard, hating kind of love.

The morning came up wet and blurry. Everything seemed part of everything else, the fog and Martha and the deepening rain.

He was a soldier, after all.

Half smiling, Lieutenant Jimmy Cross took out his maps. He shook his head hard, as if to clear it, then bent forward and began planning the day's march. In ten minutes, or maybe twenty, he would rouse the men and they would pack up and head west, where the maps showed the country to be green and inviting. They would do what they had always done. The rain might add some weight, but otherwise it would be one more day layered upon all the other days.

He was realistic about it. There was that new hardness in his stomach. He loved her but he hated her.

No more fantasies, he told himself.

Henceforth, when he thought about Martha, it would be only to think that she belonged elsewhere. He would shut down the daydreams. This was not Mount Sebastian, it was another world, where there were no pretty poems or mid-term exams, a place where men died because of carelessness and gross stupidity. Kiowa was right. Boom-down, and you were dead, never partly dead.

Briefly, in the rain, Lieutenant Cross saw Martha's gray eyes gazing back at him.

He understood.

It was very sad, he thought. The things men carried inside. The things men did or felt they had to do.

He almost nodded at her, but didn't.

Instead he went back to his maps. He was now determined to perform his duties firmly and without negligence. It wouldn't help Lavender, he knew that, but from this point on he would comport himself as an officer. He would dispose of his good-luck pebble. Swallow it, maybe, or use Lee Strunk's slingshot, or just drop it along the trail. On the march he would impose strict field discipline. He would be careful to send out flank security, to prevent straggling or bunching up, to keep his troops moving at the proper pace and at the proper interval. He would insist on clean weapons. He would confiscate the remainder of Lavender's dope. Later in the day, perhaps, he would call the men together and speak to them plainly. He would accept the blame for what had happened to Ted Lavender. He would be a man about it. He would look them in the eyes, keeping his chin level, and he would issue the new SOPs in a calm, impersonal tone of voice, a lieutenant's voice, leaving no room for argument or discussion. Commencing immediately, he'd tell them, they would no longer abandon equipment along the route of march. They would police up their acts. They would get their shit together, and keep it together, and maintain it neatly and in good working order.

He would not tolerate laxity. He would show strength, distancing himself.

Among the men there would be grumbling, of course, and maybe worse, because their days would seem longer and their loads heavier, but Lieutenant Jimmy Cross reminded himself that his obligation was not to be loved but to lead. He would dispense with love; it was not now a factor. And if anyone quarreled or complained, he would simply tighten his lips and arrange his shoulders in the correct command posture. He might give a curt little nod. Or he might not. He might just shrug and say, Carry on, then they would saddle up and form into a column and move out toward the villages west of Than Khe.

Cynthia Ozick

Cynthia Ozick was born in 1928 in New York. The recipient of numerous awards and honors, Ozick's subjects range from Judaism and mysticism to politics and history to family and character, spanning the genres of fiction, criticism, and poetry. Her short fiction collections include The Pagan Rabbi, and Other Stories *(1971),* Bloodshed and Three Novellas *(1976),* Levitation: Five Fictions *(1982), and* The Shawl *(1989). Her novels include* The Messiah of Stockholm *(1987),* The Puttermesser Papers *(1997), and* Heir to the Glimmering World *(2004). Her essay collections are* Art and Ardor *(1983),* Metaphor and Memory *(1989),* Fame and Folly *(1996), and* Quarrel and Quandary *(2000). On Bookbrowse.com Ozick spoke about the process of fiction writing versus essay writing: "Fiction is all risk, all discovery, all confidentiality—even secrecy. Essay writing verges on being a public act and is driven more by the intellectual faculty than by the imaginative. But fiction . . . when I say secrecy, I mean not only the long, long immersion in privacy and isolation, and the wooing of phantoms out of the air, but those bodiless concealments and disclosures of language that lurk in certain turns of dialogue, or the turn of an eye, or a hand, or a shaft of sky. A watchfulness, an almost perilous vigilance."*

The Shawl

Stella, cold, cold, the coldness of hell. How they walked on the roads together, Rosa with Magda curled up between sore breasts, Magda wound up in the shawl. Sometimes Stella carried Magda. But she was jealous of Magda. A thin girl of fourteen, too small, with thin breasts of her own, Stella wanted to be wrapped in a shawl, hidden away, asleep, rocked by the march, a baby, a round infant in arms. Magda took Rosa's nipple, and Rosa never stopped walking, a walking cradle. There was not enough milk; sometimes Magda sucked air; then she screamed. Stella was ravenous. Her knees were tumors on sticks, her elbows chicken bones.

Rosa did not feel hunger; she felt light, not like someone walking but like someone in a faint, in trance, arrested in a fit, someone who is already a floating angel, alert and seeing everything, but in the air, not there, not touching the road. As if teetering on the tips of her fingernails. She looked into Magda's face through a gap in the shawl: a squirrel in a nest, safe, no one could reach her inside the little house of the shawl's windings. The face, very round, a pocket mirror of a face: but it was not Rosa's bleak complexion, dark like cholera, it was another kind of face altogether, eyes blue as air, smooth feathers of hair nearly as yellow as the Star sewn into Rosa's coat. You could think she was one of *their* babies.

Rosa, floating, dreamed of giving Magda away in one of the villages. She could leave the line for a minute and push Magda into the hands of any woman on the side of the road. But if she moved out of line they might shoot. And even if she fled the line for half a second and pushed the shawl-bundle at a stranger, would the woman take it? She might be surprised, or afraid; she might drop the shawl, and Magda would fall out and strike her head and die. The little round head. Such a good child, she gave up screaming, and sucked now only for the taste of the drying nipple itself. The neat grip of the tiny gums. One mite of a tooth tip sticking up in the bottom gum, how shining, an elfin tombstone of white marble gleaming there. Without complaining, Magda relinquished Rosa's teats, first the left, then the right; both were cracked, not a sniff of milk. The duct-crevice extinct, a dead volcano, blind eye, chill hole, so Magda took the corner of the shawl and milked it instead. She sucked and sucked, flooding the threads with wetness. The shawl's good flavor, milk of linen.

It was a magic shawl, it could nourish an infant for three days and three nights. Magda did not die, she stayed alive, although very quiet. A peculiar smell, of cinnamon and almonds, lifted out of her mouth. She held her eyes open every moment, forgetting how to blink or nap, and Rosa and sometimes Stella studied their blueness. On the road they raised one burden of a leg after another and studied Magda's face. "Aryan," Stella said, in a voice grown as thin as a string; and Rosa thought how Stella gazed at Magda like a young cannibal. And the time that Stella said "Aryan," it sounded to Rosa as if Stella had really said "Let us devour her."

But Magda lived to walk. She lived that long, but she did not walk very well, partly because she was only fifteen months old, and partly because the spindles of her legs could not hold up her fat belly. It was fat with air, full and round. Rosa gave almost all her food to Magda, Stella gave nothing; Stella was ravenous, a growing child herself, but not growing much. Stella did not menstruate. Rosa did not menstruate. Rosa was ravenous, but also not; she learned from Magda how to drink the taste of a finger in one's mouth. They were in a place without pity, all pity was annihilated in Rosa, she looked at Stella's bones without pity. She was sure that Stella was waiting for Magda to die so she could put her teeth into the little thighs.

Rosa knew Magda was going to die very soon; she should have been dead already, but she had been buried away deep inside the magic shawl, mistaken there for the shivering mound of Rosa's breasts; Rosa clung to the shawl as if it covered only herself. No one took it away from her. Magda was mute. She never cried. Rosa hid her in the barracks, under the shawl, but she knew that one day someone would inform; or one day someone, not even Stella, would steal Magda to eat her. When Magda began to walk Rosa knew that Magda was going to die very soon, something would happen. She was afraid to fall asleep; she slept with the weight of her thigh on Magda's body; she was afraid she would smother Magda under her thigh. The weight of Rosa was becoming less and less; Rosa and Stella were slowly turning into air.

Magda was quiet, but her eyes were horribly alive, like blue tigers. She watched. Sometimes she laughed—it seemed a laugh, but how could it be? Magda had never seen anyone laugh. Still, Magda laughed at her shawl when the wind blew its corners, the bad wind with pieces of black in it, that made Stella's and Rosa's eyes tear. Magda's eyes were always clear and tearless. She watched like a tiger. She guarded her shawl. No one could touch it; only Rosa could touch it. Stella was not allowed. The shawl was Magda's own baby, her pet, her little sister. She tangled herself up in it and sucked on one of the corners when she wanted to be very still.

Then Stella took the shawl away and made Magda die.

Afterward Stella said: "I was cold."

And afterward she was always cold, always. The cold went into her heart: Rosa saw that Stella's heart was cold. Magda flopped onward with her little pencil legs scribbling this way and that, in search of the shawl; the pencils faltered at the barracks opening, where the light began. Rosa saw and pursued. But already Magda was in the square outside the barracks, in the jolly light. It was the roll-call arena. Every morning Rosa had to conceal Magda under the shawl against a wall of the barracks and go out and stand in the arena with Stella and hundreds of others, sometimes for hours, and Magda, deserted, was quiet under the shawl, sucking on her corner. Every day Magda was silent, and so she did not die. Rosa saw that today Magda was going to die, and at the same time a fearful joy ran in Rosa's two palms, her fingers were on fire, she was astonished, febrile: Magda, in the sunlight, swaying on her pencil legs, was howling. Ever since the drying up of Rosa's nipples, ever since Magda's last scream on the road, Magda had been devoid of any syllable; Magda was a mute. Rosa believed that something had gone wrong with her vocal cords, with her windpipe, with the cave of her larynx; Magda was defective, without a voice; perhaps she was deaf; there might be something amiss with her intelligence; Magda was dumb. Even the laugh that came when the ash-stippled wind made a clown out of Magda's shawl was only the air-blown showing of her teeth. Even when the lice, head lice and body lice, crazed her so that she became as wild as one of the big rats that plundered the barracks at daybreak looking for carrion, she rubbed and scratched and kicked and bit and rolled without a whimper. But now Magda's mouth was spilling a long viscous rope of clamor.

"Maaaa—"

It was the first noise Magda had ever sent out from her throat since the drying up of Rosa's nipples.

"Maaaa . . . aaa!"

Again! Magda was wavering in the perilous sunlight of the arena, scribbling on such pitiful little bent shins. Rosa saw. She saw that Magda was grieving for the loss of her shawl, she saw that Magda was going to die. A tide of commands hammered in Rosa's nipples: Fetch, get, bring! But she did not know which to go after first, Magda or the shawl. If she jumped out into the arena to snatch Magda up, the howling would not stop, because Magda would still not have the shawl; but if she ran back into the barracks to find the shawl, and if she found it, and if she came after Magda holding it and shaking it, then she would get Magda back, Magda would put the shawl in her mouth and turn dumb again.

Rosa entered the dark. It was easy to discover the shawl. Stella was heaped under it, asleep in her thin bones. Rosa tore the shawl free and flew—she could fly, she was only air—into the arena. The sunheat murmured of another life, of butterflies in summer. The light was placid, mellow. On the other side of the steel fence, far away, there were green meadows speckled with dandelions and deep-colored violets; beyond them, even farther, innocent tiger lilies, tall, lifting their orange bonnets. In the barracks they spoke of "flowers," of "rain": excrement, thick turd-braids, and the slow stinking maroon waterfall that slunk down from the upper bunks, the stink mixed with a bitter fatty floating smoke that greased Rosa's skin. She stood for an instant at the margin of the arena. Sometimes the electricity inside the fence would seem to hum; even Stella said it was only an imagining, but Rosa heard real sounds in the wire: grainy sad voices. The farther she was from the fence, the more clearly the voices crowded at her. The lamenting voices strummed so convincingly, so passionately, it was impossible to suspect them of being phantoms. The voices told her to hold up the shawl, high; the voices told her to shake it, to whip with it, to unfurl it like a flag. Rosa lifted, shook, whipped, unfurled. Far off, very far, Magda leaned across her air-fed belly, reaching out with the rods of her arms. She was high up, elevated, riding someone's shoulder. But the shoulder that carried Magda was not coming toward Rosa and the shawl, it was drifting away, the speck of Magda was moving more and more into the smoky distance. Above the shoulder a helmet glinted. The light tapped the helmet and sparkled it into a goblet. Below the helmet a black body like a domino and a pair of black boots hurled themselves in the direction of the electrified fence. The electric voices began to chatter wildly. "Maamaa, maaamaaa," they all hummed together. How far Magda was from Rosa now, across the whole square, past a dozen barracks, all the way on the other side! She was no bigger than a moth.

All at once Magda was swimming through the air. The whole of Magda traveled through loftiness. She looked like a butterfly touching a silver vine. And the moment Magda's feathered round head and her pencil legs and balloonish belly and zigzag arms splashed against the fence, the steel voices went mad in their growling, urging Rosa to run and run to the spot where Magda had fallen from her flight against the electrified fence; but of course Rosa did not obey them. She only stood, because if she ran they would shoot, and if she tried to pick up the sticks of Magda's body they would shoot, and if she let the wolf's screech ascending now through the ladder of her skeleton break out, they would shoot; so she took Magda's shawl and filled her own mouth with it, stuffed it in and stuffed it in, until she was swallowing up the wolf's screech and tasting the cinnamon and almond depth of Magda's saliva; and Rosa drank Magda's shawl until it dried.

Z. Z. Packer

Z. Z. Packer was born in 1973 in Chicago and raised in Atlanta and Louisville. After receiving degrees from Yale University, Johns Hopkins University, and the Iowa Writers Workshop, she became a Stegner Fellow at Stanford University. Her stories soon began to appear in publications such as The New Yorker, Harper's, *and* The Best American Short Stories *series. In 2003, she published her short story collection* Drinking Coffee Elsewhere *to wide critical acclaim. In the 2003 Best American Short Stories anthology, Packer writes, "'Every Tongue Shall Confess' started as a need; I grew up in a southern black Pentecostal church, and I wanted—needed—to portray its vibrancy without judging it. My prior attempts at this story, however, ended up too cartoonish, too flip, too something. . . . I decided that [Clareese's] viewpoint was the all-important one: she watches (mostly without observing), she does her duty, she sits back down in her choice mistress's seat, she goes to work. I know so many women like Clareese, in and out of the world of the Pentecostal Church—women who must keep moving and doing because reflection for them is tantamount to idleness. I am drawn to these lonely, soldierly women like Clareese, whose unwavering sense of rectitude is the fount to both comedy and tragedy in the story—or so I hope."*

Every Tongue Shall Confess

As Pastor Everett made the announcements that began the service, Clareese Mitchell stood with her choir members, knowing that once again she had to Persevere, put on the Strong Armor of God, the Breastplate of Righteousness, but she was having her monthly womanly troubles and all she wanted to do was curse the Brothers' Church Council of Greater Christ Emmanuel Pentecostal Church of the Fire Baptized, who'd decided that the Sisters had to wear *white* every Missionary Sunday, which was, of course, the day of the month when her womanly troubles were always at their absolute worst! And to think that the Brothers' Church Council of Greater Christ Emmanuel Pentecostal Church of the Fire Baptized had been the first place she'd looked for guidance and companionship nearly ten years ago when her aunt Alma had fallen ill. And why not? They were God-fearing, churchgoing men; men like Deacon Julian Jeffers, now sitting in the first row of pews, closest to the altar, right under the leafy top of the corn plant she'd brought in to make the sanctuary more homey. Two months ago she'd been reading the book of Micah and posed the idea of a Book of Micah discussion group to the Deacon Jeffers and he'd said, "Oh, Sister Clareese! We should make *you* a deacon!" Which of course they didn't. Deacons, like pastors, were men—not that she was complaining. But it still rankled that Jeffers had said he'd get back to her about the Micah discussion group and he never had.

Clareese's cross-eyes roved to the back of the church where Sister Drusella and Sister Maxwell sat, resplendent in their identical wide-brimmed, purple-flowered hats, their unsaved guests sitting next to them. The guests wore frightened smiles, and Clareese tried to shoot them reassuring looks. The gold-lettered banner behind them read: "We Are More Than Conquerors in Christ Our Lord" and she tried to use this as a focal point. But her cross-eyes couldn't help it; they settled, at last, on Deacon McCreedy, making his way down the aisle for the second time. Oh, how she hated him!

She would *never* forget—*never, never, never*—the day he came to the hospital where she worked; she was still wearing her white nurse's uniform and he'd said he was concerned about her spiritual well-being—Liar!—then drove her to where she lived with her aunt Alma, whose room resounded with perpetual snores and hacking and wheezing—as if Clareese didn't have enough of this at the hospital—and while Alma slept, Clareese poured Deacon McCreedy some fruit punch, which he drank between forkfuls of chicken, plus half their pork roast. No sooner than he'd wiped his hands on the napkin—didn't bother using a fork—he stood and walked behind her, covering her cross-eyes as though she were a child, as though he were about to give her a gift—a Bible with her very own name engraved on it, perhaps—but he didn't give her anything, he'd just covered her wandering eyes and said, "Sing 'On Christ the Solid Rock I Stand.' Make sure to do the Waterfall." And she was happy to do it, happy to please Deacon McCreedy, so she began singing in her best, cleanest voice until she felt his hand slide up the scratchy white pantyhose of her nurse's uniform and up toward the control-top of her pantyhose. Before she could stop him, one finger was wriggling around inside, and by then it was too late to tell him she was having her monthly womanly troubles. He drew back in disgust—no, *hatred*—then rinsed his hand in the kitchen sink and left without saying a word, not a thanks for the chicken or the pork roast or her singing. Not a single word of apology for anything. But she could have forgiven him—if Sisters could even forgive Deacons—for she could have understood that an unmarried man might have *needs,* but what really bothered her was how he ignored her. How a few weeks later she and Aunt Alma had been waiting for the bus after

Wednesday-night prayer meeting and he *drove past*. That's right. No offer of a ride, no slowing down, no nothing. Aunt Alma was nearly blind and couldn't even see it was him, but Clareese recognized his car at once.

Yes, she wanted to curse the Brothers' Church Council of Greater Christ Emmanuel Pentecostal Church of the Fire Baptized, but Sisters and Brothers could not curse, could not even swear or take an oath, for *neither shalt thou swear by thy head, because thou canst not make one hair white or black*. So no oath, no swearing, and of course no betting—an extension of *swearing*—which was why she'd told the other nurses at University Hospital that she would not join their betting pool to predict who would get married first, Patty or Edwina. She told them about the black and white hairs and all Nurse Holloway did was clomp her pumps—as if she was too good for the standard orthopedically correct shoes—down the green tiles of the hall and shout behind her back, "Somebody sure needs to get laid." Oh, how the other RNs tittered in their gossipy way.

Now everyone applauded when Pastor Everett announced that Sister Nina would be getting married to Harold, one of the Brothers from Broadway Tongues of Spirit Church. Then Pastor Everett said, "Sister Nina will be holding a Council so we can get husbands for the rest of you hardworking Sisters." Like Sister Clareese, is what he meant. The congregation laughed at the joke. Ha ha. And perhaps the joke *was on her*. If she'd been married, Deacon McCreedy wouldn't have dared do what he did; if she'd been married perhaps she'd also be working fewer shifts at the hospital, perhaps she would have never met that patient—that man—who'd almost gotten her fired! And at exactly that moment, it hit her, right below the gut, a sharp pain, and she imagined her uterus, that Texas-shaped organ, the Rio Grande of her monthly womanly troubles flushing out to the Gulf.

Pastor Everett had finished the announcements. Now it was time for testimony service. She tried to distract herself by thinking of suitable testimonies. Usually she testified about work. Last week, she'd testified about the poor man with a platelet count of seven, meaning he was a goner, and how Nurse Holloway had told him, "We're bringing you more platelets," and how he'd said, "That's all right. God sent me more." No one at the nurses' station—to say nothing of those atheist doctors—believed him. But when Nurse Holloway checked, sure enough, Glory be to God, he had a count of sixteen. Clareese told the congregation how she knelt on the cold tiled floor of University Hospital's corridor, right then and there, arms outstretched to Glory. And what could the other nurses say to that? Nothing, that's what.

She remembered her testimony from a month ago, how she'd been working the hotline, and a mother had called to say that her son had eaten ants, and Sister Clareese had assured the woman that ants were God's creatures, and though disturbing, they wouldn't harm the boy. But the Lord told Clareese to stay on the line with the mother, not to rush the way other nurses often did, so Clareese stayed on the line. And Glory be to God that she did! Once the mother had calmed down she'd said, "Thank goodness. The insecticide I gave Kevin must have worked." Sister Clareese had stayed after her shift to make sure the woman brought her boy into Emergency. Afterward she told the woman to hold hands with Kevin and give God the Praise he deserved.

But she had told these stories already. As she fidgeted in her choir-mistress's chair, she tried to think of new ones. The congregation would-n't care about how she had to stay on top of codes, or how she had to triple-check patients' charts. The only patients who stuck in her mind were Mrs. Geneva Bosma, whose toe was rotting off, and Mr. Toomey, who had prostate cancer. And, of course, Mr. Cleophus Sanders, the cause of all her current problems. Cleophus was an amputee who liked to turn the volume of his television up so high that his channel-surfing sounded as if someone were being electrocuted, repeatedly. At the nurses' station she'd overheard that Cleophus Sanders was once a musi-cian who in his heyday went by the nickname "Delta Sweetmeat." But he'd gone in and out of the music business, sometimes taking construc-tion jobs. A crane had fallen on his leg and he'd been amputated from the below the knee. No, none of these cases was Edifying in God's sight. Her run-in with Cleophus had been downright un-Edifying.

When Mr. Sanders had been moved into Mr. Toomey's room last Monday, she'd told them both, "I hope everyone has a blessed day!" She'd made sure to say this only after she was safely inside with the door closed behind her. She had to make sure she didn't mention God until the door was closed *behind* her, because Nurse Holloway was always clomping about, trying to say that this was a *university* hospi-tal, as well as a *research* hospital, one at the very *forefront* of medicine, and didn't Registered Nurse Clareese Mitchell recognize and *respect* that not everyone shared her beliefs? That the hospital catered not only to Christians, but to people of the Jewish faith? To Muslims, Hindus, and agnostics? Atheists, even?

This Clareese knew only too well, which was why it was all the more important for her to to Spread the Gospel. So she shut the door, and said to Mr. Toomey, louder this time, "I HOPE EVERYONE HAS A BLESSED DAY!"

Mr. Toomey grunted. Heavy and completely white, he reminded Sister Clareese of a walrus: everything about him drooped, his eyes like twin frowns, his nose, perhaps even his mouth, though it was hard to make out because of his frowning blond mustache. Well, Glory be to God, she expected something like a grunt from him, she couldn't say she was surprised: junkies who detox scream and writhe before turning clean; the man with a hangover does not like to wake to the sun. So it was with sinners exposed to the harsh, curing Light of the Lord.

"Hey, sanctified lady!" Cleophus Sanders called from across the room. "He got cancer! Let the man alone."

"I *know* what he *has*," Sister Clareese said. "I'm his *nurse*." This wasn't how she wanted the patient–RN relationship to begin, but Cleophus had gotten the better of her. Yes, that was the problem, wasn't it? *He'd* gotten the better of *her*. This was how Satan worked, throwing you off a little at a time. She would have to Persevere, put on the Strong Armor of God. She tried again.

"My name is Sister Clareese Mitchell, your assigned registered nurse. I can't exactly say that I'm pleased to meet you, because that would be a lie and 'lying lips are an abomination to the Lord.' I will say that I am pleased to do my duty and help you recover."

"*Me oh my!*" Cleophus Sanders said, and he laughed big and long, the kind of laughter that could go on and on, rising and rising, restarting itself if need be, like yeast. He slapped the knee of his amputated leg, the knee that would probably come off if his infection didn't stop eating away at it. But Cleophus Sanders didn't care. He just slapped that infected knee, hooting all the while in an ornery, backwoods kind of way that made Clareese want to hit him. But of course she would never, never do that.

She busied herself by changing Mr. Toomey's catheter, then remaking his bed, rolling the walrus of him this way and that, with little help on his part. As soon as she was done with Mr. Toomey, he turned on the Knicks game. The whole time she'd changed Mr. Toomey's catheter, however, Cleophus had watched her, laughing under his breath, then outright, a waxing and waning of hilarity as if her every gesture were laughably prim and proper.

"Look, Mr. *Cleophus Sanders*," she said, glad for the chance to bite on the ridiculous name, "I am a professional. You may laugh at what I do, but in doing so you laugh at the Almighty who has given me the breath to do it!"

She'd steeled herself for a vulgar reply. But no. Mr. Toomey did the talking.

"I tell *you* what!" Mr. Toomey said, pointing his remote at Sister-Clareese. "I'm going to sue this hospital for lack of peace and quiet. All your 'Almighty this' and 'Oh Glory that' is keeping me from watching the game!"

So Sister Clareese murmured her apologies to Mr. Toomey, the whole while Cleophus Sanders put on an act of restraining his amusement, body and bed quaking in seizure-like fits.

Now sunlight filtered through the yellow-tinted windows of Greater Christ Emmanuel Pentecostal Church of the Fire Baptized, lighting Brother Hopkins, the organist, with a halo-like glow. The rest of the congregation had given their testimonies, and it was now time for the choir members to testify, starting with Clareese. Was there any way she could possibly turn her incident with Cleophus Sanders into an edifying testimony experience? Just then, another hit, and she felt a cramping so hard she thought she might double over. It was her turn. Cleophus's laughter and her cramping womb seemed one and the same; he'd inhabited her body like a demon, preventing her from thinking up a proper testimony. As she rose, unsteadily, to her feet, all she managed to say was, "Pray for me."

It was almost time for Pastor Everett to preach his sermon. To introduce it, Sister Clareese had the choir sing "Every Knee Shall Bow, Every Tongue Shall Confess." It was an old-fashioned hymn, unlike the hopped-up gospel songs churches were given to nowadays. And she liked the slow unfolding of its message: how without people uttering a word, all their hearts would be made plain to the Lord; that He would know you not by what you said or did, but by what you'd hoped and intended. The teens, however, mumbled over the verses, and older choir members sang without vigor. The hymn ended up sounding like the national anthem at a school assembly: a stouthearted song rendered in monotone.

"Thank you, thank you, thank you, Sister Clareese," Pastor Everett said, looking back at her, "for that wonderful tune."

Tune? She knew that Pastor Everett thought she was not the kind of person a choirmistress should be; she was quiet, nervous, skinny in all the wrong places, and completely cross-eyed. She knew he thought of her as something worse than a spinster, because she wasn't yet old.

Pastor Everett hunched close to the microphone, as though about to begin a forlorn love song. From the corners of her vision she saw him smile—only for a second but with every single tooth in his mouth. He was yam-colored, and given to wearing epaulets on the shoulders of his robes and gold braiding all down the front. Sister Clareese felt no attraction to him, but she seemed to be the only one who didn't; even the Sisters going on eighty were charmed by Pastor Everett, who, though not entirely handsome, had handsome moments.

"Sister Clareese," he said, turning to where she stood with the choir. "Sister Clareese, I know y'all just sang for us, but I need some *more* help. Satan got these Brothers and Sisters putting m'Lord on hold!"

Sister Clareese knew that everyone expected her and her choir to begin singing again, but she had been alerted to what he was up to; he had called her yesterday. He had thought nothing of asking her to unplug her telephone—her *only* telephone, her *private* line—to bring it to church so that he could use it in some sermon about call-waiting. Hadn't even asked her how she was doing, hadn't bothered to pray over her aunt Alma's sickness. Nevertheless, she'd said, "Why certainly, Pastor Everett. Anything I can do to help."

Now Sister Clareese produced her Princess telephone from under her seat and handed it to the Pastor. Pastor Everett held the telephone aloft, shaking it as if to rid it of demons. "How many of y'all—Brothers and Sisters—got telephones?" the Pastor asked.

One by one, members of the congregation timidly raised their hands.

"All right," Pastor Everett said, as though this grieved him, "almost all of y'all." He flipped through his huge pulpit Bible. "How many of y'all—Brothers and Sisters—got call-waiting?" He turned pages quickly, then stopped, as though he didn't need to search the scripture after all. "Let me tell ya," the Pastor said, nearly kissing the microphone, "there is *Someone!* Who won't *accept* your call-waiting! There is *Someone!* Who won't *wait,* when you put Him on hold!" Sister Nancy Popwell and Sister Drusella Davies now had their eyes closed in concentration, their hands waving slowly in the air in front of them as though they were trying to make their way through a dark room.

The last phone call Sister Clareese had made was on Wednesday, to Mr. Toomey. She knew both he and Cleophus were likely to reject the Lord, but she had a policy of sorts, which was to call patients who'd been in her care for at least a week. She considered it her Christian duty to call—even on her day off—to let them know that Jesus cared, and that she cared. The other RNs resorted to callous catchphrases that they bandied about the nurses' station: "Just because I care *for* them doesn't mean I have to care *about* them," or, "I'm a nurse, not a nursery." Not Clareese. Perhaps she'd been curt with Cleophus Sanders, but she had been so in defense of God. Perhaps Mr. Toomey had been curt with her, but he was going into O.R. soon, and grouchiness was to be expected.

Nurse Patty had been switchboard operator that night and Clareese had had to endure her sighs before the girl finally connected her to Mr. Toomey.

"Praise the Lord, Mr. Toomey!"

"Who's this?"

"This is your nurse, Sister Clareese, and I'm calling to say that Jesus will be with you through your surgery."

"Who?"

"Jesus," she said.

She thought she heard the phone disconnect, then, a voice. Of course. Cleophus Sanders.

"Why ain't you called *me?*" Cleophus said.

Sister Clareese tried to explain her policy, the thing about the week.

"So you care more about some white dude than you care about good ol' Cleophus?"

"It's not that, Mr. Sanders. God cares for white and black alike. Acts 10:34 says, 'God is no respecter of persons.' Black or white. Red, purple, or green—he doesn't care, as long as you accept his salvation and live right." When he was silent on the other end she said, "It's that I've only known you for two days. I'll see you tomorrow."

She tried to hang up, but he said, "Let me play something for you. Something interesting, since all you probably listen to is monks chanting and such."

Before she could respond, there was a noise on the other end that sounded like juke music. Then he came back on the phone and said, "Like that, don't you?"

"I had the phone away from my ear."

"I thought you said 'lying is the abominable.' Do you like or do you don't?" When she said nothing he said, "Truth, now."

She answered yes.

She didn't want to answer yes. But she also didn't want to lie. And what was one to do in that circumstance? If God looked into your heart right then, what would He think? Or would He have to approve because He made your heart that way? Or were you obliged to train it against its wishes? She didn't know what to think, but on the other end Cleophus said, "What you just heard there was the blues. What you just heard there was me."

"... Let me tell ya!" Pastor Everett shouted, his voice hitting its highest octave, "*Jeeeee-zus*—did not *tell* his *Daddy*— 'I'm sorry, Pops, but my girlfriend is on the other line'; *Jeeeee-zus*—never *told* the Omnipotent One, 'Can you wait a sec, I think I got a call from the electric company!' *Jeeeeeeee-zus*—never told Matthew, Mark, Luke, or John, 'I'm *sorry*, but I got to put you on hold; I'm sorry, Brother Luke, but I got some mac and cheese in the oven; I'm *sorry*, but I got to eat this fried chicken'"—and at this, Pastor Everett paused, grinning in anticipation of his own punch line—"'cause it's finger-licking good!"

Drops of sweat plunked onto his microphone.

Sister Clareese watched as the congregation cheered, the women flagging their Bibles in the air as though the Bibles were as light and yielding as handkerchiefs; their bosoms jouncing as though they were harboring sacks of potatoes in their blouses. They shook tambourines, scores of them all going at once, the sound of something sizzling and frying.

That was it? That was The Message? Of course, she'd only heard part of it, but still. Of course she believed that one's daily life shouldn't outstrip one's spiritual one, but there seemed no place for true belief at Greater Christ Emmanuel Pentecostal Church of the Fire Baptized. Everyone wanted flash and props, no one wanted the Word itself, naked in its fiery glory.

Most of the Brothers and Sisters were up on their feet. "Tell it!" yelled some, while others called out, "Go 'head on!" The organist pounded out the chords to what could have been the theme song of a TV game show.

She looked to see what Sister Drusella's and Sister Maxwell's unsaved guests were doing. Drusella's unsaved guest was her son, which made him easy to bring into the fold: he was living in her shed and had no car. He was busy turning over one of the cardboard fans donated by Hamblin and Sons Funeral Parlor, reading the words intently, then flipping it over again to stare at the picture of a gleaming casket and grieving family. Sister Donna Maxwell's guest was an ex-con she'd written to and tried to save while he was in prison. The ex-con seemed to watch the scene with approval, though one could never really know what was going on in the criminal mind. For all Sister Clareese knew, he could be counting all the pockets he planned to pick.

And they called themselves missionaries. Family members and ex-cons were easy to convince of God's will. As soon as Drusella's son took note of the pretty young Sisters his age, he'd be back. And everyone knew you could convert an ex-con with a few well-timed pecan pies.

Wednesday was her only day off besides Sunday, and though a phone call or two was her policy on days off, she very seldom visited the hospital. And yet, last Wednesday, she'd had to. The more she'd considered Cleophus's situation—his loss of limb, his devil's music, his unsettling laughter—the more she grew convinced that he was her Missionary Challenge. That he was especially in need of Saving.

Minutes after she'd talked with him on the phone, she took the number 42 bus and transferred to the crosstown H, then walked the rest of the way to the hospital.

Edwina had taken over for Patty as nurses' station attendant, and she'd said, "We have an ETOH in—where's your uniform?"

"It's not my shift," she called behind her as she rushed past Edwina and into Room 204.

She opened the door to find Cleophus sitting on the bed, still plucking chords on his unplugged electric guitar that she'd heard him playing over the phone half an hour earlier. Mr. Toomey's bed was empty; one of the nurses must have already taken him to O.R., so Cleophus had the room to himself. The right leg of Cleophus's hospital pants hung down limp and empty, and it was the first time she'd seen his guitar, curvy and shiny as a sportscar. He did not acknowledge her when she entered. He was still picking away at his guitar, singing a song about a man whose woman had left him so high and dry, she'd taken the car, the dog, the furniture. Even the wallpaper. Only when he'd strummed the final chords did Cleophus look up, as if noticing her for the first time.

"Sister *Clare-reeeese!*" He said it as if he were introducing a show-girl.

"It's your soul," Clareese said. "God wants me to help save your soul." The urgency of God's message struck her so hard, she felt the wind knocked out of her. She sat on the bed next to him.

"Really?" he said, cocking his head a little.

"Really and truly," Clareese said. "I know I said I liked your music, but I said it because God gave you that gift for you to use. For Him."

"Uhnn-huh," Cleophus said. "How about this, little lady. How about if God lets me keep this knee, I'll come to church with you. We can go out and get some dinner afterwards. Like a proper couple."

She tried not to be flattered. "The Lord does *not make* deals, Mr. Sanders. But I'm sure the Lord would love to see you in church regardless of what happens to your knee."

"Well, since you seem to be His receptionist, how about you ask the Lord if he can give you the day off. I can take you out on the town. See, if I go to church, I *know* the Lord won't show. But I'm positive you will."

"Believe you me, Mr. Sanders, the Lord is at every service. *Where two or three are gathered together in my name, there am I in the midst of them.*" She sighed, trying to remember what she came to say. "*He is the Way, the Truth and the Life. No man—*"

". . .*cometh to the father,*" Cleophus said, "*but by me.*"

She looked at him. "You know your Bible."

"Naw. You were speaking and I just heard it." He absently strummed his guitar. "You were talking, saying that verse, and the rest of it came to me. Not even a voice," he said, "more like. . .kind of like music."

She stared. Her hands clapped his, preventing him from playing further. For a moment, she was breathless. He looked at her, suddenly seeming to comprehend what he'd just said, that the Lord had actually spoken to him. For a minute, they sat there, both overjoyed at what the Lord had done, but then he had to go ruin it. He burst out laughing his biggest, most sinful laugh yet.

"Awww!" he cried, doubled over, and then flopped backward onto his hospital bed. Then he closed his eyes, laughing without sound.

She stood up, chest heaving, wondering why she even bothered with him.

"Clareese," he said, trying to clear his voice of any leftover laughter, "don't go." He looked at her with pleading eyes, then patted the space beside him on the bed.

She looked around the room for some cue. Whenever she needed an answer, she relied on some sign from the Lord; a fresh beam of sunlight through the window, the hands of a clock folded in prayer, or the flush of a commode. These were signs that whatever she was thinking of doing was right. If there was a storm cloud, or something in her path, then that was a bad sign. But nothing in the room gave her any indication whether she should stay and witness to Mr. Sanders, or go.

"What, Mr. Sanders, do you want from me? It's my day off. I decided to come by and offer you an invitation to my church because God has given you a gift. A musical gift." She dug into her purse, then pulled out a pocket-sized Bible. "But I'll leave you with this. If you need to find us—our church—the name and number is printed inside."

He took the Bible with a little smile, turning it over, then flipping through it, as if some money might be tucked away inside. "Seriously, though," he'd said, "let me ask you a question that's gonna seem dumb. Childish. Now, I want you to think long and hard about it. Why the hell's there so much suffering in the world if God's doing his job? I mean, look at me. Take old Toomey, too. We done anything *that* bad to deserve all this put on us?"

She sighed. "Because of people, that's why. Not God. It's *people who allow suffering, people who create* it. Perpetrate it."

"Maybe that explains Hitler and all them others, but I'm talking about—" He gestured at the room, the hospital in general.

Clareese tried to see what he saw when he looked at the room. At one time, the white and pale green walls of the hospital rooms had given her solace; the way everything was clean, clean, clean; the many patients that had been in each room, some nice, some dying, some willing to accept the Lord. But most, like Mr. Toomey, cast the Lord aside

like wilted lettuce, and now the clean hospital room was just a reminder of the emptiness, the barrenness, of her patients' souls. Cleophus Sanders was just another patient who disrespected the Lord.

"Why does He allow natural disasters to kill people?" Clareese
said, knowing that her voice was raised louder than what she meant it
to be. "Why are little children born to get some rare blood disease and
die? Why," she yelled, waving her arms, "does a crane fall on your leg
and smash it? I don't know, Mr. Sanders. And I don't like it. But I'll say
this! No one has a *right* to live! The only right we have is to die. That's
it! If you get plucked out of the universe and given a chance to become
a life, that's more than not having become anything at all, and for that,
Mr. Sanders, you should be grateful!"

She had not known where this last bit had come from, and, she
could tell, neither had he, but she could hear the other nurses coming
down the hall to see who was yelling, and though Cleophus Sanders
looked to have more pity on his face than true belief, he had come after
her when she turned to leave. She'd heard the clatter of him gathering
his crutches, and even when she heard the meaty weight of him slam
onto the floor, she did not turn back.

Then there it was. Pastor Everett's silly motion of cupping his hand to his
ear, like he was eavesdropping on the choir, his signal that he was waiting
for Sister Clareese to sing her solo, waiting to hear the voice that would
send the congregation shouting, "Thank you, Jesus, Blessed Savior!"

How could she do it? She thought of Cleophus on the floor and felt
ashamed. She hadn't seen him since; her yelling had been brought to the
attention of the administrators, and although the hospital was under-
staffed, the administration had suggested that she not return until next
week. They handed her the card of the staff psychiatrist. She had not
told anyone at church what had happened. Not even her aunt Alma.

She didn't want to sing. Didn't feel like it, but, she thought, *I will
freely sacrifice myself unto Thee: I will praise Thy name, O Lord, for it
is good.* Usually thinking of a scripture would give her strength, but this
time it just made her realize how much strength she was always needing.

She didn't want to, but she'd do it. She'd sing a stupid solo part—
the Waterfall, they called it—not even something she'd *invented* or
planned to do who knows how many years ago when she'd had to
sneeze her brains out, but oh no, she'd tried holding it in, and when she
had to sing her solo, those years ago, her near-sneeze had made the
words come out tumbling in a series of staccato notes that were almost
fluid, and ever since then, she'd had to sing *all* solos that way, it was

expected of her, everyone loved it, it was her trademark. She sang: "All-hall other-her her grooouund—is sink-king sand!"

The congregation applauded.

"Saints," the Pastor said, winding down, "you know this world will soon be *over*! Jesus will come back to this tired, sorry Earth in *a moment and a twinkling of an eye*! So you can't use call-waiting on the Lord! *Jeeee-zus*, my friends, does not accept conference calls! You are Children of God! You need to PRAY! Put down your phone! Say goodbye to AT&T! You cannot go in God's *direction*, without a little—*genuflection*!"

The congregation went wild, clapping and banging tambourines, whirling in the aisles. But the choir remained standing in case Pastor Everett wanted another song. For the first time, Clareese found that her monthly troubles had settled down. And now that she had the where-withal to concentrate, she couldn't. Her cross-eyes wouldn't keep steady, they roamed like the wheels of a defective shopping cart, and from one roving eye she saw her aunt Alma, waving her arms as though listening to leftover strains of Clareese's solo.

What would she do? She didn't know if she'd still have her job when she went back on Monday, didn't know what the staff psychia-trist would try to pry out of her. More important, she didn't know what her aunt Alma would do without the special medical referrals Clareese could get her. What was a Sister to do?

Clareese's gaze must have found him just a moment after everyone else's had. A stranger at the far end of the aisle, standing directly oppo-site Pastor Everett as though about to engage him in a duel. There was Cleophus Sanders with his crutches, the right leg of his pinstriped pants hollow, wagging after him. Over his shoulder was a strap, attached to which was his guitar. Even Deacon McCreedy was looking.

What in heaven's name was Cleophus doing here? To bring his soul to salvation? To ridicule her? For another argument? Perhaps the doctors had told him he did not need the operation after all, and Cleophus was keeping his end of the deal with God. But he didn't seem like the type to keep promises. She saw his eyes search the congregation, and when he saw her, they locked eyes as if he had come to claim her. He did not come to get Saved, didn't care about his soul in that way, all he cared about was—

Now she knew why he'd come. He'd come for her. He'd come *despite* what she'd told him, despite his disbelief. Anyhow, she disapproved. It was God he needed, not her. Nevertheless, she remained standing for a few moments, even after the rest of the choir had already seated them-selves, waving their cardboard fans to cool their sweaty faces.

Annie Proulx

Born in 1935 in Norwich, Connecticut, Anne Proulx spent much of her youth moving with her family to various towns in the east, following her father's job in the textile trade. Proulx has written that she has "continued the restless shifting, traveling around North America with favorite stops in Newfoundland and Wyoming," locales where much of her work is set. Proulx credits her mother, a painter, for teaching her the "art of observation." Her story collections include Heart Songs and Other Stories *(1988),* Close Range: Wyoming Stories *(1999), and* Bad Dirt: Wyoming Stories 2 *(2004). Her novels include* Postcards *(1992), the Pulitzer-Prize and Pen/Faulkner Award-winning* The Shipping News *(1993), and* Accordion Crimes *(1996). Discussing setting with* The Guardian, *Proulx said: "It's a big interesting world, so I just took rurality as my ground. Wyoming and Newfoundland and the outback of Australia are not that different—the landscapes are different, but the economic situations and the beliefs of the people who live in the places are quite similar, because they are all commanded by powers in urban centers. But because they can't see who's making the rules and the economic strategies that govern them, they continue to believe in the independent rural life, which is deliciously ironic and very sad."*

Job History

Leeland Lee is born at home in Cora, Wyoming, November 17, 1947, the youngest of six. In the 1950s his parents move to Unique when his mother inherits a small dog-bone ranch. The ranch lies a few miles outside town. They raise sheep, a few chickens and some hogs. The father is irascible and, as soon as they can, the older children disperse. Leeland can sing "That Doggie in the Window" all the way through. His father strikes him with a flyswatter and tells him to shut up. There is no news on the radio. A blizzard has knocked out the power.

Leeland's face shows heavy bone from his mother's side. His neck is thick and his red-gold hair plastered down in bangs. Even as a child his eyes are as pouchy as those of a middle-aged alcoholic, the brows rod-straight above wandering, out-of-line eyes. His nose lies broad and close to his face, his mouth seems to have been cut with a single chisel blow into easy flesh. In the fifth grade, horsing around with friends, he falls off the school's fire escape and breaks his pelvis. He is in a body cast for three months. On the news an announcer says that the average

American eats 8.6 pounds of margarine a year but only 8.3 pounds of butter. He never forgets this statistic.

When Leeland is seventeen he marries Lori Bovee. They quit school. Lori is pregnant and Leeland is proud of this. His pelvis gives him no trouble. She is a year younger than he, with an undistinguished, oval face, hair of medium length. She is a little stout but looks a confection in pastel sweater sets. Leeland and his mother fight over this marriage and Leeland leaves the ranch. He takes a job pumping gas at Egge's Service Station. Ed Egge says, "You may fire when ready, Gridley," and laughs. The station stands at the junction of highway 16 and a county road. Highway 16 is the main tourist road to Yellowstone. Leeland buys Lori's father's old truck for fifty dollars and Ed rebuilds the engine. Vietnam and Selma, Alabama, are on the news.

The federal highway program puts through the new four-lane interstate forty miles south of highway 16 and parallel with it. Overnight the tourist business in Unique falls flat. One day a hundred cars stop for gas and oil, hamburgers, cold soda. The next day only two cars pull in, both driven by locals asking how business is. In a few months there is a for sale sign on the inside window of the service station. Ed Egge gets drunk and, driving at speed, hits two steers on the county road.

Leeland joins the army, puts in for the motor pool. He is stationed in Germany for six years and never learns a word of the language. He comes back to Wyoming heavier, moodier. He works with a snow-fence crew during spring and summer, then moves Lori and the children—the boy and a new baby girl—to Casper where he drives oil trucks. They live in a house trailer on Poison Spider Road, jammed between two rioting neighbors. On the news they hear that an enormous diamond has been discovered somewhere. The second girl is born. Leeland can't seem to get along with the oil company dispatcher. After a year they move back to Unique. Leeland and his mother make up their differences.

Lori is good at saving money and she has put aside a small nest egg. They set up in business for themselves. Leeland believes people will be glad to trade at a local ranch supply store that saves a long drive into town. He rents the service station from Mrs. Egge who has not been able to sell it after Ed's death. They spruce it up, Leeland doing all the carpenter work, Lori painting the interior and exterior. On the side Leeland raises hogs with his father. His father was born and raised in Iowa and knows hogs.

It becomes clear that people relish the long drive to a bigger town where they can see something different, buy fancy groceries, clothing, bakery goods as well as ranch supplies. One intensely cold winter when everything freezes from God to gizzard, Leeland and his father lose 112 hogs. They sell out. Eighteen months later the ranch supply business goes under. The new color television set goes back to the store.

After the bankruptcy proceedings Leeland finds work on a road construction crew. He is always out of town, it seems, but back often enough for what he calls "a good ride" and so makes Lori pregnant again. Before the baby is born he quits the road crew. He can't seem to get along with the foreman. No one can, and turnover is high. On his truck radio he hears that hundreds of religious cult members have swallowed Kool-Aid and cyanide.

Leeland takes a job at Tongue River Meat Locker and Processing. Old Man Brose owns the business. Leeland is the only employee. He has an aptitude for sizing up and cutting large animals. He likes wrapping the tidy packages, the smell of damp bone and chill. He can throw his cleaver unerringly and when mice run along the wall they do not run far if Leeland is there. After months of discussion with Old Man Brose, Leeland and Lori sign a ten-year lease on the meat locker operation. Their oldest boy graduates from high school, the first in the family to do so, and joins the army. He signs up for six years. There is something on the news about school lunches and ketchup is classed as a vegetable. Old Man Brose moves to Albuquerque.

The economy takes a dive. The news is full of talk about recession and unemployment. Thrifty owners of small ranches go back to doing their own butchering, cutting and freezing. The meat locker lease payments are high and electricity jumps up. Leeland and Lori have to give up the business. Old man Brose returns from Albuquerque. There are bad feelings. It didn't work out, Leeland says, and that's the truth of it.

It seems like a good time to try another place. The family moves to Thermopolis where Leeland finds a temporary job at a local meat locker during hunting season. A hunter from Des Moines, not far from where Leeland's father was born, tips him $100 when he loads packages of frozen elk and the elk's head onto the man's single-engine plane. The man has been drinking. The plane goes down in the Medicine Bow range to the south-east.

During this long winter Leeland is out of work and stays home with the baby. Lori works in the school cafeteria. The baby is a real crier and Leeland quiets him down with spoonsful of beer.

In the spring they move back to Unique and Leeland tries truck driving again, this time in long-distance rigs on coast-to-coast journeys that take him away two and three months at a time. He travels all over the continent, to Texas, Alaska, Montreal and Corpus Christi. He says every place is the same. Lori works now in the kitchen of the Hi-Lo Café in Unique. The ownership of the café changes three times in two years. West Klinker, an elderly rancher, eats three meals a day at the Hi-Lo. He is sweet on Lori. He reads her an article from the newspaper—a strange hole has appeared in the ozone layer. He confuses ozone with oxygen.

One night while Leeland is somewhere on the east coast the baby goes into convulsions following a week's illness of fever and cough. Lori makes a frightening drive over icy roads to the distant hospital. The baby survives but he is slow. Lori starts a medical emergency response group in Unique. Three women and two men sign up to take the first aid course. They drive a hundred miles to the first aid classes. Only two of them pass the test on the first try. Lori is one of the two. The other is Stuttering Bob, an old bachelor. One of the failed students says Stuttering Bob has nothing to do but study the first aid manual as he enjoys the leisured life that goes with a monthly social security check.

Leeland quits driving trucks and again tries raising hogs with his father on the old ranch. He becomes a volunteer fireman and is at the bad February fire that kills two children. It takes the fire truck three hours to get in to the ranch through the wind-drifted snow. The family is related to Lori. When something inside explodes, Leeland tells, an object flies out of the house and strikes the fire engine hood. It is a Nintendo player and not even charred.

Stuttering Bob has cousins in Muncie, Indiana. One of the cousins works at the Muncie Medical Center. The cousin arranges for the Medical Center to donate an old ambulance to the Unique Rescue Squad although they had intended to give it to a group in Mississippi. Bob's cousin, who has been to Unique, persuades them. Bob is afraid to drive through congested cities so Leeland and Lori take a series of buses to Muncie to pick up the vehicle. It is their first vacation. They take the youngest boy with them. On the return trip Lori leaves her purse on a chair in a restaurant. The gas money for the return trip is in the purse. They go back to the restaurant, wild with anxiety. The purse has been turned in and nothing is missing. Lori and Leeland talk about the goodness of people, even strangers. In their absence Stuttering Bob is elected president of the rescue squad.

A husband and wife from California move to Unique and open a taxidermy business. They say they are artists and arrange the animals in unusual poses. Lori gets work cleaning their workshop. The locals make jokes about the coyote in their window, posed lifting a leg against sagebrush where a trap is set. The taxidermists hold out for almost two years, then move to Oregon. Leeland's and Lori's oldest son telephones from overseas. He is making a career of the service.

Leeland's father dies and they discover the hog business is deeply in debt, the ranch twice-mortgaged. The ranch is sold to pay off debts. Leeland's mother moves in with them. Leeland continues long-distance truck driving. His mother watches television all day. Sometimes she sits in Lori's kitchen, saying almost nothing, picking small stones from dried beans.

The youngest daughter baby-sits. One night, on the way home, her employer feels her small breasts and asks her to squeeze his penis, because, he says, she ate the piece of chocolate cake he was saving. She does it but runs crying into the house and tells Lori who advises her to keep quiet and stay home from now on. The man is Leeland's friend; they hunt elk and antelope together.

Leeland quits truck driving. Lori has saved a little money. Once more they decide to go into business for themselves. They lease the old gas station where Leeland had his first job and where they tried the ranch supply store. Now it is a gas station again, but also a convenience store. They try surefire gimmicks: plastic come-on banners that pop and tear in the wind, free ice cream cones with every fill-up, prize drawings. Leeland has been thinking of the glory days when a hundred cars stopped. Now highway 16 seems the emptiest road in the country. They hold on for a year, then Leeland admits that it hasn't worked out and he is right. He is depressed for days when San Francisco beats Denver in the Super Bowl.

Their oldest boy is discharged from the service and will not say why but Leeland knows it is chemical substances, drugs. Leeland is driving long-distance trucks again despite his back pain. The oldest son is home, working as a ranch hand in Pie. Leeland studies him, looking for signs of addiction. The son's eyes are always red and streaming.

The worst year comes. Leeland's mother dies, Leeland hurts his back, and, in the same week. Lori learns that she has breast cancer and is pregnant again. She is forty-six. Lori's doctor advises an abortion. Lori refuses.

The oldest son is discovered to have an allergy to horses and quits the ranch job. He tells Leeland he wants to try raising hogs. Pork prices are high. For a few days Leeland is excited. He can see it clearly: Leeland Lee & Son, Livestock. But the son changes his mind when a friend he knew in the service comes by on a motorcycle. The next morning both of them leave for Phoenix.

Lori spontaneously aborts in the fifth month of the pregnancy and then the cancer burns her up. Leeland is at the hospital with her every day. Lori dies. The daughters, both married now, curse Leeland. No one knows how to reach the oldest son and he misses the funeral. The youngest boy cries inconsolably. They decide he will live in Billings, Montana, with the oldest sister who is expecting her first child.

Two springs after Lori's death a middle-aged woman from Ohio buys the café, paints it orange, renames it Unique Eats and hires Leeland to cook. He is good with meat, knows how to choose the best cuts and grill or do them chicken-fried style to perfection. He has never cooked anything at home and everyone is surprised at this long-hidden skill. The oldest son comes back and next year they plan to lease the old gas station and convert it to a motorcycle repair shop and steak house. Nobody has time to listen to the news.

June Spence

June Spence was born in 1969 in Raleigh, North Carolina. She received a B.A. from Southwest Missouri State and an M.F.A. from Bowling Green. Her short stories have been published in magazines and journals such as Southern Review, The Oxford American, *and* Seventeen. *Her first collection,* Missing Women and Others: Stories *(1998), explores the lives of southern girls and women living on the margins. Spence's first novel,* Change Baby, *was published in 2004. In a note following her selection by Annie Proulx for the* 1997 Best American Short Stories, *Spence explained that "Missing Women" grew out of her own experience one summer when she was working as an editorial assistant at a college town paper. Three women from a house near where she lived disappeared, sending the entire town into a panic. "Working at the paper," Spence explains, "I was privy to all manner of possible facts and odd details and downright misinformation about the women. The way the local media presented every tidbit seemed sensationalistic at times, but it was just as much a way of keeping those lost women at the front of all our minds when there were so few actual clues to what happened. The media seemed to answer our collective need to ponder over it, to not forget."*

Missing Women

Three women have vanished, a mother, her teenage daughter, and the daughter's friend—purses and cars left behind, TV on, door unlocked. The daughter had plans to spend the day at the lake with friends and never showed. The phone has rung and rung all morning, unanswered.

Puzzled friends walk through the interrupted house, sweep up broken glass from a porch light before calling the police. Broom bristles, shoe soles, finger pads smearing, tamping down, obscuring possibilities. Neighbors come forward, vague. It was late, they say. A green van, a white truck seen in the area, trolling. A man with longish brown hair, army jacket, slight to medium build. Down by the train tracks, panties. A single canvas sneaker.

Details are not clues. What happened? Police conjecture an intruder or intruders intended only to deal with the mother, to rob or to rape. The girls' arrival was unexpected. Panicking, the perpetrator(s) abducted all three. Haste should have made the abductor(s) sloppy, dribbling evidence all the way to some lair. But little is found: a single drop of blood in the foyer, but it belongs to a friend—she nicked her finger while sweeping glass. We're aghast at all the friends who tidied up. No alarm in broken glass? Those purses; women don't leave their purses.

There is truth and there is rumor. The missing daughter, Vicki, has not been particularly close to the missing friend, Adelle, since junior high. They went in different directions—the stocky, glossy Vicki somewhat of a party girl, her hair bleached yellow-white against iodine skin; Adelle the more academic and wholesomely cheerleaderish one, willowy and fine-boned. Graduation party nostalgia brought them back together that night, where they let bygones be bygones, forgiving the small betrayals. Adelle called home to say she'd be spending the night at Vicki's, the first time in almost four years. Her shiny compact car blocks the driveway to show she made it as far as that.

In her abandoned purse is medicine Adelle must take every day. Early on, this is what worries her parents most. They circle the town doggedly, their station wagon filled with fliers, her face emblazoned on their sweatshirts. *Please. If you know anything, anything at all.* In a video they lend to the TV stations, she is modeling gauzy, diaphanous wedding gowns for a local dressmaker. With her skirts and hair swirling, her perfect pearly teeth, we feel that she is innocent and doomed.

Of the missing mother Kay and daughter Vicki, we are not so sure. Their estranged husband/father cannot immediately be located. Vicki once had a restraining order against her ex-boyfriend, and he is taken in for questioning. He is at first sullen and uncooperative with investigators. With grim confidence we await his confession, but he foils us: a punched timecard and security video corroborate his third-shift presence in the chicken-parts processing plant that night. The husband/father likewise disappoints. He is not on the lam but simply lives out of state. Someone calls him and he comes, and the son/brother too. They are briefly suspected, then cleared. But there is another shady matter. Kay ran a beauty parlor with increasingly disreputable ties. Some say she laundered money for drug dealers and got greedy, funneling too large a share for herself. The police deny all that, but we note her expensive tastes, the leather in her daughter's wardrobe, and conclude the worst.

Still, each of the three might have her own reasons for wanting to disappear. Kay had maxed out her credit cards and was falling behind in her mortgage payments. Was Vicki pregnant? Some say police found an unopened urine-test kit in her bureau. Adelle the consummate per-fectionist was failing precalculus. Running off might have been easier to contemplate as a group: the girls plotting new looks in better towns; Kay mulling the practical details of bus tickets and low-profile jobs. We cannot rule out anything, but the strongest current is foul play, not the gentle fantasy of escape that we all have entertained.

Seventy-two hours pass without a trace, and the search kicks into high gear. Divers slick in neoprene suits bob the shallow lake as if for apples, rake the algaed muck along the bottom. City workers sonar the reservoir. The waters yield nothing, but the surrounding woods still swarm promisingly with hunters and hounds. We admire those who have volunteered to don orange caps and peer through binoculars, their dogs fanning out ahead and weaving through trees, loyal noses snuffling the ground. We admire the highway patrolmen in their thin summer khakis, poised in the roadside gravel, persistent but polite at the roadblocks checking licenses. The churchwomen bring pies and fried chicken and cold cans of soda to everyone tired and hungry from searching, and we admire them too.

All of us admirable, the way we rally together. We say, "We." We say, "Our community," "Our women," basking in the evidence of so many heroes lured out by tragedy: storefronts papered by high school kids with fliers provided free by local print shops, reward donations quietly accruing, information streaming through the phone lines, the cards and letters of commiseration. Surely this abundance of goodwill, mercy, and selfless volunteerism will prevail over the darker elements that abide here. For there are certain haggard people on the street, there are certain pockets of immigrants who will not master our gram-mar, whose children are insolent and fearless. There are people who look and sound uncannily like the rest of us, but if you shine a light in their crawlspaces, you might find the difference. Any might have stared with longing and hatred into the bright windows of pretty blondes.

There are leads. A reporter gets an anonymous call about a box, hidden in the park, containing information about the missing women. The caller will not disclose the nature of this information, will not linger on the line. Police are dispatched to the park, locate said box nestled amid gazebo shrubbery, examine it for explosives, dust it for prints, pry it open to find: a map, hastily sketched, of a floor plan. A park official recognizes the U shape of the building, the tiny hexagonal kitchen and bathroom appendages flanking individual units. Police converge on the apartment building. Excited tenants cluster in the halls as rooms are searched. Nothing. Wild goose chase, read the headlines. Police vexed by fruitless search. Again Adelle's parents appear on television.

Their anguish chastens other would-be pranksters, but was it just a prankster? Someone who could snatch three women away without a trace might then goad the searchers. No person of authority will come right out and say so, but there it is. We feel it, huddled indoors, or venturing out in twos and threes.

A Waffle Hut waitress comes forward. She is fairly certain she served the three women omelets, french toast, and coffee around two a.m. on the day of the disappearance. They seemed quietly anxious, not like the raucous post-bar crowd she usually waits on around that time. The cheerleader type asked for boysenberry syrup and, told there was none, sank into a sullen lassitude.

A SuperDairy QuikMart clerk comes forward. Around two that same morning, a woman resembling the missing mother burst into the store, asked if he had seen two teenage girls, and stormed out when he said he hadn't. She sometimes bought cigarettes there, and milk in single-serving containers.

The graduation party attendees are questioned further. The girls were spotted leaving the party together at one, two, and three A.M. The hostess thought she heard them arguing in the bathroom, something about a borrowed necklace. The hostess's parents said both girls were polite and charming but seemed troubled. The hostess's boyfriend saw them hugging on the lawn. Others said the lawn embrace was a brawl; Vicki had Adelle in a chokehold. Or Adelle held Vicki while she vomited malt liquor onto the zinnias. Unless it wasn't those two at all. The salutatorian has his doubts. Around one-thirty, he says, he was sitting alone on the back patio. He had turned down a joint only to have the smoke blown into his ear, leaving him giddy and fretful and confused. He is going to Yale in the fall, and the prospect was then lying heavily on his mind. Now he feels relief and a delightful anticipation of leaving, but that night he brooded while the full moon silhouetted two figures dancing together on the lawn. The salutatorian watched in darkness two moving bodies he could identify as female by their shapes, the pitch of the laughter. It's possible they kissed or only whispered. He is pale and stammering in recall. Police seize his journals but return them the next day, almost dejected. His nervous intelligence seemed so promising—a budding sociopath?—but his journals hold only the sex-obsessed ramblings of run-of-the-mill adolescence: "May 5—Would absolutely rut Bethany R. given half a chance. Tits like grapefruit, and she smells like bubble-gum-flavored suntan lotion and sex."

The time is ripe for confessions, so people start to confess, as if in fits of misguided volunteerism. Some march right into the police station or the newspaper editor's office. Some hold press conferences. A man calling himself a freelance private eye and soldier of fortune says he helped the women conceal their identities and relocate, to where he is forbidden to disclose, but rest assured they are alive and well, enjoying lucrative careers in finance. A youth generally regarded as troubled leads police and reporters to an empty culvert, an empty railcar, and on a hike through acres of empty field. A woman claiming to be one of the missing women comes forward but will not specify which one she is—she resembles none—and is vague about the other two, saying only that they ditched her. Her parents persuade her to recant. A group calling itself the Urban Tide says they have taken the women hostage in belated protest of the U.S. invasion of Grenada.[1] They are revealed to be performance artists living off college fellowships. They say their intention was to "tweak the media and thereby tweak collective perceptions." There is talk of dismantling the university's theater arts program altogether, which is hotly debated until the diversion of Vicki's ex-boyfriend's appearance in a television interview.

He reaffirms his innocence and describes their first date: they had agreed to meet at the football game. She had not permitted him to kiss her that night. The first thing he admired about her was how she blew smoke rings "like she was forty years old or something." They dated for two years and got pre-engaged. She loved redhots and for him to knead her shoulders after a long day of school and sweeping up her mother's shop. The restraining order grew out of a misunderstanding, he explains. He was a jealous guy, he admits. She could be sort of a flirt, but no more than that, he is careful to emphasize. No speaking ill

[1] The United States invaded Grenada, a small island in the southern Caribbean, in October 1983 to eliminate a Marxist regime that had allied itself with Castro's Cuba. (JHP)

of the missing. He has grown up a lot since then, he swears, and his former guidance counselor agrees in a pre-taped clip. What's next for this wrongly accused young fellow who has stolen all our hearts? He's studying for his General Equivalency Diploma and plans to enter technical school. Weekends he fishes with Dad and brothers.

Lovely Adelle had (*has?* we must be careful with what tenses imply) no boyfriend. She seemed unapproachable, schoolmates say. Boys were intimidated by her height and her perfect smile. She carried herself as if maybe she thought she was a little better than everyone else. We detect the trace of a smirk in her wedding-dress video. Her parents start to seem a little *too* perfect in their televised worry, forever circling the town, meeting with the police chief, presiding over candlelight vigils. We can't help but wonder: don't they have to work? The friendly wood panels on their station wagon begin to come across as less than sincere. When Adelle's face appears alone on a billboard and a separate award fund is established from her college savings, we say they are elitist. Someone rents a billboard featuring only the faces of the other two, and passers through unfamiliar with the case think they are unrelated disappearances.

The paper still presents them as a united front, the Missing Women, and prints their photos side by side in equal rectangles. The rectangles have shrunk, though, and are relegated to the B section, except on Sundays, when a summary appears on the front page featuring the best of the tip cards and the psychic *du jour.* In the absence of verifiable fact, reporters track the psychics' emanations and contribute wispy, artful meditations on the nature of truth. One suggests that the women never existed at all except as modern local archetypes: Kay the divorced mom, Vicki the short-skirted slattern, Adelle the model child from a better neighborhood. Cruise any strip mall in town, muses the reporter, and you will see several of their ilk. Subscriptions to the paper take a nose-dive until the reporter resigns and a larger-format, full-color TV schedule is introduced.

How we are holding up: Summer presses on, August flares. As the phones' ringing wanes, crime-line volunteers drop off reluctantly, like rose petals. Friends and relatives of the missing women who have flocked here must return to their towns, jobs, more immediate families. There is no such thing as indefinite leave unless you are the missing women. Fliers in windows start to flap at the edges, tape losing its tack. Still, church attendance remains up. Moonlight strolls are kept to a minimum. Locksmiths can't install deadbolts quickly enough. Neighborhoods stay illuminated by floodlights and seething with attack dogs.

Psychologists from the university advise us, in these prolonged times of stress, to be absolutely forthright with one another and to get plenty of rest and light to moderate exercise. Sixty-four percent of residents polled believe there will be more disappearances. Seventy-nine percent say the missing women are dead. Eleven percent believe the supernatural was involved. Two percent suggest they know something about the disappearance that the rest of us don't, and they aren't telling. The poll has a two percent margin of error.

Our police chief is often spotted raking a hand through his thin, whitening hair, loosening his collar. He has gained thirty pounds. We worry that the ordeal will force him into early retirement. For the most part we appreciate what he has done for the town, keeping both the leftist fringe and the religious zealots at bay to preserve our moderate sensibilities. Whereas our mayor is perceived to be an ineffectual weasel, the apprehended drunk drivers, college rowdies, neo-Nazis, drug dealers, and other riffraff can attest that our police chief has kept the peace. But even he cannot collar this invisible threat, this thief who whisks our women into the night, leaving only their plaintive, flat faces pressed against yellowing planes of paper, asking everyone: *Have you seen us?*

August simmering down, the newspaper finally succumbs to investigative inertia. No news is no news; they've been carrying the missing women for weeks now without a new development. Journalism must prevail; the women's photos are sponged from the B pages. Without the newspaper's resolve, we let the fair distract us, then a strike at the chicken-parts processing plant, then the college students' return to town. There's talk of rebuilding the stadium. We have our hands full.

The mayor orates, finally. This tragedy has torn at the heart of our community, he says. We are shocked, saddened, and bewildered, he says. Grappling for clues. Desperate for answers. Neighbor pitted against neighbor in suspicion and fear. We are momentarily stirred by the drama of his speech, but he is voicing sentiments of weeks ago. A belated coda. We've gotten on with it. That's his problem: no finger on the pulse. He's slow to evaluate, even slower to act. We resent his jowly, bow-tied demeanor. He proposes a monument in the square, a small gas torch that will stay lit, eternally vigilant, until the women return. Donations trickle in, guiltily.

From this, the newspaper enjoys a brief second wind of missing-women coverage. After the press conference, there are additional quotes to be gleaned from the mayor, the locally available friends and family of the missing, and the major contributors to the gas torch. There is even a statement from the fire marshal attesting to the relative safety of the proposed monument. The newspaper's cartoonist, known for her acid social commentary, draws bums and bag ladies toasting skewered rats over the torch's flame—to call attention to the downtown homeless. This is generally derided as tasteless, and the editor prints what amounts to an apology under CORRECTIONS, saying the paper "regrets the error." The cartoonist resigns under pressure and files suit. She donates part of her settlement to the torch fund, part to the soup kitchen. There will be other occasional flare-ups. Adelle's parents will reemerge woefully from time to time, but in retrospect we will see that it was here the story's last traces turned to ash.

And what of the missing women? They do turn up, but only in dreams. We're at a party, and though the dream seems intended only to air private anxieties (we find ourselves naked in a room full of people), there are the three of them, lingering over the bean dip. Or we walk into an alcove filled with light and see Adelle in her wedding dress, spinning, spinning, her face aging with each rotation, the smile lined and straining, G forces undulating her cheeks. Or from the reception area of her beauty shop we watch Kay cutting hair that drops in soft heaps, the yellow-blond hair of her daughter, black at the root. Or the girls are wearing graduation caps and robes and clutching scrolls. The scrolls are not diplomas but maps of their whereabouts. They offer us a peek, but when we lean in to look, they pull away, snickering with teenage disdain, and vanish. Or, in the one we don't speak of, we are running down a familiar forest path, hunted, and we sense them beneath the pads of our feet, planted deep in the dark, green woods, bones cooling, and we wake, knowing they've been here all along.

Appendix I

A Brief History of the Short Story

Edgar Allan Poe is widely regarded as having established the short story as a serious form in America. Though stories had been published by writers such as Washington Irving (1783–1859) and Nathaniel Hawthorne (1804–1864), it was Poe, in his 1842 review of Hawthorne's *Twice-Told Tales* (1837) who defined a short story as a work that had a "unity of effect": a short story, he asserted, worked toward a unique single effect, idea, or meaning about the nature of life, that was to be conveyed through every element of the story; every word was written around and toward that one meaning. This definition can be applied to some of Poe's most famous stories, including "The Tell-Tale Heart" and "The Cask of Amontillado," in which language, dialogue, mood, and plot all cohere to deliver powerful statements on guilt and revenge.

Poe's theory would soon be challenged by other writers. But in the mid-1800s the short story form was still developing, with direction and influence flowing in from other countries. "We have all come out from under Gogol's 'Overcoat,'" Dostoyevsky famously said of "The Overcoat," published in 1842. Nikolai Gogol's (1809–1852) classic story about a clerk whose dreams and identity are crushed by a harsh, bureaucratic system ushered in an era of Russian realism, going against a tide of poetry that had celebrated the country's history and folklore. Gogol's stories contained subjective experiences and points of view, often mingling stark realities of everyday life with dream-like, surreal leaps of imagination. Like Poe, his stories made use of both archetype and realism to shed insight on common human conditions and experiences.

Also focusing on lives of ordinary people, as opposed to lives of courtesans and the wealthy, were Guy de Maupassant (1850–1893) in France and O. Henry (William Sidney Porter, 1862–1910) in the United States. Their objective stories—in which the narrator is a pure storyteller and not a character—avoided religion and philosophy, themes prevalent in 19th-century literature, as well as elements of the surreal. Focusing on the lives of the working and middle class, their plot-driven stories—classics such as Maupassant's "The

Necklace" and O. Henry's "The Gift of the Magi"—often center around a pivotal moment in which the ironies and follies of human behavior are revealed.

But it is the Russian writer Anton Chekhov (1860–1904) who is generally cited as the father of the modern short story. In his stories, such as "The Darling" and "The Lady with the Pet Dog," we see an emphasis on the craft of character over plot, and his realistic writing style is filled with tension, compressed language, and aspects of ordinary characters' lives that require examination beneath the surface of literal events. Chekhov's quiet focus on character development and the complexities of human behavior continues to influence contemporary writers.

In the Introduction we discussed the popularity of short stories as entertainment in 19th-century America. These stories, usually filled with great heroes and elements of fantasy, tended to be soap-operatic, escapist, or moralistic rather than crafted stories with a "unity of effect." Realism rose partly as a counterpoint to these escapist stories, as well as to Romanticism's (generally, 1780–1830) extravagance of language, feeling, nature, and spirituality. Realism also made way for the exploration of point of view beyond omniscient third person. Limited points of view allowed the reader to see the world of a story through one character's perspective and experiences.

From the mid- to late 1800s through the turn of the century, America saw a swell of writers working in realism. Sarah Orne Jewett and Alice Dunbar-Nelson focused on the setting and geography around them in a style of close observation and immersion that has come to be known as *regional fiction*. Willa Cather explored, among other subjects, the landscapes of the American West and the life of pioneers. In New York and Boston, the realism of Henry James and Edith Wharton observed the mores of the Late Victorian Period (Queen Victoria 1837–1901) and the Edwardian Period (1901–1914), which emphasized manners, social customs, repression, and responsibility. James and Wharton wrote intricate accounts of family, class, and, often, high society, subtly revealing political and cultural undercurrents in America and Europe. At the same time, writers such as Jack London and Stephen Crane were developing a form of realism that has come to be called *naturalism*, in which human behavior is viewed as a function of instincts, birth, and environment.

It was inevitable that, with the advent of the 20th century, the end of Victorianism, and the entrance into a world war, a shift would occur in American fiction. So began the *modernist* period, generally encompassing the years 1910–1945. Rejecting the social dictates of the Victorian era and reacting to the wars, many stories of this period deal with themes of alienation, opposition, skepticism, and chaos—multiplicity in place of "unity of effect." In Europe, modernism was established by writers such as James Joyce, Virginia Woolf, D. H. Lawrence, and Franz Kafka, who experimented with voice, style, discontinuous narratives, subjectivity, and perception—how something is perceived rather than what is perceived—and the idea that what is perceived may not be certain. Other hallmarks of modernism include formal innovation, psychological complexity, and stories built around feelings or moods.

In America, major modern fiction writers included Gertrude Stein, Ralph Ellison, Sherwood Anderson, and William Faulkner. We can see in each of these writer's works different styles encompassed by the general term of modernism. Faulkner, for instance, worked with gothic archetypes, while Anderson's classic "Winesburg, Ohio," is modernist in its structure around associations of thought rather than linear plot. Modernism also saw a rise of writers responding to environments of isolation, dislocation, and confusion; Ernest Hemingway, Richard Wright, and Katherine Anne Porter are some of the writers who explored such themes through their own modes of realism.

In the postwar era, fiction expanded to include a diverse range of voice, styles, subjects, and narrative approaches. One of these styles is *postmodernism*. While the postmodern period can be said to encompass the end of World War II to the present day, the term itself, coined in the 1980s, does not involve a set definition or application; it refers more to a style than to an era. In general, postmodernists eschew the traditional narrative; they question the nature of realism and explore the instability and subjectivity of storytelling and perception. Aspects of postmodernism include pushing modernist ideas to further and more experimental extremes; rejecting traditional distinctions between genres; and emphasizing irony, ambiguity, subjectivity, fragmentation, discursiveness, self-consciousness, satire, and an interest in popular culture. Donald Barthelme's "The School" and Percival Everett's "The Fix" may be considered postmodern. Both stories weave realism with surrealism and contain elements of narrative playfulness.

While we may refer to our current era as postmodern, the majority of stories written between the postwar period and today would most likely not be considered truly postmodernist stories in terms of style. The years after the end of World War II have yielded a rich variety: the minimalist, working-class focused realism of Raymond Carver; the depictions of jaded suburbanization by Ann Beattie; the lyrical style of Jamaica Kincaid and Sandra Cisneros, who infuse their work with the music and vividness of poetry; the voice-driven stories of Dorothy Allison and Junot Díaz. As writers push the envelope of character and style, we see ever more dynamic and challenging stories that reshape and reinvigorate the craft of story-writing.

One consistent thread is the way in which writers continue to write in response to the times in which they live, to personal experience, to culture and society, to established literary methods, and to other writers. A major defining factor of contemporary American fiction is the explosion of literature from ethnic, diasporic, and minority groups in America, many of whom explore and criticize themes of identity, "otherness," and place. Sherman Alexie, Gish Jen, Jhumpa Lahiri, and Z. Z. Packer are some of the writers at this forefront.

Short stories have always revealed truths about the cultural and political times in which they were written. The past thirty years of short story writing in America have shown us an expansion of craft possibilities, both affirming and challenging traditional ideas of what makes a story a story. Perhaps the best way to describe the contemporary American short story is to say that it is as varied in style, subject, and sensibility as the population of America is today.

Appendix II

Writing Prompts

1. Character

Character Counterpoint. In one of his essays on narrative craft, Charles Baxter discusses how, in "counterpointed characterization . . . certain kinds of people are pushed together, people who bring out a crucial response to each other." By putting two opposed characters into the same scene, writers can create an energy or conflict that will bring about change or revelation in one or both characters. Begin a story or write a scene in which you have two characters who are in some way opposed to each other. Their differences and friction should propel the scene forward. Examples of character counterpoint from *30/30:* the narrator and Robert in Raymond Carver's "Cathedral"; the narrator and Sister Leopolda in Louise Erdrich's "Saint Marie"; the narrator and Marvin Pruitt in Reginald McKnight's "The Kind of Light That Shines on Texas."

2. Character

Family Secrets. Write a story in which a family secret drives the narrative, conflict, and tension. Your central character should know a secret or have a secret of his or her own; part of the tension should involve why the secret is buried, or should lead toward its telling. The secret should get at the heart of a family dispute, misunderstanding or missed connection. Be sure to include flashback and memory in your story to establish the weight of the past. The focus here is not on plot but rather on character, on the ways in which people's private thoughts and public actions are so often at odds. Examples of family secrets from *30/30:* Dorothy Allison, "River of Names"; Junot Díaz, "Fiesta, 1980"; Mary Gaitskill, "Tiny, Smiling Daddy."

3. Voice and Point of View

Boys and Girls. Certain phrases and sayings stay in our mind, from idioms to lines of song lyrics to commercial jingles. Write down some of these phrases, reaching for ones that evoke a memory or feeling or that defines a person's character. Rick Moody has said that "Boys" originated from a single line ("then the boys entered the house"). Jamaica Kincaid's "Girl" is propelled by the mother's demands, especially the instructional phrase "this is how." Choose the most interesting, quirky, and evocative phrase from your list, and use it as the first line in the first paragraph of a voice-driven scene or monologue. This exercise should bring back memories of particular childhood moments—focus on ones that involve tension and discovery—and help you develop a character's voice. Additional example from *30/30:* Stuart Dybek, "We Didn't."

4. Voice and Point of View

We and You. Using the stories from this collection as models, write part of or a whole story from either a second-person ("you") point of view or third-person collective ("we") point of view. If you use second person, take Lorrie Moore's lead and write a "how to" story; or take Jamaica Kincaid's lead and write a compressed short-short story involving a list of commands. If you use a third-person collective point of view, follow Ursula K. Le Guin and June Spence's examples and write from the perspective of a town, community, or group.

5. Setting

Coming Home to Find That Everything and Nothing Has Changed. Many writers are obsessed with place—a city, a home, a neighborhood. A place becomes an immediate metaphor and a way to begin thinking about characters: How are they defined by where they're from? What emotions are stirred up when a character comes home? Donald Barthelme's "The School," Sandra Cisneros's "The House on Mango Street," and Z. Z. Packer's "Every Tongue Shall Confess" explore, respectively, school, home, and church as specific places. Keeping in mind the sense of place in these stories, write a story about a character who comes home to find that everything and nothing has changed. Focus on a concrete place for your character to return to—home, school, church, and so on. Be sure to describe the place visually and sensually, and to depict the people who inhabit it, drawing out the tensions between the one returning and the place to which he or she returns.

6. Setting

Job Histories. In "Job History," Annie Proulx tracks the working life of Leeland Lee, showing how character can be indistinguishable from work in the
hardscrabble West. With this story in mind, put your protagonist in a specific
workplace and give us the sounds, smells, and feeling of that environment.
What is your protagonist's attitude toward the work? Enthusiastic? Obsessive?
Frustrated? Demeaned? How is your protagonist defined by his or her job(s)?
Show him or her in a combination of thought and action, reflection and dialogue, giving a sense of your character's position in the workplace. Additional
examples from *30/30* are Percival Everett's "The Fix" and Aleksandar Hemon's
"A Coin."

7. Plot

Narrative Journeys. A classic (and classical) way to craft a story is to set your
characters on a journey or quest. Allow them to meet new people and see new
places, all of which help them discover something about themselves and their
relationships. In this prompt, follow one of three specific "journey" ideas from
stories in our text: (1) Using an hour-by-hour structure, write about a protagonist who travels around town in an attempt to complete a specific task (Sherman Alexie, "What You Pawn I Will Redeem"); (2) Using a combination of exposition, flashback, and dramatization, write a story about a family trip gone
wrong (Jhumpa Lahiri, "Interpreter of Maladies"); (3) Using segmentation or
nonlinear structure, write a story about a trip that ends in the same place it began, as if in a circle (Tim O'Brien, "The Things They Carried").

8. Plot

Lost and Found. One liberating exercise a fiction writer can undertake is to
step outside of himself or herself and try to imagine other people's lives. While
our best writing often comes from re-imagining and fictionalizing our personal
histories, we often need distance from certain events in order to write about
them in moving, telling, and evocative ways. Here is a prompt that can help
you leave yourself behind for a while, or give you a new perspective on your
own memories. Step 1: Go to http://www.foundmagazine.com. Step 2: Browse
the site for the found object that interests you. The objects are in three cate-
gories, which you'll find on a band of links at the bottom of the main page:
notes, photos, find of the week. Take your time and linger over the items until
one inspires you. Look for elements of mystery and wonder—objects, words,
or images that make you want to know their context: who wrote a particular

note, for instance, and why? Step 3: Once you've decided on a found object, print it out and use it as the catalyst for a short story. The object you choose should set a plot or conflict in motion or should be a source of your protagonist's motivation.

9. Image and Symbol

A Thousand Words for Snow. Read Charles Baxter's "Snow" and Ann Beattie's "Snow." Compare and contrast how each writer uses snow as a symbol, paying particular attention to subtlety, setting, and character development. Next write down your own specific memories evoked by the very word "snow." Perhaps, like Baxter and Beattie, your memories of snow will also be infused with a sense of the ephemeral and transformative. Or perhaps you will have a completely different take on the meaning of the word. Start a story, titled "Snow," with one of these memories, being sure to use snow as the descriptive and symbolic foundation. As you write and revise the story, allow the symbol, rather than the actual memory, to guide the progress of the story. You could also try this prompt with other concrete words either of your own choosing, randomly pulled out of a hat, or borrowed from story titles in this anthology, such as "Milk" by Ron Carlson.

10. Image and Symbol

The Emotionality of Objects. Think about a moment of childhood or adolescence that can be defined or illuminated by a specific concrete object. What did this object (symbol) reveal to you about the world, about a relationship, or about yourself? Consider David Wong Louie's use of the refrigerator in "Cold-Hearted" and T. C. Boyle's use of the car in "Greasy Lake." Write a story or scene that revolves around this concrete object. Use it as the central symbol for one of the central characters in your story.

Acknowledgments

Alexie, Sherman, "What You Pawn I Will Redeem" from *Ten Little Indians* by Sherman Alexie. Copyright © 2003 by Sherman Alexie. Used by permission of Grove/Atlantic, Inc.

Allison, Dorothy, "River of Names" from *Trash* by Dorothy Allison. Copyright © 1988 by Dorothy Allison. Reprinted by permission of Frances Goldin Literary Agency, Inc.

Barthelme, Donald, "The School" by Donald Barthelme. Copyright © 1976 by Donald Barthelme, reprinted with the permission of The Wylie Agency, Inc.

Baxter, Charles, "Snow", from *A Relative Stranger* by Charles Baxter. Copyright © 1990 by W.W. Norton & Company, Inc.

Beattie, Ann, "Snow" by Ann Beattie. Copyright © 1983 by Ann Beattie. Reprinted by permission of International Creative Management, Inc.

Boyle, T.C., "Greasy Lake", from *Greasy Lake and Other Stories* by T. Coraghessan Boyle, © 1979, 1981, 1982, 1983, 1984, 1985 by T. Coraghessan Boyle. Used by permission of Viking Penguin, a division of Penguin Group (USA) Inc. —Song lyrics by Bruce Springsteen, embedded in "Greasy Lake." "Spirit In The Night" by Bruce Springsteen. Copyright © 1972 Bruce Springsteen, renewed © 2000 Bruce Springsteen (ASCAP). Reprinted by permission. International copyright secured. All rights reserved.

Carlson, Ron, "Milk", from *A Kind of Flying: Selected Stories* by Ron Carlson. Copyright © 2003, 1997, 1992, 1987 by Ron Carlson. Used by permission of W.W. Norton & Company, Inc.

Carver, Raymond, "Cathedral" from *Cathedral* by Raymond Carver, copyright © 1983 by Raymond Carver. Used by permssion of Alfred A. Knopf, a division of Random House, Inc.

Cisneros, Sandra, "The House on Mango Street" from *The House on Mango Street*. Copyright © 1984 by Sandra Cisneros. Published by Vintage Books, a division of Random House, Inc., and in hardcover by Alfred A. Knopf in 1994. Reprinted by permission of Susan Bergholz Literary Services, New York. All rights reserved.

Davis, Lydia, "Story" from *Break It Down* by Lydia Davis. Copyright © 1983 by Lydia Davis. First appeared in *Story and Other Stories* (The Figures: Great Barrington). Reprinted by permission of the Denise Shannon Agency, Inc.

Díaz, Junot, "Fiesta 1980", from *Drown* by Junot Díaz, copyright © 1996 by Junot Diaz. Used by permission of Riverhead Books, an imprint of Penguin Group (USA) Inc.

Dybek, Stuart, "We Didn't" from *I Sailed With Magellan* by Stuart Dybek. Copyright © 2003 by Stuart Dybek. Reprinted by permission of Farrar, Straus and Giroux, LLC. Three lines from "We Did It", used as story opener, from *Songs of Jerusalem and Myself* by Yehuda Amichai and translated by Harold Schimmel. Copyright © 1973 by Yehuda Amichai. English translation copyright © 1973 by Harold Schimmel. Reprinted by permission of HarperCollins Publishers.

Erdrich, Louise, "Saint Marie" from *Love Medicine* new and expanded version by Louise Erdrich, © 1984, 1993 by Louise Erdrich. This story originally appeared in *The Atlantic Monthly*. Reprinted by permission of Henry Holt and Company, LLC.

Everett, Percival, "The Fix", copyright © 2003 by Percival Everett. Reprinted from

Damned If I Do with the permission of Graywolf Press, Saint Paul, Minnesota.

Gaitskill, Mary, "Tiny, Smiling Daddy" by Mary Gaitskill. Reprinted with the permission of Simon & Schuster Adult Publishing Group, from *Because They Wanted To* by Mary Gaitskill. Copyright © 1997 by Mary Gaitskill. All rights reserved.

Hemon, Aleksandar, "A Coin" from *The Question of Bruno* by Aleksandar Hemon, copyright © 2000 by Aleksandar Hemon. Used by permission of Nan A. Talese/Doubleday, a division of Random House, Inc.

Jen, Gish, "Birthmates", copyright © 1994 by Gish Jen. First published in *Ploughshares*. From the collection *Who's Irish?* by Gish Jen, published by Alfred A. Knopf in 1999. Reprinted by permission of the author.

Kincaid, Jamaica, "Girl" from *At the Bottom of the river* by Jamaica Kincaid. Copyright © 1983 by Jamaica Kincaid. Re-printed by permission of Farrar, Straus and Giroux, LLC.

Lahiri, Jhumpa, "Interpreter of Maladies", from *Interpreter of Maladies* by Jhumpa Lahiri. Copyright © 1999 by Jhumpa Lahiri. Reprinted by permission of Houghton Mifflin Company. All rights reserved.

Leavitt, David, "Gravity" from *A Place I've Never Been* by David Leavitt. Copyright © 1990 by David Leavitt, reprinted with the permission of the Wylie Agency Inc.

Le Guin, Ursula K., "The Ones Who Walk Away from Omelas" by Ursula K. Le Guin. Copyright © 1973, 2001 by Ursula K. Le Guin; first appeared in *New Dimensions 3*. Reprinted by permission of the author and the author's agent, Virginia Kidd Agency, Inc.

Louie, David Wong, "Cold-hearted" by David Wong Louie. Copyright © 1994 by David Wong Louie. Originally published in the *Los Angeles Times Magazine*, 1994. Reprinted by permission of the author.

McKnight, Reginald, "The Kind of Light that Shines on Texas" from *The Kind of Light that Shines on Texas*. Boston: Little, Brown and Co., 1992. Copyright © 1992 by Reginald McKnight. Originally appeared in the *Kenyon Review*. Reprinted by permission of the Christina Ward Literary Agency and the author.

Moody, Rick, "Boys" from *Demonology* by Rick Moody. Copyright © 2001 by Rick Moody. By permission of Little, Brown and Co., Inc.

Moore, Lorrie, "How to Talk to Your Mother (Notes)" from *Self-Help* by Lorrie Moore, copyright © 1985 by M.L. Moore. Used by permission of Alfred A. Knopf, a division of Random House, Inc.

O'Brien, Tim, "The Things They Carried", from *The Things They Carried* by Tim O'Brien. Copyright © 1990 by Tim O'Brien. Reprinted by permission of Houghton Mifflin Company. All rights reserved.

Ozick, Cynthia, "The Shawl" from *The Shawl* by Cynthia Ozick, copyright © 1980, 1983 by Cynthia Ozick. Used by permission of Alfred A. Knopf, a division of Random House, Inc.

Packer, Z. Z., "Every Tongue Shall Confess", from *Drinking Coffee Elsewhere*, by ZZ Packer, copyright © 2003 by ZZ Packer. Used by permission of Riverhead Books, an imprint of Penguin Group (USA) Inc.

Proulx, Annie, "Job History" by Annie Proulx. Reprinted with the permission of Scribner, an imprint of Simon & Schuster Adult Publishing Group, from *Close Range: Wyoming Stories* by Annie Proulx. Copyright © 1999 by Dead Line Ltd.

Spence, June, "Missing Women," from *Missing Women And Others: Stories* by June Spence, copyright © 1998 by June Spence. Used by permission of Riverhead Books, an imprint of Penguin Group (USA) Inc.

Index of Authors and Titles

Additional Titles of Interest

Note to Instructors: Any of these Penguin-Putnam, Inc., titles can be packaged with this book at a special discount. Contact your local Allyn & Bacon/Longman sales representative for details on how to create a Penguin-Putnam, Inc., Value Package.

Albee, *Three Tall Women*
Allison, *Bastard Out of Carolina*
Alvarez, *How the Garcia Girls Lost Their Accents*
Bellow, *Adventures of Augie March*
Cather, *My Antonia*
Cather, *O Pioneers!*
Chopin, *Awakening*
Coraghessan Boyle, *Tortilla Curtain*
DeLillo, *White Noise*
Hawthorne, *Scarlet Letter*
Hwang, *M. Butterfly*
Jen, *Typical American*
Kerouac, *On the Road*
Kesey, *One Flew Over the Cuckoo's Nest*
Sinclair, *Babbit*
Melville, *Moby Dick*

Miller, *Crucible*
Miller, *Death of a Salesman*
Morrison, *The Bluest Eye*
Naylor, *Women of Brewster Place*
O'Brien, *The Things They Carried*
Parker, *Portable Dorothy Parker*
Silko, *Ceremony*
Steinbeck, *Grapes of Wrath*
Steinbeck, *Of Mice and Men*
Steinbeck, *The Pearl*
Stowe, *Uncle Tom's Cabin*
Terrell, *The Huntsman*
Twain, *Huckleberry Finn*
Wallace, *Big Fish*
Wharton, *Ethan Frome*
Wilson, *Fences*
Wilson, *Joe Turner's Come & Gone*